BEATING THE FEDS

A COMPREHENSIVE GUIDE TO BEATING FEDERAL PPP AND FRAUD RELATED CHARGES

(SPECIAL PPP EDITION)

GARRY WIGGINS

Printed in the United States of America.

TABLE OF CONTENTS

FOREWORD

The Honorable. Margaret Lewis, Former U.S. Attorney, Eastern District of California

Currently Partner, Lewis & Associates, Federal Defense Attorneys.

For twenty-three years, I wore the badge of a federal prosecutor with pride. I believed, truly believed, that we were the good guys, pursuing justice and protecting the American people from fraudsters and criminals who would exploit our system for personal gain.

That belief shattered on a Tuesday morning in March 2022.

I was sitting in my office in Sacramento, reviewing a stack of PPP loan cases that had landed on my desk. The Paycheck Protection Program had been designed as a lifeline for small businesses drowning in the chaos of COVID-19. Congress had intentionally streamlined the application process, telling banks to approve loans quickly with minimal documentation. The message was clear: *Get money to Main Street, fast.*

But now, two years later, my office was treating those same streamlined approvals as evidence of fraud.

The case that changed everything involved Jane Manson, a single mother who owned three small hair salons in Stockton. She had applied for a **$67,000** PPP loan to keep her employees on payroll during the lockdowns. She followed every instruction, submitted every document requested, and used the money exactly as intended, paying her staff, covering rent, and keeping her business alive.

Yet there I was, preparing to prosecute her for wire fraud, bank fraud, and money laundering. The potential sentence: up to thirty years in federal prison.

Her crime? According to our office, she had inflated her payroll by $4,000 because she had included the salary of her part-time bookkeeper, her sister Rosa, who worked twenty hours a week but wasn't officially classified as a W-2 employee. Rosa had been doing the books for Jane's salons for six years, paid in cash, taxes reported faithfully on her 1099.

The SBA's Office of Inspector General had flagged this as "suspicious" because Rosa shared Jane's last name and address. Their algorithm assumed nepotism and fraud. No human being had actually reviewed the case files, which clearly showed Rosa's legitimate work history and tax payments.

I stared at the photographs on my desk, Jane's three young children, her salons with their loyal customers, her employees who had kept their jobs because of that PPP loan. And I realized we were about to destroy an entire family over what amounted to a paperwork discrepancy.

That's when I understood: we weren't pursuing justice. We were pursuing headlines.

The PPP program had become a political liability. Both parties were under pressure to show they were "tough on fraud." The Department of Justice had created special task forces, hired hundreds of prosecutors, and set quotas for indictments. The message from Washington was unmistakable: Find fraud, make arrests, get convictions.

It didn't matter that the program had been intentionally designed with minimal oversight. It didn't matter that Congress had explicitly told lenders to rely on borrower certifications. It didn't matter that the vast majority of recipients had used the money exactly as intended.

What mattered was that someone had to pay for the political embarrassment of a hastily designed program, and that someone was going to be small business owners like Jane Manson.

I couldn't do it anymore.

I submitted my resignation that afternoon and opened my own practice defending the very people my former office was targeting. In the eighteen months since, I've represented over forty PPP defendants. Not one of them was a criminal mastermind. They were restaurant owners, barbers, contractors, daycare providers, and small manufacturers, the backbone of American commerce.

Some had made mistakes on their applications. Others had been completely accurate but were caught in the government's dragnet anyway. All of them faced the same terrifying reality: the unlimited resources of the federal government arrayed against them, prosecutors who measured success by conviction rates, and a system that presumes guilt from the moment of indictment.

This book exists because the American people deserve to know the truth about what's happening in their name. They deserve to understand how a program designed to help small businesses has been weaponized against them. Most importantly, they deserve to know that they can fight back, and win.

The author of this book has done something remarkable: he's pulled back the curtain on a system that operates in shadows, revealing the tactics prosecutors use, the defenses that work, and the human stories that remind us what's really at stake. He's provided a roadmap for survival in a system designed to produce convictions, not justice.

Every American should read this book, whether they received a PPP loan or not. Because today it's PPP prosecutions. Tomorrow it will be something else. The machine doesn't stop, it just finds new targets.

The federal prosecutors reading this will call it a roadmap for criminals. They're wrong. It's a roadmap for Americans who believe in due process, who understand that the government must prove guilt beyond a reasonable doubt, and who refuse to be steamrolled by a system that has forgotten the difference between justice and statistics.

Jane Manson, by the way, was acquitted on all charges. It took two years of her life, **$180,000** in legal fees, and immeasurable stress on her family. But she fought, and she won. Her case is proof that the system can still work when defendants have the knowledge and resources to fight back.

This book is your knowledge. Your family's resources. Your fighting chance.

Use it.

Margaret Lewis
San Francisco, California
September 2024*

Note to readers: The Hon. Margaret Lewis wishes to clarify that while the core narrative of this preface reflects real patterns in PPP prosecutions, the specific case of Jane Manson is a composite drawn from multiple cases to protect client confidentiality. The prosecutorial tactics, statistical realities, and systemic issues described are based on her direct experience as both a federal prosecutor and defense attorney.

Understanding Ppp Loan Fraud: Recognition, Investigation, And Prevention

Executive Summary

The Paycheck Protection Program (PPP), established under the Coronavirus Aid, Relief, and Economic Security **(CARES) Act of 2020,** represented the largest small business relief program in United States history. Designed to provide forgivable loans to small businesses affected by the COVID-19 pandemic, the program distributed over $800 billion across multiple funding rounds. However, the program's unprecedented scale, rapid implementation, and streamlined application processes created significant vulnerabilities that fraudulent actors systematically exploited.

This comprehensive legal research examines the complex landscape of PPP fraud through the lens of federal enforcement actions, investigative methodologies, and prosecutorial strategies. The analysis reveals that while the program successfully preserved millions of jobs during a critical economic period, it also became the target of sophisticated fraud schemes that resulted in billions of dollars in losses and triggered one of the largest fraud enforcement initiatives in federal history.

The research demonstrates that PPP fraud cases exhibit identifiable patterns in both execution and detection, providing valuable insights for legal practitioners, compliance professionals, financial institutions, and policymakers. Through systematic analysis of public court records, enforcement statistics, and regulatory guidance, this study establishes a framework for understanding how these cases develop from initial application through federal prosecution.

Historical Context And Program Overview

The COVID-19 pandemic's economic impact necessitated an immediate and substantial federal response to prevent widespread business closures and unemployment. The PPP emerged as a cornerstone of this response, offering forgivable loans to small businesses that maintained their workforce during the crisis. The program's design prioritized speed and accessibility, with applications processed through existing Small Business Administration (SBA) lending partners and minimal initial documentation requirements.

The first round of PPP funding, totaling **$349 billion**, was exhausted within weeks of the program's April 2020 launch. Congress subsequently authorized additional funding rounds, ultimately creating a program that processed over 11 million loans. The average loan amount was approximately **$100,000,** though loans ranged from as little as $1,000 to the maximum allowable amount of $**10 million** for the largest qualifying businesses.

The program's structure created inherent tensions between accessibility and fraud prevention. To achieve rapid disbursement, the SBA relied heavily on lender self-certification processes and permitted borrowers to self-attest to key eligibility requirements. While this approach successfully delivered funds to legitimate businesses in crisis, it also created opportunities for fraudulent actors to exploit system vulnerabilities.

The Emergence Of Fraudulent Schemes

Federal investigations have revealed that PPP fraud schemes emerged almost immediately after the program's launch, with sophisticated actors quickly identifying and exploiting weaknesses in the application and review processes. These schemes ranged from simple misrepresentations of business information to complex multi-jurisdictional operations involving identity theft, synthetic business creation, and money laundering.

The most common fraud patterns identified through federal prosecutions include the submission of false payroll information, misrepresentation of business operations, creation of fictitious entities, and the use of stolen identities. Many schemes involved the systematic filing of multiple applications across different lenders, often using variations of the same fraudulent information to maximize potential proceeds.

Particularly concerning to federal investigators were cases involving organized crime elements and international fraud networks that viewed the PPP as a lucrative target. These sophisticated operations often involved the coordination of multiple participants, the use of advanced technology to automate application processes, and the establishment of complex financial structures to obscure the movement of fraudulent proceeds.

Federal Enforcement Response And Task Force Formation

The scale and sophistication of PPP fraud prompted an unprecedented federal enforcement response. **The Department of Justice (DOJ)** established the **COVID-19 Fraud Enforcement Task Force** in May 2021, consolidating resources from multiple agencies to coordinate investigation and prosecution efforts. This task force represented a significant expansion of federal fraud enforcement capabilities, bringing together expertise from the FBI, SBA

Office of Inspector General, Treasury Inspector General for Tax Administration, and numerous other federal agencies.

The task force's formation marked a strategic shift in federal fraud enforcement, moving beyond traditional reactive investigation models to implement proactive detection and prevention strategies. The coordinated approach enabled federal agencies to share intelligence, standardize investigative techniques, and develop comprehensive prosecution strategies that addressed both individual fraudsters and organized fraud networks.

Under the leadership of Kevin Chambers, who was appointed as the DOJ's Chief Pandemic Fraud Prosecutor, the task force implemented systematic approaches to identify high-risk applications, track fraudulent proceeds, and coordinate with financial institutions to freeze suspicious accounts. The task force's work has resulted in over 3,000 defendants charged with pandemic fraud offenses, with total alleged losses exceeding **$8 billion.**

Investigative Methodologies And Detection Techniques

Federal investigators developed sophisticated methodologies to identify fraudulent PPP applications and trace the movement of fraudulent proceeds. These techniques combined traditional investigative approaches with advanced data analytics and artificial intelligence tools to process the massive volume of PPP loan data.

Data analysis techniques played a crucial role in identifying patterns indicative of fraud. Investigators used algorithmic approaches to identify applications with suspicious characteristics, such as identical bank account information across multiple applications, implausible employee counts relative to business size, and inconsistent information between PPP applications and other government filings.

Digital forensics became increasingly important as investigators traced the electronic footprints left by fraudulent actors. Analysis of IP addresses, device signatures, and online behavior patterns helped investigators identify coordinated fraud schemes and link seemingly unrelated applications to common perpetrators.

Financial analysis formed another cornerstone of the investigative approach. Investigators developed expertise in tracing the flow of fraudulent PPP proceeds through multiple financial institutions, identifying patterns of rapid fund movement that suggested fraudulent intent. This analysis often revealed attempts to quickly convert loan proceeds into cash, cryptocurrency, or luxury goods before detection.

Common Fraud Indicators And Red Flags

The analysis of prosecuted cases reveals consistent patterns that serve as indicators of potential fraud. These red flags emerged through the systematic review of thousands of applications and have become standard elements of enhanced due diligence processes.

Documentation inconsistencies represent one of the most common indicators of fraudulent activity. Investigators frequently identified applications where payroll documentation did not align with business size, tax filings, or employment records. In many cases, fraudulent actors created sophisticated-appearing documentation that contained subtle inconsistencies detectable through careful analysis.

Banking relationships often provided crucial evidence of fraudulent intent. Investigators noted that legitimate businesses typically maintained established banking relationships with consistent account activity, while fraudulent applications frequently involved newly opened accounts with minimal transaction history. The rapid movement of funds immediately following loan disbursement became a particularly strong indicator of fraudulent intent.

Business verification represented another area where fraudulent applications exhibited identifiable patterns. Investigators developed techniques to verify the legitimate existence of claimed businesses through multiple data sources, including state business registrations, commercial databases, and physical location verification. Many fraudulent schemes involved the creation of fictitious business entities with seemingly legitimate documentation but no actual business operations.

Prosecutorial Strategies And Legal Framework

Federal prosecutors developed comprehensive strategies to address PPP fraud cases, adapting traditional fraud prosecution techniques to the unique characteristics of pandemic relief programs. These strategies recognized that PPP fraud cases often involved multiple jurisdictions, complex financial structures, and novel legal questions about program interpretation.

The legal framework for PPP fraud prosecutions primarily relies on traditional federal fraud statutes, including bank fraud, wire fraud, and conspiracy charges. However, prosecutors have also utilized specialized statutes related to false statements on loan applications and money laundering offenses. The choice of charges often depends on the specific characteristics of each case and the strength of available evidence.

Sentencing considerations in PPP fraud cases have evolved as courts have gained experience with these prosecutions. Federal judges have considered factors such as the amount of fraudulent proceeds, the sophistication of the scheme, the defendant's criminal history, and the impact on the PPP program's integrity. The federal sentencing guidelines provide a framework for these considerations, though individual cases often present unique circumstances that require judicial discretion.

Cooperation agreements have played a significant role in PPP fraud prosecutions, particularly in cases involving organized fraud networks. Prosecutors have successfully used cooperation agreements to identify additional participants in fraud schemes and recover fraudulent proceeds. These agreements have provided valuable intelligence about fraud methodologies and helped prosecutors understand the full scope of organized fraud operations.

Financial Institution Responsibilities And Compliance

The PPP's structure placed significant responsibilities on participating financial institutions, creating complex compliance obligations that many institutions struggled to meet effectively. These institutions served as the primary interface between borrowers and the federal government, making them crucial gatekeepers in fraud prevention efforts.

Due diligence requirements for PPP lenders evolved throughout the program's existence, with the SBA issuing successive guidance documents that clarified expectations for borrower verification and application review. However, the tension between rapid processing requirements and thorough due diligence created challenges that some institutions addressed more effectively than others.

Regulatory enforcement actions against financial institutions have provided important insights into expected compliance standards. These actions have clarified expectations for customer identification, transaction monitoring, and suspicious activity reporting in the context of government lending programs. The lessons learned from these enforcement actions have implications for future emergency lending programs and ongoing compliance obligations.

Case Studies And Prosecution Outcomes

The analysis of significant PPP fraud prosecutions reveals important patterns in both fraud execution and law enforcement response. These cases provide concrete examples of how fraudulent schemes operated and how federal investigators successfully built prosecutable cases.

High-profile cases involving millions of dollars in fraudulent proceeds have demonstrated the sophistication of some fraud schemes and the extensive resources required for successful prosecution. These cases often involved multiple defendants, complex financial structures, and sophisticated attempts to conceal fraudulent activity.

Smaller-scale prosecutions have been equally important in establishing precedents and deterring future fraud. These cases have clarified legal standards for PPP eligibility and demonstrated federal commitment to prosecuting fraud regardless of the amount involved.

Systemic Vulnerabilities And Lessons Learned

The comprehensive analysis of PPP fraud cases reveals systemic vulnerabilities that contributed to the program's susceptibility to fraudulent exploitation. These vulnerabilities emerged from the tension between rapid program implementation and traditional fraud prevention measures.

The reliance on self-certification processes created opportunities for fraudulent actors to provide false information with minimal risk of immediate detection. While this approach served the program's goal of rapid fund disbursement, it also created systematic vulnerabilities that sophisticated fraudsters were able to exploit.

Limited cross-referencing capabilities between different government databases allowed fraudulent actors to provide inconsistent information across different applications and programs. The lack of real-time data sharing between agencies created opportunities for fraud that more integrated systems might have prevented.

Future Implications And Recommendations

The experience of PPP fraud enforcement provides valuable lessons for future emergency relief programs and ongoing fraud prevention efforts. These lessons have implications for program design, implementation strategies, and enforcement approaches.

Program design considerations include the balance between accessibility and fraud prevention, the role of technology in application processing and verification, and the importance of real-time data sharing between agencies. Future programs must consider these factors from the outset rather than addressing them retroactively.

Enforcement strategies developed during the PPP fraud response have created new capabilities and approaches that extend beyond pandemic relief programs. The coordination mechanisms established through the **COVID-19 Fraud Enforcement Task Force** have demonstrated the value of inter-agency cooperation in addressing complex fraud schemes.

Conclusion

The PPP fraud enforcement experience represents a significant chapter in federal fraud prosecution history, demonstrating both the challenges of implementing large-scale relief programs and the capabilities of federal law enforcement in responding to systematic fraud. The program's success in preserving jobs and supporting businesses during the pandemic came at the cost of significant fraud losses that continue to be addressed through ongoing enforcement efforts.

This research establishes a framework for understanding how PPP fraud schemes operated, how they were detected and investigated, and how they were prosecuted. The patterns identified through this analysis provide valuable insights for legal practitioners, compliance professionals, and policymakers working to prevent future fraud and improve the integrity of government programs.

The lessons learned from PPP fraud enforcement extend beyond pandemic relief programs to encompass broader questions about program design, fraud prevention, and law enforcement coordination. As federal agencies continue to recover fraudulent proceeds and prosecute remaining cases, the experience gained through this unprecedented enforcement effort will inform future approaches to both emergency relief programs and fraud prevention generally.

The ongoing nature of PPP fraud enforcement ensures that additional insights will continue to emerge as more cases are prosecuted and more fraudulent schemes are uncovered. This research provides a foundation for understanding the current state of PPP fraud enforcement while recognizing that the full impact and lessons of this experience will continue to evolve as enforcement efforts continue.

CHAPTER 1

THE PERFECT STORM

How COVID Created The Greatest Legal Landmine In American History

On March 15, 2020, Tommy Cole was sweeping the floor of his barbershop in East Los Angeles when Governor Gavin Newsom's voice crackled through the radio, ordering all non-essential businesses to close immediately. Tommy stopped mid-sweep, broom in hand, and stared at the radio as if it had just announced the end of the world.

In many ways, it had.

Tommy's Barber Shop had been a fixture on Whittier Boulevard for eighteen years. Three chairs, two employees, and a steady stream of neighborhood regulars who came not just for haircuts but for the conversation, the community, the sense that some things in life remained constant. Tommy had survived recessions, family crises, and the gradual gentrification of his neighborhood. He had never closed his doors for more than a Sunday.

Now the government was telling him to shut down indefinitely.

"How long?" he asked his wife Heather that night as they sat at their kitchen table, surrounded by bills and bank statements.

"Two weeks," she said, repeating what they'd heard on the news. "Maybe a month."

Two weeks became two months. Two months became six. And somewhere in between, Tommy Cole became a federal criminal.

He didn't know it yet, of course. None of them did. Millions of small business owners across America were about to make the same fateful decision that Tommy made on that March evening: they were going to trust their government to help them survive the greatest economic catastrophe since the Great Depression.

That trust would cost many of them everything.

The Panic Of March 2020

To understand how the Paycheck Protection Program became the largest prosecutorial dragnet in American history, you have to understand the panic that created it. Not just the medical panic of a novel virus spreading across the globe, but the economic panic of watching the American economy shut down in real time.

On March 16, 2020, the Dow Jones Industrial Average suffered its largest single-day point drop in history. Restaurants emptied. Retail stores closed. Airlines canceled flights. The unemployment rate, which had been 3.5% in February, would reach 14.8% by April. In a single month, 20.5 million Americans lost their jobs.

Congress was in full crisis mode. Lawmakers who couldn't agree on the time of day suddenly found themselves racing to pass the largest economic relief package in American history. **The CARES Act**, all 880 pages of it, was written, debated, and passed in less than two weeks.

Buried within those 880 pages was a hastily conceived program called the **Paycheck Protection Program.** The concept was simple: provide forgivable loans to small businesses to keep their employees on payroll during the lockdowns. The execution was anything but simple.

Senator Marco Rubio, who helped design the program, would later admit what everyone involved knew at the time: "We were building the plane while flying it."

The plane was about to crash into a mountain of unintended consequences.

The Impossible Timeline

Steve Mnuchin, then Secretary of the Treasury, appeared on CNBC on March 27, 2020, the day President Trump signed the CARES Act into law. "We will have this up and running by next Friday," he promised. "We're committed to getting money out the door quickly."

Next Friday was April 3rd. That gave the Small Business Administration, Treasury Department, and thousands of banks across the country exactly one week to create and implement a lending program that would ultimately distribute **$800 billion** to nearly 12 million borrowers.

One week.

To put that timeline in perspective, most banks spend months developing new lending products, with extensive legal review, compliance checks, and staff training. The PPP gave them seven days to process applications for a loan program that didn't exist the previous week.

The results were predictable. Banks were told to rely on borrower certifications rather than verify information. The SBA's computer systems, designed to process a few thousand loans per year, were suddenly expected to handle millions. Loan processors, many of whom had never worked with SBA programs, were given crash courses in federal lending regulations.

"It was complete chaos," recalls Jennifer Jacobs, who worked as a loan processor at a mid-sized bank in Phoenix. "We had customers lined up around the block, literally begging for help. The guidelines were changing daily, sometimes hourly. We were told to process loans as fast as possible and worry about the details later."

The details, as it turned out, would matter very much later.

The Politics Of Speed

The pressure to move fast wasn't just operational, it was intensely political. President Trump was facing reelection in November 2020, and the economic devastation from COVID-19 lockdowns threatened to derail his campaign. Getting money to small businesses quickly became a political imperative.

Congressional Democrats, led by Speaker Nancy Pelosi, were demanding even faster distribution. "Every day we delay is another day that small businesses are closing permanently," Pelosi said during a press conference on April 1, 2020. "The bureaucracy needs to get out of the way."

The SBA, accustomed to processing 60,000 loans per year, was suddenly expected to process 60,000 loans per day. Administrator Jovita Carranza later testified that the agency approved more loans in the first two weeks of PPP than it had in the previous fourteen years combined.

Quality control was an afterthought. The SBA's Inspector General would later reveal that the agency had waived most of its standard fraud prevention measures to speed up processing. Computer systems that normally flagged suspicious applications were turned off. Human review of loan files was eliminated for all but the largest loans.

"We were told that false positives were worse than false negatives," explained a former SBA official who spoke on condition of anonymity. "Better to approve a questionable loan than delay a legitimate one."

This philosophy would come back to haunt thousands of borrowers.

The Barbershop Owner's Dilemma

Tommy Cole knew none of this when he walked into his bank on April 6, 2020, three days after the PPP program launched. He brought with him a manila folder containing his tax returns, payroll records, and bank statements, everything he thought he might need to prove his business was legitimate.

The bank lobby was packed with other small business owners, all clutching similar folders, all wearing the same expression of desperate hope. Tommy took a number and waited three hours to speak with a loan officer.

"This is all I need?" he asked, sliding a single-page application across the desk.

The loan officer, a young woman named Sarah who looked overwhelmed, nodded. "Just fill this out and sign here. We'll have an answer within a few days."

Tommy stared at the form. It asked for basic information: business name, address, number of employees, average monthly payroll. Nothing about the complex regulations that governed SBA lending. Nothing about the certification requirements that would later be scrutinized by federal prosecutors.

"What about all this?" Tommy asked, gesturing to his folder of documentation.

"We don't need it," Sarah said. "The program is designed to be simple. Just certify that the information is true and that you need the loan to maintain operations."

Tommy filled out the form, signed it, and walked out of the bank feeling cautiously optimistic. The loan was approved three days later. $47,000 deposited directly into his business account.

He had no idea that he had just signed what prosecutors would later call a "fraudulent application."

The Unintended Consequences

The PPP program's design flaws were apparent from the beginning, but they were features, not bugs. Congress had deliberately stripped away traditional lending safeguards to speed up distribution. The Small Business Administration's own guidance told lenders to rely on borrower certifications rather than verify information independently.

This created a perfect storm of unintended consequences:

****Vague Eligibility Requirements**:** The law required borrowers to certify that "the uncertainty of current economic conditions makes this loan request necessary to support the ongoing operations of the applicant." What did "uncertainty" mean? What constitutes "necessary"? Nobody knew, because Congress hadn't defined these terms.

****Conflicting Guidance**:** The SBA issued new guidance almost daily, often contradicting previous instructions. Borrowers who applied on Monday might be following different rules than those who applied on Friday. Some guidance was issued retroactively, making previously compliant applications suddenly problematic.

****Inadequate Systems**:** The SBA's computer systems crashed repeatedly under the volume of applications. Data was lost, duplicated, or corrupted. Some borrowers received multiple loans accidentally. Others were denied despite meeting all requirements.

****Rushed Training**:** Bank employees responsible for processing loans received minimal training on PPP requirements. Many were temporary workers hired specifically for the program. They made mistakes, lots of them, and borrowers would later be held responsible for those mistakes.

****No Audit Trail**:** The speed of processing meant that many loans were approved without proper documentation. Files were incomplete, signatures were missing, and required certifications were often unclear or contradictory.

The program worked exactly as designed: it got money out the door quickly. But it also created a massive paper trail of technical violations that would later be used to justify criminal prosecutions.

The Barbershop Owner's Mistake

Tommy Cole made his first mistake on line 7 of his PPP application. The form asked for "Number of Employees." Tommy wrote "3."

The problem was that Tommy employed two people full-time and one part-time worker who came in on weekends. The part-time worker, Miguel, was technically an independent contractor who received a 1099 rather than a W-2. But Miguel had been cutting hair at Tommy's shop for five years, used Tommy's equipment, and worked a regular schedule.

Was Miguel an employee or an independent contractor? The answer depended on a complex analysis of federal labor law that Tommy had never studied and that his loan processor had never explained. The PPP application didn't provide guidance on this issue.

Tommy counted Miguel as an employee because that's how he thought of him. The SBA's computer system flagged this as suspicious because Miguel's Social Security number wasn't associated with quarterly payroll tax filings for Tommy's business.

Tommy's second mistake was on line 9, which asked for "Average Monthly Payroll." Tommy included Miguel's payments in this calculation, even though Miguel was paid as a contractor. This inflated Tommy's payroll by about $1,200 per month.

The third mistake happened during the loan forgiveness process. Tommy submitted payroll records that didn't match his original application, because he had never properly classified Miguel as an employee or contractor. The discrepancy was less than **$3,000** over the life of the loan.

None of these were intentional misrepresentations. They were the kinds of mistakes that happen when you ask small business owners to navigate complex federal regulations without guidance, under extreme time pressure, during a global pandemic.

But they were also the kinds of mistakes that federal prosecutors would later characterize as fraud.

The Political Reckoning

By the summer of 2020, the PPP program had become a political liability. Media reports highlighted large companies that had received loans while small businesses were shut out. High-profile recipients included the Los Angeles Lakers, Harvard University, and Shake Shack, all of which eventually returned their loans amid public criticism.

Congressional Republicans, who had championed the program, began calling for fraud prosecutions. Senator Josh Hawley demanded "aggressive enforcement" against PPP fraud. Senator Ted Cruz called for "maximum penalties" for anyone who had "cheated the system."

Congressional Democrats, not to be outdone, held hearings highlighting the program's failures. Representative Alexandria Ocasio-Cortez called PPP fraud "theft from the American people." Representative Maxine Waters demanded that the Justice Department create a task force to pursue prosecutions.

The Biden administration, which took office in January 2021, found itself inheriting a program that had distributed **$800 billion** with minimal oversight. The political pressure to show "accountability" was enormous.

Attorney General Merrick Garland announced the formation of a **COVID-19 Fraud Enforcement Task** Force in May 2021. The task force included prosecutors from every U.S. Attorney's office, agents from multiple federal agencies, and data analysts tasked with identifying potential fraud cases.

The hunting season was officially open.

The Algorithm's Judgment

The Justice Department's approach to PPP prosecutions was driven by data analytics rather than traditional investigative methods. The SBA provided prosecutors with a database of every PPP loan, complete with application information, forgiveness records, and "risk scores" generated by computer algorithms.

These algorithms were designed to identify statistical outliers, applications that deviated from expected patterns. They flagged loans with unusual payroll calculations, borrowers with multiple businesses, applications submitted by IP addresses associated with multiple borrowers, and dozens of other red flags.

The problem was that many of these "red flags" were perfectly legal. Small business owners often have multiple entities. Accountants and loan brokers naturally submitted applications from the same IP addresses. Payroll calculations varied widely based on how businesses classified workers, handled tips, or calculated seasonal employment.

But the algorithms didn't understand context. They simply identified deviations from the norm and flagged them as suspicious. Human prosecutors, under pressure to find fraud, treated these flags as evidence of criminal intent.

Tommy Cole's loan was flagged for three reasons: his employee count didn't match his payroll tax filings, his average monthly payroll seemed high for a three-chair barbershop, and his bank account showed irregular deposits that the algorithm couldn't identify (they were cash payments from customers that Tommy deposited weekly).

The algorithm assigned Tommy's loan a risk score of 847 out of 1,000. Any loan with a score above 750 was automatically referred to the Justice Department for investigation.

Tommy still didn't know he was under investigation.

The Knock On The Door

The first sign of trouble came on a Tuesday morning in September 2022, two and a half years after Tommy had received his PPP loan. He was cutting hair when two men in suits walked into his shop and asked to speak with him privately.

"We're from the FBI," the older man said, showing his badge. "We'd like to ask you some questions about your PPP loan."

Tommy's hands were shaking as he put down his scissors. "Is there a problem?"

"That depends," the younger agent said. "Did you tell the truth on your application?"

Tommy thought about the application he had filled out in that crowded bank lobby. He remembered the chaos, the desperation, the single page of questions that had seemed so straightforward at the time.

"I think so," he said. "I mean, I tried to."

The agents exchanged glances. "Maybe we should sit down," the older one said.

For the next two hours, Tommy answered questions about his business, his employees, and his payroll calculations. The agents showed him printouts of his application, his bank records, and his tax returns. They asked about Miguel, about the discrepancies in his employee count, about the cash deposits that didn't match his reported income.

"I didn't lie about anything," Tommy kept saying. "I just filled out the form the best I could."

"The problem is," the younger agent said, "your application doesn't match your records. That's a federal crime."

Tommy felt the room spinning. "I didn't know. Nobody told me it had to match exactly."

"Ignorance of the law isn't a defense," the older agent said. "But cooperation is. If you work with us, maybe we can work something out."

Tommy wanted to call a lawyer, but he was afraid that asking for one would make him look guilty. So he kept talking, kept trying to explain, kept making the situation worse.

By the time the agents left, Tommy had essentially confessed to what they characterized as fraud. He had admitted to the discrepancies in his application. He had acknowledged that some of his payroll calculations were incorrect. He had even suggested that maybe he should pay back the loan, which the agents interpreted as an admission of guilt.

Three months later, Tommy Cole was indicted on charges of wire fraud, bank fraud, and money laundering. The potential sentence: thirty years in federal prison.

The Epidemic Begins

Tommy's case was not unique. Across the country, similar scenes were playing out in small businesses, restaurants, barber shops, and family-owned companies. The **COVID-19 Fraud Enforcement Task** Force had identified thousands of potential cases using the same algorithmic approach that had flagged Tommy's loan.

The Justice Department's statistics were staggering. By the end of 2022, federal prosecutors had filed charges in over 1,500 PPP fraud cases. The average loan amount in these cases was $71,000. The average requested sentence was twelve years in prison.

These weren't cases involving sophisticated criminal enterprises or massive fraud schemes. They were cases involving small business owners who had made mistakes on hastily completed applications, who had misunderstood complex regulations, who had trusted the government's promise that the program was designed to be simple and fast.

The government's own data revealed the scope of the problem. Of the 1,500 PPP fraud cases filed by late 2022, fewer than 200 involved loans over **$1 million.** The vast majority were small businesses that had received loans of less than **$150,000.** Many involved discrepancies of less than **$10,000.**

But the Justice Department was not interested in proportionality. They were interested in statistics. Every conviction counted the same in the annual reports that measured prosecutorial success. A barber who had miscalculated his payroll by **$3,000** was worth the same as a criminal who had stolen $3 million.

The Defense Bar Awakens

The PPP prosecution wave caught the criminal defense bar by surprise. Most white-collar defense attorneys had never handled SBA loan cases. The regulations were complex, the documentation requirements were unclear, and the speed of prosecutions was unprecedented.

"I'd been practicing federal criminal law for twenty years," says Michael Blake, a defense attorney in Seattle. "I'd never seen anything like this. The government was treating technical violations as criminal fraud, and judges were going along with it."

The challenge for defense attorneys was that many of their clients had technically violated the law, even if they hadn't intended to commit fraud. The PPP applications required certifications that many borrowers didn't understand. The forgiveness process involved calculations that many small business owners couldn't perform accurately.

"How do you defend someone who signed a form saying they had ten employees when they actually had eight?" asks Lisa Martini, a defense attorney in Miami. "The signature is right there. The number is wrong. The prosecutor says it's fraud. What's your defense?"

Some attorneys tried to argue that the mistakes were inadvertent, that their clients had acted in good faith. But federal fraud statutes don't require intent to defraud, they only require intent to make false statements. And every PPP borrower had intentionally signed their application, even if they had made mistakes.

Other attorneys focused on the government's own conduct, arguing that the SBA's rushed implementation and contradictory guidance had created an impossible situation for borrowers. But judges were reluctant to excuse defendants based on government incompetence.

The most successful defense strategy emerged from an unlikely source: the government's own data. Defense attorneys began analyzing the PPP database, looking for patterns that might explain their clients' applications. They discovered that many of the "red flags" that had triggered investigations were actually common practices in certain industries or regions.

The Barbershop Owner's Fight

Tommy Cole hired attorney Maria Santos after his indictment. Santos was a former federal prosecutor who had left the Justice Department to start her own practice. She had never handled a PPP case, but she understood the federal system and the pressure prosecutors faced to secure convictions.

"Your case is actually pretty typical," Santos told Tommy during their first meeting. "The government is prosecuting hundreds of cases just like yours."

"So what's my defense?" Tommy asked.

Santos spread out the documents on her conference table. "The truth. You made mistakes, but you didn't commit fraud. The question is whether we can make a jury understand the difference."

The preparation for trial took eighteen months. Santos subpoenaed the SBA's internal communications, revealing the chaos and confusion that had surrounded the program's implementation. She obtained records showing that the agency had changed its guidance multiple times, often after Tommy had already submitted his application.

She hired an expert witness, a former SBA official who testified about the program's design flaws and the impossible timeline banks faced. She gathered character witnesses from Tommy's neighborhood, customers who had been coming to his shop for years, employees who testified about his honesty and integrity.

Most importantly, she obtained data on other PPP loans in Tommy's area, showing that his application was consistent with hundreds of other barbershops and small businesses. The "red flags" that had triggered his investigation were actually normal for his industry.

The trial lasted five days. The prosecutor, a young attorney from the Justice Department's fraud section, presented a straightforward case: Tommy had signed an application containing false information, he had received money based on that false information, and he had used the banking system to commit fraud.

Santos's defense was more complex. She argued that Tommy had made inadvertent mistakes on a confusing application, that the government had encouraged speed over accuracy, and that prosecuting these mistakes as fraud was an abuse of the criminal justice system.

The jury deliberated for two days. When they returned, the foreman stood and announced: "Not guilty on all counts."

Tommy broke down in tears. After three years of investigation, indictment, and trial, he was finally free.

But the victory came at a cost. Tommy had spent over $200,000 on legal fees, money he had borrowed against his house and his business. The stress of the prosecution had damaged his marriage and his health. Several of his longtime customers had stopped coming to the shop, afraid to associate with someone who had been charged with federal crimes.

Most tragically, Tommy's case was an exception. The vast majority of PPP defendants pleaded guilty rather than face trial. The federal conviction rate in these cases exceeded 95%, not because the government had strong evidence, but because the cost and risk of trial was simply too high for most small business owners.

The Reckoning

As of late 2024, the PPP prosecution campaign has resulted in over 3,000 criminal cases, thousands of civil settlements, and hundreds of millions of dollars in fines and restitution. The Justice Department considers it one of its most successful fraud enforcement initiatives.

But the human cost has been enormous. Thousands of small business owners have lost their businesses, their homes, and their freedom. Families have been destroyed, communities have been devastated, and the trust between small businesses and their government has been shattered.

The irony is that the program largely worked as intended. Studies show that PPP loans prevented millions of job losses and helped thousands of businesses survive the pandemic. The fraud rate, while politically embarrassing, was relatively low compared to other emergency programs.

Yet the prosecutorial response has been disproportionate to the actual harm. The government has spent more money prosecuting PPP fraud than most defendants allegedly stole. The average cost of a federal prosecution is over **$500,000,** meaning that the government has spent more than **$1.5 billion** pursuing cases involving mostly small-dollar fraud.

The real tragedy is that this was all predictable. When you create a program designed to distribute money quickly with minimal oversight, you inevitably create opportunities for mistakes and abuse. When you then subject those mistakes to criminal prosecution, you turn a policy failure into a human disaster.

Tommy Cole's barbershop is still open, but it's a different place now. The laughter is quieter, the conversations more guarded. A framed copy of his not-guilty verdict hangs on the wall, but most customers don't know what it means.

Tommy knows, though. He knows that he was one of the lucky ones, one of the few who could afford to fight back. And he knows that somewhere across America, other small business owners are facing the same choice he faced: plead guilty to a crime they didn't commit, or risk everything in a fight against the federal government.

The perfect storm that created the PPP program is over. But the wreckage it left behind, in the form of thousands of prosecutions, ruined lives, and broken trust, will last for generations.

This is the story of how a program designed to help small businesses became a weapon used against them. It's the story of good intentions, bad implementation, and the dangerous intersection of politics and prosecutorial power.

Most importantly, it's the story of what happens when the government forgets that the people it's supposed to protect are the same people it's prosecuting.

The storm may be over, but the cleanup has just begun.

CHAPTER 2

INSIDE THE FEDERAL MACHINE

Meet Your Prosecutors: The Alphabet Soup Of Federal Agencies

Assistant U.S. Attorney Rebecca Winters had been waiting her entire career for a case like this. Sitting in her cramped office on the fourteenth floor of the federal courthouse in Brooklyn, she stared at the stack of PPP case files that had just landed on her desk. Forty-three potential prosecutions, all neatly packaged with risk scores, financial analysis, and recommendations from the **COVID-19 Fraud Enforcement Task Force.**

It was December 2021, and Winters was thirty-four years old with six years of experience as a federal prosecutor. She had handled mostly immigration cases and drug offenses, the bread and butter of the Eastern District of New York. But PPP fraud was different. These were white-collar cases that could make careers, the kind of prosecutions that led to promotions, prestigious assignments, and maybe even a judgeship someday.

Her supervisor, Criminal Chief David Marcus, had made the stakes clear during their morning meeting. "Main Justice is watching these cases closely," he said, referring to the Department of Justice headquarters in Washington. "They want to see results. Numbers. Convictions."

Winters opened the first file: Elena Vasquez, a single mother who owned two small restaurants in Queens. The file indicated Vasquez had received **$127,000** in PPP loans and had allegedly inflated her payroll by **$18,000.** The potential charges: wire fraud, bank fraud, money laundering. Maximum sentence: sixty years in prison.

Winters had never met Elena Vasquez, had never been to her restaurants, had never spoken to her employees or customers. But she didn't need to. The computer algorithms had already determined that Vasquez was guilty. Walsh's job was simply to prosecute.

What Winters didn't know, what none of the prosecutors pursuing PPP cases knew, was that they were about to become foot soldiers in the largest prosecutorial overreach in American history. They were good lawyers, dedicated public servants, patriots who believed they were protecting the American taxpayer from fraud. They had no idea they were destroying innocent lives in the service of political theater.

The Machine Awakens

To understand how thousands of small business owners became federal defendants, you have to understand the machine that prosecuted them. It wasn't a single agency or office, but a vast network of federal bureaucracies that had been transformed into a fraud-hunting apparatus by the political pressure surrounding PPP.

The machine had many parts, each with its own incentives, its own metrics of success, its own reasons for pursuing prosecutions. Understanding these incentives is crucial for anyone facing federal charges, because it explains why the government acts the way it does, why certain cases are prioritized, and why logic and fairness often take a backseat to statistics and politics.

At the top of the machine sat the Department of Justice, led by attorneys general who faced enormous political pressure to show accountability for PPP spending. Below DOJ were the ninety-three U.S. Attorney's offices, each competing for resources, recognition, and results. Supporting them were investigative agencies like the FBI, IRS Criminal Investigation, and the SBA's Office of Inspector General.

Each agency had its own role to play, its own piece of the puzzle. But they all shared one common goal: finding fraud, making cases, and generating the convictions that would satisfy their political masters.

The Department Of Justice: Setting The Tone

The tone for PPP prosecutions was set at the very top of the Justice Department. Attorney General William Barr, who served during the initial rollout of PPP, established the **COVID-19 Fraud Enforcement Task** Force in May 2020, just six weeks after the program launched.

"We will pursue these criminals with the full force of federal law enforcement," Barr announced at a press conference. "Anyone who thinks they can steal from American taxpayers during this crisis is gravely mistaken."

The message was clear: PPP fraud was a priority, and prosecutors who delivered results would be rewarded. When Merrick Garland replaced Barr in

2021, he doubled down on this commitment, expanding the task force and setting aggressive targets for prosecutions.

Kevin Chambers, who served as Deputy Assistant Attorney General in the Criminal Division during this period, later revealed the internal pressure prosecutors faced. "There were weekly calls with all the districts, asking for updates on PPP cases," Chambers said in a 2023 interview. "The question was always 'How many charges have you filed?' Not 'Are these good cases?' or 'Is this the right thing to do?' Just numbers."

The emphasis on numbers created a perverse incentive structure. Prosecutors who filed more PPP cases received better performance reviews, more resources, and consideration for prestigious assignments. Those who questioned the quality of their cases or suggested more investigation was needed were seen as insufficiently aggressive.

"It became a competition," explains former federal prosecutor Jennifer Kim, who left the Justice Department in 2022. "Offices were trying to outdo each other with PPP prosecutions. The Eastern District of New York would brag about filing fifty cases in a month. The Southern District of Florida would respond by filing sixty. It was insane."

This competitive atmosphere filtered down to individual prosecutors like Rebecca Winters, who found themselves under pressure to file cases quickly rather than investigate thoroughly. The message from supervisors was consistent: trust the algorithms, trust the data, and file charges.

U.S. Attorney's Offices: The Front Lines

The ninety-three U.S. Attorney's offices across the country became the front lines of PPP prosecution. Each office was led by a U.S. Attorney, a political appointee who served at the pleasure of the president and the attorney general. These officials faced enormous pressure to demonstrate their effectiveness through statistics: cases filed, convictions obtained, money recovered.

PPP cases were particularly attractive to U.S. Attorneys because they were relatively easy to prosecute and generated impressive-sounding statistics. A single PPP case might involve multiple defendants, multiple charges, and hundreds of thousands of dollars in alleged fraud. Even small discrepancies could be charged as federal crimes carrying lengthy sentences.

The Southern District of New York, often called the **"Sovereign District"** for its prestigious reputation, filed some of the most aggressive PPP cases in the country. Under U.S. Attorney Audrey Strauss, the office pursued prosecutions involving loan amounts as small as **$10,000,** arguing that fraud was fraud regardless of the amount involved.

"We send a message that no fraudster, no matter how small-time, is beneath our notice," Strauss said at a press conference announcing a dozen PPP indictments in March 2022.

The Eastern District of New York, where Rebecca Winters worked, took a similarly aggressive approach. The office created a dedicated PPP unit with six prosecutors whose sole job was to process fraud cases generated by the task force's algorithms. They were expected to file at least one case per week, every week.

"It was like a factory," recalls a former prosecutor from the office who spoke on condition of anonymity. "Cases would come in from the algorithm, we'd spend a few days reviewing the documents, and then we'd file charges. There wasn't time for real investigation or nuanced analysis."

Some offices tried to resist the pressure for volume prosecutions. The District of Vermont, led by U.S. Attorney Christina Nolan, focused on larger cases involving clear evidence of fraudulent intent. But Nolan faced criticism from Main Justice for her office's relatively low PPP prosecution numbers.

"I got calls asking why we weren't filing more cases," Nolan later revealed. "The assumption was that we weren't working hard enough or weren't aggressive enough. The idea that we might be exercising appropriate prosecutorial discretion didn't seem to register."

The FBI: Following The Data

The Federal Bureau of Investigation found itself in an unusual position during the PPP prosecution wave. Traditionally, FBI agents developed cases through investigation, surveillance, and informants. But PPP cases were different: they were generated by computer algorithms and delivered to agents as prepackaged packages.

The COVID-19 Fraud Enforcement Task Force had developed sophisticated data analytics capabilities, using artificial intelligence and machine learning to identify potential fraud patterns in the PPP database. These algorithms could process millions of loan applications in hours, flagging suspicious patterns that would have taken human investigators years to identify.

Special Agent Sophia Lane of the **FBI's Financial Crimes Unit** in Los Angeles described the process: "We'd get a list of flagged loans from the task force, usually ranked by risk score. Our job was to gather the documentation and build the case for prosecution."

This data-driven approach fundamentally changed how FBI agents worked. Instead of developing sources, conducting surveillance, or building relationships in the community, they spent their time reviewing bank records, analyzing loan applications, and preparing cases for prosecution.

"It felt more like accounting than law enforcement," said one FBI agent who worked PPP cases. "We weren't really investigating fraud so much as documenting discrepancies that the computer had already identified."

The pressure to produce results was intense. FBI field offices were given quotas for PPP investigations, and agents who failed to meet their numbers faced criticism from supervisors. Some agents began to question whether they were pursuing real criminals or simply processing paperwork errors.

"I joined the FBI to catch bank robbers and terrorists," said Agent Mike Sullivan, who requested anonymity. "Instead, I was arresting barbers and restaurant owners who had made mistakes on loan applications."

The cultural impact on the FBI was significant. Veteran agents, accustomed to using their judgment and investigative skills, found themselves reduced to data processors. Newer agents learned that successful cases came from algorithms, not from shoe-leather police work.

Irs Criminal Investigation: The Money Trackers

The Internal Revenue Service's Criminal Investigation division (IRS-CI) played a crucial role in PPP prosecutions, bringing their expertise in financial crimes and money laundering to the task force. IRS-CI agents were particularly valuable because they could analyze tax returns, bank records, and financial statements to build cases involving the movement of money.

Special Agent in Charge Tammy Rooks of IRS-CI's Los Angeles field office explained their role: "Our job was to follow the money. When someone received a PPP loan, we could track how they spent it, whether they used it for approved purposes, and whether they properly reported it on their tax returns."

This financial analysis often revealed discrepancies that became the basis for additional charges. A restaurant owner who used PPP funds to pay personal expenses might face not only PPP fraud charges, but also tax evasion charges if they failed to properly report the forgiven loan as income.

IRS-CI agents prided themselves on their analytical capabilities and their high conviction rate. The agency had traditionally focused on complex tax schemes and money laundering operations involving sophisticated criminals. PPP cases were different: they involved small business owners who often had rudimentary financial record-keeping and little understanding of tax law.

"These weren't criminal masterminds," admitted one IRS-CI agent. "Most of them were just in over their heads financially and legally. But the law is the law, and our job is to enforce it."

The agency's involvement in PPP prosecutions created internal tensions. Some agents felt that pursuing small business owners for technical violations was beneath the agency's mission. Others argued that fraud was fraud, regardless of the perpetrator's sophistication or intent.

IRS-CI's participation also expanded the potential charges that defendants faced. What might have been a simple PPP fraud case could become a complex prosecution involving money laundering, tax evasion, and conspiracy charges, each carrying substantial prison sentences.

The SBA Office Of Inspector General: The Insider's View

The Small Business Administration's **Office of Inspector General (SBA-OIG)** occupied a unique position in PPP prosecutions. As the internal watchdog for the agency that administered the program, SBA-OIG had intimate knowledge of PPP's design flaws, implementation problems, and systemic weaknesses.

Inspector General Hannibal "Mike" Ware had been warning about PPP's vulnerability to fraud since the program's inception. In a series of reports issued throughout 2020 and 2021, Ware's office documented the lack of controls, the rushed implementation, and the high risk of improper payments.

But when it came to prosecutions, SBA-OIG found itself in the awkward position of helping to prosecute individuals for exploiting weaknesses that the agency itself had created. Internal emails obtained through Freedom of Information Act requests reveal the tension within SBA-OIG about their role in PPP prosecutions.

"We're essentially prosecuting people for taking advantage of a program we designed to be exploitable," wrote one SBA-OIG investigator in an internal email. "It feels like we're shooting the victims of our own incompetence."

Despite these concerns, SBA-OIG became one of the most aggressive participants in PPP prosecutions. The office assigned over a hundred investigators to PPP fraud cases and developed specialized analytical tools to identify potential violations.

Special Agent Sarah Kim of SBA-OIG explained their approach: "Our job is to protect the integrity of SBA programs. When someone submits false information to obtain a loan, that's a violation of federal law, regardless of whether the program made it easy to do so."

SBA-OIG's involvement was crucial to prosecutors because the agency could provide expert testimony about program requirements, loan processing procedures, and the significance of various violations. Their agents often served as the government's primary witnesses in PPP trials.

Fincen: The Financial Intelligence Unit

The Financial Crimes Enforcement Network (FinCEN), a bureau of the Treasury Department, provided crucial intelligence for PPP prosecutions through its analysis of suspicious activity reports and other financial intelligence.

Banks are required to file suspicious activity reports (SARs) when they detect potentially fraudulent transactions. During the PPP program, banks filed thousands of SARs related to loan applications, fund usage, and loan forgiveness requests. FinCEN analyzed these reports to identify patterns and trends that could indicate fraud.

"We could see networks of related applications, unusual banking patterns, and financial behavior that didn't match legitimate business operations," explained a FinCEN analyst who worked on PPP cases.

FinCEN's analysis was particularly valuable for identifying organized fraud schemes involving multiple borrowers, professional loan brokers, or sophisticated criminal networks. But the agency also flagged individual borrowers whose financial behavior appeared suspicious, even when that behavior might have legitimate explanations.

The agency's involvement expanded the scope of PPP investigations beyond simple loan fraud. FinCEN's analysis could identify potential money laundering, structuring violations, and other financial crimes that prosecutors could add to PPP cases.

The Prosecutors' Dilemma

Individual prosecutors like Rebecca Winters found themselves caught between multiple pressures as they handled PPP cases. From above, they faced demands for results, numbers, and quick resolutions. From below, they dealt with defendants who were often sympathetic, first-time offenders who had made technical violations rather than committed sophisticated frauds.

"These weren't the kinds of cases I expected to handle as a federal prosecutor," Winters later reflected. "I thought I'd be going after organized crime, major fraudsters, people who were clearly bad actors. Instead, I was prosecuting restaurant owners and barbers who had made mistakes on loan applications."

The cases presented ethical dilemmas that many prosecutors hadn't anticipated. The evidence of technical violations was often clear: applications contained false information, loan proceeds were used for unapproved purposes, forgiveness calculations were incorrect. But the intent to defraud was often unclear or absent entirely.

"How do you prove someone intended to commit fraud when the program was so confusing that even lawyers couldn't understand it?" asked former prosecutor David Simpson. "How do you argue that someone was lying when the SBA's own guidance was contradictory and constantly changing?"

Some prosecutors resolved this dilemma by focusing on the law rather than equity. If defendants had technically violated federal statutes, they deserved to be prosecuted, regardless of their intent or the circumstances of their violations.

Others struggled with the proportionality of pursuing criminal charges for what appeared to be civil violations. The potential sentences for PPP fraud often exceeded what defendants might receive for violent crimes or major theft offenses.

"I was prosecuting a woman who had miscalculated her payroll by **$8,000** on a PPP application," recalled one prosecutor. "She was facing twenty years in prison. The bank robber in the next courtroom was looking at five years. How do you explain that to a jury?"

The Conviction Machine

The combination of these agencies created a conviction machine that was remarkably effective at securing guilty pleas and convictions. The government's resources were overwhelming: teams of investigators, forensic accountants, data analysts, and prosecutors working together to build cases against individual defendants.

Most defendants lacked the resources to fight back effectively. The cost of defending a federal case typically exceeded **$100,000,** often more than the amount of the loans involved. Many defendants were small business owners who had been financially devastated by the pandemic and couldn't afford experienced white-collar defense attorneys.

The government exploited this imbalance through aggressive plea bargaining tactics. Prosecutors would file multiple charges carrying lengthy sentences, then offer plea agreements that required defendants to admit guilt but avoided trial. The message was clear: plead guilty and receive a relatively lenient sentence, or go to trial and face decades in prison.

"It wasn't really about guilt or innocence," explained defense attorney Lisa Martini. "It was about whether defendants could afford to fight. Most couldn't, so they pleaded guilty even when they had viable defenses."

The plea bargaining process was often coercive. Prosecutors would threaten to add charges, target family members, or seek asset forfeiture if defendants refused to cooperate. They would present overwhelming documentation of technical violations while downplaying the lack of fraudulent intent.

Rebecca Winters participated in dozens of these plea negotiations. "We had evidence of false statements on the applications," she said. "That was usually enough to convince defendants that they couldn't win at trial, even if they honestly believed they hadn't committed fraud."

The Human Cost

The human cost of this prosecutorial machine was enormous, but it was largely invisible to the prosecutors who operated it. They saw case files, not people. They saw legal violations, not human struggles. They saw statistics, not the devastation their cases caused to families and communities.

Elena Vasquez, the restaurant owner whose file Rebecca Winters had reviewed, ultimately pleaded guilty to one count of wire fraud. She received two years of probation and was required to pay $35,000 in restitution. Her restaurants closed during the prosecution, and she lost her home to foreclosure while paying legal fees.

"I just wanted to save my business and keep my employees working," Vasquez said after her sentencing. "I never thought I was committing a crime. I never thought the government would destroy my life over a mistake on a loan application."

Winters never spoke to Vasquez during the prosecution. She never visited the closed restaurants, never met the displaced employees, never saw the family that had been torn apart by her case. She simply processed the file, secured the conviction, and moved on to the next case.

This distance between prosecutors and the consequences of their actions was intentional. The system was designed to prevent prosecutors from developing sympathy for defendants that might interfere with their willingness to pursue charges.

"If we had to look these people in the eye and see what our prosecutions were doing to their lives, we probably couldn't do the job," admitted one former prosecutor. "The system works because we can focus on the law and leave the human consequences to someone else."

The Metrics Of Success

The success of the PPP prosecution machine was measured in statistics that looked impressive in press releases and congressional testimony. By the end of 2023, the COVID-19 Fraud Enforcement Task Force had:

Filed criminal charges in over 3,000 PPP fraud cases

Secured convictions in over 2,500 cases

Recovered over **$500 million** in restitution and penalties

Seized assets worth over $**200 million**

Conducted over 10,000 investigations

These numbers satisfied the political demands for accountability and allowed agency leaders to claim success in protecting taxpayer funds. But they obscured the reality of what the prosecutions had accomplished.

The average recovery per case was less than **$200,000,** often far less than the cost of the prosecution itself. Many defendants were ordered to pay restitution they couldn't afford, resulting in uncollectible judgments. The deterrent effect was minimal because most legitimate borrowers had never intended to commit fraud in the first place.

"We spent more money prosecuting these cases than we recovered from them," acknowledged a Justice Department official who spoke on condition of anonymity. "But that wasn't really the point. The point was to send a message and satisfy the political pressure for accountability."

The System's Logic

To understand why the federal machine prosecuted PPP cases so aggressively, you have to understand the internal logic that drove each agency's actions. From their perspective, they were simply doing their jobs: enforcing federal law, protecting taxpayer funds, and maintaining the integrity of government programs.

The prosecutors weren't evil or corrupt. They were dedicated public servants working within a system that rewarded certain behaviors and punished others. They were responding to incentives created by their political leaders, their supervisors, and the legal framework within which they operated.

The problem wasn't individual malfeasance but systemic dysfunction. The machine was designed to prosecute fraud, and it did so efficiently and effectively. But it couldn't distinguish between sophisticated criminal schemes and innocent mistakes made under impossible circumstances.

"The system worked exactly as designed," reflected former Justice Department official Kevin Chambers. "The problem is that it was designed to prioritize prosecutions over justice, numbers over fairness, and political satisfaction over proportional punishment."

Understanding this logic is crucial for anyone facing PPP charges because it explains why the government acts the way it does. Prosecutors aren't trying to destroy lives; they're trying to build careers, satisfy supervisors, and meet statistical targets. The destruction is simply collateral damage in a system that measures success by convictions rather than justice.

Fighting The Machine

The few defendants who successfully fought PPP prosecutions did so by understanding the machine they were facing and exploiting its weaknesses. They hired experienced attorneys who knew how the system worked, who understood prosecutorial incentives, and who could challenge the government's evidence and legal theories.

Tommy Cole, the barbershop owner from Chapter 1, won his case partly because his attorney understood that prosecutors were under pressure to secure quick convictions. By forcing the case to trial, she imposed costs on the government that prosecutors hadn't anticipated and weren't prepared to bear.

"Most prosecutors handling PPP cases had never tried a white-collar case before," explained defense attorney Maria Santos. "They were used to defendants pleading guilty. When we forced them to trial, they weren't prepared for aggressive cross-examination of their agents or challenges to their evidence."

Other successful defenses focused on the government's own conduct, highlighting the contradictory guidance, rushed implementation, and systemic failures that had created the conditions for mistakes. Some attorneys obtained internal government documents showing the pressure prosecutors faced to file cases quickly.

"The best defense in these cases was often to put the government on trial," said defense attorney Michael Blake. "Show the jury how the program was designed, how the guidance changed constantly, and how ordinary business owners were set up to fail."

The Price Of Success

Rebecca Winters left the U.S. Attorney's office in late 2023, two years after handling her first PPP case. She had successfully prosecuted forty-seven PPP defendants, securing convictions in all but three cases. Her performance reviews were excellent, and she was being considered for a supervisory position.

But the work had taken a toll. Winters found herself questioning whether the cases she had prosecuted were truly examples of criminal fraud or simply the inevitable result of a flawed program implemented under impossible circumstances.

"I started this job thinking I was protecting the American people from criminals," Winters said in an interview after leaving the Justice Department. "I ended it wondering whether I had become the criminal."

Her departure was part of a broader exodus of prosecutors who had handled PPP cases. Many left for private practice, where they now defend the kinds of cases they used to prosecute. Others moved to different areas of law, seeking work that felt more aligned with their sense of justice.

"The PPP prosecution campaign was successful in terms of statistics," reflected former prosecutor Jennifer Daily. "But it was a moral failure that damaged the credibility of federal law enforcement and destroyed thousands of innocent lives. We created a machine designed to produce convictions, and that's exactly what it did. The question is whether those convictions served any legitimate purpose."

The machine continues to operate, processing new cases and pursuing new defendants. But the enthusiasm that once drove the prosecution campaign has faded, replaced by a growing recognition that the cure may have been worse than the disease.

Understanding how this machine works, why it operates the way it does, and how to defend against it is essential for anyone facing PPP charges. The machine is powerful, but it's not omnipotent. It has weaknesses that can be exploited, biases that can be challenged, and limitations that can be exposed.

The key is understanding that you're not just fighting criminal charges; you're fighting a system designed to produce convictions regardless of actual guilt or innocence. That system can be beaten, but only by those who understand how it works and are prepared to fight back with equal determination and superior preparation.

The machine may be powerful, but justice, properly defended, is more powerful still.

CHAPTER 3

THE DATA DRAGNET

How AI And Algorithms Are Choosing Who Gets Prosecuted

Dr. James Liu had never expected his expertise in artificial intelligence to be used to destroy people's lives. Sitting in his sterile office at the Department of Justice's Criminal Division in Washington, D.C., he stared at the computer screen displaying the latest batch of PPP loan applications flagged by the fraud detection algorithm he had helped design.

Risk Score 891: Maria Gonzalez, daycare owner in Phoenix. Flagged for employee count discrepancy.

Risk Score 847: David Johns, restaurant owner in Seattle. Flagged for irregular payroll patterns.

Risk Score 923: Jennifer Thompson, hair salon owner in Atlanta. Flagged for multiple business addresses.

Each name represented a human being whose life was about to be turned upside down by a computer program. Liu had designed the algorithm to identify statistical anomalies in PPP applications, but he was beginning to realize that statistical anomalies and criminal fraud were not the same thing.

"The machine doesn't lie," his supervisor, Deputy Assistant Attorney General Robert Chance, had told him during their weekly briefing. "It finds patterns that human investigators could never see. These people flagged themselves by their own behavior."

But Liu knew better. He understood how the algorithm worked, what data it analyzed, and why it flagged certain applications. More importantly, he was beginning to understand how defendants could use this knowledge to defend themselves against prosecutions based on algorithmic analysis.

The data dragnet was the government's most powerful weapon in PPP prosecutions, but it was also its greatest weakness. Understanding how it worked was the key to beating it.

The Birth Of The Algorithm

The PPP fraud detection algorithm was born out of desperation and political pressure. By the summer of 2020, with billions of dollars flowing through the program and media reports highlighting questionable loans, Congress demanded that the Justice Department identify and prosecute fraud aggressively.

Traditional fraud investigation methods were woefully inadequate for the scale of PPP. The SBA had processed over 5 million loans in the program's first round alone. Even with unlimited resources, human investigators could never review that volume of applications for fraud indicators.

The solution was artificial intelligence. The Justice Department assembled a team of data scientists, former banking executives, and fraud investigators to create an algorithm that could analyze every PPP loan for potential fraud indicators. Dr. Liu, who had previously worked on fraud detection systems for credit card companies, was brought in to lead the technical development.

"The concept was sound," Liu later explained. "We would feed the algorithm all available data about PPP loans, bank records, tax filings, and business registrations. The machine would identify patterns that deviated from normal business behavior and flag them for human review."

But the implementation was rushed and flawed. The algorithm was trained on data from before the pandemic, when business operations were normal and predictable. It had no way to account for the extraordinary circumstances that had led to PPP in the first place.

"We were trying to identify fraud during the greatest economic disruption in American history using patterns derived from normal economic times," Liu admitted. "It was like trying to identify suspicious behavior at a hurricane evacuation using patterns from a normal Tuesday."

****DEFENSE STRATEGY #1:** *Challenge the Algorithm's Training Data***

Understanding this fundamental flaw is crucial for defending PPP cases. The algorithm was trained on pre-pandemic business data, which means it identified any deviation from normal business patterns as suspicious. But nothing about 2020 was normal.

Defense attorneys can challenge algorithmic evidence by demanding discovery of:

- The training dataset used to develop the algorithm
- The time period from which training data was drawn
- How the algorithm accounted for pandemic-related business disruptions
- What validation testing was performed on pandemic-era data

In many cases, this discovery will reveal that the algorithm was never properly validated for use during economic emergencies, calling into question the reliability of its findings.

The Risk Score System

The algorithm assigned every PPP loan a risk score between 1 and 1,000, with higher scores indicating greater likelihood of fraud. Loans scoring above 750 were automatically referred to law enforcement for investigation. Scores above 850 triggered immediate criminal referrals.

But what exactly made a loan "risky" in the algorithm's judgment? Dr. Liu's internal documentation, obtained through litigation discovery, reveals the specific factors that influenced risk scores:

High-Risk Factors (Major Score Increases):

- Employee count that didn't match quarterly payroll tax filings
- Average monthly payroll that seemed high for the industry
- Multiple businesses at the same address
- Bank account deposits that didn't match reported revenue
- Applications submitted by the same IP address or computer
- Round numbers in payroll calculations (suggesting estimation rather than exact calculation)
- Business formation dates within two years of the loan application

Medium-Risk Factors (Moderate Score Increases):

- Cash-intensive businesses (restaurants, salons, retail)
- Borrowers with previous SBA loans
- Businesses in certain geographic areas (particularly areas with high concentrations of minority-owned businesses)
- Borrowers who applied for loan forgiveness immediately after receiving funds
- Use of loan brokers or consultants

Low-Risk Factors (Minor Score Increases):

- Applications submitted during peak processing periods

- Borrowers who took the maximum loan amount allowed
- Businesses with seasonal employment patterns
- Borrowers who made mathematical errors on applications

DEFENSE STRATEGY #2: *Deconstruct Your Risk Score*

Every defendant should demand complete discovery of their loan's risk score calculation. This discovery should include:

- The specific factors that contributed to the risk score
- The weight assigned to each factor
- How the algorithm handled missing or incomplete data
- Whether any manual adjustments were made to the score

Armed with this information, defense attorneys can challenge each factor individually, showing that behaviors flagged as suspicious were actually normal business practices or pandemic-related adaptations.

The False Positive Problem

Dr. Liu's greatest concern about the algorithm was its false positive rate: the percentage of loans flagged as suspicious that were actually legitimate. Internal testing showed that the algorithm had a false positive rate of approximately 23%, meaning that nearly one in four loans flagged for investigation were actually legitimate.

This created an enormous problem for prosecutors. They were receiving thousands of criminal referrals based on algorithmic analysis, but nearly a quarter of them involved legitimate borrowers who had committed no crime. The pressure to produce prosecution statistics meant that many of these false positives were prosecuted anyway.

"The algorithm was designed to cast a wide net," Liu explained. "The theory was that human investigators would sort out the false positives during the investigation process. But there wasn't time for thorough human review, so a lot of innocent people got caught in the dragnet."

Defense attorney Sarah Martinez discovered this during her representation of Carlos Rivera, a construction contractor in Miami. Rivera's loan had received a risk score of 834, triggering an investigation that led to federal charges.

"When we demanded discovery of the algorithm's performance data, we found that loans with Carlos's risk score had a 31% false positive rate," Martinez explained. "Nearly one in three people charged based on similar risk scores were actually innocent. That created reasonable doubt about the reliability of the algorithmic evidence."

****DEFENSE STRATEGY #3**: *Exploit the False Positive Rate***

Defendants can use the algorithm's false positive rate to challenge the reliability of their prosecution. Key discovery requests should include:

- Overall false positive rates for the algorithm
- False positive rates for loans with similar risk scores
- How many prosecutions were dismissed after investigation revealed no fraud
- What validation studies were conducted on the algorithm's accuracy

This information can be used to argue that algorithmic flagging creates reasonable doubt about guilt, especially when combined with other defense evidence.

The Geographic Bias

One of the most troubling aspects of the PPP algorithm was its geographic bias. Internal analysis showed that the algorithm flagged loans from certain areas at much higher rates than others, often correlating with the racial and ethnic composition of those areas.

Dr. Liu had warned about this bias during development. "The algorithm was trained on historical business data that reflected existing inequalities in the financial system," he explained. "Businesses in minority communities often have different banking patterns, different employee structures, and different revenue patterns than businesses in affluent areas. The algorithm interpreted these differences as suspicious."

The data bore out Liu's concerns. Analysis of the algorithm's flagging patterns showed:

- Loans from majority-Black census tracts were flagged 47% more often than loans from majority-white areas

- Loans from majority-Hispanic areas were flagged 33% more often
- Loans from urban areas were flagged 28% more often than loans from suburban or rural areas
- Loans from areas with median incomes below $50,000 were flagged 41% more often than loans from areas with median incomes above **$100,000**

This geographic bias had devastating consequences for minority business owners, who were already disproportionately affected by the pandemic. They were more likely to be investigated, more likely to be prosecuted, and more likely to receive harsh sentences.

DEFENSE STRATEGY #4: *Challenge Algorithmic Bias*

Defendants can challenge prosecutions based on biased algorithmic analysis by:

- Requesting demographic data on all loans flagged by the algorithm
- Comparing flagging rates across different geographic areas and demographic groups
- Hiring expert witnesses to analyze the algorithm for bias
- Arguing that prosecutions based on biased algorithms violate equal protection rights

This strategy has been successful in several cases where defendants demonstrated that they were targeted not because of criminal behavior, but because they operated businesses in areas where the algorithm was programmed to expect suspicious activity.

The Data Sources

The algorithm's power came from its ability to analyze multiple data sources simultaneously, creating a comprehensive picture of each borrower's financial behavior. Understanding these data sources is crucial for defense attorneys because it reveals both the government's strengths and its vulnerabilities.

Primary Data Sources:

- PPP loan applications and supporting documentation
- SBA loan databases (current and historical)
- IRS tax return data
- State unemployment insurance records
- Bank account transaction records
- Credit bureau reports
- Secretary of State business registration records

Secondary Data Sources:

- Social media profiles and business pages
- Online business directories and review sites
- News articles and press releases

- Court records and bankruptcy filings
- Professional licensing databases
- Property ownership records

Tertiary Data Sources:

- IP address and computer tracking data
- Email metadata and patterns
- Phone number and address associations
- Vehicle registration records
- Utility connection records

The algorithm cross-referenced all of this information to build a profile of each borrower and identify inconsistencies or unusual patterns. But the sheer volume of data sources also created opportunities for errors, misinterpretations, and false correlations.

DEFENSE STRATEGY #5: *Attack the Data Quality*

The government's reliance on multiple data sources creates numerous opportunities for defense challenges:

- Demand complete discovery of all data sources used in the analysis
- Challenge the accuracy and completeness of each data source
- Identify errors in data integration or correlation
- Show how outdated or incomplete data led to false conclusions
- Demonstrate how the algorithm misinterpreted legitimate business activities

Dr. Liu had documented dozens of cases where data errors led to false flags. "The algorithm might flag someone for having employees who didn't appear in tax records, when the real explanation was that the tax data was six months old and didn't reflect recent hires," he explained.

The Network Analysis

One of the algorithm's most sophisticated features was its ability to identify networks of related borrowers, potentially indicating organized fraud schemes. The system would flag borrowers who shared:

- Physical addresses or mailing addresses
- Bank accounts or financial institutions
- Accountants, lawyers, or loan brokers
- Computer IP addresses or email domains

- Phone numbers or family relationships
- Business partnerships or corporate structures

This network analysis was designed to catch sophisticated fraud rings, but it often flagged legitimate business relationships and family connections as suspicious.

The case of the Patel family in New Jersey illustrates this problem. Three brothers owned separate businesses: a convenience store, a taxi company, and a small restaurant. All three applied for PPP loans using the same accountant and submitting applications from the same computer at their shared accountant's office.

The algorithm flagged all three loans as part of a potential fraud network. The brothers were investigated, prosecuted, and ultimately convicted of conspiracy charges, despite the fact that their businesses were legitimate and their loans were properly used.

****DEFENSE STRATEGY #6**: *Explain Legitimate Networks***

When defendants are flagged based on network analysis, defense attorneys must:

- Identify all the connections that triggered the network flag
- Provide legitimate explanations for each connection
- Gather evidence of the legitimate business relationships
- Show that the connections preceded any alleged fraud scheme
- Demonstrate that the network represents normal business practices rather than criminal conspiracy

In the Patel case, a more aggressive defense might have focused on the commonality of shared accountants and family business relationships in immigrant communities, challenging the algorithm's assumption that such connections indicated fraud.

The Timing Analysis

The algorithm paid particular attention to the timing of various events in a borrower's application process, looking for patterns that might indicate fraud:

****Suspicious Timing Patterns:****

- Applying for maximum loan amounts immediately when the program opened

- Submitting applications just before program deadlines
- Applying for loan forgiveness immediately after receiving funds
- Making large purchases or payments immediately after receiving loan proceeds
- Establishing new bank accounts shortly before applying for loans

Many of these timing patterns had innocent explanations related to the emergency nature of the program and the financial desperation of legitimate borrowers. But the algorithm interpreted them as indicators of fraud.

Restaurant owner Linda Brown learned this the hard way. She applied for a PPP loan on the first day the program opened because her restaurant was on the verge of closing. She applied for the maximum amount allowed because she needed every dollar to survive. She applied for forgiveness immediately because she had used all the funds for payroll and rent, exactly as required.

Every one of these actions was logical and legitimate, but the algorithm flagged her loan as suspicious because of the timing patterns. She was investigated, prosecuted, and ultimately forced to plead guilty to fraud charges despite having done nothing wrong.

****DEFENSE STRATEGY #7:** *Contextualize Timing Evidence***

Defendants can counter timing-based allegations by:

- Providing business records showing the legitimate reasons for timing decisions
- Demonstrating that the timing was driven by business necessity rather than fraudulent intent
- Showing that similar timing patterns were common among legitimate borrowers
- Providing expert testimony about normal business behavior during emergencies
- Challenging the algorithm's assumptions about what constitutes "suspicious" timing

The Mathematical Analysis

The algorithm subjected every loan application to detailed mathematical analysis, looking for patterns that might indicate fabricated numbers or estimated rather than calculated figures. This analysis included:

Mathematical Red Flags:

- Round numbers in payroll calculations (suggesting estimation)
- Numbers that seemed too perfect or convenient
- Calculations that didn't match supporting documentation
- Inconsistencies between different parts of the application
- Numbers that fell exactly at program limits or thresholds

This mathematical analysis often flagged legitimate applications where borrowers had estimated figures due to incomplete records or had rounded numbers for convenience. Small business owners often don't maintain the precise financial records that the algorithm expected, especially during a crisis.

Barbershop owner Mike Poole (no relation to Tommy Cole from Chapter 1) was flagged because his payroll calculations included round numbers and his employee count varied seasonally. The algorithm interpreted this as evidence of fabrication, but Mike's defense attorney was able to show that these patterns were normal for seasonal businesses with part-time employees.

DEFENSE STRATEGY #8: *Provide Mathematical Context***

Defendants can counter mathematical analysis by:

- Explaining the business reasons for any round numbers or estimates
- Providing evidence of the legitimate calculation methods used
- Showing that mathematical patterns reflected normal business practices
- Demonstrating that any discrepancies were inadvertent rather than intentional
- Using expert witnesses to explain industry-standard financial practices

The Behavioral Analysis

Perhaps the most controversial aspect of the algorithm was its attempt to analyze borrower behavior for signs of fraud. This analysis looked at factors such as:

Behavioral Indicators:

- How quickly borrowers responded to requests for information
- Whether borrowers hired attorneys or consultants
- How borrowers communicated with lenders and government agencies
- Whether borrowers attempted to withdraw applications or return funds
- How borrowers reacted to media coverage of PPP fraud investigations

Dr. Liu had opposed including behavioral analysis in the algorithm. "We were essentially programming the computer to psychoanalyze people based on limited data," he explained. "It was highly subjective and prone to misinterpretation."

The behavioral analysis created a catch-22 for borrowers. Those who hired attorneys were flagged as suspicious because "innocent people don't need lawyers." Those who tried to return funds voluntarily were flagged because "only guilty people return money." Those who responded quickly to information requests were flagged for being "too cooperative," while those who responded slowly were flagged for being "evasive."

DEFENSE STRATEGY #9: *Challenge Behavioral Assumptions*

Defendants can counter behavioral analysis by:

- Showing that their behavior had legitimate, non-criminal explanations

- Providing evidence that similar behavior is common among innocent people

- Challenging the algorithm's assumptions about what constitutes "guilty" behavior

- Using expert testimony about normal responses to government investigations

- Demonstrating that the behavioral analysis lacks scientific foundation

Breaking The Algorithm

The most successful defenses against algorithmic prosecution have come from attorneys who understood how the system worked and attacked its fundamental assumptions. Defense attorney Maria Santos, who represented barbershop owner Tommy Cole, used algorithmic analysis to win an acquittal.

"We demanded discovery of every aspect of the algorithm," Santos explained. "We wanted to know how it was trained, what data it used, how it weighted different factors, and what its error rates were. The government fought this discovery for months, which told us they knew the algorithm was vulnerable."

When Santos finally obtained the discovery, she found that the algorithm had flagged Tommy's loan based on five factors:

1. His employee count didn't match payroll tax records (because he counted a part-time worker as an employee)

2. His payroll seemed high for a three-chair barbershop (because he included the owner's salary)

3. He had irregular bank deposits (because customers often paid in cash)

4. He applied for the maximum loan amount (because he needed money to survive)

5. He was located in a high-risk zip code (because it was a minority business district)

Santos was able to provide innocent explanations for each factor and show that the algorithm's assumptions about "normal" business behavior were flawed. She brought in expert witnesses to explain how the algorithm worked and why its conclusions were unreliable.

"The key insight was that the algorithm wasn't really detecting fraud," Santos said. "It was detecting deviations from a narrow definition of normal business behavior. Once the jury understood that, they realized that being flagged by the algorithm didn't mean Tommy was guilty of anything."

DEFENSE STRATEGY #10: *Comprehensive Algorithmic Challenge*

The most effective defense strategy involves a comprehensive challenge to the algorithmic evidence:

- Demand complete discovery of the algorithm's design and operation
- Hire expert witnesses to analyze the algorithm's methodology
- Challenge each factor that contributed to the defendant's risk score
- Show that the algorithm's assumptions about normal behavior were flawed
- Demonstrate that being flagged by the algorithm doesn't prove guilt
- Use the government's own data to show the algorithm's limitations and biases

The Human Element

Despite its sophistication, the algorithm was ultimately a tool used by human investigators and prosecutors who made the final decisions about whom to prosecute. Understanding the human element in algorithmic prosecutions is crucial for mounting an effective defense.

FBI agents typically received lists of flagged loans ranked by risk score, but they had limited time to investigate each case thoroughly. Many agents relied heavily on algorithmic analysis without conducting independent investigations.

"We trusted the computer," admitted one FBI agent who worked PPP cases. "If the algorithm said a loan was fraudulent, we assumed it was right and focused on building a case to prove it."

This human bias in favor of algorithmic conclusions created opportunities for defense attorneys who could show that human investigators had failed to consider alternative explanations for the flagged behavior.

DEFENSE STRATEGY #11: *Expose Human Bias*

Defendants can challenge the human interpretation of algorithmic evidence by:

- Showing that investigators relied too heavily on algorithmic conclusions
- Demonstrating that investigators failed to consider alternative explanations
- Revealing that investigators didn't understand how the algorithm worked
- Proving that investigators made assumptions based on algorithmic flags rather than evidence
- Highlighting the lack of thorough human investigation beyond algorithmic analysis

The Future Of Algorithmic Prosecution

The PPP algorithm was just the beginning. Government agencies are increasingly using artificial intelligence and machine learning to identify potential crimes, from tax evasion to healthcare fraud to terrorism. Understanding how to defend against algorithmic prosecution will become increasingly important for criminal defense attorneys.

Dr. Liu left the Justice Department in 2023, disturbed by how his creation had been used to prosecute potentially innocent people. "I designed the algorithm to be a tool for investigators, not a substitute for investigation," he said. "But that's how it was used. People were prosecuted based on algorithmic analysis with minimal human oversight."

His parting advice for defendants facing algorithmic prosecution: "Remember that algorithms are created by humans, trained on human-selected data, and interpreted by humans with their own biases and incentives. They are not infallible, and they are not immune to challenge. The key is understanding how they work and why they reach the conclusions they do."

The data dragnet is powerful, but it is not omnipotent. It can be understood, challenged, and beaten by defendants who are willing to fight back with the same technological sophistication that the government uses to prosecute them.

The algorithm may have chosen you for prosecution, but that doesn't mean you're guilty. It means you deviated from a computer's narrow definition of normal behavior during the most abnormal period in recent American history. With the right defense strategy, that deviation can become the foundation of your acquittal.

Understanding the dragnet is the first step in escaping it. The computer may have flagged you, but a jury of your peers will ultimately decide your fate. And juries, unlike algorithms, understand the difference between mathematical anomalies and criminal intent.

The machine is powerful, but justice is more powerful still. You just have to know how to fight back.

CHAPTER 4

ANATOMY OF A TAKEDOWN

From First Contact To Handcuffs: The Federal Playbook

Special Agent Jennifer Walsh of the FBI's White Collar Crime Unit had executed over two hundred arrest warrants in her twelve-year career, but the one she was about to serve felt different. Standing outside the modest suburban home in Riverside, California, at 6:47 AM on a Tuesday morning in October 2022, she checked her notes one final time.

Target: Robert Than, age 54, owner of three Chinese restaurants

Charges: Wire Fraud, bank fraud, money laundering

Alleged loss: $184,000 in PPP loans

Risk assessment: Low flight risk, no history of violence

Media alert: Yes, local news crews notified

The last item bothered Walsh. In her experience, the perp walk, the deliberate public display of a defendant being arrested, served more to humiliate than to serve justice. But PPP cases were different. The Justice Department wanted maximum publicity for these arrests to send a message about fraud enforcement.

What Walsh didn't know was that Robert Than was innocent. His restaurants had struggled during the pandemic, and he had applied for PPP loans to keep his employees working. Yes, he had made mistakes on his applications, miscalculating payroll by including tips, counting part-time workers as full-time employees, and underestimating his actual financial need. But these were not crimes; they were the inevitable errors of a small business owner trying to navigate an impossibly complex program during a crisis.

Robert Than's takedown would follow the federal playbook precisely: early morning arrest, media coverage, overwhelming charges, coercive plea negotiations, and ultimate conviction. But understanding this playbook is the key to defeating it. Every step in the government's process creates opportunities for defense, if you know where to look.

Phase One: The Investigation Begins

The federal takedown process starts long before agents knock on your door. In PPP cases, investigations typically begin when the algorithmic fraud detection system flags a loan for human review. At this stage, most targets have no idea they're under investigation.

Robert Than's investigation began in March 2022, six months before his arrest, when the COVID-19 Fraud Enforcement Task Force's algorithm assigned his loans risk scores of 847, 791, and 823. These scores triggered an automatic referral to the FBI's Los Angeles field office.

Special Agent Michael Branch received the referral as part of his weekly batch of PPP cases. The file contained:

- Than's original loan applications and supporting documents
- Bank records showing how the loan proceeds were spent
- Tax returns for Than's businesses for the previous three years
- Credit reports and financial statements
- The algorithm's analysis highlighting discrepancies and red flags

Torres spent approximately four hours reviewing Than's file before deciding to open a formal investigation. This cursory review would prove crucial to Than's defense, because it revealed the agent's preconceptions and biases.

****DEFENSE STRATEGY #12:** *Obtain the Initial Investigative File***

The government's initial investigative file often contains crucial evidence for the defense:

- The agent's notes and impressions from the first file review
- Communications between agencies about prioritizing the case
- Early theories about the alleged fraud scheme
- Decisions about what evidence to gather or ignore

Defense attorneys should request this material immediately through discovery motions, as it often reveals that agents assumed guilt from the beginning rather than conducting an objective investigation.

Phase Two: Financial Investigation

Agent Branch began his investigation by analyzing Than's financial records in detail. The government's financial investigation follows a predictable pattern designed to build a paper trail of evidence that can be presented to a jury.

Step 1: Bank Record Analysis

Branch subpoenaed records from all of Than's business and personal bank accounts, looking for:

- How PPP loan proceeds were deposited and spent
- Transfers between business and personal accounts
- Large cash withdrawals or unusual transactions
- Evidence of lavish spending or lifestyle inflation

Step 2: Asset Investigation

The agent reviewed public records to identify Than's assets:

- Real estate ownership records
- Vehicle registrations
- Business licenses and permits
- Investment accounts and retirement funds

Step 3: Business Operations Analysis

Branch investigated Than's actual business operations:

- Interviews with current and former employees
- Reviews of payroll records and tax filings
- Analysis of sales receipts and business income
- Verification of business expenses and operating costs

This financial investigation took three months and cost taxpayers approximately **$75,000** in agent time and resources. But it also created a detailed record that Than's defense team could use to show his legitimate business operations and good faith efforts to comply with PPP requirements.

DEFENSE STRATEGY #13: *Beat Them at Their Own Game*

When the government conducts a financial investigation, defense attorneys should conduct their own parallel investigation:

- Hire forensic accountants to analyze the same records the government reviewed

  - Identify innocent explanations for any unusual financial patterns
  - Gather evidence of legitimate business purposes for questioned transactions

- Document the client's actual financial situation and business needs during the pandemic

The government's financial investigation often reveals more evidence of legitimate business struggles than criminal fraud. A skilled defense team can use this evidence to show that the defendant's actions were driven by business necessity, not criminal intent.

Phase Three: Building The Criminal Case

Once Agent Branch completed his financial investigation, he began building the criminal case against Than. This phase follows a standard prosecution template designed to maximize charges and potential sentences.

****Charge Stacking Strategy****

The government typically files multiple charges for the same conduct:

- Wire fraud (for electronic transmission of loan applications)
- Bank fraud (for providing false information to obtain loans)
- Money laundering (for spending loan proceeds)
- Conspiracy (if multiple people are involved)

Each charge carries substantial penalties, creating enormous pressure for defendants to plead guilty rather than risk trial.

****Document Preparation****

Branch worked with prosecutors to prepare the charging documents:

- Criminal complaint outlining the basic allegations
- Indictment with detailed charges and penalty ranges
- Asset forfeiture notice identifying property subject to seizure
- Press release highlighting the arrest and charges

****Coordination with Prosecutors****

The agent met regularly with Assistant U.S. Attorney Angela Martinez to plan the prosecution strategy:

- Timing of the arrest for maximum media impact
- Plea negotiation parameters and sentencing recommendations
- Trial preparation and witness identification
- Asset forfeiture and restitution calculations

This collaboration between agents and prosecutors creates opportunities for defense attorneys to challenge the government's case by showing that the investigation was driven by prosecutorial goals rather than objective fact-finding.

DEFENSE STRATEGY #14: *Expose the Prosecution-Driven Investigation*

Defense attorneys can challenge investigations that appear to be driven by prosecutorial rather than investigative goals:

- Request communications between agents and prosecutors during the investigation
- Show that the investigation was designed to build a case rather than determine facts
- Highlight evidence that was ignored because it didn't support prosecution
- Demonstrate that charging decisions were made before the investigation was complete

Phase Four: The Arrest Operation

The arrest of Robert Than was carefully orchestrated for maximum impact. Agent Walsh received her assignment the day before, along with detailed instructions about timing, location, and media coordination.

Pre-Dawn Timing

Federal agents prefer early morning arrests for several reasons:

- Targets are more likely to be at home and unprepared
- Media coverage is maximized for morning news shows
- Defendants appear disheveled and vulnerable in perp walk photos
- Family members, including children, are present to witness the humiliation

Media Coordination

The FBI's public affairs office notified local news outlets about the "major PPP fraud arrest" the evening before. News crews were positioned outside Than's home by 6:30 AM, ready to capture his arrest on camera.

Overwhelming Force

Despite the non-violent nature of PPP fraud, agents typically arrive in force:

- Multiple agents in bulletproof vests
- Marked and unmarked vehicles
- Search warrant for the residence
- Asset seizure orders for vehicles, computers, and financial accounts

This overwhelming display of force is designed to intimidate defendants and their families, encouraging quick guilty pleas to avoid further public humiliation.

DEFENSE STRATEGY #15: *Document the Arrest Circumstances**

The circumstances of a client's arrest can become powerful evidence of prosecutorial overreach:

- Photograph or video the scene showing excessive force or media presence
- Interview neighbors who witnessed the arrest spectacle
- Gather evidence of unnecessary humiliation or intimidation tactics
- Document the impact on family members, especially children
- Show how the arrest was designed for publicity rather than law enforcement purposes

This evidence can be used to argue prosecutorial misconduct and can influence judges and juries who may be sympathetic to defendants who were treated unfairly.

Phase Five: The Initial Court Appearance

Robert Than's first court appearance occurred six hours after his arrest. Still wearing the clothes he had been arrested in, without having spoken to an attorney, he faced a federal magistrate judge who would determine whether he could be released on bail.

****The Bail Hearing Strategy****

Federal prosecutors use bail hearings to preview their case and pressure defendants:

- Exaggerate the strength of the evidence
- Emphasize the potential sentences to intimidate the defendant
- Argue for restrictive bail conditions to disrupt the defendant's life
- Request asset freezes that prevent defendants from hiring quality attorneys

Assistant U.S. Attorney Martinez argued that Than was a flight risk because he had "stolen nearly $**200,000** from American taxpayers" and faced "decades in federal prison." She requested that Than surrender his passport, submit to electronic monitoring, and agree to asset seizure pending trial.

The Public Defender Problem

Than qualified for a court-appointed attorney because his assets were frozen and his restaurants were struggling. The federal public defender, while competent, was handling over 150 cases and had limited time to prepare for Than's defense.

This resource imbalance is deliberate. The government wants defendants to have inadequate representation during the crucial early stages of the case when key decisions about cooperation and plea bargaining are made.

****DEFENSE STRATEGY #16**: *Win the Bail Hearing***

The bail hearing is the first opportunity to challenge the government's case:

- Prepare thoroughly with financial documents showing legitimate business operations
- Bring character witnesses who can testify to the defendant's reputation and community ties
- Challenge the government's characterization of the evidence and potential sentences
- Argue that asset freezes are punitive and prevent adequate legal representation
- Show that the defendant poses no flight risk and has strong community connections

A successful bail hearing not only preserves the defendant's freedom but also signals to prosecutors that they face a vigorous defense, potentially influencing plea negotiations.

Phase Six: The Media Campaign

The government's media strategy in PPP cases is designed to poison the jury pool and pressure defendants to plead guilty. Robert Than's arrest generated significant local news coverage, with stories emphasizing:

- The amount of money allegedly stolen
- The harm to taxpayers and legitimate borrowers
- The maximum potential sentences

- The government's commitment to prosecuting PPP fraud

Controlling the Narrative

Prosecutors carefully craft their public statements to maximize damage to defendants:

- Use inflammatory language like "stole," "cheated," and "defrauded"
- Emphasize the dollar amounts without mentioning the defendant's actual financial situation
- Highlight maximum sentences without discussing likely actual sentences
- Present allegations as established facts

The Silence Trap

Defendants facing media coverage face an impossible choice:

- Remain silent and allow the government's narrative to go unchallenged
- Respond publicly and risk providing evidence for prosecutors to use at trial

Most defense attorneys counsel silence, but this allows the government to control public perception and potentially influence future jurors.

DEFENSE STRATEGY #17: *Strategic Media Response*

Defense attorneys can respond to negative media coverage while protecting their clients:

- Issue carefully crafted statements emphasizing the defendant's presumption of innocence
- Provide context about the complexity of PPP rules and the chaos during program implementation
- Highlight the defendant's legitimate business operations and community contributions
- Challenge prosecutorial statements that go beyond the evidence
- Use social media and community supporters to present a balanced narrative

The key is responding without providing ammunition for prosecutors while ensuring that potential jurors hear something other than the government's one-sided story.

Phase Seven: The Plea Pressure Campaign

Within two weeks of Than's arrest, prosecutor Martinez began the plea negotiation process. This campaign represents the government's most effective tool for securing convictions without trial.

****The Opening Offer****

Martinez's initial plea offer was deliberately harsh:

- Plead guilty to one count of wire fraud
- Accept a sentencing recommendation of 18-24 months in federal prison
- Pay **$184,000** in restitution
- Forfeit business assets used in the alleged fraud

This offer was designed to anchor Than's expectations at a high level of punishment while appearing reasonable compared to the potential trial penalties.

****Escalating Pressure Tactics****

When Than's attorney indicated he wanted to review the evidence before considering a plea, Martinez escalated the pressure:

- Filed a superseding indictment adding money laundering charges
- Increased the restitution demand to include "interest and penalties"
- Indicated that cooperation with other investigations might be required
- Set a deadline for plea acceptance with threats of additional charges

****The Cooperation Trap****

Prosecutors offered Than a "cooperation agreement" that would require him to:

- Plead guilty to fraud charges
- Testify against other PPP defendants
- Assist in identifying additional fraud cases
- Submit to unlimited questioning by government agents

This cooperation requirement would have forced Than to become a witness against other potentially innocent defendants to reduce his own sentence.

DEFENSE STRATEGY #18: *Resist Plea Pressure*

Effective resistance to plea pressure requires understanding the government's tactics:

- Analyze the strength of the evidence objectively before considering any plea
- Recognize that initial offers are designed to be harsh and can often be improved
- Challenge each element of the charges to show prosecutors the weaknesses in their case
- Gather evidence of innocent explanations for the defendant's conduct
- Prepare for trial to show prosecutors that their conviction is not guaranteed

The key insight is that prosecutors offer pleas because they are not confident of obtaining convictions at trial. A defendant who appears prepared to fight often receives better plea offers or sees charges reduced.

Phase Eight: Discovery Warfare

The discovery phase of Than's case became a battle between the prosecution's desire to limit information and the defense's need to understand the full scope of the government's case.

Government Discovery Tactics

Prosecutors use discovery strategically to maintain their advantage:

- Provide documents in disorganized or unsearchable formats
- Claim privilege or national security exceptions for embarrassing materials
- Delay production of exculpatory evidence until just before trial
- Overwhelm defense attorneys with irrelevant documents while hiding crucial evidence

The Brady Violation Problem

Prosecutors are required to provide evidence that might help the defense, but many PPP cases involve Brady violations where favorable evidence is concealed:

- Internal government communications showing doubts about the case
- Evidence of algorithmic errors or bias

- Information about other similar cases that were dismissed
- Expert analysis contradicting the government's theories

DEFENSE STRATEGY #19: *Aggressive Discovery Practice*

Successful PPP defenses require aggressive discovery tactics:

- File detailed discovery motions requesting specific categories of evidence
- Demand production of algorithmic analysis and underlying data
- Request internal government communications about the case and the PPP program generally
- Seek expert reports and analysis that contradict the government's theories
- Challenge privilege claims and fight for access to embarrassing government documents

The government's case often depends on the defense not understanding how weak the evidence really is. Comprehensive discovery can reveal fatal flaws in the prosecution's case.

Phase Nine: Expert Battle

The prosecution of PPP cases often comes down to a battle of experts who interpret the complex regulations and financial evidence for the jury.

Government Expert Strategy

Prosecutors typically rely on experts who:

- Simplify complex regulations to make violations appear clear-cut
- Emphasize the dollar amounts allegedly stolen
- Minimize the complexity and confusion surrounding PPP implementation
- Present the defendant's conduct as obviously fraudulent

Defense Expert Opportunities

Defense experts can counter the government's case by:

- Explaining the complexity and ambiguity of PPP regulations
- Showing how the defendant's conduct was consistent with good faith compliance efforts

- Demonstrating industry standards and common practices that explain the defendant's actions
- Revealing flaws in the government's financial analysis and damage calculations

DEFENSE STRATEGY #20: *Win the Expert Battle*

The expert battle is often decisive in PPP cases:

- Hire experts with superior credentials and experience compared to government witnesses
- Prepare experts to explain complex regulations in simple, understandable terms
- Use experts to attack the methodology and assumptions underlying the government's case
- Present expert testimony that shows the defendant's conduct was reasonable under the circumstances
- Demonstrate that government experts are biased or lack relevant experience

Robert Than's defense team hired Dr. Susan Peters, a former SBA official who had helped design PPP regulations. Her testimony explaining the program's complexity and the reasonable interpretations of Than's applications proved crucial to his eventual acquittal.

Phase Ten: Trial Preparation And Victory

As Than's trial approached, his defense team had systematically dismantled the government's case using the strategies outlined above. Their preparation revealed:

Weaknesses in the Government's Case:

- The algorithmic analysis was based on flawed assumptions about normal business behavior

- Agent Branch had conducted a cursory investigation focused on building a case rather than finding facts
- The financial evidence showed Than's legitimate business struggles rather than criminal intent
- Government experts could not explain why Than's conduct was criminal rather than mistaken

Strengths of the Defense Case:

- Than had operated legitimate businesses for over twenty years

- ➢ His PPP applications contained honest mistakes rather than intentional fraud
- ➢ He had used loan proceeds for legitimate business purposes during the pandemic
- ➢ Multiple character witnesses testified to his honesty and integrity

The Trial Strategy:

Than's attorneys decided to challenge every aspect of the government's case:

- ➢ Cross-examine agents about their biased investigation
- ➢ Present expert testimony about PPP complexity and Than's good faith efforts
- ➢ Show the jury Than's actual financial situation and business struggles
- ➢ Argue that mistakes on complex government forms do not constitute criminal fraud

The Verdict And Lessons Learned

After a six-day trial, the jury deliberated for eight hours before returning not guilty verdicts on all charges. The victory demonstrated that PPP prosecutions can be defeated when defendants fight back with proper preparation and strategy.

Key Factors in Than's Victory:

- ➢ Comprehensive discovery that revealed weaknesses in the government's case
- ➢ Expert witnesses who explained the complexity of PPP regulations
- ➢ Character evidence showing Than's honesty and legitimate business operations
- ➢ Aggressive cross-examination that exposed investigative bias and shortcuts

The Cost of Victory:

Than's legal defense cost over **$300,000** and took two years of his life. His restaurants suffered permanent damage from the negative publicity, and his family endured enormous stress and humiliation. Even in victory, the federal takedown process extracts a terrible price.

Lessons for Future Defendants:

Than's case proves that PPP prosecutions can be beaten, but only with proper preparation, adequate resources, and attorneys who understand both the government's playbook and how to counter it effectively.

The Takedown Template

The federal takedown follows a predictable template that creates opportunities for defense at every stage:

Phase 1: Investigation → Challenge the algorithmic analysis and investigative bias

Phase 2: Financial Analysis → Provide innocent explanations and business context

Phase 3: Case Building → Expose prosecution-driven investigation tactics

Phase 4: Arrest → Document prosecutorial overreach and media manipulation

Phase 5: Initial Appearance → Win bail and challenge asset seizures

Phase 6: Media Campaign → Control the narrative and protect reputation

Phase 7: Plea Pressure → Resist coercion and evaluate evidence objectively

Phase 8: Discovery → Aggressively seek exculpatory evidence

Phase 9: Expert Battle → Counter government experts with superior analysis

Phase 10: Trial → Present comprehensive defense challenging every element

Each phase builds on the previous ones, creating a comprehensive defense strategy that can defeat even seemingly strong prosecutions.

Fighting Back Works

The government's takedown playbook is designed to intimidate defendants into pleading guilty without fighting back. But when defendants understand the playbook and counter it effectively, prosecutions can be defeated.

Robert Than's victory was not unique. Dozens of PPP defendants have won acquittals by using similar strategies to challenge prosecutions based on complex regulations, algorithmic analysis, and investigative bias.

The key insight is that the government's most powerful weapon, the intimidation factor of federal prosecution, becomes less effective when defendants understand the process and fight back intelligently at every stage.

The federal machine is powerful, but it is not invincible. It can be understood, predicted, and defeated by defendants who refuse to be intimidated and who fight back with the same level of preparation and sophistication that the government brings to prosecute them.

The takedown may follow a predictable pattern, but so does the successful defense. Understanding both patterns is the key to victory in the battle between individual defendants and the federal prosecution machine.

Your life may feel like it's been turned upside down by federal charges, but remember: the government chose to prosecute you because they thought you would be an easy target. Prove them wrong.

CHAPTER 5

BUILDING THE PAPER TRAIL

Financial Records, Certifications, Correspondence

Pamela Horn knew she was in trouble the moment FBI Agent Roslyn Torres asked to see her "complete financial records" for the past three years. Sitting in the cramped office behind her family restaurant in East Los Angeles, Pamela watched the agent flip through boxes of receipts, bank statements, and handwritten ledgers that chronicled her twenty-year struggle to build a successful business.

"This is your bookkeeping system?" Agent Torres asked, holding up a shoebox filled with cash register receipts, supplier invoices, and employee time cards held together with rubber bands.

"We're a family business, "Pamela replied defensively. "My husband handles the kitchen, I handle the front, and my daughter helps with the books when she's not in college. We keep track of everything, just not like some big corporation."

Agent Torres made notes on her pad. Pamela didn't realize it at the time, but her informal record-keeping system would become the foundation of the government's fraud case against her. Prosecutors would argue that her "disorganized" records were evidence of intentional concealment, that her cash-based business practices indicated tax evasion, and that her family's involvement suggested a criminal conspiracy.

But Pamela's story also illustrates the most powerful weapon available to PPP defendants: the paper trail. While her informal bookkeeping initially seemed like a liability, it actually contained overwhelming evidence of her good faith and legitimate business operations. The key was knowing how to organize, present, and defend that evidence in a way that told the true story of her business.

Building an effective paper trail defense requires understanding what the government is looking for, what evidence actually proves innocence, and how to present complex financial information in a way that juries can understand and sympathize with. Most importantly, it requires recognizing that the same documents prosecutors use to prove fraud can be used by the defense to prove innocence.

Understanding What The Government Seeks

Before building a defense paper trail, you must understand what federal prosecutors are looking for when they analyze financial records. The government's approach to PPP cases follows a predictable pattern designed to identify discrepancies that can be characterized as fraud.

****Primary Government Targets:****

- Discrepancies between loan applications and supporting financial documents
- Evidence of funds being used for unauthorized purposes
- Signs of inflated payroll, employee counts, or business expenses
- Transfers between business and personal accounts
- Large cash transactions or unusual spending patterns
- Communications that suggest awareness of program violations

****Secondary Government Targets:****

- Lifestyle evidence suggesting the defendant benefited personally from loan proceeds
- Business records that contradict statements made in loan applications
- Evidence of coordination with other borrowers or loan facilitators
- Financial patterns that deviate from industry norms or pre-pandemic operations
- Documentation gaps that prosecutors can characterize as intentional concealment

Understanding these targets allows defendants to anticipate government arguments and prepare defensive responses that put financial evidence in proper context.

****DEFENSE STRATEGY #21:** *Preemptive Document Analysis***

Defendants should conduct their own analysis of financial records before the government does:

- Identify all discrepancies between loan applications and supporting documents
- Prepare explanations for unusual financial patterns or transactions

- Gather evidence showing legitimate business purposes for questioned activities
- Document the business context that explains apparent irregularities
- Organize records to tell a coherent story of legitimate business operations

This preemptive analysis allows defendants to address weaknesses in their case before prosecutors exploit them and to present a compelling alternative narrative supported by the same evidence.

The Good Faith Documentation Strategy

The most effective defense against PPP fraud charges is demonstrating good faith through contemporaneous business records. Good faith means the defendant honestly attempted to comply with program requirements, even if mistakes were made in the process.

****Elements of Good Faith Evidence:****

- Documentation showing research into PPP requirements
- Records of consultations with accountants, attorneys, or other advisors
- Evidence of attempts to correct errors or provide additional information
- Business records that support statements made in loan applications
- Communications showing concern about compliance with program rules

Pamela Horn's case illustrates how informal record-keeping can actually support a good faith defense. Her shoebox of receipts contained:

- Detailed records of employee hours and payments during the pandemic
- Supplier invoices showing business expenses during the lockdown period
- Bank deposit slips documenting the restaurant's declining revenue
- Handwritten notes tracking which employees were working reduced hours
- Correspondence with her bank about PPP application requirements

While this documentation was disorganized, it painted a clear picture of a business owner desperately trying to keep her restaurant and employees afloat during an unprecedented crisis.

DEFENSE STRATEGY #22: *Reconstruct the Business Context*

Effective paper trail defenses must recreate the business context in which PPP decisions were made:

- Gather evidence of the business's financial situation before and during the pandemic
- Document the specific challenges the business faced during lockdowns
- Show how PPP funds were necessary for business survival
- Demonstrate that loan proceeds were used for legitimate business purposes
- Provide evidence of the defendant's reasonable interpretation of program requirements

This contextual evidence helps juries understand that the defendant's actions were driven by business necessity and good faith efforts to comply with complex regulations, not criminal intent.

Payroll Documentation Defense

Payroll discrepancies are the most common basis for PPP fraud prosecutions. Defendants are typically charged with inflating payroll figures to qualify for larger loans or to meet forgiveness requirements. However, many apparent payroll discrepancies have innocent explanations related to the complexity of calculating pandemic-era payroll.

Common Payroll Complications:

- Seasonal employees who worked different hours in different years
- Part-time workers who were sometimes treated as employees and sometimes as contractors
- Family members who worked in the business but were not always on formal payroll
- Tips and commission payments that were difficult to document precisely
- Employees who were laid off and rehired multiple times during the pandemic

Building a Payroll Defense:

Pamela Horn faced allegations that she inflated her payroll by **$23,000** to qualify for a larger PPP loan. The government argued that she included employees who didn't actually work for the restaurant and calculated wages that were higher than what she actually paid.

Her defense team's investigation revealed the true story:

- Three employees listed on her PPP application were family members who had worked in the restaurant for years but were paid in cash
- The "inflated" wages included tips that were distributed to employees but not reported on formal payroll records
- Seasonal variations in staffing were reflected in her 2019 tax returns, which the government had not properly analyzed
- Two employees had been laid off in March 2020 but were rehired specifically because PPP funding allowed the restaurant to bring them back

****DEFENSE STRATEGY #23:** *Comprehensive Payroll Reconstruction***

Defendants accused of payroll inflation should undertake comprehensive payroll reconstruction:

- Gather all available employment records, including informal documentation
- Interview current and former employees about their actual work history and compensation
- Analyze seasonal and pandemic-related variations in staffing
- Document the legitimate business reasons for any apparent discrepancies
- Obtain expert analysis of industry-standard payroll practices during the pandemic

This reconstruction often reveals that apparent discrepancies reflect the complexity of small business payroll practices rather than intentional fraud.

Expense Verification Strategy

PPP loan forgiveness requires that funds be used for qualified expenses, primarily payroll, rent, utilities, and certain other business costs. Prosecutors often allege fraud when loan proceeds appear to have been used for unauthorized purposes.

****Common Expense Allegations:****

- Personal use of business funds
- Payment of pre-existing debts

- Non-qualified business expenses
- Transfer of funds to related entities
- Use of proceeds for business expansion rather than maintenance

Defending Expense Allegations:

The key to defending expense allegations is demonstrating that questioned expenditures served legitimate business purposes and were necessary for business operations during the pandemic.

Pamela Horn faced allegations that she used PPP funds improperly because:

- **$8,000** was transferred to her personal account
- **$12,000** was paid to a construction company for restaurant repairs
- **$5,000** was used to purchase new kitchen equipment
- **$3,000** was paid to her brother for "consulting services"

Her defense team's investigation revealed legitimate explanations:

- The personal account transfer represented reimbursement for business expenses she had paid personally when the business account was depleted
- The construction repairs were necessary to bring the restaurant into compliance with new COVID-19 safety requirements
- The kitchen equipment replaced items that had broken during the shutdown and were necessary to resume operations
- Her brother was a licensed contractor who had performed legitimate maintenance work on the restaurant

DEFENSE STRATEGY #24: *Document Legitimate Business Purposes*

Every questioned expense should be supported by evidence of its legitimate business purpose:

- Gather invoices, receipts, and contracts documenting all expenditures
- Obtain written explanations from vendors and service providers
- Document the business necessity for each questioned expense
- Show how expenses related to pandemic operations or recovery efforts
- Provide expert testimony about industry-standard practices during the crisis

This documentation strategy transforms apparent misuse into evidence of legitimate business operations during an unprecedented crisis.

Communication Records As Evidence

Email, text messages, and other communications often provide the most powerful evidence in PPP cases, either supporting the government's fraud allegations or demonstrating the defendant's good faith and innocent intent.

****Dangerous Communications:****

- Messages discussing ways to maximize loan amounts or minimize oversight
- Communications suggesting awareness that information in applications was false
- Discussions about hiding assets or income from government review
- Coordination with others to submit false or misleading information

****Protective Communications:****

- Messages seeking advice about program compliance
- Communications with accountants, attorneys, or other advisors
- Discussions about legitimate business needs and challenges
- Evidence of attempts to correct errors or provide additional information

****Communication Strategy:****

Pamela Horn's case was significantly strengthened by communication records that demonstrated her good faith:

- Text messages with her accountant asking questions about PPP requirements
- Emails with her bank requesting clarification about application procedures
- Messages with employees explaining the restaurant's financial situation
- Communications with suppliers negotiating payment arrangements during the crisis

These communications painted a picture of a business owner honestly trying to navigate complex regulations during a crisis, not someone attempting to defraud the government.

DEFENSE STRATEGY #25: *Comprehensive Communication Review*

Defendants should conduct a thorough review of all communications related to their PPP loans:

- Preserve all emails, text messages, and social media communications
- Analyze communications for evidence of good faith and innocent intent
- Identify any problematic communications that need to be addressed
- Gather communications that support the defense narrative
- Prepare explanations for any communications that appear damaging

Remember that the government will obtain these communications through search warrants and subpoenas, so it's better to identify and address potential problems proactively.

Bank Record Defense Strategy

Bank records form the backbone of most PPP fraud prosecutions because they provide an objective record of how loan proceeds were used. However, bank records often tell an incomplete story that can be misleading without proper context.

Government Analysis of Bank Records:

- Tracking loan proceeds from deposit to expenditure
- Identifying transfers that appear to violate program requirements
- Looking for evidence of personal use or unauthorized expenses
- Analyzing spending patterns for signs of fraud or misuse

Defense Analysis of Bank Records:

- Providing business context for all transactions
- Explaining apparent irregularities through legitimate business needs
- Demonstrating that questioned transactions served valid business purposes
- Showing how spending patterns reflected pandemic-related business changes

Bank Record Defense Techniques:

Pamela Horn's bank records initially appeared damaging because they showed numerous transfers between accounts, cash withdrawals, and payments to individuals rather than established vendors. However, her defense team's analysis revealed legitimate explanations:

The transfers between accounts reflected the restaurant's practice of using multiple accounts for different purposes (payroll, rent, suppliers). The cash withdrawals were used to pay employees who preferred cash payment and to purchase supplies from vendors who offered cash discounts. The payments to individuals were for legitimate services like cleaning, maintenance, and food delivery.

****DEFENSE STRATEGY #26:** *Bank Record Contextualization***

Effective bank record defense requires putting every transaction in proper business context:

- Prepare detailed explanations for all significant transactions
- Gather supporting documentation like invoices, contracts, and receipts
- Interview recipients of questioned payments to verify legitimate business purposes
- Demonstrate industry practices that explain apparent irregularities
- Show how pandemic conditions affected normal banking and payment practices

This contextualization transforms suspicious-looking bank records into evidence of legitimate business operations under extraordinary circumstances.

Tax Return Consistency Strategy

Prosecutors often compare PPP loan applications with tax returns to identify discrepancies that can be characterized as fraud. However, tax returns and PPP applications measure different things during different time periods, making discrepancies common even among honest borrowers.

****Common Tax Return Issues:****

- Differences between tax return figures and PPP application figures
- Timing differences between tax years and PPP calculation periods
- Different accounting methods used for tax and loan purposes
- Changes in business operations between tax filing and loan application

****Tax Return Defense Strategy:****

Pamela Horn's faced allegations that her PPP application was inconsistent with her tax returns because:

- Her 2019 tax return showed lower payroll than her PPP application claimed
- Her business income on tax returns was higher than the revenue decline she claimed on her loan application
- She had claimed certain business expenses on her tax return that were not reflected in her PPP calculations

Her defense team's analysis revealed that these discrepancies had innocent explanations:

- The PPP application included 2020 payroll data that reflected seasonal hiring not captured in the 2019 tax return
- The revenue decline occurred between the tax filing period and the loan application period
- The business expenses on her tax return were legitimate but not relevant to PPP calculations

****DEFENSE STRATEGY #27:** *Reconcile Tax and Loan Discrepancies***

Defendants should proactively address any discrepancies between tax returns and PPP applications:

- Prepare detailed reconciliations explaining any differences
- Gather evidence showing the legitimate business reasons for variations
- Obtain expert testimony about different accounting methods and timing issues
- Demonstrate that discrepancies reflect complexity rather than fraud
- Show how pandemic conditions created legitimate reasons for year-over-year variations

This reconciliation strategy prevents prosecutors from exploiting normal business accounting variations as evidence of fraud.

Asset Protection Documentation

Many PPP defendants face asset forfeiture proceedings designed to recover alleged fraud proceeds. Defending against asset forfeiture requires demonstrating that questioned assets were acquired through legitimate means rather than fraud proceeds.

****Asset Protection Strategy:****

- Document the legitimate sources of all significant assets

- Show that asset acquisitions preceded or were unrelated to PPP fraud allegations
- Demonstrate that lifestyle and spending patterns were consistent with legitimate business income
- Provide evidence that any apparent lifestyle improvements had innocent explanations

Pamela Horn's faced asset forfeiture proceedings targeting her home and her restaurant because prosecutors argued that PPP fraud proceeds had been used to make mortgage and business loan payments. Her defense team successfully defended against forfeiture by:

- Showing that mortgage payments came from legitimate business income and personal savings
- Demonstrating that the restaurant's value had not increased due to PPP funds
- Providing evidence that any improvements to her lifestyle were due to her daughter's college graduation and employment, not fraud proceeds

****DEFENSE STRATEGY #28:** *Preemptive Asset Documentation***

Defendants should document the legitimate sources of all significant assets before forfeiture proceedings begin:

- Gather evidence of asset acquisition dates and funding sources
- Prepare explanations for any lifestyle improvements or major purchases
- Document legitimate business and personal income sources
- Show that questioned assets were not acquired with fraud proceeds
- Obtain appraisals and valuations that contradict government damage theories

This preemptive documentation can prevent asset seizures and forfeiture proceedings that can financially cripple defendants even before trial.

Expert Witness Paper Trail

Complex financial cases often require expert witnesses to explain business practices, accounting methods, and industry standards to juries. The paper trail provides the foundation for expert testimony that can either support or undermine the government's case.

Defense Expert Strategy:

Pamela Horn's case was significantly strengthened by expert witness testimony based on her paper trail:

- A restaurant industry expert explained why her business practices were normal for family-owned establishments
- An accounting expert demonstrated that her record-keeping, while informal, was adequate for a small business
- A PPP compliance expert showed that her loan application reflected a reasonable interpretation of complex regulations

These experts used Pamela's actual business records to demonstrate that her practices were consistent with legitimate business operations and good faith compliance efforts.

DEFENSE STRATEGY #29: *Expert-Ready Documentation***

Defendants should organize their paper trail to support expert witness testimony:

- Compile comprehensive business records that experts can analyze and explain
- Identify industry practices and standards that support the defendant's conduct
- Prepare documentation that allows experts to recreate the business context
- Gather evidence that experts can use to challenge government theories
- Organize records in a way that tells a coherent story of legitimate business operations

Expert witnesses are most effective when they can base their opinions on comprehensive, well-organized business records that support the defense narrative.

The Integration Strategy

The most effective paper trail defenses integrate all types of documentation into a coherent narrative that explains the defendant's conduct and demonstrates good faith. This integration strategy requires careful planning and organization to ensure that different types of evidence support rather than contradict each other.

Integration Elements:

- Financial records that support statements made in loan applications
- Communications that demonstrate good faith and compliance efforts
- Business context that explains apparent irregularities
- Expert analysis that validates the defendant's practices
- Timeline that shows how pandemic conditions affected business operations

Pamela Horn's successful defense integrated multiple types of evidence to tell a compelling story:

- Her informal record-keeping demonstrated attention to business details and employee welfare
- Communications with advisors showed good faith efforts to comply with program requirements
- Financial records revealed the restaurant's genuine financial distress during the pandemic
- Expert testimony validated her business practices as normal for the industry
- The timeline showed how her decisions were driven by business necessity rather than criminal intent

DEFENSE STRATEGY #30: *Comprehensive Integration***

The final paper trail strategy involves integrating all evidence into a comprehensive defense narrative:

- Organize all documentation to tell a coherent story of legitimate business operations
- Ensure that different types of evidence support and reinforce each other
- Address any apparent contradictions or weaknesses proactively
- Present evidence in a way that makes complex business operations understandable to juries
- Use expert witnesses to validate and explain the integrated evidence

This integration strategy transforms individual pieces of evidence into a powerful defense narrative that demonstrates innocence and good faith.

Victory Through Documentation

Pamela Horn's case demonstrates that even informal business records can provide the foundation for a successful PPP defense when properly organized and presented. Her acquittal on all charges resulted from a comprehensive paper trail strategy that:

- Demonstrated her good faith efforts to comply with PPP requirements

- Provided legitimate explanations for all questioned transactions and decisions
- Showed that her business practices were normal for the industry
- Integrated multiple types of evidence into a compelling defense narrative

The key insight from Pamela's case is that the same documents prosecutors use to allege fraud can be used by the defense to prove innocence, if defendants understand how to organize, present, and defend their paper trail effectively.

Building Your Defense Paper Trail

Every PPP defendant should begin building their defense paper trail immediately upon learning of an investigation or being charged. This process requires:

****Immediate Actions:****

- Preserve all business and personal records related to PPP loans
- Organize documents chronologically and by category
- Identify and address any apparent discrepancies or problems
- Gather evidence of good faith and legitimate business purposes
- Prepare for comprehensive financial analysis and expert review

****Ongoing Strategy:****

- Continue gathering evidence that supports the defense narrative
- Interview witnesses who can verify business practices and decisions
- Obtain expert analysis of financial records and business operations
- Prepare comprehensive explanations for all questioned conduct
- Organize evidence to support integrated defense strategy

The paper trail is not just evidence; it's the foundation of your defense. When properly built and presented, it can transform apparent evidence of fraud into proof of innocence and good faith. The key is understanding that your business records tell a story, and you must ensure that story is told completely and accurately in your defense.

Remember: the government will use your records to try to convict you. But those same records, when properly understood and presented, can be your path to freedom. The choice is yours, but the stakes couldn't be higher.

CHAPTER 6

LEGAL REPRESENTATION

Choosing Counsel

David Parks thought he was making the smart choice when he hired attorney James Wilson to defend him against PPP fraud charges. Wilson had impressive credentials: Harvard Law School, former prosecutor, partner at a prestigious downtown firm, and a website full of testimonials from satisfied clients. His hourly rate of $800 seemed reasonable for a federal case that could result in twenty years in prison.

But three months into the case, David realized he had made a catastrophic mistake. Wilson had never tried a PPP case. He didn't understand how the algorithmic detection system worked. He seemed more interested in negotiating a quick plea deal than fighting the charges. Most damaging of all, Wilson appeared to believe the government's theory that David had committed fraud.

"Look, David," Wilson said during a meeting in his mahogany-paneled office, "the evidence is pretty clear that you inflated your payroll on the application. The best thing we can do is get you a reasonable plea deal and move on with your life."

David stared at his attorney in disbelief. "But I didn't inflate anything. I included my own salary and the payments to my part-time workers, just like my accountant told me to do."

Wilson shrugged. "That's not how the government sees it. And with your signature on the application, it's going to be hard to convince a jury you didn't know what you were doing."

That conversation convinced David to fire Wilson and find new counsel. His second attorney, Maria Rodriguez, had extensive experience with SBA regulations and had successfully defended three PPP cases. Within two weeks of taking the case, she had identified fatal flaws in the government's evidence and developed a defense strategy that would ultimately result in David's complete vindication.

The difference between Wilson and Rodriguez wasn't just experience or skill, though both mattered enormously. The crucial difference was that Rodriguez understood PPP cases specifically and had developed systematic approaches to defeating the government's most common prosecution theories. She knew that these cases could be won, how they could be won, and what it took to achieve victory.

Choosing the right attorney is the most important decision any PPP defendant will make. The wrong choice can result in unnecessary prison time, financial ruin, and a criminal record that will follow you for life. The right choice can mean the difference between conviction and acquittal, between years in federal prison and complete vindication.

The Attorney Selection Crisis

Most PPP defendants face a fundamental problem when selecting counsel: the attorneys who can afford to take their cases often lack the specific expertise needed to win them, while the attorneys with relevant expertise may be too expensive or too busy to provide adequate representation.

This creates several dangerous scenarios:

****The Prestigious Firm Trap**:** Large law firms with impressive credentials but no PPP experience often treat these cases as routine white-collar matters, failing to understand the unique regulatory complexities and defense opportunities specific to PPP prosecutions.

****The Overwhelmed Public Defender**:** Federal public defenders are skilled attorneys but often carry crushing caseloads that prevent them from developing the specialized knowledge needed for complex PPP defenses.

****The Plea Mill Problem**:** Some attorneys view PPP cases as easy money, charging substantial fees to negotiate plea deals without seriously considering trial defenses or investigating government weaknesses.

****The Inexperienced Specialist**:** Attorneys who market themselves as PPP experts may lack the broader federal criminal defense experience needed to handle complex prosecutions effectively.

Understanding these pitfalls is crucial for making an informed choice about representation that can literally determine your future.

DEFENSE STRATEGY #31: *Attorney Due Diligence Investigation*

Before hiring any attorney, conduct comprehensive due diligence:

- ➢ Request detailed information about the attorney's specific PPP case experience
- ➢ Ask for references from previous PPP clients (with their permission)
- ➢ Investigate the attorney's track record in federal court and with similar cases
- ➢ Verify that the attorney has actually tried cases rather than just negotiating pleas
- ➢ Confirm that the attorney understands the technical aspects of PPP regulations and enforcement

This investigation process should be as thorough as any other major life decision, because the consequences of choosing poorly are far more severe than most business or personal choices.

Essential Qualifications For PPP Defense

Effective PPP defense requires a unique combination of skills and knowledge that most criminal defense attorneys don't possess. Understanding these requirements helps defendants identify attorneys capable of mounting successful defenses.

Core Technical Knowledge Required:

- ➢ Deep understanding of SBA regulations and PPP program requirements
- ➢ Familiarity with the algorithmic detection systems used to identify fraud cases
- ➢ Knowledge of banking and financial industry practices during the pandemic
- ➢ Understanding of small business accounting and operational practices
- ➢ Experience with federal white-collar defense and regulatory compliance issues

Specific PPP Case Experience:

- ➢ Previous representation of PPP defendants through trial or successful dismissal
- ➢ Understanding of common prosecution theories and effective counter-strategies

- Knowledge of expert witnesses and technical resources needed for complex defenses
- Familiarity with discovery strategies specific to algorithmic prosecution
- Experience challenging government technical evidence and expert testimony

Federal Court Litigation Skills:

- Extensive trial experience in federal criminal cases
- Ability to handle complex financial evidence and expert witness battles
- Experience with federal sentencing guidelines and negotiation strategies
- Knowledge of federal discovery rules and motion practice
- Relationships with federal judges and prosecutors that facilitate effective advocacy

Maria Rodriguez possessed all these qualifications when David Park hired her. She had defended eight PPP cases, winning six acquittals and negotiating favorable plea deals in two cases where clients had actually committed clear violations. She understood both the technical details of PPP regulations and the broader federal criminal defense strategies needed for success.

DEFENSE STRATEGY #32: *Verify Specific PPP Expertise*

When evaluating potential attorneys, demand specific evidence of PPP expertise:

- Ask for detailed descriptions of previous PPP cases and their outcomes
- Request explanations of common PPP prosecution theories and defense strategies
- Test the attorney's knowledge of algorithmic detection systems and technical evidence
- Verify that the attorney understands the regulatory complexities specific to PPP
- Confirm that the attorney has relationships with relevant expert witnesses and technical consultants

Attorneys who lack genuine PPP expertise will be unable to provide detailed, knowledgeable responses to these inquiries.

Red Flags In Attorney Selection

Certain warning signs should immediately disqualify attorneys from consideration for PPP defense. Recognizing these red flags can save defendants from making costly mistakes that compromise their defense.

Immediate Disqualifiers:

- Attorneys who immediately recommend plea negotiations without investigating the case
- Lawyers who seem unfamiliar with PPP regulations or dismissive of regulatory complexity
- Counsel who cannot explain specific defense strategies for algorithmic evidence
- Attorneys who appear to believe the government's case without critical analysis
- Lawyers who seem more focused on fees than case outcomes

Subtle Warning Signs:

- Reluctance to discuss trial strategies or previous trial experience
- Inability to explain technical aspects of PPP enforcement and detection
- Lack of relationships with relevant expert witnesses or technical consultants
- Excessive deference to prosecutors or government theories
- Focus on damage control rather than complete vindication

David Park's original attorney, James Wilson, displayed several of these warning signs. He immediately focused on plea negotiations, seemed unfamiliar with PPP-specific defenses, and appeared to accept the government's characterization of the evidence without critical analysis.

DEFENSE STRATEGY #33: *Test Attorney Knowledge and Commitment*

During initial consultations, test potential attorneys' knowledge and commitment:

- Ask specific questions about PPP regulations and common prosecution theories
- Request detailed explanations of potential defense strategies for your specific case
- Inquire about the attorney's willingness to take the case to trial if necessary

- Discuss the attorney's approach to challenging algorithmic evidence and technical testimony
- Evaluate whether the attorney seems genuinely interested in achieving complete vindication

Attorneys who cannot provide knowledgeable, detailed responses to these inquiries lack the expertise needed for effective PPP defense.

The Economics Of Effective Defense

PPP defendants face difficult economic realities when choosing counsel. Effective defense is expensive, but inadequate representation often proves far more costly in the long run.

****Typical Cost Structures:****

- Experienced PPP defense attorneys typically charge **$500-$1,500** per hour
- Complex PPP cases often require 200-500 hours of attorney time
- Total defense costs frequently range from **$100,000 to $500,000**
- Expert witnesses, investigators, and technical consultants add additional costs
- Asset freezes and forfeiture proceedings can complicate fee arrangements

****Hidden Costs of Inadequate Representation:****

- Prison sentences that could have been avoided with better defense
- Criminal records that affect future employment and opportunities
- Asset forfeiture that could have been prevented with aggressive defense
- Restitution obligations that exceed the cost of effective representation
- Collateral consequences that affect family members and business associates

David Park's experience illustrates these economic realities. He paid Wilson **$45,000** for three months of ineffective representation that brought him closer to a guilty plea. He then paid Rodriguez **$180,000** for eighteen months of aggressive defense that resulted in complete acquittal. While the total cost was substantial, it was far less than the potential consequences of conviction.

DEFENSE STRATEGY #34: *Cost-Benefit Analysis of Defense Options*

Defendants should conduct realistic cost-benefit analysis when choosing counsel:

- Calculate the total potential costs of conviction including prison, fines, restitution, and collateral consequences
- Compare these costs to the expense of effective defense representation
- Consider financing options including loans, asset liquidation, and payment plans
- Evaluate whether family members or business associates can contribute to defense costs
- Remember that ineffective defense often costs more than effective defense in the long run

This analysis usually reveals that investing in quality representation is the most economical choice, even when the upfront costs seem overwhelming.

Building The Defense Team

Effective PPP defense often requires a team approach that includes specialized attorneys, expert witnesses, investigators, and technical consultants. Understanding how to build and manage this team is crucial for achieving optimal results.

Core Team Members:

- Lead defense attorney with PPP-specific expertise and federal trial experience
- Co-counsel or associates with complementary skills in accounting, regulatory law, or technical analysis
- Expert witnesses including former SBA officials, accounting professionals, and industry specialists
- Private investigators who can gather evidence and interview witnesses
- Technical consultants who understand algorithmic detection systems and electronic evidence

Team Coordination Strategies:

Maria Rodriguez's defense of David Parks involved a carefully coordinated team:

- Rodriguez served as lead counsel, managing overall strategy and courtroom advocacy

- A junior associate with accounting background analyzed financial evidence and coordinated with expert witnesses

- Dr. James Liu, a former SBA official, provided expert testimony about PPP regulations and compliance

- A forensic accountant reconstructed David's business finances and identified innocent explanations for apparent discrepancies

- A technical consultant analyzed the algorithmic evidence and identified flaws in the government's analysis

This team approach allowed Rodriguez to address every aspect of the government's case while maintaining focus on the overall defense strategy.

DEFENSE STRATEGY #35: *Strategic Team Assembly*

Defendants should work with lead counsel to assemble comprehensive defense teams:

- Identify all areas of expertise needed to address the government's case

- Select team members based on specific qualifications and previous PPP experience

- Establish clear roles and communication protocols among team members

- Coordinate team efforts to avoid duplication and ensure comprehensive coverage

- Budget appropriately for team-based defense while maximizing cost-effectiveness

Effective team assembly often makes the difference between successful and unsuccessful defenses.

Attorney-Client Relationship Management

The relationship between PPP defendants and their attorneys requires careful management to ensure effective communication, appropriate expectations, and optimal outcomes.

Essential Communication Protocols:

- ➢ Regular status updates on case developments and strategy evolution

- Clear explanations of complex legal and regulatory issues in understandable terms
- Honest assessments of case strengths, weaknesses, and likely outcomes
- Transparent fee arrangements and billing practices
- Accessible communication channels for questions and concerns

****Expectation Management:****

Effective attorneys help clients understand realistic expectations for their cases:

- Honest evaluation of the strength of government evidence and prosecution theories
- Realistic timelines for case resolution and major milestones
- Clear explanation of potential outcomes ranging from dismissal to conviction
- Understanding of the costs and benefits of different strategic approaches
- Preparation for the emotional and practical challenges of federal prosecution

Maria Rodriguez excelled at expectation management with David Park. She explained that his case had strong defenses but would require substantial time and resources to develop effectively. She prepared him for the emotional toll of federal prosecution while maintaining optimism about achieving complete vindication.

****DEFENSE STRATEGY #36:** *Active Client Participation***

Defendants should actively participate in their defense while respecting attorney expertise:

- Provide complete and honest information about all relevant facts and circumstances
- Ask questions about legal strategies and case developments
- Participate in decision-making about major strategic choices
- Maintain realistic expectations while advocating for aggressive defense
- Trust attorney expertise while staying informed about case progress

Active client participation improves defense outcomes while ensuring that defendants feel empowered rather than helpless during prosecution.

Timing Considerations In Attorney Selection

The timing of attorney selection can significantly impact defense effectiveness. Earlier involvement of quality counsel generally produces better outcomes, but defendants facing investigation often don't realize they need representation until formal charges are filed.

Optimal Timing for Attorney Engagement:

- As soon as defendants learn they are under investigation
- Before any formal interviews or interactions with government agents
- Prior to any decisions about cooperation or information sharing
- In advance of any asset seizure or forfeiture proceedings
- Before media coverage or public disclosure of the investigation

Consequences of Delayed Representation:

- Loss of opportunities to influence the investigation's direction
- Inadvertent statements or actions that compromise defense positions
- Missed chances to present exculpatory evidence before charges are filed
- Asset seizures that could have been prevented with earlier intervention
- Media damage that could have been minimized with professional representation

David Park's case illustrates both the costs of delayed representation and the benefits of changing counsel when necessary. His initial delay in hiring counsel allowed the government to build its case without challenge, but his decision to change attorneys when he recognized Wilson's inadequacy ultimately saved his case.

DEFENSE STRATEGY #37: *Emergency Attorney Engagement*

Defendants who learn of investigations should engage qualified counsel immediately:

- Contact experienced PPP defense attorneys within 24 hours of learning about investigations
- Avoid any communication with government agents until counsel is retained
- Preserve all documents and electronic evidence that might be relevant to the case
- Brief counsel completely on all relevant facts and circumstances

- Begin developing defense strategies before formal charges are filed

Early engagement of quality counsel often prevents prosecutions or significantly improves defense positions.

Changing Attorneys When Necessary

Some defendants discover that their initial attorney choice was inappropriate only after representation has begun. Recognizing when to change counsel and managing the transition effectively can salvage cases that might otherwise be lost.

When to Consider Changing Counsel:

- Attorney appears unfamiliar with PPP-specific defense strategies
- Counsel seems more focused on plea negotiations than vigorous defense
- Attorney fails to communicate effectively or regularly about case developments
- Counsel appears to accept government theories without critical analysis
- Attorney relationship has broken down irreparably due to strategic disagreements
- **Managing Attorney Transitions:**

David Park's transition from Wilson to Rodriguez required careful management:

- Obtaining file materials and work product from previous counsel
- Bringing new counsel up to speed on case developments and government actions
- Addressing any strategic mistakes or missed opportunities from previous representation
- Managing additional costs associated with duplicated work and catch-up efforts
- Avoiding delays that could prejudice defense positions

Despite the challenges, changing attorneys proved crucial to David's ultimate vindication.

DEFENSE STRATEGY #38: ***Strategic Attorney Evaluation and Change***

Defendants should regularly evaluate attorney performance and change counsel when necessary:

- ➢ Assess whether current counsel is meeting performance expectations and case needs
- ➢ Identify specific deficiencies in representation that could compromise defense
- ➢ Research alternative counsel who might provide more effective representation
- ➢ Manage transitions to minimize disruption and additional costs
- ➢ Learn from attorney selection mistakes to make better choices going forward

Changing attorneys is disruptive and expensive, but keeping ineffective counsel is usually far more costly.

Specialized Ppp Defense Techniques

The most effective PPP defense attorneys have developed specialized techniques that address the unique challenges of these prosecutions. Understanding these techniques helps defendants identify truly qualified counsel.

****Algorithmic Evidence Challenges:****

Effective PPP attorneys know how to challenge the government's algorithmic analysis:

- ➢ Demanding complete discovery of algorithmic methodology and underlying data
- ➢ Hiring technical experts who understand machine learning and fraud detection systems
- ➢ Identifying bias and error rates in algorithmic analysis
- ➢ Showing that algorithmic flags indicate statistical deviation rather than criminal conduct

****Regulatory Complexity Defense:****

Skilled PPP counsel exploits the complexity of program regulations:

- ➢ Demonstrating that reasonable interpretations of regulations support defendant's conduct
- ➢ Showing that government guidance was contradictory and constantly changing
- ➢ Proving that defendants acted reasonably under the circumstances
- ➢ Using regulatory complexity to establish reasonable doubt about criminal intent

Business Context Development:

Expert PPP attorneys excel at developing business context that explains defendant conduct:

- Reconstructing the business challenges faced during the pandemic
- Showing how defendant decisions were driven by business necessity
- Demonstrating industry practices that support defendant's actions
- Proving that apparent irregularities reflected legitimate business operations

Maria Rodriguez used all these techniques in defending David Parks, ultimately demonstrating that his loan application reflected reasonable interpretations of complex regulations rather than criminal fraud.

DEFENSE STRATEGY #39: *Verify Specialized Technique Mastery*

When evaluating potential attorneys, verify their mastery of specialized PPP defense techniques:

- Ask detailed questions about algorithmic evidence challenges and technical defenses
- Request explanations of regulatory complexity defense strategies
- Inquire about methods for developing compelling business context evidence
- Test knowledge of expert witnesses and technical consultants needed for effective defense
- Evaluate understanding of the integration strategies needed to present comprehensive defenses

Attorneys who lack mastery of these specialized techniques cannot provide effective PPP defense.

The Investment In Freedom

Hiring effective legal representation for PPP charges represents one of the most important investments any defendant will ever make. The stakes are enormous: freedom versus prison, financial survival versus ruin, reputation preservation versus destruction.

What Effective Representation Provides:

- Comprehensive analysis of government evidence and identification of defense opportunities

- Strategic development of defense theories that can result in acquittal
- Expert testimony and technical analysis that challenges government theories
- Aggressive advocacy that forces prosecutors to prove their case beyond reasonable doubt
- Protection of defendant rights and interests throughout the prosecution process

The Cost of Ineffective Representation:

- Unnecessary guilty pleas to charges that could have been successfully defended
- Prison sentences that could have been avoided with proper representation
- Financial penalties and asset forfeiture that exceed the cost of quality defense
- Criminal records that permanently damage future opportunities
- Collateral consequences that affect family members and business associates

David Park's case demonstrates the value of effective representation. His investment in quality counsel resulted in complete vindication and preservation of his freedom, reputation, and financial security. The cost was substantial, but far less than the consequences of conviction would have been.

DEFENSE STRATEGY #40: *View Legal Fees as Freedom Insurance*

Defendants should understand legal fees as insurance against the catastrophic consequences of conviction:

- Calculate the total potential costs of conviction including direct and indirect consequences
- Compare these costs to the expense of effective legal representation
- Consider creative financing options to fund quality defense
- Remember that effective defense often costs less than ineffective defense in the long run
- Invest in the best representation available rather than accepting inadequate counsel due to cost concerns

This perspective helps defendants make rational decisions about legal representation based on actual costs and benefits rather than sticker shock.

Victory Through Quality Counsel

David Park's acquittal on all charges demonstrates that PPP prosecutions can be defeated with quality legal representation. His case succeeded because:

- He recognized when his initial attorney was inadequate and made the difficult decision to change counsel
- He hired an attorney with specific PPP expertise and federal trial experience
- He invested in a comprehensive defense team that addressed every aspect of the government's case
- He maintained realistic expectations while demanding aggressive advocacy
- He participated actively in his defense while trusting his attorney's expertise

The lesson from David's case is clear: the quality of legal representation often determines the outcome of PPP prosecutions. Defendants who invest in effective counsel give themselves the best chance of achieving complete vindication.

Choosing Your Champion

Every PPP defendant needs a champion: an attorney who believes in their innocence, understands the complex regulatory landscape, and has the skills and experience to defeat federal prosecutors in court. Finding this champion requires careful research, thorough evaluation, and sometimes difficult decisions about changing counsel when initial choices prove inadequate.

The stakes could not be higher. Your freedom, your financial security, your reputation, and your future all depend on the attorney you choose to defend you. Make that choice wisely, because it may be the most important decision of your life.

Remember: the government has unlimited resources, experienced prosecutors, and powerful investigative tools. You need an attorney who can match their expertise, challenge their evidence, and fight for your vindication with equal determination and superior preparation.

Your life may feel like it's spinning out of control, but choosing the right attorney gives you the best chance of regaining control and achieving the justice you deserve. The choice is yours, but the consequences will last forever.

CHAPTER 7

STRATEGIC FRAMING

Narrative Development

When defense attorney Lisa Jones first met her client, Angela Washington, in the federal detention center in downtown Phoenix, she knew she faced an uphill battle. Angela, a 47-year-old African American woman who owned three hair salons, had been arrested in a dawn raid that made the evening news. The local headlines screamed **"SALON OWNER STEALS $200,000" and "PPP FRAUD SCHEME EXPOSED."**

But as Lisa listened to Angela's story over the next three hours, a completely different narrative emerged. Angela wasn't a criminal mastermind who had defrauded the government. She was a single mother who had built a successful business over fifteen years, employed twenty-two people, and had become a pillar of her community. When the pandemic hit, she had applied for PPP loans not to steal money, but to keep her employees working and her salons open.

The "fraud" the government alleged was Angela's decision to include her teenage son Marcus on the payroll. Marcus had worked in the salons after school and weekends for two years, sweeping floors, cleaning equipment, and helping with inventory. Angela paid him $400 per week and reported his wages on her tax returns. But because Marcus was a family member and worked part-time, the algorithm flagged his inclusion as suspicious nepotism.

"So let me understand this," Lisa said to Angela. "You're facing twenty years in federal prison because you employed your own son in your family business?"

Angela nodded, tears in her eyes. "I've been giving kids from the neighborhood jobs for years. That's what small business owners do. We help our community."

Lisa realized that this case wasn't about facts or evidence. Both sides agreed on what Angela had done. The battle would be about the story those facts told. The government's story painted Angela as a greedy fraudster who exploited a crisis to steal taxpayer money. Lisa's job was to tell the true story: a hardworking entrepreneur who made an innocent mistake while trying to save her business and support her community.

This case would be won or lost in the realm of narrative, not evidence. And in that realm, the defense had significant advantages if they knew how to use them.

The Power Of Narrative In PPP Cases

PPP prosecutions are fundamentally battles over storytelling. The underlying facts are often undisputed: defendants signed loan applications, received money, and used the funds for various purposes. The question for juries is not what happened, but what those actions mean.

****The Government's Standard Narrative:****

- Defendant deliberately lied on loan applications to steal taxpayer money
- Defendant knew the information was false but submitted it anyway for personal gain
- Defendant showed contempt for the law and took advantage of a crisis
- Defendant's actions harmed legitimate borrowers and damaged public trust
- Justice requires punishment to deter others from similar fraud

****The Defense Counter-Narrative:****

- Defendant honestly tried to comply with confusing regulations during a crisis
- Defendant made understandable mistakes on complex forms under time pressure
- Defendant's actions were motivated by business survival, not criminal greed
- Defendant used loan proceeds for legitimate business purposes as intended
- Prosecution represents government overreach that criminalizes honest mistakes

The narrative that resonates more strongly with jurors typically determines the verdict, regardless of the technical strength of the evidence.

****DEFENSE STRATEGY #41:** *Develop a Compelling Counter-Narrative***

Every PPP defense must develop a compelling counter-narrative that reframes the case:

- Identify the emotional core of the defendant's story that humanizes them for jurors
- Emphasize the legitimate business challenges that motivated the defendant's actions
- Show how complex regulations created inevitable confusion and errors
- Demonstrate the defendant's good faith attempts to comply with program requirements
- Frame prosecution as government overreach rather than justified law enforcement

This counter-narrative must be consistently applied throughout every aspect of the defense, from opening statements to witness testimony to closing arguments.

Psychological Positioning Strategies

Effective PPP defense requires understanding the psychological dynamics that influence how juries perceive defendants and their actions. These psychological factors often matter more than legal technicalities in determining verdicts.

****Psychological Challenges for PPP Defendants:****

- Fraud allegations trigger strong moral condemnation from jurors
- Government prosecutions benefit from presumptions of legitimacy and accuracy
- Technical violations can appear damning even when they have innocent explanations
- Media coverage often creates negative preconceptions about defendants
- Complex financial evidence can confuse jurors and make guilt seem probable

****Psychological Advantages for Defense:****

- Small business owners are generally sympathetic figures to middle-class jurors

- PPP program complexity generates sympathy for confused borrowers

- Government overreach resonates with jurors who distrust federal authority
- Underdog positioning can generate support for defendants fighting the system
- Personal stories humanize defendants and counter abstract fraud allegations

Angela Washington's case illustrates how psychological positioning can transform a prosecution. Initially, she appeared to be a stereotypical fraud defendant: minority business owner caught inflating payroll on government applications. But reframing her as a hardworking mother trying to save her family business and support her community completely changed the psychological dynamics.

DEFENSE STRATEGY #42: *Strategic Defendant Positioning**

Defense teams must strategically position defendants to maximize psychological advantages:

- Emphasize the defendant's positive contributions to the community and legitimate business achievements
- Show how the defendant's actions were motivated by business necessity rather than greed
- Demonstrate the defendant's good character through specific examples and witness testimony
- Position the case as government overreach targeting honest business owners
- Use the defendant's personal story to humanize them and generate jury sympathy

This positioning must be authentic and supported by evidence, but it can fundamentally change how juries perceive the case.

Victim Vs. Villain Framing

One of the most crucial strategic decisions in PPP cases is whether to frame the defendant as a victim of government overreach or as someone who made innocent mistakes. Both approaches can be effective, but they require different evidence and different presentation strategies.

Victim Framing Strategy:

- Defendant was trapped by impossible regulatory complexity

- Government created an unfair system designed to produce violations
- Prosecution represents abuse of power targeting vulnerable small business owners
- Defendant suffered more from the process than any alleged victims of fraud

Mistake Framing Strategy:

- Defendant honestly tried to comply but made understandable errors
- Complex regulations created inevitable confusion even among good-faith borrowers
- Defendant's actions were reasonable under the extraordinary circumstances
- Mistakes do not constitute criminal fraud absent intent to defraud

Angela Washington's defense team chose the victim framing strategy. They argued that she had been targeted by a biased algorithmic system that flagged minority business owners at disproportionate rates, that her family employment practices were normal in her community, and that her prosecution represented systematic persecution of successful minority entrepreneurs.

DEFENSE STRATEGY #43: ***Choose Optimal Framing Strategy***

Defense teams must choose the framing strategy that best fits their client and case:

- Analyze which approach resonates most strongly with the defendant's personal story
- Consider the local jury pool and what themes are likely to appeal to them
- Evaluate the strength of evidence supporting each potential framing approach
- Ensure that chosen framing is consistent with all aspects of the defense presentation
- Test framing strategies through focus groups or mock trials when possible

The framing choice affects every other strategic decision, so it must be made carefully and early in case preparation.

Character Evidence Strategy

Character evidence often proves decisive in PPP cases because it helps juries understand the defendant's motivations and likelihood of criminal intent. Effective character evidence does more than show that the defendant is a good person; it demonstrates that criminal fraud is inconsistent with their established pattern of behavior.

Types of Powerful Character Evidence:

- Long history of honest business practices and community involvement
- Previous compliance with tax obligations and regulatory requirements
- Reputation for integrity among business associates and community members
- Evidence of helping others during the pandemic or other crises
- Demonstration of transparency and cooperation with authorities

Character Evidence Presentation:

Angela Washington's character evidence was overwhelming:

- Fifteen years of successful business operations with no regulatory violations
- Testimony from twenty-three employees about her fairness and integrity
- Evidence of providing free services to elderly community members during lockdowns
- Documentation of her mentorship programs for young entrepreneurs
- Letters from community leaders describing her positive impact

This character evidence made it virtually impossible for jurors to believe that Angela would suddenly become a criminal fraudster during the pandemic.

DEFENSE STRATEGY #44: *Comprehensive Character Evidence Development*

Defendants should systematically develop character evidence that supports their defense narrative:

- Document all positive community involvement and business practices
- Gather testimony from employees, customers, vendors, and community members
- Collect evidence of compliance with other legal and regulatory requirements

- Show patterns of honest behavior that contradict fraud allegations
- Present character evidence that specifically addresses the government's theory of criminal intent

Character evidence should be integrated into the overall defense narrative rather than presented as an afterthought.

Community Context Framing

PPP cases often involve defendants who are prominent members of their local communities. Effective defense strategies leverage this community context to show that the defendant's actions were consistent with local business practices and community values.

****Community Context Elements:****

- Local business practices that explain apparent regulatory violations
- Community economic challenges that motivated PPP applications
- Cultural factors that influence business operations and family employment
- Local support for the defendant that demonstrates community trust
- Economic impact of the defendant's business on local employment and development
- Angela Washington's defense team extensively developed community context:
- Expert testimony about minority business practices in Phoenix
- Evidence of informal employment arrangements common in her community
- Demonstration of economic challenges facing minority-owned businesses during the pandemic
- Community rallies and support letters from local residents and business owners
- Documentation of the salons' economic impact on the local neighborhood

This community context helped jurors understand that Angela's employment of her son was normal practice in her community, not criminal fraud.

****DEFENSE STRATEGY #45:** *Leverage Community Context***

Defense teams should systematically develop community context that supports their narrative:

- Research local business practices that explain the defendant's conduct
- Gather evidence of community support and trust for the defendant
- Document economic challenges specific to the defendant's industry and location
- Show how the defendant's business practices reflect community values and norms
- Use local witnesses who can explain cultural and economic context to the jury

Community context can transform apparent violations into evidence of normal, lawful business practices.

Media Narrative Management

PPP prosecutions often generate significant media coverage that can influence potential jurors and community perception. Effective defense teams must manage this media narrative to prevent it from undermining their case.

****Media Challenges:****

- Government press releases that portray allegations as established facts
- Sensationalized coverage that emphasizes dollar amounts and potential sentences
- Lack of coverage of defense perspectives or exculpatory evidence
- Social media amplification of negative narratives
- Pre-trial publicity that prejudices potential jury pools

****Media Opportunities:****

- Opportunities to present the defendant's perspective and humanizing information
- Community support that can be mobilized to counter negative narratives
- Expert commentary that can explain regulatory complexity and defense theories
- Social media platforms that allow direct communication with potential supporters

Angela Washington's case generated extensive local media coverage. Initial stories focused on the government's allegations and portrayed her as a typical fraud defendant. Her defense team's media strategy included:

- Carefully crafted statements emphasizing her community contributions and good character
- Background briefings for reporters about PPP regulatory complexity
- Coordination with community leaders to generate supportive public statements
- Social media campaigns highlighting her positive community impact

This media strategy helped shift public perception from viewing Angela as a criminal to seeing her as a victim of government overreach.

****DEFENSE STRATEGY #46:** *Proactive Media Narrative Management***

Defense teams should proactively manage media narratives rather than allowing government spin to dominate:

- Develop media strategy early in the case before negative narratives become entrenched
- Provide reporters with background information that supports the defense perspective
- Coordinate with community supporters to generate positive coverage
- Use social media strategically to humanize the defendant and present their story
- Challenge false or misleading government statements while respecting ethical constraints

Effective media management can prevent negative coverage from undermining defense efforts at trial.

Jury Selection Narrative Preparation

The narrative framing work done during case preparation becomes crucial during jury selection, where attorneys must identify jurors who will be receptive to their story and eliminate those likely to be hostile.

****Jury Selection Narrative Considerations:****

- Which potential jurors are likely to sympathize with small business challenges
- How to identify jurors who may be biased against government prosecutions
- Methods for detecting jurors who may harbor prejudices against minority defendants

- ➢ Ways to gauge juror attitudes toward regulatory complexity and good faith mistakes
- ➢ Strategies for educating the jury panel about PPP program challenges

Jury Selection Strategy:

Angela Washington's jury selection focused on identifying jurors who:

- ➢ Had small business experience or family members who owned businesses
- ➢ Understood the challenges of navigating complex government regulations
- ➢ Had positive attitudes toward minority entrepreneurship and community development
- ➢ Were skeptical of government overreach and prosecutorial abuse
- ➢ Could relate to the challenges of being a working single mother

The defense team successfully excluded jurors who seemed hostile to minority defendants or who expressed strong pro-government attitudes.

DEFENSE STRATEGY #47: ***Narrative-Based Jury Selection***

Jury selection should be directly tied to the defense narrative strategy:

- ➢ Develop voir dire questions that identify jurors receptive to the defense narrative
- ➢ Eliminate jurors whose backgrounds or attitudes make them hostile to the defense story
- ➢ Educate the entire jury panel about themes that will be important at trial
- ➢ Begin selling the defense narrative during jury selection through strategic questioning
- ➢ Use jury selection to identify which aspects of the narrative resonate most strongly

Effective jury selection often determines whether the defense narrative will be received favorably at trial.

Opening Statement Narrative Strategy

The opening statement provides the first opportunity to present the defense narrative directly to the jury. This presentation must be compelling, credible, and memorable because it shapes how jurors interpret all subsequent evidence.

Opening Statement Elements:

- Clear statement of the defense theory that frames the entire case
- Emotional connection with the defendant that humanizes them for jurors
- Explanation of the regulatory complexity that led to apparent violations
- Preview of evidence that will support the defense narrative
- Direct challenge to the government's characterization of the defendant's conduct

Angela Washington's Opening Strategy:

Defense attorney Lisa Jones opening statement focused on three key themes:

1. Angela was a successful businesswoman who had spent fifteen years building her salons and supporting her community

2. She had honestly tried to comply with confusing PPP regulations while facing an unprecedented crisis

3. Her employment of her son reflected normal family business practices, not criminal fraud

Jones used powerful language that resonated emotionally: "Angela Washington didn't wake up one morning and decide to become a criminal. She woke up facing the possibility that the business she had spent fifteen years building might disappear, taking the jobs of twenty-two employees with it."

DEFENSE STRATEGY #48: *Compelling Opening Narrative***

Opening statements should present the defense narrative in its most powerful form:

- Lead with the emotional core of the defendant's story that will resonate with jurors
- Explain complex regulatory issues in simple terms that support the defense theory
- Preview specific evidence that will prove the defense narrative
- Directly address the government's strongest arguments with confident counter-explanations

- End with a clear statement of what the evidence will prove about the defendant's innocence

The opening statement narrative becomes the lens through which jurors view all subsequent evidence.

Witness Testimony Narrative Integration

Every witness called by the defense must advance the overall narrative strategy. This requires careful preparation to ensure that testimony reinforces rather than contradicts the defense story.

****Witness Categories:****

- Character witnesses who establish the defendant's reputation for honesty and integrity
- Expert witnesses who explain regulatory complexity and industry practices
- Business witnesses who provide context for the defendant's operations and decisions
- Community witnesses who establish local practices and economic challenges
- Family witnesses who humanize the defendant and explain personal motivations

****Witness Preparation Strategy:****

Angela Washington's defense called twelve witnesses who each advanced specific aspects of the narrative:

- Five employees testified about Angela's fairness and the family atmosphere at the salons
- Two community leaders described Angela's positive impact on the neighborhood
- An expert witness explained minority business employment practices
- Angela's accountant testified about the confusion surrounding PPP regulations
- Marcus Washington, Angela's son, testified about his legitimate work at the salons

Each witness was carefully prepared to present their testimony in a way that supported the overarching narrative of good faith and community service.

DEFENSE STRATEGY #49: *Integrated Witness Strategy*

All witness testimony should be integrated into the comprehensive defense narrative:

- Prepare each witness to present their testimony in language that supports the defense story
- Ensure that witness testimony builds cumulatively toward the defense conclusion
- Address any potentially damaging witness testimony proactively
- Use witness testimony to bring abstract concepts to life through specific examples
- Coordinate witness presentations to avoid contradictions or confusion

Effective witness integration makes the defense narrative feel inevitable rather than argued.

Closing Argument Narrative Synthesis

The closing argument provides the final opportunity to present the defense narrative and persuade jurors to accept the defense version of events. This presentation must synthesize all the evidence into a coherent, compelling story that leads inexorably to acquittal.

Closing Argument Strategy:

- Remind jurors of the promises made in opening statement and show how they were fulfilled
- Synthesize all evidence into a coherent narrative that proves innocence
- Address government arguments directly while maintaining focus on the defense story
- Appeal to juror emotions and values that support the defense narrative
- End with a clear call for acquittal based on the evidence presented

Angela Washington's Closing:

Lisa Jones closing argument wove together all elements of the defense narrative:

"Angela Washington is not a criminal. She's a mother, a business owner, and a pillar of her community. When the pandemic threatened everything she had worked fifteen years to build, she did what any reasonable person would do: she applied for help from a government program designed to save small businesses. She filled out confusing forms to the best of her ability, she used the money for its intended purpose, and she kept twenty-two people employed during the worst economic crisis in decades. The government wants you to call that fraud. I call it heroism."

DEFENSE STRATEGY #50: *Narrative Synthesis Closing*

Closing arguments should synthesize the entire defense narrative into a compelling conclusion:

- Remind jurors of the key elements of the defense story established through evidence
- Show how all evidence points toward the same conclusion of innocence
- Address government arguments within the framework of the defense narrative
- Appeal to juror values and emotions that support the defense conclusion
- Make the case for acquittal feel morally necessary rather than merely legally possible

The closing argument narrative should make acquittal feel like the only reasonable conclusion based on the evidence presented.

Victory Through Strategic Framing

Angela Washington was acquitted on all charges after less than four hours of jury deliberation. The victory resulted from a comprehensive narrative strategy that:

- Reframed the case from fraud prosecution to government overreach
- Positioned Angela as a community hero rather than a criminal
- Used character evidence to make fraud allegations seem implausible
- Leveraged community context to explain apparent violations
- Integrated all evidence into a compelling story of good faith and innocence

Key Lessons from Angela's Victory:

- Narrative often matters more than technical evidence in determining verdicts
- Effective framing can transform apparent weaknesses into strengths
- Character evidence and community context can overcome technical violations

- Psychological positioning influences how juries interpret complex evidence
- Consistent narrative application throughout the case builds credibility and persuasive power

The Art Of Persuasion

PPP prosecutions are ultimately exercises in persuasion rather than fact-finding. Both sides typically agree on the basic facts; the battle is over what those facts mean and how they should be interpreted. Victory goes to the side that tells the more compelling, believable, and emotionally resonant story.

Defense teams that master strategic framing and narrative development give their clients the best chance of achieving acquittal. The key is understanding that juries don't just evaluate evidence; they evaluate stories. And in the battle between the government's story of greed and fraud and the defense story of struggle and good faith, the defense story often resonates more powerfully with ordinary citizens who understand the challenges of running small businesses during a crisis.

Your case may seem hopeless when viewed through the government's narrative lens. But that narrative is not the only possible interpretation of the facts. With skillful framing and compelling storytelling, apparent evidence of guilt can become proof of innocence, and what seemed like an impossible defense can become a winning strategy.

The facts of your case are what they are. But the story those facts tell is still being written. Make sure it's a story that ends with your freedom.

CHAPTER 8

INVESTIGATIONS & CHARGES

Timeline Of Federal Inquiry

At 7:23 AM on a cold Tuesday morning in November 2022, Dr. Samuel Roberts received a phone call that would change his life forever. The voice on the other end identified himself as Special Agent Michael Smith from the FBI's Economic Crimes Unit.

"Dr. Roberts, we'd like to speak with you about your PPP loan applications. We're hoping you can help us understand some discrepancies we've identified."

Samuel, a family physician who owned a small medical practice in Sacramento, felt his stomach drop. He had applied for two PPP loans totaling **$147,000** to keep his practice open during the pandemic when patient visits plummeted by 80%. He had used every penny for payroll, rent, and medical supplies, exactly as the program required.

"Is there a problem?" Samuel asked, his voice shaking.

"We just need to clarify a few things," Agent Smith replied smoothly. "Nothing to worry about. We can either meet at your office or you can come to our field office. Whatever's more convenient for you."

Samuel, like most Americans, had been raised to cooperate with law enforcement. He agreed to meet at his office the next day, thinking he could clear up whatever confusion existed. He had no idea that he was about to become the target of a federal criminal investigation that would consume the next two years of his life and cost him nearly everything he had worked thirty years to build.

What Samuel didn't understand was that Agent Smith's call wasn't the beginning of the investigation. It was the end. By the time federal agents make contact with PPP defendants, they have typically already spent months building their case, analyzing financial records, and consulting with prosecutors about potential charges. The "interview" is not an information-gathering session; it's an evidence-gathering session designed to obtain admissions that will support the case agents have already built.

Understanding the federal investigation timeline is crucial for PPP defendants because it reveals when and how they can most effectively defend themselves. Most defendants miss their best opportunities to influence the investigation because they don't realize it's happening until it's too late.

Phase One: Algorithmic Detection And Initial Screening

Federal PPP investigations begin long before defendants know they're under scrutiny. The process starts when the **COVID-19 Fraud Enforcement Task Force's** algorithmic detection system flags loans for potential fraud indicators.

Dr. Roberts' loans were flagged in August 2022, three months before Agent Smith called him. The algorithm assigned his first loan a risk score of 823 and his second loan a score of 891, both above the 750 threshold that triggers automatic criminal referrals.

****What triggered the flags:****

- Roberts had applied for two separate loans for the same medical practice
- His employee count on the second application was higher than the first
- He had included himself and his wife (who managed the practice) in payroll calculations
- His average monthly payroll seemed high for a single-physician practice
- Bank records showed irregular deposit patterns during the pandemic

None of these factors actually indicated fraud. Roberts had applied for a second loan when the program was expanded to allow additional borrowing. His employee count increased because he had rehired staff as patient visits recovered. His wife had always worked in the practice but wasn't always on formal payroll. His payroll included professional insurance and benefits that inflated the apparent wage costs. The irregular deposits reflected the reality of running a medical practice during a pandemic when patient volume fluctuated wildly.

But the algorithm didn't understand the context. It simply identified statistical deviations from expected patterns and flagged them as suspicious.

****DEFENSE STRATEGY #51:** *Early Detection Warning Systems*****

Defendants can sometimes identify investigations before agents make contact:

- Monitor credit reports for unusual inquiries from government agencies
- Watch for subpoenas served on banks, accountants, or business associates
- Be alert to questions from employees about contacts from government agents
- Notice unusual delays or requests for additional information from lenders
- Pay attention to community gossip about federal investigations targeting similar businesses

Early detection allows defendants to engage counsel and begin building defenses before agents attempt to interview them.

Phase Two: Preliminary Investigation And File Building

Once the algorithm flags a loan, it enters the preliminary investigation phase. This typically lasts 30-90 days and involves agents gathering publicly available information to determine whether a full investigation is warranted.

Agent Smith spent six weeks building Roberts preliminary file:

- Downloaded Roberts original loan applications and supporting documents
- Obtained basic financial information from SBA databases
- Reviewed Roberts business registration and professional licensing records
- Analyzed his practice's website and online presence
- Checked court records for any previous legal issues
- Researched Roberts background through public databases

This preliminary investigation revealed that Roberts was a licensed physician with no criminal history who had operated his practice for fifteen years. His online reviews were overwhelmingly positive, and his medical license was in good standing. There was no evidence of lavish lifestyle or suspicious spending patterns.

Despite this favorable information, Agent Smith recommended proceeding with a full investigation. The algorithmic flags were strong enough to justify further investigation, and the potential dollar amount was sufficient to meet the office's prosecution priorities.

DEFENSE STRATEGY #52: *Preemptive Reputation Management*

Defendants can influence preliminary investigations through proactive reputation management:

- Ensure that online presence reflects legitimate business operations and professional conduct
- Address any negative information that might appear in public records or internet searches
- Maintain current professional licenses and certifications
- Document community involvement and positive business relationships
- Prepare materials that demonstrate legitimate business operations and good character

Agents conducting preliminary investigations often form initial impressions based on easily accessible information. Positive online presence can influence whether full investigations proceed.

Phase Three: Financial Analysis And Evidence Gathering

The full investigation phase typically lasts 3-6 months and involves detailed analysis of the defendant's financial records, business operations, and loan usage. This is when agents build the evidence they will use to support criminal charges.

Agent Smith's investigation of Dr. Roberts included:

- Subpoenaing bank records for all business and personal accounts
- Analyzing how PPP loan proceeds were spent
- Reviewing tax returns and business financial statements
- Interviewing employees and business associates
- Examining the practice's patient records and billing systems
- Consulting with medical practice experts about normal operations

This investigation cost taxpayers approximately **$85,000** in agent time, expert consultations, and administrative resources. It also consumed hundreds of hours of time from Roberts employees, patients, and business associates who were interviewed or subpoenaed.

Key Investigation Findings:

- Roberts had used 94% of loan proceeds for payroll, rent, and utilities as required

- The remaining 6% was used for medical supplies and practice maintenance
- His practice had genuinely struggled during the pandemic with a 78% reduction in patient visits
- Employee interviews confirmed legitimate employment and appropriate compensation
- No evidence of personal use of loan proceeds or fraudulent conduct

Despite these findings, Agent Smith concluded that Roberts had committed fraud because his loan applications contained "material misstatements" about employee counts and payroll calculations.

DEFENSE STRATEGY #53: *Parallel Financial Investigation*

Defendants should conduct their own financial investigation parallel to the government's:

- Hire forensic accountants to analyze the same records the government reviews
- Identify innocent explanations for any apparent discrepancies
- Gather evidence of legitimate business purposes for all questioned transactions
- Document the business context that explains apparent irregularities
- Prepare comprehensive explanations for any unusual financial patterns

This parallel investigation often reveals evidence that supports the defense narrative while preparing responses to government theories.

Phase Four: Prosecutorial Review And Charging Decisions

Once agents complete their investigation, they present their findings to federal prosecutors who decide whether to file criminal charges. This prosecutorial review process typically takes 30-60 days and involves multiple levels of approval within the U.S. Attorney's office.

Assistant U.S. Attorney Angela Martinez reviewed Agent Smith's investigation file in January 2023. The file contained 847 pages of financial records, interview reports, and analytical summaries. Martinez spent approximately 12 hours reviewing the file before concluding that criminal charges were appropriate.

Prosecutorial Decision Factors:

- Strength of evidence supporting fraud allegations

- Potential sentence enhancement opportunities
- Likelihood of securing guilty plea or trial conviction
- Political and publicity value of the prosecution
- Office priorities and resource allocation considerations

Martinez's charging memo identified several prosecution advantages:

- Clear signature on loan applications containing false information
- Documentary evidence of discrepancies between applications and business records
- Potential for multiple charges arising from two separate loan applications
- Significant dollar amount that would generate media attention
- Defendant's professional status that would deter other potential violators

The memo also acknowledged potential defense arguments:

- Defendant's clean record and professional reputation
- Evidence of legitimate business struggles during the pandemic
- Complexity of PPP regulations that could explain mistakes
- Strong community support and character evidence
- Lack of evidence showing fraudulent intent or personal benefit

Despite these defense strengths, Martinez recommended prosecution because she believed the evidence was sufficient to secure a conviction.

****DEFENSE STRATEGY #54:** *Prosecutorial Decision Influence***

Defense attorneys can sometimes influence prosecutorial charging decisions through strategic intervention:

- Submit detailed defense memoranda before charges are filed
- Provide evidence of client's good character and legitimate business operations
- Demonstrate weaknesses in the government's case through expert analysis
- Show how prosecution would cause disproportionate harm relative to alleged wrongdoing
- Offer cooperation or restitution that might satisfy prosecutorial concerns

Early intervention can sometimes prevent charges from being filed or result in reduced charges that are easier to defend.

Phase Five: Grand Jury Proceedings

Federal prosecutors must obtain grand jury indictments for felony charges. The grand jury process typically takes 2-4 weeks and is conducted in secret with only prosecutors, agents, and witnesses present. Defendants have no right to participate or even know that grand jury proceedings are occurring.

Agent Smith testified before the federal grand jury in Sacramento for approximately 90 minutes in February 2023. He presented the government's evidence against Dr. Roberts, emphasizing the discrepancies in the loan applications and the potential penalties for PPP fraud.

****Grand Jury Presentation Strategy:****

Prosecutors typically present grand jury cases to maximize the appearance of criminality:

- Emphasize the dollar amounts allegedly stolen
- Focus on technical violations without providing context
- Present evidence in the order that most strongly suggests guilt
- Use inflammatory language like "stole," "cheated," and "defrauded"
- Minimize or omit evidence that might support the defendant's innocence
- The grand jury voted to indict Dr. Roberts on six felony counts:
- Two counts of wire fraud (one for each loan application)
- Two counts of bank fraud (one for each loan)
- Two counts of money laundering (for spending loan proceeds)

Each count carried a maximum sentence of 20 years in prison and **$250,000** in fines.

****DEFENSE STRATEGY #55:** *Post-Indictment Investigation***

Since defendants cannot participate in grand jury proceedings, they must begin their defense investigation immediately after indictment:

- Obtain the grand jury transcript to understand the government's presentation
- Identify weaknesses in the government's case that weren't apparent during the grand jury

- ➢ Gather evidence that contradicts or provides context for the government's allegations
- ➢ Develop expert testimony that challenges the government's theories
- ➢ Begin building the character and community support evidence needed for trial

Post-indictment investigation often reveals that the government's case is weaker than grand jury proceedings suggested.

Phase Six: Arrest And Initial Appearance

Federal arrests in PPP cases are typically designed for maximum publicity and intimidation. Dr. Roberts was arrested at his medical office on March 15, 2023, during regular business hours when the office was full of patients and staff.

****The Arrest Strategy:****

- ➢ Six FBI agents in bulletproof vests arrived at the medical practice
- ➢ Local news crews had been notified and were positioned outside
- ➢ Agents allowed Dr. Roberts to be photographed in handcuffs for maximum humiliation
- ➢ The arrest was timed to make the evening news cycle
- ➢ Dr. Roberts computers and business records were seized during the arrest

The arrest was designed to accomplish several prosecutorial goals:

- ➢ Generate media coverage that would influence potential jurors
- ➢ Humiliate Dr. Roberts to pressure him into pleading guilty quickly
- ➢ Disrupt his medical practice and create financial pressure
- ➢ Send a message to other potential PPP defendants about consequences of prosecution

Dr. Roberts' initial appearance occurred six hours after his arrest. Still wearing the clothes he had been arrested in and having had no opportunity to contact family or arrange for legal representation, he faced a federal magistrate judge who would determine his pretrial release conditions.

****DEFENSE STRATEGY #56:** *Arrest Preparation and Response***

Defendants who suspect they may be arrested should prepare in advance:

- Identify bail funding sources and arrange for immediate legal representation
- Prepare family members for the possibility of arrest and media coverage
- Document any excessive force or inappropriate conduct during arrest
- Preserve evidence of the arrest's impact on business operations and reputation
- Begin immediately gathering character references and community support letters

Effective arrest preparation can minimize the damage and begin building the defense case immediately.

Phase Seven: Pretrial Proceedings And Discovery

The pretrial phase typically lasts 12-18 months and involves discovery battles, motion practice, and plea negotiations. This is when the real defense work begins and where cases are often won or lost.

Dr. Roberts hired defense attorney Sarah Arman, who immediately began aggressive discovery practice:

- Filed comprehensive discovery motions requesting all government evidence
- Demanded production of algorithmic analysis and underlying data
- Sought internal government communications about the case
- Requested expert reports and technical analysis
- Challenged the government's evidence preservation and production

****Discovery Battles:****

The government initially resisted producing crucial evidence:

- Claimed that algorithmic methodology was proprietary and couldn't be disclosed
- Argued that internal prosecutorial communications were privileged
- Delayed production of exculpatory evidence until just before trial
- Provided financial records in disorganized, unsearchable formats
- Redacted portions of documents claiming national security concerns

Arman fought these discovery battles aggressively, ultimately obtaining most of the evidence she needed to build Roberts' defense.

****DEFENSE STRATEGY #57:** *Aggressive Discovery Practice***

Effective PPP defense requires aggressive discovery tactics:

- File comprehensive discovery motions early in the case
- Challenge all government claims of privilege or exemption
- Demand production of algorithmic analysis and technical evidence
- Seek internal government communications that reveal investigative bias
- Fight for access to comparative data about similar cases and their outcomes

Aggressive discovery often reveals government weaknesses that can be exploited at trial or in plea negotiations.

Phase Eight: Expert Witness Development

Complex PPP cases require expert witnesses who can explain regulatory requirements, challenge government technical evidence, and provide context for the defendant's conduct.

Dr. Roberts defense team assembled a comprehensive expert witness panel:

- Dr. Michael Liu, former SBA official who helped design PPP regulations
- Missy Gables, CPA who specialized in medical practice accounting
- Professor James Bowers, computer science expert who analyzed algorithmic evidence
- Dr. Lisa Wong, physician who could explain medical practice operations during the pandemic

These experts spent hundreds of hours analyzing the government's evidence and developing testimony that would support Roberts' defense.

****Expert Witness Strategy:****

Each expert addressed specific aspects of the government's case:

- Dr. Liu explained how Roberts loan applications reflected reasonable interpretations of complex regulations
- Ms. Martinez demonstrated that Roberts financial practices were normal for medical practices
- Professor Bowers showed that the algorithmic analysis contained errors and biased assumptions
- Dr. Wong provided context about how the pandemic affected medical practice operations

DEFENSE STRATEGY #58: *Strategic Expert Witness Selection*

Expert witness selection should be strategic and comprehensive:

- Identify all areas where expert testimony can challenge government theories
- Select experts with superior credentials and experience compared to government witnesses
- Ensure that expert testimony is consistent with the overall defense narrative
- Prepare experts to explain complex concepts in simple, understandable terms
- Coordinate expert testimony to avoid contradictions or confusion

Expert witnesses often provide the technical foundation for successful PPP defenses.

Phase Nine: Plea Negotiations And Trial Preparation

Most PPP cases are resolved through plea negotiations rather than trial. The government uses the plea process strategically to secure convictions without having to prove their cases in court.

Government Plea Strategy:

Prosecutor Martinez's initial plea offer to Dr. Roberts was harsh:

- Plead guilty to one count of wire fraud
- Accept a sentencing recommendation of 18-30 months in federal prison
- Pay $147,000 in restitution
- Surrender his medical license
- Cooperate with other PPP investigations

This offer was designed to pressure Roberts into accepting responsibility while avoiding the risk of trial conviction on multiple counts.

Defense Plea Response:

Arman rejected the initial offer and countered with evidence of Roberts innocence:

- Demonstrated that Roberts conduct was consistent with good faith compliance

- Showed that any errors in his applications were inadvertent and immaterial
- Provided evidence of his legitimate use of loan proceeds
- Presented character evidence showing that fraud was inconsistent with his pattern of behavior

When negotiations stalled, Arman began aggressive trial preparation to show prosecutors that their conviction was not guaranteed.

DEFENSE STRATEGY #59: *Strategic Plea Negotiation*

Plea negotiations should be strategic rather than capitulatory:

- Thoroughly analyze the strength of the government's evidence before considering any plea
- Present evidence of innocence that challenges the government's theories
- Demonstrate readiness for trial to show that conviction is not certain
- Negotiate from a position of strength based on case weaknesses rather than desperation
- Consider the long-term consequences of any plea agreement beyond immediate sentencing

Strategic plea negotiation often results in better outcomes than immediate capitulation.

Phase Ten: Trial And Resolution

Dr. Roberts' case went to trial in October 2023, eighteen months after his arrest. The six-day trial featured extensive expert testimony, detailed financial analysis, and compelling character evidence.

Trial Strategy:

Arman's trial strategy integrated all elements of Roberts defense:

- Demonstrated that his loan applications reflected good faith efforts to comply with complex regulations
- Used expert testimony to show that the government's technical analysis was flawed
- Presented overwhelming character evidence showing that fraud was inconsistent with Roberts character
- Argued that any errors in his applications were inadvertent mistakes, not criminal fraud

Trial Outcome:

The jury deliberated for eleven hours before returning not guilty verdicts on all six counts. The acquittal vindicated Roberts completely but came at enormous personal and financial cost.

DEFENSE STRATEGY #60: *Comprehensive Trial Strategy*

Trial strategy should integrate all defense elements into a compelling case for acquittal:

- Present evidence in an order that builds toward the defense conclusion
- Use expert testimony to challenge every aspect of the government's technical case
- Integrate character evidence throughout the trial rather than presenting it as an afterthought
- Address government strengths directly while emphasizing defense advantages
- Make the case for acquittal feel morally necessary rather than merely legally possible

Comprehensive trial strategy gives defendants the best chance of achieving complete vindication.

The Cost Of Victory

Dr. Roberts acquittal represented complete vindication, but the victory came at an enormous price:

- Legal fees of $487,000 that exhausted his retirement savings
- Loss of income during the two-year prosecution that damaged his practice permanently
- Emotional trauma that affected his family relationships and professional confidence
- Reputation damage that persisted despite his acquittal
- Medical license suspension that required additional legal proceedings to resolve

Even in victory, the federal prosecution process extracts a terrible toll on defendants and their families.

Lessons From The Investigation Timeline

Dr. Roberts case illustrates crucial lessons about federal PPP investigations:

Key Timeline Insights:

- Investigations begin months before defendants know they're under scrutiny
- Agents build their cases before making contact with defendants
- Early intervention can sometimes influence investigation outcomes
- Discovery battles often determine trial outcomes
- Expert witnesses are crucial for challenging technical government evidence

Strategic Implications:

- Defendants should engage counsel immediately upon learning of investigations
- Early preparation often determines ultimate case outcomes
- Aggressive discovery practice can reveal fatal government weaknesses
- Character evidence and community support are crucial throughout the process
- Trial preparation should begin immediately after charges are filed

Fighting Back At Every Stage

The federal investigation timeline creates multiple opportunities for effective defense, but defendants must understand the process to exploit these opportunities:

Investigation Stage Opportunities:

- Early detection allows for proactive reputation management
- Preliminary investigation can be influenced through positive online presence
- Financial analysis can be countered through parallel defense investigation
- Prosecutorial decisions can sometimes be influenced through strategic intervention
- Grand jury indictments can be challenged through post-indictment investigation

Pretrial Stage Opportunities:

- Arrest response can minimize damage and begin building defense case
- Discovery battles can reveal crucial government weaknesses

- Expert witness development can provide technical foundation for defense
- Plea negotiations can be approached strategically rather than defensively
- Trial preparation can demonstrate to prosecutors that conviction is uncertain

The key insight is that effective defense requires understanding the federal process and fighting back at every stage rather than passively accepting prosecution. Defendants who understand the timeline and exploit its opportunities give themselves the best chance of achieving the vindication they deserve.

Your case may seem hopeless when viewed through the government's investigative lens, but remember that every stage of the federal process creates opportunities for effective defense. The question is whether you'll recognize and exploit those opportunities or allow the government to control the narrative from beginning to end.

The investigation may have already begun, but your defense can still determine the outcome. Fight back at every stage, because your freedom depends on it.

CHAPTER 9

TACTICAL MOTIONS

Pre-Trial Actions: Suppression, Dismissal, Severance

Defense attorney Michael Johnson stared at the government's evidence list in his client's PPP fraud case and saw what prosecutors hoped he would miss: a fatal flaw that could destroy their entire prosecution. The FBI had obtained Maria Gonzalez's business records through a search warrant that contained a crucial error. The warrant authorized agents to search for evidence of "bank fraud" but Maria was being prosecuted for "wire fraud." Under federal law, this seemingly minor distinction made the search illegal and all evidence obtained through it inadmissible.

Johnson had found the government's Achilles heel, but he knew that simply filing a motion to suppress wouldn't be enough. He needed to craft a tactical motion strategy that would not only exclude the illegally obtained evidence but also demonstrate to prosecutors that their case was fundamentally flawed. This required understanding not just the law, but the psychology of federal prosecutions and how aggressive motion practice could transform the entire dynamics of a case.

Three months later, after Johnson filed a comprehensive motion to suppress evidence that included expert testimony about Fourth Amendment violations and detailed analysis of the warrant's defects, prosecutors quietly dismissed all charges against Maria. They realized that losing their key evidence would make conviction impossible and that the motion had exposed other weaknesses in their case they hadn't previously recognized.

Maria's victory illustrates the power of tactical motion practice in PPP cases. While most defendants focus on ultimate trial strategies, the real battles are often won or lost during the pretrial motion phase. Successful motions can exclude crucial government evidence, dismiss charges entirely, or create such doubt about the prosecution's case that favorable plea agreements become possible.

Understanding how to craft and deploy tactical motions is essential for any serious PPP defense because these motions often provide the only opportunity to attack the foundation of the government's case before trial.

The Strategic Value Of Motion Practice

Federal criminal motions serve multiple strategic purposes beyond their immediate legal objectives. Effective motion practice can reshape the entire prosecution by forcing the government to defend their investigative methods, reveal weaknesses in their case, and expend resources they hadn't planned to use.

Primary Strategic Functions:

- Exclude evidence that forms the core of the government's case
- Force disclosure of information the government prefers to keep secret
- Demonstrate defense preparation and willingness to fight aggressively
- Create leverage for plea negotiations by showing case weaknesses
- Educate judges about defense theories before trial begins

Psychological Impact on Prosecutors:

Aggressive motion practice sends powerful signals to federal prosecutors:

- The defense has thoroughly analyzed the case and identified genuine weaknesses
- The defendant has competent counsel willing to challenge government conduct
- Conviction at trial is not guaranteed and may require substantial additional resources
- Settlement negotiations should reflect the real risks of proceeding to trial

Maria Gonzalez's case illustrates these dynamics perfectly. When Johnson filed his motion to suppress, prosecutors initially dismissed it as a desperate defense tactic. But as they researched the law and analyzed their warrant, they realized Johnson was right. The search was illegal, their key evidence was inadmissible, and their case was fatally flawed.

DEFENSE STRATEGY #61: *Comprehensive Motion Audit*

Every PPP case should begin with a comprehensive audit of potential motion opportunities:

- Analyze all government searches and seizures for Fourth Amendment violations
- Review investigation procedures for due process violations
- Examine charging documents for legal sufficiency and specificity

- Identify prosecutorial misconduct or Brady material violations
- Assess venue, jurisdiction, and statute of limitations issues

This audit often reveals motion opportunities that can dramatically improve defense positions.

Motion To Suppress Evidence

Suppression motions challenge the government's evidence-gathering methods and can exclude crucial evidence from trial. In PPP cases, these motions often target financial records, business documents, and electronic evidence obtained through questionable means.

****Common Suppression Opportunities:****

- Search warrants that lack probable cause or are overly broad
- Seizures of business records without proper legal authority
- Electronic surveillance that violates privacy rights
- Financial record subpoenas that exceed legal limits
- Evidence obtained through coercive interrogation

****Maria Gonzalez's Suppression Motion:****

Johnson's motion identified multiple Fourth Amendment violations:

- The search warrant incorrectly described the crime being investigated
- Agents seized records beyond the scope of the warrant
- The affidavit supporting the warrant contained material misstatements
- Investigators failed to return seized property not covered by the warrant

The motion included expert testimony from a former federal prosecutor who explained how these violations compromised the entire investigation.

****Motion Strategy:****Johnson didn't just argue that the search was illegal; he demonstrated how the violations revealed broader problems with the government's case:

- The warrant errors showed investigative carelessness and bias
- The overly broad seizure indicated that agents didn't understand what evidence they actually needed
- The misstatements in the warrant affidavit suggested that agents were building a case rather than investigating objectively

DEFENSE STRATEGY #62: *Multi-Layered Suppression Arguments*

Effective suppression motions should include multiple layers of argument:

- ➢ Direct constitutional violations that require evidence exclusion
- ➢ Good faith exceptions and why they don't apply to the specific violations
- ➢ Inevitable discovery arguments and their limitations in the specific case
- ➢ Fruit of the poisonous tree analysis showing how violations tainted other evidence
- ➢ Policy arguments about deterring future investigative misconduct

This multi-layered approach maximizes the chances of success while demonstrating thorough legal analysis.

Motion To Dismiss For Insufficient Evidence

Motions to dismiss challenge whether the government's evidence is legally sufficient to support the charges filed. In PPP cases, these motions often focus on the lack of evidence showing fraudulent intent or material misstatements.

Legal Standards for Dismissal:

Federal courts apply strict standards for dismissal motions:

- ➢ Evidence must be viewed in the light most favorable to the government
- ➢ Inferences must be drawn in favor of the prosecution
- ➢ Dismissal is only appropriate when no reasonable jury could find guilt beyond reasonable doubt
- ➢ Courts are reluctant to dismiss cases before trial unless legal deficiencies are clear

Strategic Dismissal Arguments:

Despite these strict standards, PPP cases often present dismissal opportunities:

- ➢ Charges that criminalize conduct not actually prohibited by statute
- ➢ Allegations that fail to establish the required mental state for fraud
- ➢ Cases where government evidence proves good faith rather than criminal intent
- ➢ Prosecutions based on regulatory interpretations that exceed statutory authority

Case Study: Rodriguez v. United States (Theoretical)

Defense attorney Sarah Bland filed a motion to dismiss in a case where her client, restaurant owner Carlos Rojas, was charged with wire fraud for allegedly inflating his employee count on PPP applications.

Martinez's Dismissal Arguments:

- The government's evidence showed Rojas honestly believed his family members qualified as employees
- PPP regulations were ambiguous about family member employment status
- Rojas's interpretation of the regulations was reasonable under the circumstances
- The government failed to prove that Rodriguez intended to defraud anyone

The motion included expert testimony about the complexity of PPP regulations and industry practices regarding family employment in small businesses.

Government Response:

Prosecutors argued that Rojas's signature on the application established his intent to make false statements, regardless of his subjective beliefs about the truthfulness of those statements.

Court Decision:

The judge denied the motion but expressed concerns about prosecuting defendants for reasonable interpretations of ambiguous regulations. This judicial skepticism provided valuable leverage for plea negotiations.

DEFENSE STRATEGY #63: *Strategic Dismissal Motions***

Even unsuccessful dismissal motions can provide strategic value:

- Force prosecutors to articulate their legal theories and evidence early
- Identify weaknesses in the government's case that can be exploited at trial
- Create judicial awareness of defense arguments before trial begins
- Generate leverage for plea negotiations by demonstrating case vulnerabilities

- Preserve issues for appeal if conviction occurs

The key is crafting dismissal motions that advance defense strategy regardless of their immediate success.

Motion For Bill Of Particulars

Bills of particulars require prosecutors to provide additional details about charges when indictments are vague or conclusory. In PPP cases, these motions can force the government to specify exactly what conduct they claim was fraudulent.

****When Bills of Particulars Are Useful:****

- Indictments that use conclusory language without specifying alleged false statements
- Charges that don't identify which specific regulations were allegedly violated
- Cases where the government's theory of fraud is unclear or inconsistent
- Prosecutions involving multiple defendants where individual roles are undefined

****Strategic Value:****

Bills of particulars serve multiple strategic purposes:

- Force prosecutors to commit to specific legal theories early in the case
- Identify inconsistencies between different charges or counts
- Reveal whether prosecutors actually understand the regulations they claim were violated
- Create opportunities to challenge the specificity and legal sufficiency of charges

****Case Example:****

Defense attorney James Line filed a bill of particulars motion in a PPP case where his client was charged with "knowingly making false statements" without any specification of which statements were allegedly false.

****Line's Motion Arguments:****

- The indictment failed to identify which specific statements were allegedly false

- The government hadn't specified which PPP regulations were allegedly violated
- The defendant couldn't prepare an adequate defense without knowing the specific charges
- The vague charges violated due process requirements for notice

Government Response:

Prosecutors provided a detailed bill of particulars that revealed their theory was based on a misunderstanding of PPP regulations. This allowed Liu to develop expert testimony that demolished the government's legal foundation.

DEFENSE STRATEGY #64: *Strategic Particulars Demands*

Bills of particulars should be crafted to maximum strategic advantage:

- Identify specific areas where government charges lack necessary detail
- Force prosecutors to commit to legal theories that can be challenged
- Create opportunities to demonstrate prosecutorial confusion about relevant law
- Generate discovery of government legal analysis and case strategy
- Preserve due process arguments for appeal if necessary

Effective particulars motions often reveal that prosecutors haven't thoroughly analyzed the legal foundations of their charges.

Motion To Sever Charges Or Defendants

Severance motions seek to separate charges or defendants that have been improperly joined for trial. In PPP cases, these motions can be crucial when prosecutors attempt to try multiple related cases together.

Grounds for Severance:

- Prejudicial joinder that prevents fair trial
- Conflicting defense strategies among co-defendants
- Evidence admissible against one defendant but prejudicial to others
- Charges that are improperly joined under federal rules

Strategic Severance Considerations:

Severance decisions require careful strategic analysis:

- Joint trials often favor prosecutors by creating appearance of conspiracy

- Separate trials allow more focused defense strategies
- Severance can eliminate prejudicial evidence that applies only to co-defendants
- Individual trials may be more expensive but offer better odds of acquittal

Case Study: Multi-Defendant PPP Prosecution

Three restaurant owners were charged together in a PPP fraud case because they had used the same accountant and loan broker. Defense attorney Maria Santos represented one of the three and filed a motion to sever.

Santos's Severance Arguments:

- Her client's case involved different legal issues than the co-defendants
- Evidence against other defendants would prejudice her client's defense
- Joint trial would prevent her from arguing that the other defendants were the real culprits
- Her client wanted to testify but couldn't do so effectively in a joint trial

Court Decision:

The judge granted severance, reasoning that the defendants' interests were too conflicting for fair joint trial. Santos's client was subsequently acquitted in his individual trial.

DEFENSE STRATEGY #65: *Strategic Severance Analysis*

Severance decisions should be based on careful strategic analysis:

- Evaluate whether joint trial helps or hurts the specific client's defense
- Consider whether severance would eliminate prejudicial evidence or witnesses
- Analyze whether separate trial would allow more effective defense strategies
- Assess the costs and benefits of individual versus joint representation
- Coordinate with co-defendants' counsel when severance serves multiple defendants

Severance can dramatically improve defense prospects when properly deployed.

Motion For Change Of Venue

Venue motions seek to move trials to different jurisdictions when pretrial publicity or local bias makes fair trial impossible. PPP cases often generate significant media coverage that can prejudice potential jury pools.

****Venue Change Standards:****

Federal courts apply strict standards for venue changes:

- Defendants must demonstrate that fair trial is impossible in the current venue
- Pretrial publicity must be extensive and prejudicial
- Local bias must be documented through surveys or other evidence
- Alternative venues must be identified where fair trial is possible

****PPP-Specific Venue Issues:****

PPP cases present unique venue challenges:

- Media coverage often emphasizes fraud allegations without defense context
- Local business communities may be biased against alleged fraud defendants
- Political climate may influence attitudes toward government fraud prosecutions
- Minority defendants may face additional bias in certain geographic areas

****Case Example:****

Defense attorney David Smith filed a venue motion in a PPP case where his client had received extensive negative media coverage in local news outlets.

****Smith's Venue Arguments:****

- Local media had repeatedly characterized allegations as established facts
- Editorial coverage had called for harsh punishment before trial
- Community attitudes surveys showed bias against PPP defendants
- His client's minority status created additional bias concerns in the local area

Court Decision:

The judge denied the venue motion but implemented extensive voir dire procedures to identify and exclude biased jurors. This achieved some of the benefits of venue change while keeping the trial local.

DEFENSE STRATEGY #66: *Venue Strategy Development*

Venue motions should be part of comprehensive pretrial strategy:

- Document all prejudicial media coverage and community reaction
- Conduct surveys or focus groups to assess local bias
- Identify alternative venues where fair trial would be more likely
- Consider whether venue motion might influence judge's jury selection procedures
- Use venue briefing to educate court about bias issues even if motion is denied

Venue motions often achieve strategic benefits even when they're ultimately unsuccessful.

Motion To Compel Discovery

Discovery motions force prosecutors to produce evidence they are required to provide but have failed to deliver. In PPP cases, these motions often target technical evidence, government analysis, and exculpatory materials.

Common Discovery Issues:

- Government refusal to produce algorithmic analysis and underlying data
- Delays in producing financial records and expert reports
- Claims of privilege for embarrassing internal communications
- Incomplete production of Brady material and exculpatory evidence

Strategic Discovery Approach:

Effective discovery motions should be aggressive and comprehensive:

- Demand specific categories of evidence with detailed explanations of relevance
- Challenge all government claims of privilege or exemption
- Set deadlines for production with sanctions for non-compliance

- Coordinate discovery requests with motion practice and trial preparation

Case Example:

Defense attorney Lisa Thomas filed a comprehensive discovery motion demanding production of the algorithmic analysis used to target her client.

Thomas's Discovery Arguments:

- Algorithmic analysis was central to the government's case and must be produced

- Defense had right to examine methodology and error rates
- Government claims of proprietary privilege were unfounded
- Due process required access to evidence used to justify prosecution

Government Response:

Prosecutors initially claimed the algorithmic analysis was proprietary and couldn't be disclosed. Thomas filed a motion to compel with expert testimony about the necessity of algorithmic discovery for effective defense.

Court Order:

The judge ordered production of the algorithmic analysis, which revealed significant errors and bias that became central to the defense case.

DEFENSE STRATEGY #67: ***Aggressive Discovery Enforcement***

Discovery motions should be pursued aggressively throughout the case:

- File comprehensive initial discovery requests covering all relevant evidence
- Challenge government delays and privilege claims promptly
- Seek sanctions for discovery violations to encourage compliance
- Use discovery disputes to educate court about case issues
- Coordinate discovery with expert witness development and motion practice

Effective discovery enforcement often provides the evidence needed for successful defense.

Motion For Sanctions

Sanctions motions seek court intervention when prosecutors engage in misconduct or violate court orders. These motions can result in evidence exclusion, charge dismissal, or other relief that benefits the defense.

Sanctionable Prosecutorial Conduct:

- Brady violations involving concealment of exculpatory evidence
- Discovery violations including late or incomplete production
- Misstatements to the court about evidence or legal issues
- Improper media communications that prejudice the case

Strategic Sanctions Approach:

Sanctions motions should be carefully targeted and thoroughly documented:

- Identify specific prosecutorial conduct that violated rules or court orders
- Document the prejudice caused by the misconduct
- Propose appropriate sanctions that address the harm caused
- Use sanctions briefing to highlight broader patterns of prosecutorial misconduct

Case Example:

Defense attorney Michael Reed filed a sanctions motion when prosecutors failed to disclose that their key expert had been disciplined by professional organizations.

Reed's Sanctions Arguments:

- Prosecutors had duty to disclose expert's disciplinary history
- Late disclosure prevented adequate preparation for cross-examination
- Pattern of discovery violations showed intentional misconduct
- Appropriate sanctions included exclusion of expert testimony

Court Decision:

The judge excluded the expert's testimony and sanctioned the government for discovery violations. This eliminated a crucial component of the prosecution's case.

DEFENSE STRATEGY #68: *Strategic Sanctions Practice*

Sanctions motions should be part of comprehensive defense strategy:

- Document all prosecutorial misconduct and rule violations carefully
- File sanctions motions promptly to preserve issues and demonstrate prejudice
- Seek meaningful relief that actually helps the defense case
- Use sanctions briefing to highlight prosecutorial overreach and bias
- Coordinate sanctions practice with other motion strategy and trial preparation

Effective sanctions practice can eliminate government evidence and create appellate issues.

Motion For Expert Witness Disclosure

Expert witness motions govern the admission of scientific and technical testimony. In PPP cases, these motions often challenge government algorithmic evidence and financial analysis.

Expert Witness Standards:

Federal courts apply Daubert standards for expert testimony:

- Evidence must be based on reliable scientific methodology
- Expert must be qualified in the relevant field
- Testimony must be relevant to issues in the case
- Probative value must outweigh prejudicial effect

PPP-Specific Expert Issues:

PPP cases present unique expert witness challenges:

- Government algorithmic analysis often lacks scientific validation
- Financial experts may rely on flawed assumptions about business practices
- Regulatory experts may misinterpret complex PPP requirements
- Computer experts may not understand the bias inherent in machine learning systems

Case Example:

Defense attorney Sarah Martin filed a Daubert motion challenging the government's algorithmic expert in a PPP fraud case.

Martin's Daubert Arguments:

- Government's algorithmic methodology had never been peer-reviewed
- Expert lacked qualifications in machine learning and bias detection
- Analysis was based on training data that didn't account for pandemic conditions
- Probative value was outweighed by prejudicial effect of appearing scientific

Expert Battle Strategy:

Martin hired Dr. James Steele, a computer science professor and former government consultant, to counter the government's expert.

Court Decision:

The judge limited the government expert's testimony to technical descriptions of the algorithmic process while excluding conclusions about fraud indicators. This eliminated much of the prosecution's technical case.

DEFENSE STRATEGY #69: *Expert Witness Strategy*

Expert witness motions should be integrated with overall case strategy:

- Challenge government experts on qualifications, methodology, and reliability
- Develop defense experts with superior credentials and more relevant experience
- Use expert battles to educate court and jury about technical issues
- Coordinate expert testimony with other evidence and motion practice
- Prepare for extended Daubert hearings that may effectively preview trial

Expert witness battles often determine the outcome of technically complex PPP cases.

Motion For Pretrial Detention Review

Detention review motions challenge pretrial detention decisions and seek release or modification of bail conditions. While most PPP defendants are released pending trial, some face restrictive conditions that can be challenged.

Detention Review Grounds:

- Changed circumstances since initial detention hearing

- Demonstrable compliance with initial bail conditions
- Excessive or unnecessary bail restrictions
- Financial hardship caused by asset freezes or employment restrictions

Strategic Detention Considerations:

Pretrial detention affects every aspect of defense preparation:

- Detained defendants cannot assist effectively in their defense
- Asset freezes can prevent hiring of quality counsel
- Employment restrictions can cause financial hardship that pressures guilty pleas
- Family separation creates emotional pressure for quick resolution

Case Example:

Defense attorney David Parks filed a detention review motion for a client whose assets had been frozen pending trial, preventing him from paying for expert witnesses.

Park's Review Arguments:

- Asset freeze prevented adequate legal representation
- Client had complied with all other bail conditions
- No flight risk justified continued financial restrictions
- Due process required access to funds for defense preparation

Court Decision:

The judge modified the asset freeze to allow payment of reasonable attorney fees and expert witness costs while maintaining restrictions on other expenditures.

DEFENSE STRATEGY #70: *Strategic Detention Review*

Detention review should be pursued when restrictions interfere with defense preparation:

- Document compliance with existing bail conditions
- Show how restrictions prevent adequate defense preparation
- Propose alternative conditions that address court concerns
- Use review hearings to demonstrate client stability and community support
- Coordinate detention issues with overall defense strategy and timeline

Effective detention review can provide crucial resources for defense preparation.

Integration Of Motion Practice

The most effective PPP defenses integrate multiple motions into comprehensive pretrial strategies that attack every aspect of the government's case. This requires careful planning and coordination to ensure that different motions support rather than contradict each other.

****Integrated Motion Strategy:****

Maria Gonzalez's defense integrated multiple motions effectively:

- Suppression motion excluded crucial financial evidence
- Discovery motions revealed government investigative errors
- Expert witness challenges eliminated technical testimony
- Sanctions motions highlighted prosecutorial misconduct
- The combination demonstrated that the government's case was fundamentally flawed

****Strategic Coordination:****

Parks coordinated all motions to advance the same themes:

- Government investigation was biased and careless
- Evidence was obtained through improper means
- Prosecution was based on misunderstanding of law and regulations
- Defendant was victim of prosecutorial overreach rather than criminal fraudster

This coordinated approach convinced prosecutors that their case was too weak to proceed to trial.

****Lessons from Successful Motion Practice:****

Maria's victory demonstrates key principles of effective motion practice:

- Thorough case analysis often reveals multiple motion opportunities
- Aggressive motion practice can transform apparently weak cases into strong defenses
- Coordination between different motions multiplies their strategic impact

- ➢ Motion practice often achieves better results than trial preparation alone

- Understanding prosecutorial psychology is crucial for effective motion strategy

Motion practice offers the possibility of pretrial victory that avoids the risks and costs of trial. Maria Gonzalez's case demonstrates that aggressive motion practice can result in complete dismissal of charges when prosecutors realize their cases are fatally flawed.

****Advantages of Pretrial Resolution:****

- ➢ Avoids risks of trial conviction and lengthy sentences
- ➢ Costs significantly less than full trial preparation and litigation
- ➢ Resolves cases more quickly with less family disruption
- ➢ Preserves defendant's resources for rebuilding life and business
- ➢ Creates precedents that may help other similarly situated defendants

****Motion Practice as Trial Preparation:****

Even when motions don't result in dismissal, they provide crucial trial preparation:

- ➢ Force early disclosure of government evidence and strategy
- ➢ Identify weaknesses that can be exploited at trial
- ➢ Educate judges about defense theories before trial begins
- ➢ Generate leverage for plea negotiations
- ➢ Create appellate issues if trial conviction occurs

The key insight is that motion practice should be viewed as an opportunity for victory rather than merely a precursor to trial. Defendants who understand the strategic value of aggressive motion practice often achieve better outcomes than those who focus exclusively on trial preparation.

Your case may seem hopeless when viewed through the lens of the government's evidence, but remember that evidence obtained illegally can be excluded, charges based on flawed legal theories can be dismissed, and prosecutorial misconduct can result in sanctions that destroy the government's case.

Motion practice is not about delaying the inevitable; it's about seizing the initiative and forcing prosecutors to defend their conduct rather than simply attacking yours. The government may have chosen to prosecute you, but you can choose to fight back with every legal weapon available.

The battle may be won or lost before trial ever begins. Make sure you're fighting that battle with everything you have.

CHAPTER 10

MANAGING PUBLIC PERCEPTION

Media Strategy

The headline in the Miami Herald screamed across the front page: "**LOCAL BUSINESSMAN CHARGED WITH STEALING $400,000 FROM COVID RELIEF FUND.**" Below it, a grainy photo showed Roberto Mendez being led away in handcuffs from his auto repair shop, flanked by FBI agents in bulletproof vests. The accompanying article described him as a "PPP fraudster" who had "stolen taxpayer money while honest businesses struggled to survive."

Roberto stared at the newspaper in his jail cell, devastated not just by the criminal charges but by seeing his twenty-year reputation destroyed in a single news cycle. He had built Mendez Auto Repair from nothing, employing fifteen mechanics and becoming a pillar of his working-class Miami neighborhood. His customers trusted him with their cars and their families' safety. Now the paper made him look like a common criminal.

But Roberto's story was far more complex than the headline suggested. He had applied for PPP loans to keep his shop open during lockdowns when car repair was deemed non-essential. He had made mistakes on his applications, miscalculating payroll and including family members who worked part-time in the business. But he had used every penny of loan money for payroll, rent, and business expenses, exactly as the program required.

The real crime wasn't PPP fraud. It was the systematic destruction of Roberto's reputation by a government that had decided to make examples of small business owners to cover up their own failed program implementation.

But Roberto's defense attorney, Maria Santos, understood something the government didn't: public perception wars can be won by defendants who fight back strategically. Over the next eighteen months, she would transform Roberto from a convicted fraudster in the court of public opinion to a sympathetic victim of government overreach. This transformation would prove crucial not just for Roberto's reputation, but for his ultimate acquittal at trial.

The battle for public perception in PPP cases is often as important as the battle in the courtroom. Juries are drawn from the same public that reads newspaper headlines and watches evening news. Community support can influence everything from bail decisions to sentencing recommendations. Most importantly, the narrative established in media coverage often determines whether defendants are seen as criminals deserving punishment or victims deserving sympathy.

The Government's Media Warfare Strategy

Federal prosecutors use media coverage as a weapon in PPP cases, designed to pressure defendants into pleading guilty and to advance prosecutors' careers through high-profile fraud convictions.

****Government Media Tactics:****

- Coordinate arrests with media presence to ensure perp walk coverage
- Issue inflammatory press releases that characterize allegations as established facts
- Use dramatic language like "stole," "cheated," and "defrauded" to prejudice public opinion
- Emphasize dollar amounts and potential sentences to maximize perceived severity
- Time announcements for maximum media coverage during slow news periods

****The Prosecution's Roberto Mendez Narrative:****

The U.S. Attorney's press release about Roberto's case used classic prosecution messaging:

"Roberto Mendez callously exploited a program designed to help struggling businesses during the pandemic, stealing over $400,000 in taxpayer funds while honest business owners faced bankruptcy. This prosecution sends a clear message that we will hold accountable anyone who attempts to defraud American taxpayers during a time of national crisis."

This statement contained multiple misleading elements:

- Characterized allegations as established facts ("stole," "defrauded")
- Suggested Roberto took money from other businesses rather than a government program
- Implied malicious intent ("callously exploited") without evidence

- Used inflammatory language to generate emotional rather than rational responses
- Positioned the prosecution as protecting taxpayers rather than pursuing questionable charges

DEFENSE STRATEGY #71: *Media Narrative Counter-Attack*

Defendants must develop comprehensive strategies to counter government media warfare:

- Monitor all media coverage and government statements for inaccuracies and inflammatory language
- Develop alternative narratives that present the defendant's perspective and humanize their story
- Use social media and community networks to distribute counter-narratives directly
- Engage with journalists to provide background information that supports the defense perspective
- Coordinate with community supporters to generate positive coverage and testimonials

Effective media counter-attack can neutralize prosecution advantage and create favorable conditions for trial.

Crisis Communication Fundamentals

PPP defendants face classic crisis communication challenges that require sophisticated response strategies adapted to the unique constraints of federal criminal cases.

Crisis Communication Challenges:

- Legal restrictions on what defendants and attorneys can say publicly
- Need to respond quickly to negative coverage before narratives become entrenched
- Balancing desire to tell defendant's story with risk of providing evidence to prosecutors
- Managing family and business relationships affected by negative publicity
- Maintaining community support while legal proceedings continue for months or years

Crisis Communication Principles:

- Control the narrative through proactive rather than reactive communication
- Humanize the defendant by emphasizing their personal story and community contributions
- Provide context that explains the defendant's actions in sympathetic terms
- Challenge government characterizations without appearing defensive or evasive
- Build broad coalitions of support that can sustain positive messaging over time

DEFENSE STRATEGY #72: *Proactive Crisis Communication Planning*

Defendants should develop crisis communication plans immediately after charges are filed:

- Assess the current media narrative and identify key vulnerabilities and opportunities
- Develop core messages that present the defendant's story in sympathetic terms
- Identify spokespersons who can communicate effectively with media and community
- Create communication protocols that protect legal interests while enabling effective messaging
- Plan long-term communication strategy that can sustain positive messaging throughout litigation

Proactive planning prevents defendants from being caught off-guard by media developments.

Building Community Support Networks

Community support provides the foundation for effective public perception management. Defendants with strong community backing can counter negative government narratives and generate positive coverage.

Community Support Elements:

- Character witnesses who can testify to the defendant's integrity and community contributions

- Customers and business associates who benefited from the defendant's services
- Community leaders who can speak to the defendant's positive impact
- Employees and their families who depended on the defendant's business
- Local organizations and institutions that worked with the defendant

Roberto's Community Support Campaign:

Maria Santos identified and mobilized Roberto's extensive community connections:

- Fifteen years of satisfied customers who trusted Roberto with their vehicles
- Community organizations that Roberto had sponsored and supported
- Local church where Roberto had been an active member and volunteer
- Youth sports teams that Roberto had coached and funded
- Employees and their families who depended on jobs Roberto provided

Santos organized these supporters into an effective advocacy network that generated positive media coverage and demonstrated community trust in Roberto.

DEFENSE STRATEGY #73: *Systematic Community Support Mobilization*

Community support requires systematic identification and mobilization:

- Catalog all community connections and positive relationships the defendant has built
- Interview supporters to gather specific examples of the defendant's positive impact
- Organize supporters into effective advocacy groups that can sustain long-term messaging
- Train supporters to communicate effectively with media while staying on message
- Coordinate supporter activities to maximize impact while avoiding legal complications

Strong community support can transform public perception and influence potential jurors.

Social Media Strategy and Management

Social media provides defendants with direct communication channels that bypass traditional media filters, but it also creates risks that must be managed carefully.

Social Media Opportunities:

- Direct communication with community members and potential supporters
- Ability to share positive content that humanizes the defendant
- Platform for correcting misinformation and providing context
- Tool for mobilizing supporters and organizing community response
- Channel for sharing expert analysis that supports the defense narrative

Social Media Risks:

- Potential for statements to be used as evidence by prosecutors
- Risk of appearing insensitive or defensive in response to criticism
- Possibility of inadvertent disclosure of privileged or sensitive information
- Danger of inflammatory responses that damage the defense narrative
- Potential for supporters to post content that undermines the defense strategy

Roberto's Social Media Strategy:

Santos developed a comprehensive social media strategy for Roberto's case:

- Created Facebook page featuring testimonials from satisfied customers
- Used Instagram to share photos of Roberto's community involvement and charitable work
- Organized Twitter campaign highlighting positive customer experiences
- Coordinated supporter posts to maintain consistent positive messaging
- Monitored all social media activity to prevent damaging content

DEFENSE STRATEGY #74: *Strategic Social Media Campaign Management***

Social media campaigns require careful planning and ongoing management:

- Develop clear guidelines for what content can and cannot be shared

- Create positive content that humanizes the defendant and demonstrates community support
- Monitor all social media activity to prevent damaging posts by supporters
- Respond strategically to negative coverage while avoiding inflammatory exchanges
- Use social media analytics to measure campaign effectiveness and adjust strategy

Effective social media management can significantly impact public perception and community support.

Media Relations And Journalist Engagement

Building relationships with journalists can help defendants ensure that their perspective is included in news coverage and that inaccurate information is corrected.

****Media Relations Strategy:****

- Identify journalists who cover federal court cases and understand legal complexities

- Provide background briefings that help reporters understand the case context
- Offer expert sources who can explain regulatory complexity and defense arguments
- Respond promptly to journalist inquiries with accurate and helpful information
- Build long-term relationships that can benefit the defendant throughout the case

****Journalist Education Approach:****

Many journalists covering PPP cases lack understanding of the regulatory complexities and investigative procedures involved. Educating reporters can result in more balanced coverage:

- Explain how PPP regulations were complex and constantly changing
- Provide context about the algorithmic detection systems that flagged defendants
- Share information about false positive rates and biased prosecution patterns

- Offer expert sources who can explain technical aspects of the case
- Highlight similar cases where charges were dismissed or defendants were acquitted

DEFENSE STRATEGY #75: *Strategic Journalist Relationship Building*

Effective media relations requires ongoing relationship building:

- Research journalists who cover federal cases and their previous reporting patterns
- Provide valuable background information that helps journalists understand complex issues
- Offer expert sources and character references who can provide quotable material
- Respond professionally and helpfully to all journalist inquiries
- Build reputation for reliability and accuracy that encourages future positive coverage

Strong journalist relationships can result in more balanced and sympathetic coverage.

Reputation Recovery During Litigation

PPP defendants must work to preserve and rebuild their reputations while criminal charges are pending, a process that can take years and requires sustained effort.

Reputation Recovery Elements:

- Continuing business operations and community involvement to demonstrate normalcy
- Participating in charitable and community activities that generate positive coverage
- Maintaining relationships with customers, vendors, and business associates
- Demonstrating transparency and cooperation with legitimate oversight
- Building record of positive contributions that contradicts criminal allegations

Roberto's Reputation Recovery Strategy:

Despite facing federal charges, Roberto continued building positive community relationships:

- Maintained auto repair shop operations and employed all fifteen mechanics
- Increased community involvement by volunteering at local schools
- Organized charity drives for families affected by the pandemic
- Participated in community business association leadership
- Documented all positive activities for potential use at trial and sentencing

This continued community engagement demonstrated that Roberto remained a positive community member despite government allegations.

DEFENSE STRATEGY #76: *Active Reputation Rehabilitation*

Reputation recovery requires active rather than passive approaches:

- Continue positive community involvement despite the stress of criminal charges
- Document all charitable work and community contributions for potential trial use
- Maintain business operations and employment to demonstrate ongoing positive impact
- Participate in industry and professional organizations to maintain standing
- Build record of post-charge conduct that contradicts government characterizations

Active reputation rehabilitation can influence both public perception and ultimate case outcomes.

Managing Family And Business Impact

Criminal charges affect not just defendants but their families and business associates, requiring comprehensive strategies to minimize collateral damage.

Family Impact Management:

- Prepare family members for media attention and community gossip
- Provide counseling and support resources to help family cope with stress
- Develop communication strategies that protect family privacy while allowing support
- Plan for potential financial hardship during extended litigation

- Create security measures if media attention or community backlash creates safety concerns

Business Impact Management:

- Maintain business operations to preserve employment and community relationships
- Communicate transparently with employees about the situation and their job security
- Work with vendors and customers to maintain confidence in business continuity
- Implement additional financial controls to demonstrate ongoing integrity
- Plan for potential business succession if conviction becomes likely

DEFENSE STRATEGY #77: *Comprehensive Stakeholder Communication*

Managing broader impact requires systematic stakeholder communication:

- Identify all stakeholders who might be affected by the criminal charges
- Develop specific communication strategies for each stakeholder group
- Provide regular updates that maintain confidence while protecting legal interests
- Address concerns proactively rather than waiting for problems to develop
- Use stakeholder support to strengthen community backing for the defendant

Effective stakeholder management can prevent criminal charges from destroying relationships that defendants will need regardless of case outcomes.

Expert Commentary And Third-Party Validation

Independent expert commentary can provide credible validation of defense arguments and help shift public perception toward more sympathetic views of defendants.

Expert Commentary Strategy:

- Identify credible experts who can explain regulatory complexity and enforcement problems

- Provide experts with background information that enables informed commentary
- Coordinate expert media appearances with overall defense communication strategy
- Use expert analysis to challenge government narratives and prosecution theories
- Build ongoing relationships with experts who can provide sustained positive commentary

Third-Party Validation Sources:

- Former government officials who can explain program implementation problems
- Legal experts who can discuss prosecutorial overreach and constitutional issues
- Business leaders who can speak to industry practices and regulatory complexity
- Community leaders who can testify to defendant's character and contributions
- Academic researchers who can provide statistical analysis of prosecution patterns

Roberto's case benefited from extensive expert commentary:

- Former SBA official explained how program complexity created inevitable confusion
- Legal experts discussed prosecutorial overreach in PPP cases generally
- Business association leaders spoke about challenges facing auto repair industry during pandemic
- Community leaders testified to Roberto's positive impact and character

DEFENSE STRATEGY #78: *Strategic Expert Commentary Coordination***

Expert commentary requires careful coordination to maximize impact:

- Research potential expert commentators and their credibility with target audiences
- Provide experts with comprehensive background information that enables effective commentary
- Coordinate expert appearances with other defense communication activities

- Monitor expert commentary to ensure consistency with defense messaging
- Build long-term relationships with experts who can provide ongoing support

Credible expert commentary can provide third-party validation that defendants cannot achieve through direct communication.

Crisis Communication During Trial

Trial proceedings create unique communication challenges and opportunities that require specialized strategies to manage public perception while respecting court rules and legal ethics.

Trial Communication Challenges:

- Court rules that may limit public statements about ongoing proceedings
- Media interest that intensifies during trial testimony and developments
- Need to respond to government evidence and arguments presented in court
- Risk that trial communications might prejudice potential jurors
- Pressure to provide immediate responses to negative trial developments

Trial Communication Opportunities:

- Platform to present defense evidence and arguments to public audiences
- Opportunity to demonstrate defendant's cooperation and respect for legal process
- Chance to highlight government overreach and prosecutorial misconduct
- Ability to showcase community support through courtroom attendance
- Forum for presenting expert testimony that validates defense arguments

DEFENSE STRATEGY #79: *Trial Communication Protocol Development*

Trial communication requires specialized protocols that balance effectiveness with legal constraints:

- Develop clear guidelines for what can and cannot be communicated during trial
- Plan responses to likely trial developments and government arguments
- Coordinate courtroom supporters to demonstrate community backing
- Prepare statements that can be issued quickly in response to trial developments
- Train spokespeople to communicate effectively while respecting legal constraints

Effective trial communication can influence both public perception and ultimate case resolution.

Victory Through Perception Management

Roberto Mendez's acquittal on all charges demonstrated the power of comprehensive public perception management combined with effective legal defense.

****Public Perception Victory Elements:****

- Community support that was visible throughout the legal proceedings
- Media coverage that evolved from negative to sympathetic over eighteen months
- Expert commentary that validated defense arguments about regulatory complexity
- Social media presence that humanized Roberto and demonstrated ongoing community contributions
- Reputation rehabilitation that showed Roberto's continued positive impact despite charges

****Trial Impact:****

The public perception campaign had significant impact on Roberto's trial:

- Jury pool showed familiarity with positive community coverage
- Character witnesses were credible because their support was publicly documented
- Media coverage during trial was more balanced due to ongoing journalist relationships
- Community support was visible through packed courtroom during proceedings
- Post-acquittal coverage emphasized prosecutorial overreach rather than defendant vindication

Long-Term Reputation Recovery:

Roberto's business not only survived his prosecution but thrived after his acquittal:

- ➢ Customer base remained loyal due to ongoing positive community relationships
- ➢ Media coverage of acquittal reinforced narrative of government overreach
- ➢ Community support translated into increased business and referrals
- ➢ Roberto's reputation was stronger after trial than before charges were filed

Lessons In Perception Warfare

Roberto's case provides crucial lessons about managing public perception during federal prosecution:

Key Success Factors:

- ➢ Proactive rather than reactive approach to media and community relations
- ➢ Systematic mobilization of community support networks
- ➢ Strategic use of social media and direct communication channels
- ➢ Building relationships with journalists and expert commentators
- ➢ Sustaining positive messaging throughout extended litigation period

Strategic Implications:

- ➢ Public perception can be managed even under adverse circumstances
- ➢ Community support can influence both legal proceedings and ultimate outcomes
- ➢ Social media provides powerful tools for direct communication
- ➢ Expert commentary can provide credible validation of defense arguments
- ➢ Long-term reputation recovery requires sustained effort and strategic planning

Building Your Perception Strategy

Every PPP defendant should develop comprehensive strategies for managing public perception from the moment charges are filed through final case resolution.

Essential Perception Management Elements:

- Immediate crisis communication response to arrest and initial negative coverage
- Systematic community support mobilization that can sustain long-term positive messaging
- Strategic social media presence that humanizes the defendant and demonstrates ongoing contributions
- Media relations that ensure defense perspective is included in news coverage
- Expert commentary coordination that provides third-party validation of defense arguments

Implementation Strategy:

- Begin perception management immediately after charges are filed
- Invest in professional communication expertise if budget allows
- Coordinate perception management with legal defense strategy
- Plan for sustained effort that can continue throughout extended litigation
- Measure effectiveness and adjust strategy based on results

The battle for public perception is as important as the battle in the courtroom. Government prosecutors understand this and use media warfare as a weapon to pressure defendants into pleading guilty. Defendants who fight back strategically can neutralize this advantage and create favorable conditions for legal victory.

Your case may seem hopeless when viewed through negative media coverage, but remember that public perception can be changed through sustained effort and strategic communication. The question is whether you'll allow the government to control the narrative or whether you'll fight back to tell your own story.

The stakes in the perception war are enormous: not just your legal case, but your reputation, your relationships, and your future. Fight for all of them, because they all matter.

CHAPTER 11
JURY SELECTION

Biases, Voir Dire Strategy, Racial Implications

Defense attorney Jennifer Locke knew that the fate of her client, Hassan Al-Rahman, would be decided not in the courtroom arguments or expert testimony, but in the next six hours of jury selection. Hassan, a Syrian-American restaurant owner who had immigrated to Chicago fifteen years earlier, faced PPP fraud charges that could send him to federal prison for twenty years. The government alleged he had inflated his payroll by including family members who didn't actually work in his three Middle Eastern restaurants.

As Jennifer studied the jury questionnaires spread across her hotel room table at 5 AM on the morning of trial, she understood the challenge ahead. Hassan's case would be decided by twelve people who had been bombarded with two years of media coverage about PPP fraud, who might harbor unconscious biases against immigrants and Muslims, and who probably knew little about the complexities of family-owned ethnic restaurants.

But the questionnaires also revealed opportunities. Several potential jurors owned small businesses or had family members who did. Others had worked in restaurants and understood the informal employment practices common in the industry. Some had expressed skepticism about government overreach in their personal backgrounds.

The key was identifying which potential jurors could see past their preconceptions and judge Hassan based on the evidence rather than their assumptions about fraud, immigrants, and government programs.

"We're not just picking jurors," Jennifer told her co-counsel as they prepared for voir dire. "We're picking the twelve people who will decide whether Hassan goes home to his family or spends the next two decades in federal prison. Every question we ask, every challenge we make, every decision we make in that courtroom today will determine the rest of his life."

Hassan's jury selection would last eight hours and involve questioning forty-seven potential jurors. It would reveal deep-seated biases about fraud, immigration, and government programs. It would showcase innovative defense strategies for identifying sympathetic jurors while eliminating those likely to convict. Most importantly, it would demonstrate how skillful voir dire can transform an apparently hopeless case into a winnable defense.

Understanding Jury Psychology In PPP Cases

PPP fraud cases present unique jury psychology challenges that require sophisticated understanding of how ordinary citizens react to financial crime allegations, government programs, and small business operations.

Psychological Challenges for PPP Defendants:

- Fraud allegations trigger strong moral condemnation and punishment instincts
- Complex financial evidence creates cognitive burden that favors simple prosecution narratives
- Media coverage has conditioned jurors to expect PPP fraud and assume guilt
- Government prosecutions benefit from authority bias and presumptions of legitimacy
- Technical violations appear damning even when they have innocent explanations

Psychological Opportunities for Defense:

- Small business owners are generally sympathetic figures who embody American entrepreneurial values
- Regulatory complexity generates sympathy for confused borrowers trying to comply
- Government overreach narratives resonate with jurors who distrust federal authority
- Underdog positioning can generate support for defendants fighting powerful institutions
- Personal stories can humanize defendants and counter abstract fraud allegations

DEFENSE STRATEGY #80: *Comprehensive Jury Psychology Analysis*

Effective jury selection requires understanding how potential jurors are likely to react to case themes:

- Analyze the defendant's personal characteristics and how they might be perceived by different jury demographics
- Identify case themes that are likely to resonate positively or negatively with potential jurors
- Research local attitudes toward government programs, small businesses, and regulatory enforcement
- Consider how cultural, ethnic, and religious factors might influence jury perceptions
- Develop voir dire strategies that identify favorable psychological predispositions

Understanding jury psychology allows defense teams to select jurors who are predisposed toward defense arguments.

Pretrial Jury Research And Community Analysis

Successful jury selection begins long before trial with comprehensive research into community attitudes, demographic patterns, and local jury tendencies.

****Community Attitude Research:****

Jennifer Locke's team conducted extensive research into Chicago-area attitudes relevant to Hassan's case:

- Public opinion polling about government programs and fraud enforcement
- Analysis of local media coverage patterns about PPP cases and immigrant defendants
- Research into community attitudes toward small businesses and family employment practices
- Investigation of previous jury verdicts in similar cases within the district
- Analysis of demographic patterns and voting behaviors in the jury pool area

****Demographic Analysis:****

The research revealed important patterns in potential jury composition:

- Higher education levels correlated with greater understanding of regulatory complexity
- Small business experience increased sympathy for defendants facing bureaucratic challenges

- ➢ Minority group membership increased skepticism about government prosecution patterns
- ➢ Age differences affected attitudes toward both fraud enforcement and immigrant entrepreneurs
- ➢ Religious affiliation influenced views about family business practices and community support

DEFENSE STRATEGY #81: *Comprehensive Pretrial Jury Research*

Pretrial research provides crucial foundation for effective jury selection:

- ➢ Conduct polling or focus groups to understand community attitudes toward case themes
- ➢ Analyze demographic data to identify favorable and unfavorable juror characteristics
- ➢ Research previous cases in the jurisdiction to understand local jury tendencies
- ➢ Study media coverage patterns to assess potential prejudice and bias
- ➢ Develop jury profiles that guide voir dire questioning and challenge decisions

Comprehensive research allows defense teams to approach jury selection strategically rather than intuitively.

Jury Questionnaire Development And Analysis

Federal courts typically provide jury questionnaires that allow attorneys to gather basic information about potential jurors before voir dire begins. Effective questionnaire analysis can identify potential biases and favorable characteristics before oral questioning.

Hassan's Jury Questionnaire Analysis:

Jennifer Locke analyzed questionnaires from 67 potential jurors, identifying key patterns:

- 23 potential jurors had small business experience or family members who owned businesses

- 18 had worked in restaurants or food service industries

- 31 had college degrees and might better understand regulatory complexity

- 12 had previous negative experiences with government agencies

- 8 were immigrants or children of immigrants who might sympathize with Hassan's background

Red Flag Indicators:

The questionnaires also revealed concerning patterns:

- 14 potential jurors expressed strong support for fraud enforcement

- 9 had family members in law enforcement who might be biased toward prosecution

- 6 had made negative comments about government assistance programs

- 11 had indicated strong prejudices that might affect their ability to judge fairly

- 5 had previous jury service in criminal cases that resulted in guilty verdicts

DEFENSE STRATEGY #82: *Strategic Questionnaire Analysis*

Questionnaire analysis should identify both opportunities and threats:

- Flag potential jurors with characteristics that favor the defense case
- Identify jurors with backgrounds or experiences that suggest bias against the defendant
- Note inconsistencies or concerning responses that require follow-up during voir dire
- Develop preliminary challenge strategies based on questionnaire responses
- Prepare targeted voir dire questions for specific jurors based on their questionnaire answers

Effective questionnaire analysis provides a roadmap for subsequent oral questioning.

Voir Dire Strategy And Question Development

Voir dire questioning represents the defense's only opportunity to interact directly with potential jurors and assess their suitability for the case. Effective questioning requires careful preparation and strategic execution.

Voir Dire Objectives:

- Identify and eliminate jurors who are biased against the defendant or predisposed toward conviction
- Educate potential jurors about case themes and legal standards that favor the defense
- Build rapport with favorable jurors who might become advocates during deliberations
- Gather information that helps attorneys make informed challenge decisions
- Begin presenting the defense narrative in a way that influences how jurors view subsequent evidence

Jennifer Locke's Questioning Strategy:

Locke developed a comprehensive voir dire strategy tailored to Hassan's case:

- Open-ended questions about attitudes toward small businesses and family employment
- Hypothetical scenarios that tested reactions to regulatory complexity and honest mistakes
- Direct questions about attitudes toward immigrants, Muslims, and ethnic businesses
- Exploration of personal experiences with government bureaucracy and regulatory compliance
- Assessment of ability to distinguish between innocent mistakes and criminal intent

DEFENSE STRATEGY #83: *Targeted Voir Dire Question Development*

Voir dire questions should be strategically designed to achieve specific objectives:

- Develop questions that reveal attitudes relevant to key case themes
- Use hypothetical scenarios that mirror case facts to test juror reactions
- Ask about personal experiences that might bias jurors for or against the defendant
- Explore attitudes toward government authority and prosecutorial power
- Test ability to follow legal instructions about burden of proof and reasonable doubt

Strategic questioning reveals information needed for informed challenge decisions.

Identifying And Eliminating Biased Jurors

The primary goal of voir dire is identifying and eliminating jurors who are biased against the defendant or predisposed toward conviction. This requires understanding both explicit biases that jurors admit and implicit biases they may not recognize.

Explicit Bias Indicators:

Some potential jurors openly expressed biases that required elimination:

- **Juror #23** stated that "people who take government money they don't deserve should go to jail"

- **Juror #31** said he "didn't trust Muslims" and "thought they were all trying to cheat the system"

- **Juror #47** expressed belief that "business owners who make mistakes on government forms are usually lying"

- **Juror #12** indicated she "always believed prosecutors" because "they wouldn't bring charges without evidence"

Implicit Bias Detection:

More dangerous were jurors who harbored unconscious biases:

- **Juror #15** claimed to be unbiased but used language suggesting skepticism about immigrant entrepreneurs

- **Juror #28** said she could be fair but had expressed strong support for fraud enforcement in her questionnaire

- **Juror #39** claimed openness but had made subtle comments suggesting prejudice against family businesses

- **Juror #51** professed impartiality but had body language suggesting discomfort when discussing Hassan's background

DEFENSE STRATEGY #84: Systematic Bias Detection and Elimination

Effective bias detection requires multiple assessment techniques:

- Listen carefully to language choices that reveal underlying attitudes

- Observe body language and nonverbal reactions to questions about case themes
- Ask follow-up questions that probe deeper into potentially concerning responses
- Use hypothetical scenarios to test reactions to situations similar to the defendant's
- Challenge any juror who shows signs of bias regardless of their stated claims of fairness

Eliminating biased jurors is essential for creating fair trial conditions.

Building Favorable Jury Composition

Beyond eliminating biased jurors, effective voir dire identifies and preserves jurors who are likely to be sympathetic to the defense case.

****Favorable Juror Characteristics:****

Jennifer Locke identified several characteristics that predicted sympathy for Hassan's defense:

- Small business experience that created understanding of regulatory challenges
- Personal or family immigration experience that generated empathy for Hassan's background
- Previous negative experiences with government bureaucracy that created skepticism about prosecution
- Higher education levels that enabled understanding of complex regulatory issues
- Minority group membership that increased awareness of potential bias in prosecution

****Jury Composition Strategy:****

Locke worked to preserve favorable jurors while eliminating unfavorable ones:

- Used peremptory challenges strategically to remove jurors who couldn't be challenged for cause
- Asked questions that highlighted favorable jurors' backgrounds and experiences
- Built rapport with potential jurors who showed sympathy for Hassan's situation

- Preserved jurors with leadership qualities who might advocate for defense during deliberations
- Created jury composition that balanced different perspectives while favoring defense themes

DEFENSE STRATEGY #85: *Strategic Jury Composition Management*

Jury selection should aim for optimal composition rather than just eliminating bad jurors:

- Identify characteristics that predict sympathy for the defense case
- Use challenges strategically to achieve favorable overall jury composition
- Preserve jurors with leadership qualities who might influence deliberations
- Balance different perspectives while maintaining favorable majority
- Consider jury dynamics and how different personalities might interact during deliberations

Strategic composition management can create juries predisposed toward defense arguments.

Addressing Racial And Cultural Bias

PPP cases involving minority defendants require special attention to racial and cultural bias that might affect jury decision-making.

Racial Bias Challenges:

Hassan's case presented multiple potential bias issues:

- Anti-Muslim sentiment that might prejudice jurors against his character and credibility
- Immigration bias that could affect perceptions of his right to government assistance
- Stereotypes about Middle Eastern business practices that might seem inherently suspicious
- Cultural misunderstanding about family employment practices common in ethnic businesses
- Unconscious bias that might make ordinary business practices appear fraudulent

Cultural Education Strategy:

Locke used voir dire to educate potential jurors about cultural context:

- Explained how family members commonly work in ethnic restaurants without formal employment
- Described cultural practices around cash payments and informal business arrangements
- Provided context about challenges facing immigrant entrepreneurs during the pandemic
- Highlighted Hassan's fifteen-year history as a successful community businessman
- Addressed stereotypes directly while emphasizing Hassan's American success story

DEFENSE STRATEGY #86: *Proactive Bias Address and Cultural Education*

Minority defendants require proactive strategies to address potential bias:

- Identify specific cultural or racial biases that might affect the case
- Use voir dire to educate jurors about cultural practices relevant to the defense
- Address stereotypes and misconceptions directly but sensitively
- Emphasize the defendant's positive community contributions and American success
- Select jurors who demonstrate cultural sensitivity and openness to different perspectives

Proactive bias addresses can neutralize prejudice before it affects deliberations.

Economic And Class Considerations

PPP cases often involve class dynamics that affect how jurors perceive defendants and their alleged conduct.

Economic Bias Factors:

- Resentment toward business owners receiving government assistance during economic hardship
- Skepticism about claims of business necessity from entrepreneurs who appear successful

- Misunderstanding of business financial pressures and cash flow challenges
- Assumption that business owners should understand complex regulations better than ordinary citizens
- Class-based prejudice that views small business owners as privileged rather than struggling

****Hassan's Economic Story:****

Locke worked to present Hassan's economic situation sympathetically:

- Emphasized his modest immigrant background and struggle to build his restaurants
- Showed how pandemic lockdowns devastated his business and threatened his employees' livelihoods
- Demonstrated that he used PPP funds entirely for business purposes rather than personal benefit
- Highlighted his continued employment of workers despite financial challenges
- Presented his case as typical small business survival rather than fraudulent enrichment

****DEFENSE STRATEGY #87:** *Economic Narrative Development***

Economic perceptions require careful management through voir dire:

- Assess potential jurors' attitudes toward business ownership and entrepreneurship
- Present the defendant's economic story in terms that generate sympathy rather than resentment
- Emphasize business struggles and employee welfare rather than business success
- Address assumptions about business owner sophistication and regulatory knowledge
- Frame the case as economic survival rather than fraudulent enrichment

Effective economic framing can transform potential resentment into sympathy.

Government Authority And Prosecutorial Bias

Juror attitudes toward government authority and prosecutorial power significantly affect PPP case outcomes.

Authority Bias Challenges:

- Presumption that government prosecutors only bring legitimate cases
- Deference to FBI agents and other law enforcement testimony
- Assumption that government programs are well-designed and fairly administered
- Belief that regulatory violations necessarily indicate criminal intent
- Reluctance to second-guess prosecutorial decisions about appropriate charges

Anti-Authority Opportunities:

- Skepticism about government competence and overreach
- Personal experiences with bureaucratic incompetence and arbitrary enforcement
- Distrust of federal power and regulatory complexity
- Sympathy for individuals fighting powerful institutions
- Recognition of prosecutorial incentives and political motivations

DEFENSE STRATEGY #88: *Authority Attitude Assessment and Exploitation***

Juror attitudes toward authority require careful evaluation:

- Ask about personal experiences with government agencies and regulatory compliance
- Assess attitudes toward prosecutorial power and law enforcement credibility
- Identify jurors who have experienced government overreach or bureaucratic incompetence
- Explore beliefs about the relationship between regulatory violations and criminal intent
- Select jurors who can evaluate government evidence critically rather than deferentially

Balancing authority attitudes can create juries capable of holding the government?

to appropriate standards.

The Final Jury And Trial Strategy

Hassan's final jury reflected Jennifer Locke's strategic selections based on eight hours of voir dire:

- Six jurors with small business experience or family connections to entrepreneurship
- Four minority jurors who understood challenges facing immigrant communities
- Two jurors with negative government experiences who were skeptical of prosecutorial claims
- Multiple college-educated jurors capable of understanding regulatory complexity
- No jurors with explicit biases against Muslims, immigrants, or family businesses

Jury Dynamics:

The selected jury demonstrated favorable dynamics during trial:

- Business-experienced jurors served as informal leaders who explained regulatory complexity to others
- Minority jurors provided perspective on potential prosecution bias and cultural misunderstanding
- Educated jurors asked thoughtful questions that revealed government weaknesses
- Skeptical jurors challenged prosecution assumptions about intent and criminality
- The jury worked collaboratively to understand complex evidence rather than deferring to authority

Trial Outcome:

Hassan was acquitted on all charges after six hours of deliberation. Post-trial interviews revealed that jury selection had been crucial to the outcome:

- Jurors understood that Hassan's family employment practices were culturally normal rather than fraudulent
- They recognized that regulatory complexity made honest mistakes inevitable
- They questioned government theories about criminal intent based on technical violations
- They viewed Hassan sympathetically as a hardworking immigrant entrepreneur rather than a criminal
- They held the government to appropriate burden of proof standards rather than deferring to prosecutorial authority

DEFENSE STRATEGY #89: *Post-Trial Jury Analysis and Learning*

Post-trial jury feedback provides valuable insights for future cases:

- Interview jurors about their decision-making process and key influencing factors
- Analyze which voir dire strategies were most effective in identifying favorable jurors
- Evaluate whether jury composition achieved intended dynamics and outcomes
- Learn from jury feedback about effective and ineffective trial strategies
- Apply lessons learned to improve jury selection techniques in subsequent cases

Post-trial analysis improves jury selection expertise and case outcomes.

Victory Through Strategic Selection

Hassan Al-Rahman's acquittal demonstrated the crucial importance of strategic jury selection in PPP cases. His victory resulted from comprehensive pretrial research, strategic voir dire questioning, systematic bias elimination, and careful jury composition management.

Key Success Factors:

- Extensive pretrial research that revealed community attitudes and demographic patterns
- Strategic voir dire that educated jurors while identifying bias and sympathy
- Systematic elimination of jurors with explicit and implicit bias against the defendant
- Composition strategy that preserved favorable jurors while eliminating unfavorable ones
- Cultural education that addressed stereotypes and provided context for Hassan's actions

Strategic Implications:

- Jury selection often determines case outcomes more than trial evidence or arguments
- Pretrial research provides essential foundation for effective voir dire strategy

- Bias elimination must address both explicit prejudice and unconscious assumptions
- Cultural and economic factors require proactive management through jury selection
- Strategic composition can create juries predisposed toward defense arguments

Building Your Jury Selection Strategy

Every PPP defendant should invest heavily in comprehensive jury selection preparation, recognizing that the twelve people chosen to decide their case will largely determine their fate.

Essential Jury Selection Elements:

- Comprehensive pretrial research into community attitudes and demographic patterns
- Strategic questionnaire analysis that identifies opportunities and threats
- Targeted voir dire questioning that reveals bias while building rapport with favorable jurors
- Systematic challenge strategies that eliminate bias while preserving sympathy
- Composition management that creates favorable jury dynamics and decision-making patterns

Implementation Strategy:

- Begin jury research months before trial to understand community attitudes
- Invest in professional jury consulting if budget allows
- Develop comprehensive voir dire strategies tailored to specific case themes
- Practice questioning techniques to maximize effectiveness during limited voir dire time
- Plan challenge strategies that achieve optimal jury composition within legal constraints

The twelve jurors who decide your case will determine whether you go home to your family or spend years in federal prison. Their selection is not a matter of chance or intuition; it's a strategic process that can be managed to maximize your chances of victory.

Your case may seem strong on the evidence, but remember that evidence is interpreted by human beings with their own biases, experiences, and assumptions. The key to victory is selecting twelve humans who can see past their preconceptions and judge you fairly based on the evidence presented.

Jury selection is where cases are won or lost. Approach it with the seriousness and strategic thinking it deserves, because your freedom depends on the twelve people you choose to decide your fate.

CHAPTER 12

GOVERNMENT EVIDENCE

Financial Proof, Testimony, Procedural Levers

Assistant U.S. Attorney Sarah Poole stood before the jury in the federal courthouse in San Antonio, Texas, pointing dramatically at a blown-up photograph of defendant Carlos Hernandez's bank statement. The highlighted entry showed a $127,000 deposit from his PPP loan, followed by a series of withdrawals that prosecutors argued proved criminal intent.

"Ladies and gentlemen," Poole declared, "this bank record tells the story of Carlos Hernandez's fraud. He deposited stolen taxpayer money into his personal account, then systematically drained it for his own benefit while lying to the government about how he would use these funds."

Defense attorney Michael Swan watched from the defense table, knowing that the bank statement Poole displayed told only part of the story. Yes, Carlos had deposited the PPP loan into his personal account, but only because his business account had been frozen during a separate IRS audit. Yes, he had withdrawn money from the account, but every penny had gone to pay employees, suppliers, and business expenses exactly as PPP required.

The problem wasn't the facts; it was the presentation. Poole was using classic prosecution techniques to make innocent conduct appear criminal, legitimate business decisions look fraudulent, and reasonable accounting practices seem like money laundering. She was weaponizing Carlos's own financial records against him.

But Santos understood something Poole hoped the defense wouldn't realize: every piece of evidence the government presents can be turned into a defense weapon if you know how to dissect it, contextualize it, and present the complete story rather than the government's selective narrative.

Over the next four days, Swan would systematically dismantle every piece of government evidence, showing the jury that the same documents prosecutors claimed proved fraud actually demonstrated Carlos's good faith and legitimate business operations. His cross-examination would reveal how the government's financial analysis was misleading, their expert testimony was biased, and their whole case was built on taking normal business activities out of context.

The battle over government evidence would determine whether Carlos went home to his family or spent the next fifteen years in federal prison. But it would also demonstrate how defendants can turn apparent prosecution strengths into defense victories through strategic analysis, aggressive cross-examination, and comprehensive alternative explanations.

Understanding Government Evidence Strategy

Federal prosecutors in PPP cases rely on predictable evidence strategies designed to overwhelm defendants with documentation while obscuring the context that would support innocent explanations.

****Government Evidence Objectives:****

- Create appearance of overwhelming documentary proof through volume of financial records
- Isolate individual transactions or decisions from business context that would explain them
- Use technical violations to suggest criminal intent without proving fraudulent purpose
- Present expert testimony that makes complex business practices appear inherently suspicious
- Leverage government agent credibility to validate prosecutorial theories

****Standard Government Evidence Categories:****

- Original loan applications with alleged false statements highlighted
- Bank records showing loan deposits and subsequent expenditures
- Business financial statements that contradict loan application claims
- Employee interviews that dispute defendant's payroll representations
- Expert testimony about program requirements and defendant's violations

****The Prosecution's Evidence Strategy Against Carlos:****

Poole built her case around five key evidence categories:

1. PPP applications showing alleged inflated payroll calculations

2. Bank records documenting loan proceeds and their use

3. Employee testimony about actual work performed and compensation received

4. Expert testimony about program requirements and violation significance

5. Agent testimony about investigation findings and defendant's statements

Each category was designed to support the government's theory that Carlos had deliberately misrepresented his business finances to steal government money.

DEFENSE STRATEGY #90: *Comprehensive Government Evidence Analysis*

Effective defense requires systematic analysis of all government evidence:

- Obtain complete copies of every document the government intends to use at trial
- Analyze each piece of evidence for weaknesses, omissions, and alternative interpretations
- Identify contexts and explanations that the government's presentation ignores or minimizes
- Develop counter-narratives that explain apparent irregularities through legitimate business purposes
- Prepare cross-examination strategies that expose government evidence weaknesses

Comprehensive analysis reveals that government evidence often supports defense arguments more than prosecution theories.

Deconstructing Financial Evidence

Financial records form the backbone of most PPP prosecutions, but they are particularly vulnerable to defense challenges because they typically show legitimate business activities that have been taken out of context.

Government Financial Evidence Manipulation:

Prosecutors use several techniques to make legitimate financial activities appear criminal:

- Presenting individual transactions without business context that would explain them

- Emphasizing dollar amounts without explaining normal business cash flow patterns
- Focusing on apparent discrepancies without investigating innocent explanations
- Using selective time periods that exclude exculpatory financial information
- Presenting complex business finances through oversimplified prosecution narratives

Carlos's Financial Evidence Challenges:

The government's financial evidence against Carlos appeared damning on the surface:

- His loan application claimed average monthly payroll of $34,000, but his tax returns showed lower payroll
- He deposited PPP proceeds into personal rather than business accounts
- Bank records showed large cash withdrawals that couldn't be traced to specific business expenses
- Some loan proceeds appeared to be used for personal expenses like car payments and mortgage
- His business showed profits on tax returns despite claiming financial necessity for PPP loans

Defensive Financial Analysis:

Swan's forensic accountant conducted comprehensive analysis that revealed innocent explanations:

- The payroll discrepancy reflected seasonal employment increases that weren't captured in annual tax return averages
- Personal account deposits occurred because business accounts were frozen during unrelated IRS audit
- Cash withdrawals were used to pay employees who preferred cash payment and suppliers who offered cash discounts
- Apparent personal expenses were actually reimbursements for business costs Carlos had paid personally when business accounts were frozen
- Business profits reflected successful management and legitimate business income rather than fraudulent PPP enrichment

DEFENSE STRATEGY #91: *Independent Financial Reconstruction*

Defense teams should conduct independent financial analysis that provides complete context:

- Hire forensic accountants who can analyze the same records the government reviewed
- Reconstruct complete financial picture including business context the government ignored
- Identify innocent explanations for all apparent discrepancies or irregular patterns
- Document legitimate business purposes for all questioned transactions
- Present financial evidence in chronological context that explains apparent anomalies

Independent analysis often reveals that apparent evidence of fraud actually demonstrates legitimate business operations.

Challenging Expert Testimony

Government expert witnesses are designed to lend scientific credibility to prosecutorial theories, but they are often vulnerable to challenges based on their methodology, assumptions, and bias.

Government Expert Strategy:

Prosecutors typically present experts who:

- Simplify complex regulations to make violations appear clear and intentional
- Apply rigid interpretations that don't account for business realities or regulatory ambiguity
- Emphasize technical violations without considering broader compliance efforts
- Use inflammatory language that characterizes mistakes as fraud
- Present government-favorable opinions without acknowledging reasonable alternative interpretations

Poole's Expert Witness:

The government's expert in Carlos's case was Dr. Patricia Wilson, a former SBA official who testified about PPP program requirements and Carlos's alleged violations. Her testimony included several problematic elements:

- She claimed Carlos's payroll calculations were "obviously inflated" without considering seasonal employment variations
- She testified that family member employment was "inherently suspicious" despite being explicitly permitted by regulations
- She characterized normal business practices as fraud indicators without industry context
- She applied current regulatory interpretations to Carlos's historical conduct retroactively
- She ignored evidence of Carlos's good faith compliance efforts

Expert Testimony Deconstruction:

Santos's cross-examination exposed fundamental flaws in Wilson's testimony:

- She had never operated a small business and lacked practical experience with PPP compliance challenges
- Her analysis was based on incomplete records that excluded exculpatory evidence
- She applied regulatory standards that weren't in effect when Carlos submitted his applications
- She admitted under cross-examination that reasonable interpretations could support Carlos's conduct
- She acknowledged that her conclusions were based on prosecutorial theories rather than objective analysis

DEFENSE STRATEGY #92: *Systematic Expert Testimony Challenge*

Government expert testimony requires comprehensive challenge strategies:

- Research expert qualifications and identify areas where they lack relevant experience
- Analyze expert methodology and assumptions for flaws and bias
- Identify evidence the expert ignored or misinterpreted in reaching conclusions
- Prepare counter-experts with superior qualifications and contrary opinions
- Use cross-examination to expose expert bias and methodological limitations

Effective expert challenges can eliminate crucial elements of the government's case.

Attacking Agent Credibility

FBI agents and other government investigators often serve as key prosecution witnesses, but their credibility can be undermined through strategic cross-examination that exposes investigative bias and shortcuts.

Agent Credibility Challenges:

Government agents in PPP cases are vulnerable to several types of credibility attacks:

- Demonstrating that their investigation was biased from the beginning toward finding fraud
- Showing that they failed to investigate innocent explanations for apparent discrepancies
- Exposing their lack of knowledge about business operations and industry practices
- Revealing pressure from supervisors to produce prosecutions regardless of evidence quality
- Documenting their failure to follow standard investigative procedures

Agent River's Testimony Problems:

Special Agent Michael Rivers served as the lead investigative witness against Carlos, but his testimony contained several vulnerabilities:

- He admitted that he assumed Carlos was guilty from the first day of investigation
- He acknowledged that he never interviewed Carlos's customers or suppliers who could verify legitimate business activities
- He conceded that he lacked knowledge about restaurant industry employment practices
- He revealed that he was under pressure from supervisors to complete investigations quickly
- He admitted that he never considered whether Carlos's conduct might have innocent explanations

Cross-Examination Strategy:

Santos's cross-examination of Rivers exposed the weakness of the government's investigation:

- Rivers acknowledged that he had decided Carlos was guilty before completing his investigation

- He admitted that he never verified whether Carlos's business practices were normal for the restaurant industry
- He conceded that he ignored evidence that supported Carlos's explanations for apparent discrepancies
- He revealed that his investigation took only six weeks despite the complexity of Carlos's business finances
- He acknowledged that he never consulted with business experts about industry practices

DEFENSE STRATEGY #93: *Aggressive Agent Cross-Examination*

Government agents should be cross-examined aggressively to expose investigative bias:

- Prepare detailed timeline showing how agents reached conclusions before investigating thoroughly
- Expose agents' lack of knowledge about business operations and industry practices
- Show how investigative pressure led to shortcuts and biased conclusions
- Demonstrate that agents ignored evidence supporting innocent explanations
- Reveal inconsistencies between agent reports and actual evidence

Effective agent cross-examination can undermine the credibility of the entire government case.

Document Authentication And Chain Of Custody

Government document evidence is only admissible if it is properly authenticated and its chain of custody is established. Challenges to authentication and custody can exclude crucial prosecution evidence.

Authentication Requirements:

Federal rules require that documents be authenticated through:

- Witness testimony about document creation or receipt
- Expert analysis of document characteristics and origins
- Chain of custody documentation showing document handling
- Circumstantial evidence that supports document authenticity

Chain of Custody Vulnerabilities:

PPP cases often involve complex electronic evidence that is vulnerable to custody challenges:

- Bank records obtained through subpoenas may lack proper certification
- Electronic documents may be incomplete or altered during transmission
- Government agents may fail to preserve original versions of crucial documents
- Time gaps in custody documentation may create reasonable doubt about document integrity

DEFENSE STRATEGY #94: *Systematic Document Challenge*

Every government document should be challenged for authentication and custody:

- Demand complete chain of custody documentation for all evidence
- Challenge authentication of electronic records and database information
- Object to incomplete or altered documents that may mislead the jury
- Require witness testimony establishing personal knowledge of document creation
- Move to exclude improperly authenticated evidence before trial

Document challenges can eliminate crucial prosecution evidence and create reasonable doubt.

Employee Witness Credibility

Government prosecutors often present employee witnesses who contradict defendant claims about payroll, work performed, and business operations. However, these witnesses are frequently vulnerable to credibility challenges.

Employee Witness Problems:

Employee testimony in PPP cases often contains significant vulnerabilities:

- Financial incentives for cooperation with government including potential immunity from prosecution
- Limited knowledge about overall business operations and financial necessities

- Potential bias against employers due to termination or other workplace disputes
- Confusion about legal definitions of employment versus contractor relationships
- Pressure from government agents during interviews that may have influenced testimony

Government Employee Witnesses Against Carlos:

Prosecutors called three former employees who testified that:

- They had never worked the hours Carlos claimed in his payroll calculations
- Some individuals listed as employees had never actually worked for the restaurant
- Carlos had exaggerated their compensation levels in his PPP applications
- Family members listed as employees did minimal actual work

Employee Credibility Challenges:

Swan's cross-examination revealed significant credibility problems:

- Two witnesses had been terminated for theft and had ongoing disputes with Carlos
- Government agents had interviewed witnesses multiple times until their stories aligned with prosecution theories
- Witnesses had limited knowledge about seasonal employment variations and family member roles
- One witness had received implied immunity in exchange for testimony against Carlos
- Witnesses contradicted their own earlier statements to investigators

DEFENSE STRATEGY #95: *Employee Witness Impeachment*

Employee witnesses require comprehensive credibility challenges:

- Research witness backgrounds for potential bias, criminal history, or financial incentives
- Compare witness trial testimony with their earlier statements to investigators
- Show that witnesses lack knowledge about business operations they're testifying about

- ➢ Expose any pressure or inducements offered by government for cooperation
- ➢ Present contrary evidence from other employees or business records

Employee witness impeachment can eliminate key elements of the government's factual case.

Digital Evidence And Technology Challenges

PPP cases increasingly involve digital evidence including emails, text messages, computer records, and algorithmic analysis. This evidence presents unique challenges and opportunities for defense.

Digital Evidence Vulnerabilities:

- ➢ Authentication requirements for electronic communications and computer records
- ➢ Chain of custody issues for evidence obtained from multiple digital sources
- ➢ Technical complexity that may confuse juries and create reasonable doubt
- ➢ Potential for alteration or selective preservation of digital evidence
- ➢ Need for expert testimony to explain technical aspects of digital evidence

Algorithmic Evidence Challenges:

Carlos's case involved algorithmic analysis that flagged his loan as suspicious, but this evidence contained several vulnerabilities:

- ➢ The algorithm had not been validated for accuracy in PPP fraud detection
- ➢ False positive rates were high enough to create reasonable doubt about reliability
- ➢ Algorithmic assumptions about normal business behavior were demonstrably flawed
- ➢ The system had not been tested for bias against minority-owned businesses
- ➢ Government witnesses could not explain how the algorithm actually worked

DEFENSE STRATEGY #96: *Technical Evidence Challenge and Explanation*

Digital and algorithmic evidence requires specialized challenge strategies:

- Hire technical experts who can analyze and explain complex digital evidence
- Challenge authentication and reliability of algorithmic analysis and computer records
- Show that technical evidence has been taken out of context or misinterpreted
- Use counter-experts to demonstrate flaws in government technical analysis
- Simplify complex technical concepts for jury understanding

Technical evidence challenges can eliminate sophisticated prosecution tools.

Turning Government Evidence Into Defense Evidence

The most effective strategy for dealing with government evidence is not just challenging it, but turning it into positive evidence for the defense.

Evidence Transformation Strategy:

Swan transformed each category of government evidence into defense evidence:

- Financial records that prosecutors claimed showed fraud actually demonstrated Carlos's legitimate business struggles
- Bank statements that appeared to show misuse actually revealed proper business expense payments
- Employee testimony that seemed to contradict Carlos's applications actually confirmed seasonal employment variations
- Expert testimony that characterized violations actually acknowledged regulatory complexity and ambiguity
- Agent testimony that supported prosecution theories actually revealed investigative bias and shortcuts

The PPP Application Evidence:

The government's strongest evidence was Carlos's original loan application, which contained apparent false statements about payroll and employee counts. But Swan turned this evidence around:

- Showed that application discrepancies reflected reasonable interpretations of complex regulations
- Demonstrated that Carlos had sought advice from his accountant about proper completion
- Proved that Carlos had disclosed all material information requested by the lender
- Established that any errors were inadvertent rather than intentional
- Used the application itself to show Carlos's good faith efforts to comply with program requirements

DEFENSE STRATEGY #97: *Evidence Recontextualization and Transformation*

Government evidence should be recontextualized to support defense arguments:

- Identify alternative explanations for all government evidence that support innocence
- Show how evidence presented out of context actually demonstrates legitimate conduct
- Use cross-examination to extract admissions that support defense theories
- Present additional evidence that provides context missing from government presentation
- Reframe prosecution evidence to support defense narrative of good faith and legitimate business operations

Evidence transformation converts prosecution strengths into defense advantages.

Expert Witness Counter-Strategy

Effective defense requires not just challenging government experts, but presenting superior counter-experts who can provide alternative interpretations of evidence.

Defense Expert Strategy:

Swan assembled a team of expert witnesses who countered each aspect of the government's case:

- Dr. Maria Rome, former SBA official who explained regulatory complexity and reasonable interpretations

- Professor James Keene, accounting expert who analyzed Carlos's financial records and business practices
- Sammy Martinez, restaurant industry expert who testified about normal employment and payment practices
- Dr. Michael Chen, computer science expert who challenged the algorithmic analysis

Each expert provided testimony that directly contradicted government expert opinions and offered alternative explanations for apparent evidence of fraud.

DEFENSE STRATEGY #98: *Comprehensive Counter-Expert Development*

Defense expert strategy should address every aspect of government expert testimony:

- Identify experts with superior qualifications and experience compared to government witnesses
- Prepare experts to provide specific alternative explanations for apparent evidence of fraud
- Use experts to educate jury about business practices and regulatory complexity
- Coordinate expert testimony to present comprehensive alternative narrative
- Present expert testimony that makes defense conclusions appear inevitable rather than argued

Superior expert testimony can completely undermine government theories and establish reasonable doubt.

Victory Through Evidence Mastery

Carlos Hernandez was acquitted on all charges after the jury deliberated for less than three hours. The victory resulted from systematic deconstruction of every piece of government evidence and transformation of apparent prosecution strengths into defense advantages.

Key Success Factors:

- Comprehensive financial analysis that provided innocent explanations for all apparent discrepancies
- Aggressive cross-examination that exposed government expert bias and agent investigative shortcuts

- Technical challenges that eliminated unreliable algorithmic evidence
- Employee witness impeachment that revealed credibility problems and bias
- Superior expert testimony that provided alternative explanations for all prosecution evidence

Jury Feedback:

Post-trial interviews revealed that the defense's evidence strategy had been decisive:

- Jurors understood that Carlos's financial practices reflected legitimate business operations rather than fraud
- They recognized that government experts were biased and lacked relevant business experience
- They concluded that the investigation had been superficial and biased from the beginning
- They found defense expert testimony more credible and comprehensive than government evidence
- They viewed Carlos as a victim of prosecutorial overreach rather than a criminal

Lessons In Evidence Warfare

Carlos's case demonstrates crucial principles for defending against government evidence:

Strategic Principles:

- Every piece of government evidence can be challenged, contextualized, and potentially transformed into defense evidence
- Independent analysis often reveals that apparent prosecution strengths actually support defense arguments
- Expert testimony battles are often decisive in complex financial cases
- Credibility challenges can undermine entire categories of government evidence
- Technical evidence is particularly vulnerable to challenge by superior defense experts

Tactical Implementation:

- Begin evidence analysis immediately upon receiving government discovery

- Invest in independent expert analysis of all financial and technical evidence
- Prepare comprehensive cross-examination strategies for all government witnesses
- Develop alternative narratives that explain apparent evidence of fraud through legitimate business purposes
- Present evidence transformation through superior expert testimony and comprehensive defense presentation

The government's evidence may appear overwhelming, but remember that every document, every witness, and every expert opinion can be challenged, contextualized, and potentially turned into a defense advantage. The question is whether you'll accept the government's interpretation of evidence or fight to present the complete story that supports your innocence.

Evidence warfare requires preparation, expertise, and aggressive advocacy. But as Carlos's case demonstrates, defendants who master these techniques can transform apparent prosecution strengths into complete vindication. Your evidence is telling a story. Make sure it's the right story.

CHAPTER 13

CROSS EXAMINATION STRATEGY

Undermining Credibility

Defense attorney Lisa Banks stood at the podium facing FBI Special Agent Patricia Williams, who had just finished two hours of direct examination designed to portray defendant Kim Patel as a calculating fraudster who had stolen $200,000 in PPP funds. Agent Williams had testified confidently about her "thorough investigation" that revealed Kim's "pattern of deception" in applying for loans to support her three beauty salons.

But Banks knew something the jury didn't yet realize: Agent Williams's investigation had been anything but thorough. In preparation for cross examination, Banks had discovered that Williams had never visited Kim's salons, never interviewed Kim's loyal customers, never consulted with beauty industry experts about normal business practices, and never investigated the devastating impact of pandemic lockdowns on personal care businesses.

Most damaging of all, Williams had reached her conclusion that Kim was guilty after spending only four hours reviewing the case file, then spent the next six months trying to build evidence to support that predetermined conclusion.

"Agent Williams," Banks began, her voice calm but pointed, "you testified that you conducted a thorough investigation of Ms. Patel's case. How many hours did you spend at Ms. Patel's salons observing the business operations you claim to understand so well?"

Williams shifted uncomfortably. "I didn't visit the salons personally."

"So your understanding of how beauty salons operate, which you've testified about extensively, is based entirely on paperwork rather than actual observation?"

"That's correct."

"And when you concluded that Ms. Patel's employee count was suspicious, did you speak with any current or former employees to verify whether your suspicions were accurate?"

"No, but the documentation showed..."

"Agent Williams, please answer the question I asked. Did you speak with any employees?"

"No."

Over the next ninety minutes, Banks systematically dismantled Agent Williams's credibility, revealing that her "thorough investigation" consisted of reviewing documents provided by prosecutors, accepting their theories without independent verification, and building a case designed to support a predetermined conclusion rather than discover the truth.

By the time Banks finished, Agent Williams appeared defensive, uninformed, and biased. More importantly, the jury had learned that the government's entire case was built on an investigation that avoided evidence supporting Kim's innocence while magnifying anything that could be twisted to suggest guilt.

Kim Patel would ultimately be acquitted on all charges, and post trial interviews revealed that Banks's cross examination of Agent Williams had been the turning point. The jury concluded that if the government's lead investigator couldn't be trusted to conduct a fair investigation, the prosecution itself couldn't be trusted.

The Strategic Foundation Of Cross Examination Warfare

Cross examination in PPP cases represents psychological warfare disguised as legal questioning. The objective is not merely to challenge witness testimony, but to completely destroy the government's credibility while simultaneously building the defense case through hostile witnesses.

****The Warfare Mentality:****

Effective cross examination requires understanding that you are not having a conversation with witnesses; you are conducting an assault on their credibility designed to eliminate their value to the prosecution. Every question must serve this destructive purpose while advancing specific defense objectives.

Government witnesses in PPP cases are particularly vulnerable because they typically rely on superficial investigations, biased assumptions, and prosecutorial coaching rather than genuine expertise or thorough knowledge. This creates multiple attack vectors that skilled defense attorneys can exploit systematically.

Primary Destruction Targets:

Witness credibility through exposure of bias, incompetence, or dishonesty. Investigation methodology through revelation of shortcuts and predetermined conclusions. Expert qualifications through demonstration of ignorance about relevant subject matter. Financial incentives through exposure of cooperation deals and payment arrangements. Prosecutorial coordination through revelation of coaching and scripted testimony.

DEFENSE STRATEGY #99: *Total Credibility Warfare Approach*

Cross examination should be approached as credibility warfare designed to destroy witness value to prosecution. Identify multiple attack vectors for each witness including credibility, methodology, expertise, incentives, and coordination vulnerabilities. Plan systematic destruction sequences that build cumulative damage throughout questioning. Coordinate attacks across all witnesses to create overwhelming doubt about government case reliability. Use hostile witnesses to build an affirmative defense case while destroying prosecution theories.

Total warfare approach transforms prosecution witnesses into defense assets through systematic credibility destruction.

Advanced Preparation Techniques For Witness Destruction

Devastating cross examination requires preparation that goes far beyond reading witness statements and reviewing direct examination testimony. Effective preparation involves intelligence gathering that rivals government investigative techniques.

Deep Background Investigation Protocol:

Banks's preparation for Agent Williams included comprehensive intelligence gathering that revealed numerous vulnerabilities. Professional history including previous cases where Williams's investigations were criticized by courts or defense attorneys. Performance evaluations showing pressure from supervisors to close cases quickly and produce convictions. Training records revealing gaps in knowledge relevant to small business operations and PPP regulations. Personal financial information showing career advancement motivations tied to prosecution success rates.

Document Forensics and Timeline Analysis:

Effective preparation requires forensic analysis of all documents associated with witness testimony. Original investigation reports compared with final testimony to identify changes influenced by prosecutorial pressure. Email communications between witnesses and prosecutors showing coordination and coaching. Multiple versions of witness statements revealing evolution from favorable to hostile positions. Timeline analysis showing correlation between witness cooperation and personal benefits received.

Psychological Profile Development:

Understanding witness psychology enables more effective manipulation and control during cross examination. Personality traits that can be exploited such as professional pride, desire to appear knowledgeable, or defensiveness about competence. Emotional triggers that create stress responses making witnesses more vulnerable to making damaging admissions. Communication patterns that reveal when witnesses are lying, uncertain, or uncomfortable with their testimony.

DEFENSE STRATEGY #100: *Comprehensive Witness Intelligence Gathering*

Effective cross examination requires intelligence gathering that exceeds government investigation standards. Conduct deep background investigations revealing witness vulnerabilities including professional criticism, performance pressure, and career motivations. Perform forensic analysis of all documents showing witness statement evolution and prosecutorial coordination. Develop psychological profiles identifying personality traits and emotional triggers that can be exploited during questioning. Create comprehensive attack plans targeting all identified vulnerabilities simultaneously.

Intelligence gathering provides ammunition for systematic witness destruction and reveals strategic opportunities invisible to surface preparation.

The Science Of Psychological Manipulation In Cross Examination

Cross examination effectiveness depends heavily on psychological manipulation techniques that force witnesses to provide testimony that damages their credibility while supporting defense theories.

Cognitive Dissonance Exploitation:

This technique creates psychological tension by forcing witnesses to choose between contradictory positions, both of which damage their credibility or support defense arguments.

Banks used this against Agent Williams: "Agent Williams, either you conducted a thorough investigation and are incompetent because you missed obvious evidence supporting Ms. Patel's innocence, or you conducted a superficial investigation and are lying about its thoroughness. Which description is accurate?"

Authority Undermining Protocol:

Government witnesses rely heavily on their official positions to establish credibility. Systematic undermining of their authority destroys this foundation while making their testimony appear unreliable.

Banks undermined Williams's authority by demonstrating her lack of relevant training: "Agent Williams, in your four hours of PPP training, did anyone explain the difference between normal family business employment practices and fraudulent payroll inflation?"

Professional Pride Exploitation:

Most experts and officials have strong professional pride that can be weaponized against them by questioning their competence in areas where they lack genuine expertise.

"Dr. Morrison, you've testified extensively about normal business practices in beauty salons. How many beauty salons have you personally operated or advised?" When Morrison admitted he had never worked with beauty salons, Banks followed up: "So your expert opinions about what constitutes normal versus suspicious behavior in beauty salons are based on theoretical assumptions rather than practical experience?"

DEFENSE STRATEGY #101: *Systematic Psychological Manipulation*

Cross examination should employ systematic psychological manipulation to control witness responses and extract damaging admissions. Use cognitive dissonance to force witnesses into contradictory positions that damage credibility regardless of their choice. Undermine witness authority by exposing lack of relevant training and expertise in areas crucial to their testimony.

Exploit professional pride by questioning competence in ways that force admissions of ignorance or incompetence. Create emotional stress through strategic pacing and pressure that makes witnesses more vulnerable to manipulation.

Psychological manipulation transforms hostile witnesses into unwilling defense advocates through strategic pressure and control.

Cross Examination Of Algorithmic Evidence And Technical Witnesses

PPP cases increasingly rely on algorithmic analysis and technical evidence that appears scientific but is often vulnerable to devastating challenges based on methodology, bias, and reliability concerns.

****Algorithmic Bias Exposure:****

Government fraud detection algorithms in PPP cases often contain systematic biases that can be exposed to create reasonable doubt about their reliability and fairness.

Banks confronted the government's technical witness Dr. James Ford: "Dr. Ford, are you aware that the algorithm you've testified about flags minority owned businesses at rates 40% higher than white owned businesses with identical financial profiles?"

"I wasn't aware of that specific statistic..."

"So the algorithm you're claiming reliably identifies fraud may actually be identifying race and ethnicity rather than criminal behavior?"

"I can't speak to that specific analysis..."

"Dr. Ford, if an algorithm systematically targets minority business owners, would you agree that its conclusions about any specific minority business owner are suspect?"

False Positive Rate Exploitation:

Technical witnesses often cannot explain the error rates of systems they're defending, creating opportunities to demonstrate unreliability.

"Dr. Ford, what percentage of loans flagged as suspicious by this algorithm turn out to involve innocent business owners?"

"I don't have that information readily available..."

"So for all you know, 50% or even 80% of the people flagged by this system could be completely innocent?"

"I suppose that's theoretically possible..."

"And you're asking this jury to convict Ms. Patel based on a system that might incorrectly flag innocent people more often than it correctly identifies actual fraud?"

DEFENSE STRATEGY #102: *Technical Evidence Credibility Destruction*

Technical evidence should be systematically challenged through bias exposure and reliability questioning. Demand disclosure of algorithmic bias testing and error rates that reveal system unreliability. Expose false positive rates that create reasonable doubt about conclusions applied to individual defendants. Show that technical witnesses lack knowledge about limitations and flaws in systems they're defending. Demonstrate that algorithmic analysis reflects programmer bias rather than objective fraud detection.

Technical evidence destruction eliminates sophisticated prosecution tools while creating reasonable doubt about government competence and fairness.

Employee Witness Neutralization Through Bias And Incentive Exposure

Employee witnesses often provide the most damaging testimony in PPP cases because they have personal knowledge of defendant business operations. However, they are frequently the most vulnerable to credibility attacks based on bias, incentives, and limited understanding.

Comprehensive Bias Excavation:

Employee witnesses typically have complex relationships with defendants that create multiple sources of bias that can be systematically exposed.

Banks's cross examination of former employee Martha Davis revealed multiple bias sources:

"Ms. Davis, you were terminated from Ms. Patel's salon in March 2020, correct?"

"Yes."

"You were terminated for repeatedly arriving late and missing client appointments?"

"There were some scheduling conflicts..."

"You filed for unemployment benefits claiming you were laid off due to COVID rather than terminated for cause?"

"I needed the unemployment benefits..."

"So you lied to a government agency about the reason for your termination?"

"I had to survive..."

"Ms. Davis, after your termination, did you post negative reviews about Ms. Patel's salon on social media?"

"I may have expressed my feelings..."

"You posted on Facebook that Ms. Patel was a 'greedy witch who deserved to lose her business,' correct?"

"I was upset..."

"And now you're testifying that she committed fraud, shortly after posting that she deserved to lose her business?"

****Knowledge Limitation Exposure:****

Employee witnesses often testify about business operations they don't actually understand, creating opportunities to demonstrate their lack of knowledge about legal requirements and normal business practices.

"Ms. Davis, during your employment, did you ever review Ms. Patel's tax returns or business financial statements?"

"No."

"Did you ever attend meetings with her accountant about business finances?"

"No."

"Are you familiar with PPP program requirements for employee classification and payroll calculations?"

"Not specifically..."

"So your testimony about whether Ms. Patel's PPP applications were accurate is based on your personal assumptions rather than knowledge of program requirements?"

DEFENSE STRATEGY #103: *Employee Witness Complete Neutralization**

Employee witnesses should be neutralized through systematic exposure of bias, incentives, and knowledge limitations. Reveal personal grievances, financial motivations, and credibility problems that show witness hostility toward the defendant. Expose lies told to government agencies and inconsistent statements that undermine general credibility. Demonstrate limited knowledge about business operations, legal requirements, and regulatory compliance that the witness is testifying about. Show that witness testimony is based on personal assumptions and grudges rather than factual knowledge.

Employee neutralization eliminates key prosecution testimony while demonstrating government reliance on biased and unreliable sources.

Expert Witness Annihilation Through Methodology And Qualification Challenges

Government expert witnesses in PPP cases often appear impressive but are vulnerable to complete destruction through challenges to their methodology, qualifications, and financial incentives.

****Qualification Inadequacy Exposure:****

Many government experts lack relevant experience in the specific areas they're testifying about, creating opportunities for devastating credibility attacks.

Banks's destruction of Dr. Harold Morrison began with qualification challenges:

"Dr. Morrison, you've testified extensively about normal employment practices in family owned beauty salons. How many beauty salons have you personally operated?"

"None, but I have extensive experience with government programs..."

"How many beauty salon owners have you consulted with about employment practices?"

"I haven't consulted specifically with beauty salon owners..."

"Have you ever published research on employment practices in personal care businesses?"

"No, but my general expertise..."

"Dr. Morrison, have you ever even been inside a beauty salon as a customer?"

"I don't believe that's relevant..."

"So your expert opinions about what constitutes normal versus suspicious behavior in beauty salons are based on theoretical assumptions about an industry you've never actually observed or studied?"

Financial Incentive Exposure:

Expert witnesses often receive substantial payments for testimony, creating incentives for providing prosecution favorable opinions.

"Dr. Morrison, how much are you being paid for your testimony today?"

"I receive standard expert witness compensation..."

"How much specifically?"

"Fifteen thousand dollars."

"That's more than many small business owners make in a month during the pandemic?"

"I suppose..."

"Dr. Morrison, how much of your annual income comes from testifying for government prosecutors?"

"I provide expert services to various clients..."

"What percentage of your income comes from government prosecution work?"

"Approximately sixty percent..."

"So the majority of your income depends on providing testimony that prosecutors find helpful?"

DEFENSE STRATEGY #104: *Expert Witness Complete Annihilation*

Expert witnesses should be completely destroyed through systematic challenges to qualifications, methodology, and financial incentives. Expose lack of relevant experience in specific areas they're testifying about to show opinions are based on assumptions rather than expertise. Reveal substantial financial incentives for providing prosecution favorable testimony that call independence into question. Challenge methodology and assumptions underlying expert opinions through industry statistics and standards they're unaware of. Show that expert conclusions exceed scope of actual expertise and are based on prosecutorial theories rather than objective analysis.

Expert annihilation eliminates crucial prosecution evidence while demonstrating government reliance on biased and financially motivated testimony.

Cooperating Witness Credibility Obliteration

Cooperating witnesses who have made deals with the government are among the most vulnerable prosecution witnesses because their credibility is automatically suspect due to incentives for providing favorable testimony.

Incentive Structure Complete Exposure:

Cooperating witnesses face severe consequences if prosecutors deem their cooperation inadequate, creating enormous pressure to provide helpful testimony regardless of truthfulness.

Banks's destruction of cooperating witness Marcus Cove revealed the full scope of his incentives:

"Mr. Cove, you're facing federal tax evasion charges carrying a maximum sentence of fifteen years in prison?"

"Yes."

"Prosecutors have promised to recommend no jail time if you cooperate satisfactorily against Ms. Patel?"

"They said they would consider it..."

"Mr. Cove, what happens if prosecutors decide your cooperation is not satisfactory?"

"I suppose they could recommend the full sentence..."

"So your testimony today could literally mean the difference between going home tonight and spending fifteen years in federal prison?"

"I'm telling the truth..."

"Mr. Cove, have prosecutors defined what constitutes 'satisfactory cooperation'?"

"Not specifically..."

"So you don't know whether saying Ms. Patel is innocent would be considered satisfactory cooperation?"

"I suppose not..."

"Isn't it true that you believe your only chance of avoiding prison is to tell prosecutors what they want to hear about Ms. Patel?"

Personal Grudge and Financial Motivation Exposure:

Cooperating witnesses often have personal grievances against defendants that provide additional motivation for hostile testimony beyond cooperation agreements.

"Mr. Cove, you and Ms. Patel had a business partnership that ended in litigation?"

"We had a dispute..."

"You sued her for $300,000 in damages?"

"Yes."

"You lost that lawsuit and were ordered to pay her attorney fees?"

"The judge was biased..."

"So you owed Ms. Patel money when federal agents approached you about cooperation?"

"That's one way to look at it..."

"Mr. Cove, if Ms. Patel goes to prison, she can't collect the money you owe her, correct?"

"I hadn't thought about it that way..."

"So your testimony against Ms. Patel serves both your need to avoid prison and your desire to avoid paying the debt you owe her?"

DEFENSE STRATEGY #105: *Cooperating Witness Complete Obliteration*

Cooperating witnesses should be completely obliterated through exposure of incentives, personal grudges, and credibility problems. Reveal specific benefits witnesses receive for cooperation including immunity, sentencing recommendations, and financial assistance. Show severe consequences witnesses face if cooperation is deemed inadequate to demonstrate pressure for helpful testimony regardless of truthfulness. Expose personal grievances, financial motivations, and credibility problems that provide additional incentives for hostile testimony. Demonstrate that witnesses have every reason to lie and no reason to tell truth that might hurt their cooperation deals.

Cooperating witness obliteration eliminates the government's most damaging testimony while showing prosecutorial reliance on inherently unreliable sources.

Financial Witness Industry Knowledge Destruction

Accountants, bank officials, and financial analysts often testify about defendant financial practices without understanding the industry specific context that explains apparent irregularities.

Industry Ignorance Exposure:

Financial witnesses typically apply corporate accounting standards to small family businesses without understanding how these businesses actually operate.

Banks's destruction of CPA Thomas Rogers revealed his complete ignorance about beauty salon operations:

"Mr. Rogers, how many beauty salons have you audited in your career?"

"None specifically, but financial principles are universal..."

"Are you aware that beauty salons typically operate primarily on cash transactions?"

"I understand some businesses use cash..."

"Are you aware that many beauty salon clients pay in cash and tip in cash?"

"Tips would be reported income..."

"Mr. Rogers, are you aware that family members commonly work in beauty salons without formal employment contracts?"

"That would be unusual from an accounting perspective..."

"Unusual according to what standard?"

"Generally accepted accounting principles..."

"Mr. Rogers, do generally accepted accounting principles specifically address family employment in ethnic beauty salons during pandemic lockdowns?"

"GAAP provides general guidance..."

"So your conclusion that Ms. Patel's employment practices were irregular is based on corporate accounting standards that don't account for small family business realities?"

Standard Misapplication Exposure:

Financial witnesses often misapply accounting standards designed for large corporations to small businesses operating under completely different circumstances.

"Mr. Rogers, the accounting standards you've cited were designed for publicly traded corporations, correct?"

"GAAP applies broadly..."

"But publicly traded corporations don't typically employ family members in informal arrangements?"

"That would be unusual for large corporations..."

"And publicly traded corporations don't typically operate beauty salons serving ethnic communities?"

"No..."

"So you're applying accounting standards designed for Fortune 500 companies to judge a small family owned beauty salon?"

DEFENSE STRATEGY #106: *Financial Witness Industry Knowledge Destruction*

Financial witnesses should be destroyed through exposure of industry ignorance and inappropriate standard application. Show that witnesses lack experience with the defendant's specific business type and industry practices that explain apparent irregularities. Demonstrate that witness conclusions are based on corporate accounting standards inappropriate for small family businesses. Expose ignorance about industry specific financial practices, cash flow patterns, and employment arrangements. Reveal that witnesses are judging small business practices by standards designed for large corporations operating under completely different circumstances.

Industry knowledge destruction eliminates financial expert testimony based on inappropriate standards while showing government ignorance about small business realities.

Government Agent Investigation Bias Exposure

FBI agents and other government investigators often serve as key prosecution witnesses, but their credibility can be systematically destroyed through exposure of investigative bias, shortcuts, and predetermined conclusions.

Predetermined Conclusion Timeline:

Government agents in PPP cases frequently reach conclusions about guilt before completing their investigations, then spend months building evidence to support those conclusions rather than conducting objective investigations.

Banks's exposure of Agent Williams's bias followed a systematic timeline approach:

"Agent Williams, when did you first review Ms. Patel's case file?"

"August 15th, 2022."

"How long did you spend reviewing the file that day?"

"Approximately four hours."

"What conclusion did you reach after that four hour review?"

"I believed there were indicators of fraud..."

"Did you conclude that Ms. Patel was probably guilty?"

"The evidence suggested irregularities..."

"Agent Williams, please answer my question. Did you conclude she was probably guilty after four hours?"

"Yes."

"When did you complete your investigation?"

"February 2023."

"So you spent six months after concluding she was guilty gathering evidence to support that conclusion?"

"I gathered evidence to complete the investigation..."

"Agent Williams, during those six months, did you spend any time looking for evidence that might prove Ms. Patel was innocent?"

"I investigated all relevant evidence..."

"Did you interview any customers who could testify to her good character?"

"No."

"Did you consult with beauty industry experts about normal employment practices?"

"No."

"Did you investigate whether her business practices were consistent with industry standards?"

"No."

"So your six month investigation was designed to prove guilt rather than discover truth?"

****Investigation Shortcut Exposure:****

Government agents often take shortcuts that undermine the reliability of their conclusions while creating the appearance of thorough investigation.

"Agent Williams, you testified about Ms. Patel's suspicious employee scheduling. Did you personally observe operations at any of her salons?"

"No."

"Did you interview any current employees about their actual work schedules?"

"No."

"Did you research normal scheduling practices in beauty salons?"

"No."

"So your conclusion that her scheduling was suspicious is based on paperwork review rather than actual investigation of beauty salon operations?"

DEFENSE STRATEGY #107: *Government Agent Investigation Bias Complete Exposure**

Government agents should be systematically destroyed through exposure of investigative bias and predetermined conclusions. Document timeline showing agents reached guilt conclusions before completing investigations then spent months building supporting evidence rather than seeking truth. Show that agents ignored exculpatory evidence while magnifying anything that could be construed as inculpatory. Expose investigation shortcuts including failure to interview favorable witnesses, consult industry experts, or research normal business practices. Reveal pressure from supervisors to close cases quickly and produce convictions that compromised investigation objectivity.

Agent bias exposure undermines the reliability of the entire government case while demonstrating prosecutorial predetermined outcomes rather than objective investigation.

Character Witness Reversal And Conversion

When the government calls character witnesses to rebut defense character evidence, these witnesses can often be converted into defense assets through skillful cross examination that reveals their opinions are based on media coverage rather than personal knowledge.

Media Influence Exposure:

Government character witnesses typically form negative opinions based on arrest publicity rather than personal knowledge of defendant conduct or character.

Banks's conversion of business association president Rhonda Turner into a defense asset:

"Ms. Turner, when did you first form a negative opinion about Ms. Patel?"

"When I learned about the charges..."

"How did you learn about the charges?"

"From the newspaper article..."

"So your negative opinion is based on media coverage rather than personal knowledge of her business practices?"

"The charges are serious..."

"Ms. Turner, before reading that newspaper article, what was your opinion of Ms. Patel?"

"I didn't really have one..."

"Have you ever heard any complaints about her business practices?"

"No..."

"Was she a member in good standing of your business association?"

"Yes, for seven years..."

"During those seven years, did your association ever receive any complaints about her conduct?"

"No..."

"Did other members ever express concerns about her business practices?"

"Not that I recall..."

"So your current negative opinion is based entirely on criminal charges that haven't been proven rather than any actual knowledge of misconduct?"

"I suppose that's accurate..."

****Prior Positive Relationship Documentation:****
Character witnesses often had positive relationships with defendants before criminal charges were filed, revealing that their negative opinions are based on prosecution rather than conduct.

"Ms. Turner, didn't Ms. Patel serve on your association's charity committee for three years?"

"Yes..."

"Didn't she organize the annual fundraiser for local schools?"

"Yes..."

"Didn't your association give her an award for community service in 2019?"

"Yes..."

"So the same person you now say has damaged the reputation of legitimate businesses was recognized by your organization for outstanding community service?"

DEFENSE STRATEGY #108: *Character Witness Complete Reversal***

Government character witnesses should be converted into defense assets through exposure of media bias and documentation of prior positive relationships. Show that negative opinions are based on arrest publicity rather than personal knowledge of defendant conduct or character. Reveal that witnesses had positive opinions and relationships with the defendant before criminal charges were filed. Document defendant's positive contributions to community and industry that contradict prosecution characterizations. Use witness admissions to show the defendant's excellent reputation before prosecution targeting.

Character witness reversal transforms prosecution attacks into defense character evidence while showing that negative opinions are based on prosecutorial targeting rather than actual misconduct.

Cross Examination Technology And Presentation Enhancement

Modern cross examination benefits from technology tools that enhance presentation effectiveness and provide real time access to impeachment materials.

****Digital Impeachment Systems:****

Effective cross examination requires instant access to prior statements, documents, and impeachment materials that can be quickly displayed to highlight witness inconsistencies.

Banks used comprehensive digital systems during Kim's trial:

Database containing all witness statements searchable by topic and keyword for instant impeachment access. Presentation technology allowing simultaneous display of contradictory documents and statements. Real time transcript systems enabling immediate identification of inconsistencies between direct and cross examination. Video analysis software revealing witness credibility indicators and stress responses. Communication systems enabling coordination with co counsel for strategic adjustments.

****Visual Impact Enhancement:****

Technology can make witness inconsistencies and credibility problems visually obvious to juries in ways that purely verbal questioning cannot achieve.

When Agent Williams claimed her investigation was thorough, Banks simultaneously displayed her four hour initial review timeline next to her six month evidence gathering timeline, making the bias visually obvious without additional argument.

When Dr. Morrison claimed expertise in beauty salon operations, Banks displayed his resume showing no relevant experience while listing actual beauty salon industry experts, making his lack of qualifications immediately apparent.

****DEFENSE STRATEGY #109:** *Technology Enhanced Cross Examination Presentation***

Cross examination effectiveness should be enhanced through strategic technology use. Develop comprehensive databases providing instant access to all impeachment materials including prior statements, documents, and expert qualifications. Use presentation technology to make witness inconsistencies and credibility problems visually obvious to juries. Employ real time transcript analysis to identify inconsistencies between direct and cross examination testimony. Utilize communication systems for coordination with co counsel enabling real time strategic adjustments based on witness responses.

Technology enhancement transforms cross examination from purely verbal assault into multimedia presentation that makes witness credibility problems undeniably obvious to juries.

Cumulative Destruction Strategy Across All Witnesses

Individual cross examinations should be coordinated to create cumulative destruction that undermines the entire prosecution case while building a comprehensive defense narrative.

Consistent Theme Development:

Banks coordinated all cross examinations around consistent themes that built cumulative doubt about prosecution reliability:

Government investigation was superficial and biased from the beginning. Prosecution witnesses lacked relevant knowledge about beauty salon industry operations. Expert testimony was based on inappropriate standards and financial incentives. Cooperating witnesses had personal and financial motivations for providing false testimony. Technical evidence was unreliable and potentially discriminatory against minority business owners.

Progressive Evidence Building:

Each cross examination built on previous witness admissions to create overwhelming evidence of prosecutorial overreach and government incompetence:

Agent Williams admitted predetermined conclusions and superficial investigation. Dr. Morrison acknowledged lack of industry experience and substantial financial compensation. Employee witnesses revealed personal grudges and credibility problems. Financial experts conceded ignorance about small business practices. Technical witnesses could not explain system reliability or error rates.

Narrative Integration:

Cumulative cross examination results were integrated with expert witness testimony and closing arguments to create a comprehensive defense narrative showing government persecution of innocent small business owners.

DEFENSE STRATEGY #110: *Coordinated Cumulative Destruction Campaign*

Cross examination should be coordinated across all witnesses to create cumulative destruction of the prosecution case. Develop consistent themes running through all government witness cross examinations that build comprehensive doubt about investigation quality and prosecution motives.

Plan progressive evidence building where each cross examination builds on previous witness admissions to create an overwhelming case for prosecutorial overreach. Integrate cross examination results with expert witness testimony and closing arguments to present a unified defense narrative showing government persecution rather than legitimate prosecution.

Cumulative destruction campaign transforms individual witness challenges into comprehensive cases for acquittal based on prosecutorial incompetence and bias.

Victory Through Cross Examination Mastery

Kim Patel's complete acquittal demonstrated the decisive power of masterful cross examination in PPP defense cases. Banks's systematic destruction of government witnesses achieved multiple strategic objectives that resulted in rapid jury verdict.

****Total Credibility Destruction Results:****

Agent Williams appeared incompetent and biased to the jury after admitting predetermined conclusions and superficial investigation techniques. Dr. Morrison seemed uninformed and financially motivated after acknowledging lack of industry experience and substantial payment for testimony. Employee witnesses were revealed as vindictive and unreliable after exposure of personal grudges and lies to government agencies. Financial experts appeared ignorant about small business realities after admitting unfamiliarity with beauty salon industry practices. Technical witnesses seemed uninformed about system limitations after inability to explain error rates and reliability measures.

****Jury Decision Process:****

Post trial interviews revealed that cross examination had been decisive in jury decision making process:

Jurors lost confidence in government investigation quality after witnessing Agent Williams's admissions about bias and shortcuts. They questioned prosecution motives and methods after seeing financial incentives driving expert testimony. They viewed Kim sympathetically as a victim of overreach rather than criminal after understanding industry context missing from the government's case. They applied reasonable doubt standards rigorously due to credibility concerns about all government witnesses. They concluded that the government had failed to prove guilt beyond reasonable doubt due to systematic problems with investigation and witness reliability.

Precedent Establishment:

Banks's cross examination success established important precedents for future PPP defense cases:

Demonstrated vulnerability of algorithmic prosecution evidence to bias and reliability challenges. Showed how to expose investigative shortcuts and predetermined conclusions that undermine case reliability. Provided template for expert witness destruction in financial cases through industry knowledge challenges. Established jury receptivity to prosecutorial overreach arguments in PPP cases. Created appellate record for challenging similar prosecutions based on investigation bias and witness credibility problems.

The Cross Examination Revolution In Federal Defense

Cross examination mastery represents the great equalizer in federal criminal cases where government resources vastly exceed defense capabilities. Through systematic witness destruction techniques, skilled defense attorneys can transform apparent prosecution strengths into complete defense victories.

Revolutionary Principles:

Every government witness contains multiple vulnerabilities that can be systematically exploited through proper preparation and strategic questioning. Credibility destruction often proves more effective than factual contradiction in achieving jury acquittals. Psychological manipulation and control techniques can force hostile witnesses to provide testimony supporting defense theories. Coordinated cross examination across multiple witnesses creates cumulative doubt exceeding the sum of individual witness challenges. Technology enhancement and modern presentation tools significantly amplify cross examination effectiveness.

Implementation Requirements:

Extensive preparation involving intelligence gathering that rivals government investigative techniques. Comprehensive background investigation revealing witness vulnerabilities including bias, incompetence, and financial incentives. Strategic planning coordinating individual cross examinations with overall defense theory and closing arguments. Psychological training developing ability to control witnesses and extract damaging admissions through manipulation techniques. Continuous skill development transforming competent attorneys into devastating cross examination specialists.

Your freedom may depend entirely on your attorney's ability to see through government witness facades to exploit the vulnerabilities that exist beneath every prosecution presentation. Choose counsel who understands that cross examination represents warfare conducted through words, psychology, and strategic thinking rather than mere questioning.

The witnesses who would convict you can become the witnesses who free you through skilled cross examination that exposes their bias, incompetence, and unreliability. Government prosecutors may control the charges and initial evidence presentation, but masterful cross examination allows defense attorneys to control the narrative and ultimate outcome.

Cross examination represents the battlefield where innocence is proven and freedom is won through systematic destruction of prosecution credibility. Approach it with the preparation, skill, and determination it deserves, because your life may literally depend on your ability to destroy the witnesses who would destroy you.

Remember that every question asked, every pause taken, and every admission extracted during cross examination contributes to the ultimate verdict that determines your fate. The government may appear to have overwhelming evidence, but skilled cross examination can reveal that evidence to be based on bias, incompetence, and prosecutorial overreach rather than reliable investigation and credible testimony.

Master the art of cross examination warfare, because in federal court facing PPP charges, it may represent your only path to complete vindication and freedom.

CHAPTER 14

CLOSING ARGUMENTS & VERDICT

Emotional Appeals

Defense attorney Grace Strong stood before the jury at 3:47 PM on a Friday afternoon in the federal courthouse in Phoenix, Arizona, knowing that the next sixty minutes would determine whether her client, Selena Vasquez, spent the next twenty years in federal prison or walked out of the courthouse a free woman. For the past two weeks, Elena had sat silently at the defense table while government prosecutors painted her as a greedy fraudster who had stolen $180,000 in PPP funds from American taxpayers during the worst crisis in a generation.

But Strong knew something the prosecutors didn't realize: the jury was ready to hear the truth. Over fourteen days of trial, Strong had systematically dismantled every government witness, exposed the bias and incompetence of the FBI's investigation, and revealed that Selena's supposed "fraud" was actually the desperate attempt of a single mother to save the Mexican restaurant that had been her family's livelihood for eighteen years.

Now came the moment when everything would be decided. Strong looked at the twelve jurors who would determine Elena's fate, took a deep breath, and began the most important speech of her legal career.

"Ladies and gentlemen," Strong said, her voice strong but compassionate, "two weeks ago, the government stood before you and told you a story about greed, deception, and fraud. They painted Selena Vasquez as a criminal who exploited a national crisis for personal gain. But now that you've heard all the evidence, now that you've seen the witnesses cross examined, now that you know the full truth, I'm going to tell you a very different story. A story about a hardworking mother who made honest mistakes while trying to save her family's business and her employees' jobs during the most terrifying economic crisis of her lifetime."

Strong paused, letting her words settle with the jury. She had spent months preparing for this moment, studying every detail of Selena's case, every piece of evidence, every witness statement. But more importantly, she had studied the twelve people sitting in the jury box, understanding their backgrounds, their values, and what would resonate with them as they made the most important decision in Selena's life.

"Selena Vasquez didn't wake up one morning and decided to become a criminal," Strong continued. "She woke up facing the possibility that the restaurant she had spent eighteen years building, the business that employed twelve people from her community, the dream that had brought her family to America, might disappear forever because of a virus no one understood and lockdowns no one had ever experienced."

Selena's closing argument would last fifty-eight minutes and result in a complete acquittal on all charges. But more than that, it would demonstrate how effective closing arguments can transform technical legal defenses into powerful human stories that motivate juries to find defendants innocent regardless of the complexity of the evidence or the apparent strength of the prosecution's case.

The Strategic Foundation Of Winning Closing Arguments

Closing arguments represent the final opportunity to influence jury decision making, but they are not merely summaries of evidence or legal arguments. Effective closing arguments are emotional appeals that connect with jury values while providing logical justification for acquittal.

****The Psychology of Jury Decision Making:****

Research consistently shows that juries make emotional decisions first, then use logic to justify those decisions. This means that closing arguments must appeal to jury emotions and values before addressing legal technicalities or evidence analysis.

Effective closing arguments in PPP cases must transform defendants from abstract criminal defendants into sympathetic human beings who deserve jury compassion and understanding. They must reframe complex financial evidence as human stories of struggle and survival during unprecedented circumstances.

****Emotional Connection Requirements:****

Successful closing arguments establish emotional connections between juries and defendants that make conviction feel morally wrong regardless of technical legal violations. These connections depend on presenting defendants as ordinary people facing extraordinary circumstances rather than criminals deserving punishment.

DEFENSE STRATEGY #111: *Emotional Foundation Building*

Closing arguments must establish emotional foundations that make acquittal feel morally necessary. Present defendants as sympathetic human beings facing circumstances that any reasonable person could encounter. Connect defendant experiences to universal human values like family protection, business survival, and community responsibility. Frame alleged violations as understandable responses to crisis rather than criminal conduct. Make conviction appear to punish human virtues rather than criminal behavior.

Emotional foundation building creates psychological barriers to conviction that persist despite prosecutorial arguments about technical legal violations.

Narrative Construction For Maximum Impact

The most effective closing arguments in PPP cases construct compelling narratives that reframe the entire case from criminal prosecution to human drama involving government overreach and individual struggle.

The Hero's Journey Framework:

Strong structured Selena's closing argument using classical narrative frameworks that resonate deeply with human psychology. Selena as the hero facing seemingly impossible challenges. The pandemic is the crisis that threatens everything she has built. Her PPP application is the difficult choice she makes to protect her family and employees. Government prosecution as the unjust punishment for her heroic efforts to survive.

Three Act Structure Implementation:

Act One: Selena's background and the life she built through hard work and determination. "Selena came to America with nothing but a dream and eighteen years of sixteen hour days later, she had built Vasquez Family Restaurant into a cornerstone of her community."

Act Two: The crisis that threatens everything and the impossible choices it creates. "Then came March 2020, and overnight, Selena's eighteen years of work were threatened by circumstances completely beyond her control."

Act Three: The resolution that shows Selena deserves justice rather than punishment. "Selena doesn't deserve to be punished for trying to save her family's business during the worst crisis in American history. She deserves to be celebrated for keeping twelve families employed when businesses everywhere were closing their doors."

DEFENSE STRATEGY #112: *Classical Narrative Structure Implementation*

Closing arguments should use classical narrative structures that engage human psychology and create emotional investment in defendant outcomes. Structure arguments as the hero's journey where the defendant faces impossible circumstances with courage and determination. Use a three act format that establishes the defendant's positive background, explains crisis circumstances, and resolves with a call for justice rather than punishment. Present government prosecution as unjust antagonist threatening sympathetic protagonist who deserves protection rather than condemnation.

Classical narrative structure creates emotional engagement that transcends technical legal analysis and motivates juries toward acquittal.

Evidence Recontextualization And Transformation

Effective closing arguments transform apparent evidence of guilt into proof of innocence by providing context and alternative interpretations that support defense theories.

Financial Evidence Transformation:

Government prosecutors had argued that Selena's PPP application contained false statements about her payroll and employee count. Strong transformed this evidence into proof of Selena's honesty and good faith.

"The government wants you to believe that Selena committed fraud because her PPP application showed higher payroll than her tax returns. But let me tell you what really happened. Selena included her own salary in her PPP calculations because she knew that if her restaurant closed, she wouldn't just lose employees, she would lose the person who had worked sixteen hour days for eighteen years to build that business. She included her part time workers because she knew they depended on those jobs even if they only worked weekends. She included family members because in Mexican family restaurants, everyone contributes to the business that feeds the family."

Bank Record Reinterpretation:

Prosecutors argued that Selena's use of PPP funds violated program requirements. Strong reframed the same evidence as proof of Selena's dedication to her business and employees.

"The government showed you bank records of how Selena spent her PPP money, and they want you to see fraud. I want you to see a woman desperately trying to keep her business alive. Yes, she paid her mortgage with some of the money, but that mortgage payment kept the roof over the restaurant that employed twelve people. Yes, she paid for groceries with some of the money, but those groceries fed the family that ran the restaurant eighteen hours a day. Selena didn't steal this money. She used every penny to keep her business operating and her employees working."

DEFENSE STRATEGY #113: *Evidence Transformation Through Recontextualization*

Apparent evidence of guilt should be transformed into proof of innocence through strategic recontextualization. Provide business and human context that explains apparent violations as reasonable responses to crisis circumstances. Show that questioned financial transactions served legitimate business purposes that support rather than contradict the defendant's good faith. Transform technical violations into evidence of the defendant's dedication to employees and business survival. Present alternative interpretations of evidence that support defense theories rather than prosecution allegations.

Evidence transformation turns prosecution strengths into defense advantages by providing human context that makes apparent violations appear reasonable and justified.

Government Case Deconstruction And Credibility Attack

Closing arguments must systematically deconstruct the government's case while attacking the credibility of prosecution witnesses and evidence.

Investigation Quality Challenge:

Strong attacked the quality of the government's investigation to create reasonable doubt about their conclusions.

"The FBI spent exactly twelve hours investigating Selena's case. Twelve hours to decide whether a woman who had worked honestly for eighteen years was suddenly a criminal. They never visited her restaurant. They never spoke to her employees. They never talked to her customers. They never consulted with restaurant industry experts. They took a complex small business that they didn't understand, applied corporate accounting standards that don't fit family restaurants, and called the differences "fraud."

Witness Credibility Destruction:

Strong reminded the jury of the credibility problems revealed during cross examination.

"Remember Agent Thompson's testimony? He admitted under oath that he decided Selena was guilty after four hours of reviewing paperwork. Four hours. Then he spent eight months trying to prove that predetermined conclusion instead of conducting an actual investigation. That's not law enforcement, ladies and gentlemen. That's persecution."

Expert Testimony Dismantling:

Strong highlighted the weaknesses in government expert testimony.

"The government's expert, Dr. Wilson, testified that Selena's employment practices were suspicious. But remember what we learned during cross examination? Dr. Wilson had never operated a restaurant. He had never consulted with restaurant owners. He had never published research on restaurant employment practices. He was paid fifteen thousand dollars to give opinions about an industry he had never studied. Would you trust Dr. Wilson to operate a restaurant? Then why should you trust him to judge Selena's restaurant operations?"

DEFENSE STRATEGY #114: *Systematic Government Case Deconstruction*

Closing arguments must systematically attack every element of the government's case to create comprehensive reasonable doubt. Challenge investigation quality by highlighting shortcuts, bias, and predetermined conclusions that undermine reliability. Destroy witness credibility by reminding the jury of impeachment evidence revealed during cross examination. Dismantle expert testimony by exposing lack of relevant experience and financial incentives for prosecution favorable opinions. Show that the government's case is built on assumptions and bias rather than thorough investigation and reliable evidence.

Systematic deconstruction creates overwhelming doubt about government case reliability while demonstrating prosecutorial overreach and incompetence.

Reasonable Doubt Strategy And Legal Standard Emphasis

Effective closing arguments must educate juries about the reasonable doubt standard while showing how that standard applies to the specific evidence in the case.

****Reasonable Doubt Education:****

Strong explained the reasonable doubt standard in terms that connected with jury experiences and values.

"The judge will instruct you that the government must prove Selena's guilt beyond a reasonable doubt. That means if you have reasonable questions about whether Selena intended to commit fraud, you must find her not guilty. If you have reasonable questions about whether her actions were mistakes rather than crimes, you must find her not guilty. If you have reasonable questions about whether the government's investigation was adequate and unbiased, you must find her not guilty."

****Evidence Gap Analysis:****

Strong systematically identified gaps in the government's evidence that created reasonable doubt.

"The government never proved that Selena knew her PPP application contained false information. They never proved that she intended to defraud anyone. They never proved that she used the money for unauthorized purposes. They never proved that reasonable restaurant owners wouldn't have made the same decisions Selena made. Without proof of these essential elements, you cannot convict Selena of fraud."

****Alternative Explanation Emphasis:****

Strong highlighted alternative explanations for apparent evidence of guilt that created reasonable doubt about criminal intent.

"Every single thing the government calls evidence of fraud has an innocent explanation that fits the evidence better than their theory of criminal intent. Selena's payroll calculations reflected her understanding of restaurant operations, not an intent to deceive. Her use of PPP funds reflected desperate efforts to save her business, not criminal misappropriation. Her cooperation with investigators reflected honesty and transparency, not consciousness of guilt."

DEFENSE STRATEGY #115: *Comprehensive Reasonable Doubt Development*

Closing arguments must develop comprehensive reasonable doubt about all elements of the prosecution case. Educate the jury about reasonable doubt standards using language and examples that connect with their experiences and values. Identify specific evidence gaps that prevent the government from meeting the burden of proof on essential elements of charges. Emphasize alternative explanations for apparent evidence of guilt that create doubt about criminal intent and fraudulent purpose. Show that the government's theory of the case requires the jury to make assumptions not supported by evidence.

Comprehensive reasonable doubt development provides logical justification for emotional decisions to acquit sympathetic defendants.

Community And Character Evidence Integration

Closing arguments must integrate character and community evidence to show that defendants deserve community support rather than criminal punishment.

Community Impact Emphasis:

Strong highlighted Selena's positive impact on her community to show that conviction would harm innocent people.

"Selena's restaurant isn't just a business, it's a community institution. For eighteen years, it has provided jobs for local families, served authentic Mexican food to three generations of customers, and supported local schools and charities. Selena didn't just employ twelve people, she helped support twelve families. Convicting Selena doesn't just punish her, it punishes everyone whose lives she has touched in positive ways."

Character Witness Integration:

Strong wove character evidence throughout her argument to reinforce Selena's positive character and reputation.

"You heard from Selena's employees, her customers, her suppliers, and her neighbors. Every single person who knows Selena personally testified to her honesty, her work ethic, and her dedication to her family and community.

These aren't character witnesses hired for trial. These are real people whose lives Elena has touched over eighteen years of honest work."

Future Contribution Potential:

Strong emphasized Selena's potential for continued positive community contributions to show that conviction would waste rather than protect community resources.

"Selena is fifty two years old. She has at least fifteen more years of productive work ahead of her. If you convict her, you take away not just her freedom, but her ability to continue contributing to her community. If you acquit her, she will continue employing people, serving her community, and building the American dream that brought her family here eighteen years ago."

DEFENSE STRATEGY #116: *Community and Character Evidence Integration*

Character and community evidence must be integrated throughout closing arguments to show defendants deserve community support rather than criminal punishment. Emphasize the defendant's positive impact on the community to show that conviction harms innocent people beyond the defendant. Integrate character witness testimony to reinforce the defendant's reputation for honesty and community contribution. Highlight the defendant's potential for continued positive contributions to show that conviction wastes rather than protects community resources.

Character integration humanizes defendants while showing that conviction serves no legitimate community purpose.

Emotional Peak and Call to Action

Closing arguments must build to emotional peaks that motivate juries to take action by finding defendants not guilty.

Emotional Crescendo Construction:

Strong built her argument to an emotional peak that connected Selena's personal story with universal American values.

"Selena Vasquez represents everything we admire about America. She came here with nothing but determination and a dream. She worked sixteen hour days for eighteen years to build something meaningful. She employed her neighbors and served her community. When the crisis threatened everything she had built, she fought to save it with the same courage and determination that brought her to America in the first place. The question you must answer is simple: Does America punish people for trying to save their family businesses during the worst crisis in our lifetime, or does America protect people who embody the values that make our country great?"

Justice Frame Implementation:

Strong framed acquittal as necessary for justice rather than mercy for a sympathetic defendant.

"This case isn't about sympathy for Selena, though she certainly deserves your sympathy. This case is about justice. Justice requires that the government prove criminal intent, not just technical violations. Justice requires that prosecutors investigate thoroughly before destroying someone's life with criminal charges. Justice requires that we distinguish between honest mistakes made during a crisis and criminal fraud committed for personal gain. Justice requires that you find Selena Vasquez not guilty."

Direct Call to Action:

Strong ended with a direct call for specific action that gave jurors clear instruction about what justice required.

"In a few minutes, you will go into that jury room and make the most important decision in Selena's life. You have the power to correct the injustice that brought us here. You have the power to tell the government that hard working Americans deserve better than prosecution for trying to survive impossible circumstances. You have the power to send Selena home to her family and her community where she belongs. I ask you to use that power. I ask you to find Selena Vasquez not guilty on all charges."

DEFENSE STRATEGY #117: *Emotional Peak and Direct Action Call***

Closing arguments must build to emotional peaks that motivate jury action while providing clear instruction about what justice requires. Construct emotional crescendo that connects the defendant's story with universal values that resonate with jury experiences and beliefs. Frame acquittal as a requirement of justice rather than mercy for sympathetic defendants to provide logical justification for emotional decision. End with direct call to action that gives jury specific instruction about how to implement justice through a not guilty verdict.

Emotional peak and action call transforms sympathy into motivation for specific action that results in acquittal.

Prosecution Argument Anticipation And Preemption

Effective closing arguments must anticipate and preempt prosecution rebuttal arguments to maintain jury support throughout the prosecution's response.

Prosecution Argument Prediction:

Strong anticipated that prosecutors would argue Selena's violations were clear regardless of her motivations.

"The prosecutor is going to stand up after I sit down and tell you that Selena's motivations don't matter, that technical violations of federal law require conviction regardless of circumstances. But that argument ignores the most important element of fraud charges: intent to defraud. Without proof that Selena intended to steal money rather than save her business, there is no fraud. Good motivations don't excuse criminal conduct, but they do prove that conduct wasn't criminal in the first place."

Victim Impact Preemption:

Strong anticipated arguments about harm to taxpayers and other PPP applicants.

"They might argue that Selena's actions harmed other PPP applicants or cost taxpayers money. But Selena used every penny of PPP money for its intended purpose: keeping people employed during the pandemic. She didn't buy luxury cars or take vacations. She paid rent, payroll, and business expenses. The only way Selena's actions harmed anyone is if you believe that keeping twelve families employed during lockdowns was somehow wrong."

Technical Violation Response:

Strong preempted arguments that technical violations require conviction regardless of intent.

"They will point to technical discrepancies between Selena's application and her business records as if those discrepancies prove fraud. But those same discrepancies prove that Selena was trying to honestly estimate her business needs during unprecedented circumstances. Perfect accuracy in predicting business needs during a pandemic would have been superhuman, not criminal."

DEFENSE STRATEGY #118: *Prosecution Argument Preemption and Response*

Closing arguments must anticipate and preempt prosecution rebuttal arguments to maintain jury support through prosecution response. Predict prosecution arguments about technical violations and provide preemptive responses that reframe those arguments as supporting defense theories. Address victim impact arguments by showing defendant actions served legitimate purposes that align with program goals. Preempt arguments about rule of law by distinguishing between criminal violations requiring criminal intent and technical violations reflecting honest mistakes.

Argument preemption prevents prosecution from regaining jury support through rebuttal arguments that defendants cannot respond to directly.

Cultural And Demographic Sensitivity

Closing arguments must be sensitive to jury demographics and cultural backgrounds while avoiding stereotypes or assumptions that might alienate jurors.

Cultural Bridge Building:

Strong carefully acknowledged Selena's Mexican heritage while emphasizing universal American values that transcended cultural differences.

"Selena's story is fundamentally an American story, regardless of where she was born. The courage to leave everything familiar and build something new, the determination to work harder than anyone should have to work, the commitment to family and community that drives everything she does, these are the values that built America and continue to make America great."

Economic Experience Connection:

Strong connected Selena's business struggles with experiences that jurors could relate to regardless of their backgrounds.

"Every one of you has faced unexpected bills, budget pressures, or financial emergencies that forced difficult decisions. Selena faced the same pressures, just magnified by circumstances no one had ever experienced. She made the same kinds of decisions any of you might have made: she prioritized keeping people employed over perfect paperwork, she chose business survival over regulatory compliance, she protected her employees' welfare over government forms."

Universal Value Emphasis:

Strong emphasized values that resonated across cultural and demographic differences.

"This case is about values that unite us regardless of our differences: the value of hard work, the importance of taking care of family, the responsibility to help your community, and the belief that honest people shouldn't be punished for making their best efforts under impossible circumstances."

DEFENSE STRATEGY #119: *Cultural Sensitivity and Universal Value Connection*

Closing arguments must be sensitive to cultural differences while emphasizing universal values that unite diverse juries. Acknowledge the defendant's cultural background while emphasizing values and experiences that transcend cultural differences. Connect defendant experiences with universal human challenges that any reasonable person might face. Emphasize values like hard work, family responsibility, and community service that resonate across demographic differences.

Cultural sensitivity and universal value emphasis creates broad jury support that transcends individual differences and backgrounds.

Technology And Visual Aid Integration

Modern closing arguments benefit from technology integration that enhances emotional impact while clarifying complex evidence.

Timeline Visualization:

Strong used visual timelines to show Elena's eighteen year progression from immigrant with nothing to successful business owner.

"Let me show you Selena's real story through this timeline. 2002: Selena arrives in America with her husband and young daughter. 2004: They save enough money to open a small taco stand. 2008: They expand to a full restaurant. 2015: They employ twelve people and serve hundreds of customers weekly. 2020: The pandemic threatens to destroy everything they've built. This isn't the timeline of a criminal. This is the timeline of the American dream."

Financial Evidence Simplification:

Strong used visual presentations to simplify complex financial evidence and show Selena's good faith use of PPP funds.

"The government showed you hundreds of pages of financial records trying to confuse you about Selena's use of PPP money. Let me show you the simple truth. Here's every dollar Selena received: **$180,000**. Here's how she spent it: **$95,000** for payroll, $**35,000** for rent, **$25,000** for utilities and supplies, **$25,000** for business expenses including food costs. Every dollar went to keeping her restaurant operating and people employed."

Character Evidence Visualization:

Strong used photos and videos to bring character evidence to life for the jury.

"Let me show you who Selena really is." The presentation included photos of Selena at community events, with her employees, serving customers, and working in her restaurant. "This is Selena volunteering at her daughter's school. This is Selena serving free meals to seniors during the lockdown. This is Selena at her restaurant at 5 AM preparing for another sixteen hour day. This is who the government wants you to send to prison."

DEFENSE STRATEGY #120: *Technology Integration for Emotional Enhancement*

Closing arguments should integrate technology to enhance emotional impact while clarifying complex evidence. Use visual timelines to show the defendant's positive life progression and community contributions over time. Simplify complex financial evidence through visual presentations that make the defendant's good faith obvious to juries. Use photos and videos to bring character evidence to life and humanize defendants for jury decision making.

Technology integration makes abstract legal arguments concrete and emotional while providing clear visual support for defense theories.

Verdict Psychology And Decision Framework

Effective closing arguments must understand jury decision psychology and provide frameworks that make acquittal feel like the obvious and necessary choice.

Decision Simplification:

Strong simplified the jury's decision to a clear choice between justice and injustice.

"Your decision comes down to a simple question: Does Selena Vasquez deserve to be punished for trying to save her family business during the worst crisis in American history? If your answer is no, then you must find her not guilty. If your answer is yes, then you believe that honest mistakes made under impossible circumstances should be treated as federal crimes."

Consequence Framing:

Strong helped jurors understand the consequences of their decision for Elena, her family, and her community.

"If you convict Selena, you don't just send her to prison. You close her restaurant permanently. You put twelve people out of work. You take a grandmother away from her grandchildren. You tell every small business owner in America that the government will prosecute them for making honest mistakes during emergencies. If you acquit Selena, you do justice, you preserve jobs, you keep families together, and you send a message that America protects hardworking people who embody our best values."

Legacy Consideration:

Strong asked jurors to consider how their decision would reflect their own values and principles.

"Years from now, when people ask you about this case, what will you tell them? Will you tell them that you convicted a hardworking mother for trying to save her family business? Or will you tell them that you stood up for justice when the government tried to prosecute someone for embodying American values? Your verdict will reflect not just your judgment about Selena, but your judgment about what kind of country America should be."

DEFENSE STRATEGY #121: *Decision Psychology and Legacy Framing*

Closing arguments should simplify jury decisions while helping jurors understand consequences and legacy implications of their choices. Frame decision as simple choice between justice and injustice to make acquittal feel morally necessary. Help jurors understand consequences of conviction for the defendant, family, and community to make punishment appear disproportionate and harmful. Ask jurors to consider how their decision reflects their own values and what legacy they want to create through their verdict.

Decision psychology and legacy framing creates emotional investment in acquittal while providing moral justification for not guilty verdict.

Victory Through Closing Argument Mastery

Selena Vasquez was acquitted on all charges after the jury deliberated for three hours and twenty minutes. Post trial interviews revealed that Strong's closing argument had been decisive in convincing jurors that Selena deserved compassion rather than punishment.

****Jury Decision Factors:****

Jurors reported that several elements of Strong's closing argument had been particularly persuasive:

Emotional connection with Selena's story as a hardworking immigrant pursuing the American dream. Understanding of restaurant industry context that explained apparent violations as normal business practices. Reasonable doubt about Selena's intent to commit fraud based on evidence gaps in the government's case. Character evidence showing Selena's positive community contributions over eighteen years. Recognition that conviction would harm innocent people including employees and family members.

****Immediate Impact:****

The acquittal had immediate positive consequences for Selena and her community:

Selena returned to operating her restaurant and employing twelve people. Her family remained together and continued contributing to their community. Local media coverage emphasized prosecutorial overreach rather than criminal conduct. Other PPP defendants gained hope that vigorous defense could result in acquittal. Community support for Selena increased rather than decreased after trial.

****Long Term Precedent:****

Strong's successful closing argument established important precedents for future PPP defense cases:

Demonstrated effectiveness of emotional appeals combined with reasonable doubt arguments. Showed how character and community evidence could overcome apparent technical violations. Provided template for reframing prosecution evidence as proof of good faith rather than criminal intent. Established jury receptivity to arguments about prosecutorial overreach in PPP cases. Created model for integrating cultural sensitivity with universal value appeals.

The Art And Science Of Persuasion

Selena's acquittal demonstrated that closing arguments represent both art and science, requiring emotional intelligence combined with legal expertise to motivate juries toward just verdicts.

Artistic Elements:

Successful closing arguments require artistic skills including storytelling ability, emotional intelligence, and performance capabilities that engage jury hearts as well as minds. These skills transform legal arguments into human dramas that motivate emotional investment in defendant outcomes.

Scientific Elements:

Effective closing arguments also require scientific understanding of jury psychology, decision making processes, and persuasion techniques that can be systematically applied to achieve specific outcomes. This scientific foundation ensures that emotional appeals serve strategic purposes rather than random hopes.

Integration Requirements:

Master practitioners integrate artistic and scientific elements to create closing arguments that feel spontaneous and heartfelt while serving carefully planned strategic objectives. This integration requires extensive preparation combined with courtroom adaptability and emotional authenticity.

Your freedom may depend entirely on your attorney's ability to transform legal technicalities into human stories that motivate juries to find you innocent regardless of apparent evidence of technical violations. Choose counsel who understands that closing arguments represent emotional warfare disguised as legal argument.

The closing argument may be your final opportunity to speak to the people who will determine your fate. Make sure that opportunity is used by someone who can connect with jury hearts while providing their minds with logical justification for the emotional decision to set you free.

Closing arguments are where cases are won or lost through the power of persuasion applied to human psychology. Master this art, because your life may depend on your attorney's ability to make twelve strangers care enough about your fate to risk government displeasure by finding you not guilty.

Remember that juries decide with their hearts and justify with their heads. Your closing argument must appeal to both, but it must reach their hearts first, because that's where the real decision will be made. Make them care about you as a human being, and they will find reasons to set you free. Fail to make that emotional connection, and all the legal arguments in the world won't save you.

The verdict is the culmination of everything that came before, but it's the closing argument that transforms all that preparation into the emotional experience that motivates juries to act. Approach it with the preparation and passion it deserves, because your freedom depends on it.

CHAPTER 15

SENTENCING STRATEGY

Guidelines, Mitigation, Impact Statements

Defense attorney David Martin stood before federal Judge Patricia Williams in the Northern District of California, knowing that the next hour would determine whether his client, Michael Zhang, would spend the next decade in federal prison or receive a sentence that would allow him to rebuild his life and continue supporting his family. Six months earlier, Michael had reluctantly pleaded guilty to PPP fraud charges after prosecutors threatened to add money laundering and conspiracy charges that could have resulted in a thirty year sentence.

Now, at Michael's sentencing hearing, Martin faced the most important challenge of his legal career: convincing a federal judge that Michael deserved mercy rather than the harsh punishment that federal sentencing guidelines recommended. Michael owned three small electronics repair shops that had been devastated by pandemic lockdowns. His PPP applications had contained inaccuracies about his employee count and payroll calculations that prosecutors characterized as fraud worth **$240,000.**

But Martin knew that sentencing hearings represented opportunities to present the complete human story behind criminal charges, to show judges the person rather than just the crime, and to demonstrate that justice required rehabilitation rather than retribution. Over the past three months, Martin had assembled a comprehensive mitigation package that revealed Michael's true character, his positive contributions to his community, and the devastating impact that a lengthy prison sentence would have on innocent family members and employees.

"Your Honor," Martin began, "today you have the opportunity to do justice in a case that represents everything wrong with PPP prosecutions. Michael Zhang is not a criminal who deserves years in federal prison. He is a hardworking immigrant who made honest mistakes while trying to save the businesses that employ seventeen people and support dozens of families in our community. The question before you is not whether Michael deserves punishment, but whether the punishment should fit the man rather than just the technical violations he committed."

Judge Williams listened intently as Martin presented forty-five minutes of mitigation evidence that transformed Michael from an abstract criminal defendant into a sympathetic human being who had made understandable errors during unprecedented circumstances. The presentation would result in a sentence of probation rather than prison, demonstrating how effective sentencing advocacy can achieve outcomes that seemed impossible based on the charges alone.

Understanding Federal Sentencing In PPP Cases

Federal sentencing in PPP cases involves complex calculations under the United States Sentencing Guidelines, but judges retain discretion to impose sentences below guideline ranges when circumstances justify departure or variance.

****Sentencing Guidelines Calculation:****

PPP fraud sentences are calculated based on loss amount, defendant's criminal history, and specific offense characteristics that can dramatically increase recommended sentences. Base offense levels start at level 7 for fraud cases, then increase based on loss amount calculations that often exceed actual harm caused by defendant conduct.

Loss amount calculations in PPP cases are particularly harsh because they typically include the entire loan amount rather than actual loss to the government. This means defendants who used PPP funds for legitimate business purposes face sentences based on money they never stole or misused.

****Departure and Variance Opportunities:****

Federal judges can impose sentences below guideline ranges through downward departures based on specific factors outlined in the guidelines, or through variances based on broader considerations of justice and proportionality under 18 USC Section 3553(a).

PPP cases present unique opportunities for downward departures and variances because they often involve first time offenders who committed technical violations during unprecedented circumstances rather than traditional fraud motivated by greed.

DEFENSE STRATEGY #122: *Comprehensive Sentencing Strategy Development*

Effective sentencing requires comprehensive strategy development that addresses guidelines calculations while building compelling cases for downward departures and variances. Challenge loss amount calculations that exceed actual harm caused by defendant conduct. Identify specific departure grounds including lack of criminal history, minimal harm to victims, and extraordinary circumstances. Develop variance arguments based on defendant's character, community contributions, and the unique circumstances of PPP prosecutions during pandemic emergency.

Comprehensive sentencing strategy transforms technical guidelines calculations into human stories that justify mercy rather than harsh punishment.

Mitigation Evidence Development And Presentation

Effective sentencing advocacy requires extensive mitigation evidence that shows defendants deserve compassion rather than condemnation.

Personal History and Background:

Martin's mitigation package for Michael Zhang included comprehensive personal history that explained his character and life circumstances. Immigration story showing Michael's journey from poverty in China to successful business ownership in America. Educational achievements including engineering degree and business management training that demonstrated intellectual capability and commitment to self improvement. Employment history showing steady progression from entry level technician to business owner employing seventeen people.

Family Impact Documentation:

Mitigation evidence must demonstrate how incarceration would harm innocent family members who depend on defendants for financial and emotional support. Michael's family impact evidence included detailed documentation of his role as sole financial provider for elderly parents, disabled brother, and three young children. Medical evidence showing his wife's chronic illness that required expensive treatment and constant care. Educational plans for children that would be disrupted by loss of family income and father's presence.

Community Contribution Evidence:

Effective mitigation shows defendants as positive community members whose incarceration would harm rather than protect society. Michael's community evidence included documentation of his volunteer work with Chinese American community organizations, financial support for local schools and charities, and mentorship of young immigrants pursuing business ownership. Character letters from community leaders, customers, employees, and neighbors who testified to his positive impact on their lives.

DEFENSE STRATEGY #123: *Comprehensive Mitigation Evidence Assembly*

Sentencing mitigation requires systematic assembly of evidence showing defendants deserve compassion rather than punishment. Document complete personal history including immigration story, educational achievements, and employment progression that demonstrates positive character development. Gather comprehensive family impact evidence showing how incarceration would harm innocent dependents including children, elderly parents, and disabled family members. Collect extensive community contribution evidence including volunteer work, charitable giving, and positive impact on neighbors and community organizations.

Comprehensive mitigation evidence transforms defendants from abstract criminals into sympathetic human beings whose punishment would harm rather than protect society.

Loss Calculation Challenges And Restitution Strategy

PPP fraud sentences are heavily influenced by loss calculations that often bear little relationship to actual harm caused by defendant conduct. Challenging these calculations can dramatically reduce recommended sentences.

Actual Loss versus Intended Loss:

Sentencing guidelines allow judges to consider actual loss rather than intended loss when calculating sentences. In PPP cases, this distinction can be crucial because many defendants used loan proceeds for legitimate business purposes rather than personal enrichment.

Martin challenged the government's loss calculation for Michael Zhang by demonstrating actual versus intended loss. "Your Honor, the government seeks to hold Michael responsible for **$240,000** in alleged fraud, but the evidence shows that Michael used 94% of loan proceeds for legitimate business expenses including payroll, rent, and supplies. The actual loss to the government, if any, was less than **$15,000,** not the **$240,000** the government claims."

Benefit to Government Argument:

When defendants used PPP funds for program approved purposes, courts can consider whether the government received intended benefits that reduce actual loss calculations. Michael's shops remained open during lockdowns, maintained employment for seventeen people, and continued serving essential electronics repair services in the community.

Restitution Calculation Strategy:

Restitution amounts can be negotiated to reflect actual harm rather than technical violations. Martin negotiated restitution of **$15,000** representing questionable expenses rather than the full **$240,000** loan amount, demonstrating Michael's good faith use of funds for legitimate business purposes.

DEFENSE STRATEGY #124: *Loss Calculation Challenge and Restitution Negotiation*

Sentencing advocacy must challenge loss calculations that exceed actual harm while negotiating reasonable restitution amounts. Distinguish between actual loss and intended loss by showing that defendants used loan proceeds for legitimate business purposes rather than personal enrichment. Argue benefit to government when defendants used funds for program approved purposes that achieved Congressional intent. Negotiate restitution amounts that reflect actual harm rather than technical violations to demonstrate good faith and reduce overall sentence exposure.

Loss calculation challenges can dramatically reduce sentences while restitution negotiation demonstrates defendant cooperation and good faith.

Character Evidence And Reference Letter Strategy

Character evidence is crucial in sentencing because it shows judges the person behind the charges and demonstrates that defendants deserve second chances rather than harsh punishment.

Character Letter Coordination:

Martin assembled over forty character letters from diverse sources that painted a comprehensive picture of Michael's positive character and community impact. Letters from employees describing Michael as fair and generous employer who continued paying wages during lockdowns when business income declined. Customer letters praising Michael's honesty and reliability in business dealings over many years. Community leader letters describing Michael's volunteer work and financial support for local organizations.

Letter Writing Guidelines:

Effective character letters follow specific formats that maximize their impact on judges. Personal relationship descriptions that establish the writer's credibility and knowledge of the defendant. Specific examples of the defendant's positive character traits demonstrated through concrete actions rather than general statements. Impact statements showing how the defendant's incarceration would harm letter writers and the broader community.

Letter Source Diversification:

Character letters should come from diverse sources that show the defendant's positive impact across different areas of life. Professional references including suppliers, customers, and business associates who can testify to the defendant's honesty and integrity in business dealings. Community references including neighbors, religious leaders, and volunteer organization coordinators who know the defendant's charitable work and community involvement. Personal references including friends and family who can describe the defendant's character and values in private relationships.

DEFENSE STRATEGY #125: *Strategic Character Evidence Development*

Character evidence requires strategic development that presents a comprehensive picture of the defendant's positive character and community contributions. Coordinate character letters from diverse sources including employees, customers, community leaders, and family members who can testify to different aspects of the defendant's character. Provide letter writing guidelines that ensure letters include specific examples and impact statements rather than general character assertions. Organize character evidence to show progression of positive relationships and community contributions over time.

Strategic character evidence transforms defendants from criminals deserving punishment into community members deserving second chances.

Mental Health And Addiction Issues

Many PPP defendants suffer from mental health or addiction issues that contributed to their poor decision making and should be considered in sentencing.

Mental Health Documentation:

Comprehensive mental health evaluations can reveal underlying conditions that explain defendant behavior while supporting arguments for treatment rather than incarceration. Psychological evaluations showing depression, anxiety, or other mental health conditions that impaired defendant's judgment during pandemic stress. Medical records documenting treatment for mental health conditions that preceded criminal conduct. Expert testimony explaining how mental health conditions contributed to poor decision making rather than criminal intent.

Addiction Treatment Evidence:

Defendants with substance abuse issues can present treatment evidence that shows commitment to rehabilitation and reduced likelihood of future criminal conduct. Documentation of voluntary addiction treatment programs completed before sentencing. Evidence of ongoing participation in support groups and counseling that demonstrates commitment to sobriety. Expert testimony about the relationship between addiction and criminal behavior that supports treatment rather than incarceration.

Stress and Trauma Documentation:

Pandemic related stress and trauma can provide context for defendant decision making that supports lenient sentencing. Mental health evaluations documenting pandemic related anxiety, depression, and financial stress that impaired judgment. Evidence of family health crises, business failures, or other traumatic events during the pandemic period. Expert testimony about impact of unprecedented pandemic stress on decision making capabilities.

DEFENSE STRATEGY #126: *Mental Health and Addiction Mitigation Development*

Mental health and addiction issues require careful documentation to support sentencing mitigation arguments. Obtain comprehensive psychological evaluations that document mental health conditions affecting defendant judgment during the relevant time period. Document addiction treatment participation and ongoing recovery efforts that demonstrate commitment to rehabilitation. Present expert testimony explaining the relationship between mental health issues and criminal behavior to support treatment rather than incarceration.

Mental health and addiction mitigation can explain defendant behavior while supporting treatment oriented sentences that address underlying causes of criminal conduct.

Cooperation And Acceptance Of Responsibility

Demonstrating genuine acceptance of responsibility and cooperation with authorities can significantly reduce sentences under federal guidelines.

****Acceptance of Responsibility Requirements:****

Federal sentencing guidelines provide reduction for defendants who clearly demonstrate acceptance of responsibility for their criminal conduct. This requires more than guilty pleas; defendants must show genuine remorse and understanding of harm caused by their actions.

Michael Zhang's acceptance of responsibility included detailed allocution acknowledging his mistakes and explaining how he would conduct business differently in the future. "Your Honor, I take full responsibility for the mistakes I made in my PPP applications. I should have been more careful with the paperwork and sought professional help to ensure accuracy. I understand that my actions violated federal law and I am deeply sorry for any harm I caused."

****Cooperation Credit Opportunities:****

Defendants who provide substantial assistance to government investigations can receive significant sentence reductions under federal guidelines. However, cooperation must be genuinely valuable to qualify for credit.

Some PPP defendants can provide cooperation by explaining industry practices, identifying systemic problems in loan processing, or providing information about other violations they observed. This cooperation must be balanced against potential harm to other defendants and ethical considerations.

Early Guilty Plea Advantages:

Defendants who plead guilty early in cases can receive greater acceptance of responsibility credit than those who plead guilty on eve of trial. Early pleas demonstrate genuine remorse rather than strategic calculation to avoid worse outcomes.

DEFENSE STRATEGY #127: *Acceptance of Responsibility and Cooperation Strategy*

Acceptance of responsibility and cooperation require careful strategic development to maximize sentence reduction benefits. Demonstrate genuine remorse through detailed acknowledgment of wrongdoing and understanding of harm caused by criminal conduct. Explore cooperation opportunities that provide valuable assistance to the government while protecting client interests and ethical obligations. Consider timing of guilty pleas to maximize acceptance of responsibility credit while preserving negotiation leverage.

Acceptance of responsibility and cooperation can significantly reduce sentences while demonstrating the defendant's commitment to rehabilitation and future law compliance.

Alternative Sentencing And Prison Alternative Programs

Federal courts have authority to impose creative sentences that serve justice while avoiding unnecessary incarceration costs and family disruption.

Home Confinement and Electronic Monitoring:

Home confinement allows defendants to serve sentences while maintaining employment and family responsibilities. Electronic monitoring technology enables supervision without incarceration costs.

Michael Zhang's sentence included six months home confinement with electronic monitoring that allowed him to continue operating his businesses and supporting his family while serving his sentence. This alternative protected public safety while avoiding unnecessary family separation and business disruption.

Community Service Requirements:

Community service sentences allow defendants to repay society through positive contributions rather than expensive incarceration. Service should be tailored to defendant skills and community needs.

Martin proposed community service involving Michael teaching electronics repair skills to disadvantaged youth through local community college programs. This service utilized Michael's expertise while providing valuable training opportunities for young people seeking technical careers.

Restitution Payment Plans:

Courts can structure restitution payments to accommodate defendant financial circumstances while ensuring victim compensation. Payment plans should be realistic based on defendant income and expenses.

Michael's restitution was structured as monthly payments over three years that allowed him to maintain business operations while compensating the government for actual losses. The payment schedule considered his business income variability and family financial obligations.

DEFENSE STRATEGY #128: *Alternative Sentencing Advocacy*

Alternative sentencing requires creative advocacy that demonstrates how non incarceration sentences can serve justice while reducing costs and family disruption. Propose home confinement and electronic monitoring that allows defendants to maintain employment and family responsibilities while serving sentences. Develop community service proposals that utilize defendant skills to benefit society while providing meaningful consequences for criminal conduct. Structure restitution payment plans that ensure victim compensation while accommodating defendant financial circumstances.

Alternative sentencing advocacy can achieve justice while avoiding unnecessary incarceration that serves no legitimate penological purpose.

Victim Impact And Community Harm Analysis

Effective sentencing advocacy must address victim impact while distinguishing between actual harm and theoretical violations that caused no real injury.

Actual Victim Identification:

PPP fraud cases often involve theoretical victims rather than actual individuals harmed by defendant conduct. The SBA and general taxpayers are abstract victims who suffered no direct personal harm from individual defendant actions.

Martin argued that Michael's conduct caused no actual victim harm because he used loan proceeds for program approved purposes that achieved Congressional intent. His businesses remained open, maintained employment, and continued serving community needs during pandemic lockdowns.

Community Benefit Documentation:

Defendants who used PPP funds appropriately can demonstrate community benefits that offset theoretical government harm. Michael's businesses provided essential electronics repair services, maintained employment for seventeen people, and supported local supply chains during the economic crisis.

Comparative Harm Analysis:

Sentencing advocacy should compare harm from defendant conduct with harm that would result from lengthy incarceration. Michael's imprisonment would close businesses employing seventeen people, eliminate essential community services, and force family dependence on government assistance.

DEFENSE STRATEGY #129: *Victim Impact and Community Harm Analysis*

Victim impact analysis must distinguish between actual harm and theoretical violations while demonstrating community benefits from defendant conduct. Identify actual victims harmed by defendant actions versus abstract government harm that caused no direct injury to individuals. Document community benefits from defendant's use of loan proceeds including employment maintenance and essential service provision. Compare harm from defendant conduct with harm that would result from incarceration including business closure and family hardship.

Victim impact analysis can demonstrate that punishment would cause more harm than the defendant's original conduct while showing that justice requires proportional rather than theoretical penalties.

Sentence Departure And Variance Arguments

Federal judges have authority to impose sentences below guideline ranges when circumstances justify departure from standard calculations.

Departure Ground Identification:

Specific departure grounds are outlined in sentencing guidelines and can provide basis for reduced sentences when applicable to defendant circumstances. Extraordinary family circumstances including sole financial provider status for disabled dependents. Lack of criminal history and minimal likelihood of recidivism. Extraordinary community service and charitable contributions. Unique circumstances not adequately considered in guidelines calculations.

Variance Argument Development:

Variance arguments under 18 USC Section 3553(a) allow broader consideration of justice and proportionality factors beyond specific departure grounds. The seriousness of the offense and need for just punishment. The need to afford adequate deterrence and protect public safety. The need to provide defendants with educational or vocational training and medical care. The need to avoid unwarranted sentence disparities among defendants with similar records convicted of similar conduct.

PPP Specific Variance Arguments:

PPP cases present unique circumstances that support variance arguments based on the unprecedented nature of pandemic emergency and program implementation. Extraordinary circumstances of global pandemic that created unprecedented business pressures and decision making challenges. Rushed program implementation that created regulatory confusion and inevitable compliance errors. Disproportionate sentences compared to typical fraud cases involving actual victim harm and criminal enrichment.

DEFENSE STRATEGY #130: *Departure and Variance Argument Strategy*

Departure and variance arguments require systematic identification of applicable grounds and strategic development of supporting evidence. Identify specific departure grounds including extraordinary family circumstances, lack of criminal history, and community service contributions. Develop comprehensive variance arguments under Section 3553(a) factors that address justice and proportionality concerns. Present PPP specific arguments about pandemic circumstances and program implementation problems that support below guidelines sentences.

Departure and variance arguments can achieve dramatically reduced sentences when supported by compelling evidence and strategic legal argument.

Sentencing Hearing Presentation And Advocacy

Sentencing hearings require careful orchestration that presents mitigation evidence effectively while addressing judge concerns and prosecutor arguments.

****Witness Presentation Strategy:****

Sentencing hearings allow live witness testimony that can be more compelling than written submissions alone. Character witnesses who can describe the defendant's positive impact on their lives and community. Family members who can explain hardship that incarceration would cause to innocent dependents. Mental health experts who can explain psychological factors that contributed to criminal conduct. Community leaders who can testify to the defendant's contributions and rehabilitation potential.

****Document Organization and Presentation:****

Sentencing submissions require careful organization that presents mitigation evidence persuasively while addressing all relevant factors. Comprehensive sentencing memorandum that presents legal arguments and mitigation evidence systematically. Character letter compilation organized by relationship type and impact area. Financial documentation showing restitution capability and family hardship from incarceration. Treatment and rehabilitation evidence demonstrating commitment to addressing underlying issues.

****Allocution Preparation and Delivery:****

Defendant allocution represents a crucial opportunity to speak directly to judge about remorse, understanding, and future plans. Acceptance of responsibility must be genuine and specific rather than general apology. Understanding of harm caused by criminal conduct including impact on victims and community. Specific plans for ensuring future law compliance including business practice changes and professional guidance. Expression of gratitude for support received and commitment to justifying community confidence.

DEFENSE STRATEGY #131: *Sentencing Hearing Orchestration and Presentation*

Sentencing hearings require careful orchestration that maximizes mitigation evidence impact while addressing all relevant legal and factual issues. Plan witness presentation that provides compelling live testimony from character witnesses, family members, and experts. Organize document submissions that present mitigation evidence systematically while supporting legal arguments for reduced sentences. Prepare defendant allocution that demonstrates genuine acceptance of responsibility and commitment to rehabilitation.

Effective hearing orchestration can transform sentencing from mechanical guidelines application into human drama that motivates judicial compassion and reduced punishment.

Victory Through Sentencing Advocacy

Michael Zhang received a sentence of three years probation with six months home confinement, community service, and restitution of $15,000. This outcome represented a dramatic victory considering that sentencing guidelines had recommended 18 to 24 months imprisonment.

Sentencing Success Factors:

Judge Williams explained her sentencing decision by citing several factors that Martin's advocacy had highlighted. Michael's lack of criminal history and excellent character evidence from community members. His use of loan proceeds for legitimate business purposes rather than personal enrichment. The extraordinary circumstances of the pandemic emergency that created unprecedented business pressures. The community benefited from allowing Michael to continue operating businesses that employed seventeen people. The minimal actual harm compared to theoretical guideline calculations.

Immediate Impact Benefits:

The probationary sentence had immediate positive consequences for Michael and his community. Michael continued operating his businesses and maintaining employment for seventeen people. His family remained together with father present to care for disabled brother and chronically ill wife. Community continued receiving essential electronics repair services during ongoing pandemic recovery. Michael began community service teaching technical skills to disadvantaged youth.

Long Term Rehabilitation:

The sentence structure supported Michael's rehabilitation while protecting community interests. Probation supervision ensured ongoing law compliance without unnecessary incarceration costs. Community service provided meaningful consequence while utilizing Michael's skills for public benefit. Restitution schedule allowed gradual compensation while maintaining business viability. Home confinement satisfied punishment goals while preserving family stability.

The Art Of Sentencing Advocacy

Michael's sentencing success demonstrated that effective advocacy can achieve dramatically better outcomes than mechanical application of sentencing guidelines. This requires understanding both legal requirements and human psychology that influences judicial decision making.

Legal Expertise Requirements:

Sentencing advocacy requires mastery of complex guidelines calculations, departure grounds, and variance arguments that can reduce recommended sentences. This technical expertise provides the foundation for strategic arguments but cannot alone achieve optimal outcomes.

Human Story Development:

Effective sentencing requires transforming technical legal violations into human stories that motivate judicial compassion while respecting rule of law requirements. This involves presenting defendants as complete human beings whose punishment affects entire communities rather than just individual criminals.

Strategic Integration:

Master practitioners integrate legal expertise with human story development to create sentencing presentations that satisfy both intellectual and emotional requirements for reduced punishment. This integration requires extensive preparation combined with courtroom advocacy skills.

Your freedom may depend on your attorney's ability to transform guideline calculations into human stories that motivate judicial mercy without compromising respect for law and victims. Even guilty pleas can result in dramatically different sentences based on the quality of sentencing advocacy.

Sentencing represents your final opportunity to influence the consequences of criminal charges. Make sure that opportunity is used by counsel who understands that judges are human beings who can be motivated by compelling stories of redemption, community benefit, and proportional justice.

The sentence you receive will determine not just your immediate fate, but your ability to rebuild your life, support your family, and contribute to your community. Invest in sentencing advocacy that treats this decision with the gravity it deserves, because the difference between prison and probation may determine the trajectory of the rest of your life.

Remember that sentencing judges have enormous discretion to impose sentences that serve justice rather than mechanical guideline calculations. Your challenge is motivating them to use that discretion in your favor through advocacy that appeals to their sense of justice, proportionality, and human compassion.

CHAPTER 16

APPEALS & POST-CONVICTION

Habeas Strategies, Reconsideration, Delays

Defense attorney Jennifer West stared at the computer screen in her downtown Los Angeles office, reading the devastating verdict that had just destroyed her client's life. Robert Lin, a Korean American restaurant owner who had operated his family business for twenty-three years, had been convicted on all PPP fraud charges and sentenced to forty-two months in federal prison. The jury had deliberated for less than six hours before finding him guilty of wire fraud, bank fraud, and money laundering based on discrepancies in his loan applications totaling **$67,000.**

But West knew that Robert's fight was far from over. Despite the conviction and harsh sentence, the appellate process offered multiple opportunities to challenge the verdict, reduce the sentence, or even achieve complete reversal. Over the next eighteen months, West would wage an aggressive post-conviction campaign that would ultimately result in Robert's conviction being overturned and all charges dismissed.

The key to Robert's eventual victory lay in understanding that appeals and post-conviction proceedings represent entirely different battlefields from trial, with different rules, different strategies, and different opportunities for success. While trial advocacy focuses on persuading juries through emotional appeals and witness credibility, appellate advocacy depends on identifying legal errors, constitutional violations, and procedural mistakes that can invalidate convictions regardless of factual guilt or innocence.

"Robert's conviction may seem final," West told his devastated family after the sentencing, "but we're just beginning to fight. The trial court made serious legal errors that violated Robert's constitutional rights, and we're going to use the appellate process to correct those errors and get Robert the justice he deserves."

West's appellate strategy would combine direct appeals challenging legal errors with collateral attacks through habeas corpus petitions that raised constitutional violations not addressed in the direct appeal. She would also pursue sentence reduction motions, compassionate release applications, and prosecutorial misconduct claims that could provide relief even if the conviction itself remained intact.

Robert Lin's case would establish important precedents for PPP appeals while demonstrating how persistent post-conviction advocacy can achieve victory even after apparently hopeless trial defeats.

Understanding The Appellate Landscape For PPP Cases

Federal appeals in PPP cases present unique opportunities because the rapid prosecution of these cases often resulted in legal errors, constitutional violations, and procedural shortcuts that can be challenged on appeal.

****Direct Appeal Opportunities:****

PPP prosecutions frequently contain appellable issues because prosecutors and judges were applying new legal theories to unprecedented circumstances without established precedent. Legal sufficiency challenges to fraud charges based on regulatory complexity and ambiguity. Constitutional challenges to prosecutions based on vague statutory language and regulatory uncertainty. Evidentiary challenges to admission of algorithmic evidence and expert testimony. Procedural challenges to discovery violations and prosecutorial misconduct.

****Collateral Attack Possibilities:****

Even after direct appeals are exhausted, PPP defendants can pursue collateral attacks through habeas corpus petitions that raise constitutional claims not addressed in direct appeals. Ineffective assistance of counsel claims based on attorney failures to challenge algorithmic evidence or investigate regulatory complexity. Due process violations based on prosecutions of conduct that was authorized under contemporaneous regulatory guidance. Equal protection violations based on discriminatory enforcement patterns targeting minority business owners.

****Sentence Reduction Opportunities:****

Federal law provides multiple mechanisms for reducing sentences even after appeals are complete. Compassionate release motions based on extraordinary and compelling circumstances including family hardship and community impact. Sentence reduction motions based on changes in law or guideline amendments that would reduce recommended sentences. First Step Act and other criminal justice reform provisions that provide relief for nonviolent offenders.

DEFENSE STRATEGY #132: *Comprehensive Post-Conviction Strategy Development*

Post-conviction advocacy requires a comprehensive strategy that combines direct appeals with collateral attacks and sentence reduction efforts. Identify all potential appellate issues including legal sufficiency, constitutional violations, evidentiary errors, and procedural mistakes. Develop collateral attack theories based on constitutional claims not addressed in direct appeals including ineffective assistance and due process violations. Pursue sentence reduction opportunities through compassionate release, guideline amendments, and criminal justice reform provisions.

Comprehensive post-conviction strategy provides multiple avenues for relief even after apparently final convictions and sentences.

Legal Sufficiency Challenges In PPP Appeals

Many PPP convictions are vulnerable to legal sufficiency challenges because prosecutors stretched fraud statutes beyond their intended scope to criminalize conduct that was authorized or ambiguous under program regulations.

Statutory Interpretation Challenges:

PPP prosecutions often rely on broad interpretations of fraud statutes that exceed statutory language and legislative intent. Wire fraud and bank fraud statutes require proof of schemes to defraud, but many PPP cases involve honest mistakes or regulatory violations that lack fraudulent intent. Money laundering prosecutions require proof of intent to conceal criminal proceeds, but defendants who used PPP funds for business purposes lacked such intent.

West identified multiple statutory interpretation issues in Robert Lin's case. The government had charged wire fraud based on electronic submission of loan applications, but the applications were submitted through government-approved systems that required electronic filing. Bank fraud charges were based on alleged false statements to lenders, but the lenders were following government instructions to rely on borrower certifications rather than verify information independently.

Regulatory Authorization Defense:

Many PPP prosecutions criminalize conduct that was explicitly or implicitly authorized by contemporaneous regulatory guidance. When government regulations authorize specific conduct, subsequent prosecution of that same conduct violates due process and exceeds prosecutorial authority.

Robert Lin's loan applications had followed guidance from the SBA that was in effect when he submitted his applications. The government's prosecution was based on regulatory interpretations that were developed after Robert's applications were submitted and approved.

Vagueness and Fair Notice Challenges:

Criminal prosecutions require that defendants have fair notice that their conduct violates federal law. PPP regulations were often vague, contradictory, and constantly changing, making it impossible for reasonable business owners to understand what conduct was prohibited.

DEFENSE STRATEGY #133: *Legal Sufficiency Challenge Development*

Legal sufficiency challenges require systematic analysis of statutory elements and regulatory context that demonstrates prosecutions exceed legal authority. Challenge broad interpretations of fraud statutes that criminalize conduct lacking criminal intent or fraudulent purpose. Identify regulatory authorization for defendant conduct that precludes criminal prosecution of the same behavior. Develop vagueness and fair notice challenges based on regulatory complexity and ambiguity that prevented reasonable compliance.

Legal sufficiency challenges can result in complete reversal of convictions based on legal errors rather than factual disputes.

Constitutional Challenges In PPP Appeals

PPP prosecutions raise numerous constitutional issues that can be raised on direct appeal or through habeas corpus petitions.

Due Process Violations:

The Fifth Amendment Due Process Clause prohibits prosecutions that violate fundamental fairness or criminalize conduct that was authorized when performed. PPP prosecutions often violate due process by applying current regulatory interpretations to past conduct that was compliant under contemporaneous guidance.

West's due process challenge in Robert Lin's case focused on the government's retroactive application of regulatory standards. "The government cannot prosecute Robert for violating rules that didn't exist when he submitted his applications. Due process requires fair notice of prohibited conduct, and Robert had no way of knowing that conduct explicitly authorized by SBA guidance would later be prosecuted as federal crimes."

Equal Protection Violations:

Statistical evidence shows that PPP prosecutions disproportionately target minority business owners despite similar violation rates across all demographic groups. This selective enforcement violates the Equal Protection Clause when it reflects discriminatory intent or has discriminatory impact.

Robert Lin's equal protection challenge included statistical analysis showing that Korean American business owners were prosecuted at rates 60% higher than white business owners with identical loan profiles. Expert testimony demonstrated that algorithmic detection systems contained biases that flagged minority-owned businesses more frequently than white-owned businesses.

Excessive Fines and Cruel and Unusual Punishment:

The Eighth Amendment prohibits fines and sentences that are grossly disproportionate to the offense committed. PPP sentences often violate this prohibition because they impose harsh punishment for technical violations that caused minimal or no actual harm.

DEFENSE STRATEGY #134: *Constitutional Challenge Strategy Development*

Constitutional challenges require systematic analysis of due process, equal protection, and Eighth Amendment violations that can invalidate prosecutions or sentences. Develop due process challenges based on retroactive application of regulatory standards and prosecution of authorized conduct. Present equal protection challenges using statistical evidence of discriminatory enforcement patterns and algorithmic bias. Challenge sentences as excessive under Eighth Amendment proportionality requirements.

Constitutional challenges can invalidate convictions and sentences based on fundamental violations of defendant rights rather than technical legal errors.

Ineffective Assistance Of Counsel Claims

Many PPP defendants received inadequate representation from attorneys who lacked understanding of the complex regulatory issues and defense strategies specific to these cases.

Strickland Standard Application:

Ineffective assistance claims require proof that counsel's performance was deficient and that the deficiency prejudiced the defense. PPP cases present unique opportunities for such claims because many attorneys lacked experience with SBA regulations and algorithmic evidence.

Common attorney errors in PPP cases include failure to challenge algorithmic evidence and expert testimony, failure to investigate regulatory complexity and defense theories, failure to retain appropriate expert witnesses, and failure to develop industry context evidence that could explain apparent violations.

Expert Witness Failures:

Many PPP defense attorneys failed to retain experts who could challenge government algorithmic analysis, explain industry practices, and provide regulatory guidance interpretation. These failures often constitute ineffective assistance because expert testimony is crucial in complex financial cases.

Robert Lin's original attorney had failed to retain any expert witnesses despite the complexity of restaurant industry regulations and the government's reliance on algorithmic analysis. West's post-conviction investigation revealed that available experts could have testified that Robert's conduct was consistent with industry standards and SBA guidance.

Investigation Deficiencies:

Effective PPP defense requires extensive investigation of regulatory guidance, industry practices, and government investigative procedures. Attorneys who fail to conduct adequate investigation may provide ineffective assistance.

Many PPP defense attorneys failed to investigate the regulatory guidance that was in effect when defendants submitted their applications, the bias and error rates of algorithmic detection systems, and the shortcuts and predetermined conclusions that characterized government investigations.

DEFENSE STRATEGY #135: *Ineffective Assistance Claim Development*

Ineffective assistance claims require systematic analysis of attorney performance deficiencies and resulting prejudice to defense outcomes. Document attorney failures to challenge algorithmic evidence, retain appropriate expert witnesses, and investigate regulatory complexity. Show how attorney deficiencies prejudiced defense by demonstrating what effective representation could have achieved. Develop comprehensive records that support ineffective assistance claims through post-conviction investigation and expert analysis.

Ineffective assistance claims can provide basis for new trials or sentence reductions when original representation failed to meet constitutional standards.

Evidentiary Challenges And Brady Violations

PPP prosecutions often involve evidentiary errors and Brady violations that can be challenged on appeal or through post-conviction motions.

Algorithmic Evidence Challenges:

Many PPP cases relied on algorithmic analysis that was admitted without proper foundation or reliability testing. Appellate courts are increasingly skeptical of algorithmic evidence that lacks scientific validation and transparency.

West challenged the admission of algorithmic evidence in Robert Lin's case by arguing that the government had failed to establish proper foundation for its reliability and accuracy. "The government asked the jury to convict Robert based on analysis from a computer system that they couldn't explain, hadn't validated, and refused to make available for independent testing."

Expert Testimony Challenges:

Government expert witnesses in PPP cases often provided opinions that exceeded their expertise or were based on insufficient data. These evidentiary errors can be challenged on appeal under Daubert standards.

Robert Lin's case involved government expert testimony about restaurant industry practices from a witness who had never operated a restaurant or consulted with restaurant owners. This testimony should have been excluded as unreliable and beyond the expert's qualifications.

Brady Violation Discovery:

Government prosecutors in PPP cases often failed to disclose exculpatory evidence including information about algorithmic bias, false positive rates, and similar cases that were dismissed or resulted in acquittals.

Post-conviction investigation in Robert Lin's case revealed that prosecutors had failed to disclose internal emails questioning the reliability of the algorithmic analysis and statistical data showing high false positive rates for Korean American business owners.

DEFENSE STRATEGY #136: *Evidentiary Challenge and Brady Violation Development*

Evidentiary challenges require systematic analysis of trial errors and government disclosure failures that violated defendant rights. Challenge admission of algorithmic evidence lacking proper foundation and reliability testing. Attack expert testimony that exceeded witness qualifications or was based on insufficient data. Investigate potential Brady violations through post-conviction discovery of government files and communications.

Evidentiary challenges can result in new trials or appellate reversals based on admission of unreliable evidence or suppression of exculpatory material.

Sentence Reduction And Compassionate Release Strategies

Even when convictions cannot be overturned, sentences can often be reduced through various post-conviction mechanisms.

Compassionate Release Applications:

The First Step Act expanded compassionate release provisions to allow defendants to petition directly for sentence reductions based on extraordinary and compelling circumstances. PPP defendants often qualify for compassionate release based on family hardship, community impact, and low recidivism risk.

West filed a compassionate release motion for Robert Lin based on his role as sole caregiver for elderly parents with serious medical conditions and his business's importance to the local Korean American community. The motion included medical documentation, character evidence, and economic impact analysis showing that Robert's continued incarceration served no legitimate penological purpose.

Guideline Amendment Retroactivity:

Changes to federal sentencing guidelines can sometimes be applied retroactively to reduce sentences for defendants who were sentenced under harsher provisions. PPP defendants should monitor guideline amendments that might provide relief.

Recent amendments addressing loss calculations in fraud cases could potentially reduce sentences for PPP defendants who were sentenced based on inflated loss amounts that exceeded actual harm caused by their conduct.

Criminal Justice Reform Provisions:

Various criminal justice reform initiatives provide opportunities for sentence reduction including the First Step Act, Second Chance Act, and other programs designed to reduce incarceration for nonviolent offenders.

DEFENSE STRATEGY #137: *Sentence Reduction Strategy Implementation*

Sentence reduction requires systematic pursuit of all available mechanisms including compassionate release, guideline amendments, and criminal justice reform provisions. Develop compassionate release applications based on extraordinary circumstances including family hardship, medical conditions, and community impact. Monitor guideline amendments and legal changes that might provide retroactive relief. Pursue criminal justice reform programs designed for nonviolent offenders.

Sentence reduction strategies can achieve significant custody time reductions even when convictions cannot be overturned.

Prosecutorial Misconduct Claims

PPP prosecutions involved significant prosecutorial misconduct that can be challenged through appeals and post-conviction motions.

Discovery Violations:

Many PPP prosecutors violated discovery obligations by failing to disclose exculpatory evidence, providing inadequate expert disclosures, and delaying production of crucial evidence until trial.

Robert Lin's case involved multiple discovery violations including late production of algorithmic analysis data, inadequate disclosure of expert witness qualifications, and failure to provide Brady material about similar dismissed cases.

Inflammatory Statements and Prejudicial Conduct:

PPP prosecutors often made inflammatory statements designed to prejudice juries rather than present evidence. These violations can be challenged on appeal or through misconduct claims.

The prosecutor in Robert Lin's case had made inflammatory statements about "greedy immigrants stealing American taxpayer money" that violated ethical obligations and prejudiced the jury against Robert based on his ethnicity rather than evidence.

Vindictive Prosecution Claims:

Some PPP prosecutions appear motivated by publicity and career advancement rather than legitimate law enforcement purposes. These vindictive prosecutions violate due process and can be challenged through post-conviction motions.

DEFENSE STRATEGY #138: *Prosecutorial Misconduct Challenge Development*

Prosecutorial misconduct claims require systematic documentation of ethical violations and constitutional infringements that affected trial outcomes. Document discovery violations including Brady material suppression and inadequate expert disclosures. Record inflammatory statements and prejudicial conduct that violated ethical obligations. Investigate prosecutorial motivations to identify potential vindictive prosecution claims.

Prosecutorial misconduct challenges can result in dismissals, new trials, or other relief when government attorneys violated constitutional and ethical obligations.

Habeas Corpus Petition Strategy

When direct appeals are unsuccessful, habeas corpus petitions provide additional opportunities to challenge convictions based on constitutional violations.

Habeas Grounds Development:

Federal habeas corpus petitions can raise constitutional claims that were not adequately addressed in direct appeals. Due process violations based on prosecutions that exceeded statutory authority or violated regulatory guidance. Equal protection violations based on discriminatory enforcement patterns. Ineffective assistance of counsel claims based on attorney failures that prejudiced defense outcomes.

West's habeas petition for Robert Lin raised multiple constitutional claims including due process violations based on retroactive application of regulatory standards, equal protection violations based on discriminatory targeting of Korean American business owners, and ineffective assistance claims based on his original attorney's failures.

Evidentiary Development:

Habeas petitions allow development of evidence that was not available during trial including expert analysis of algorithmic bias, statistical evidence of discriminatory enforcement, and investigation of prosecutorial misconduct.

Robert Lin's habeas petition included new expert testimony about algorithmic bias in fraud detection systems, statistical analysis of enforcement patterns showing discrimination against Korean American business owners, and evidence of prosecutorial misconduct that had not been discovered during trial.

Procedural Requirements:

Habeas petitions must comply with strict procedural requirements including exhaustion of state remedies, statute of limitations compliance, and demonstration that claims were not adequately addressed in direct appeals.

DEFENSE STRATEGY #139: *Comprehensive Habeas Corpus Strategy*

Habeas corpus petitions require strategic development of constitutional claims with supporting evidence that was not available during direct appeals. Identify constitutional violations including due process, equal protection, and ineffective assistance claims that can be raised in habeas proceedings. Develop new evidence through expert analysis, statistical studies, and investigation that supports constitutional claims. Ensure compliance with procedural requirements including exhaustion and statute of limitations.

Habeas corpus petitions provide additional opportunities to challenge convictions based on constitutional violations even after direct appeals are unsuccessful.

Appellate Brief Writing And Oral Argument Strategy

Successful appeals require sophisticated brief writing and oral argument skills that differ significantly from trial advocacy.

Appellate Brief Strategy:

Effective appellate briefs identify clear legal errors and present compelling arguments for reversal or remand. Issue identification and framing that presents strongest appellable errors first. Legal argument development that demonstrates clear violations of law or constitutional rights. Record citation that provides specific support for all factual assertions. Policy arguments that show broader implications of affirming trial court errors.

West's appellate brief in Robert Lin's case focused on three primary issues: legal insufficiency of fraud charges based on regulatory authorization, constitutional violations based on due process and equal protection, and evidentiary errors based on admission of unreliable algorithmic evidence.

Oral Argument Preparation:

Appellate oral arguments require different skills from trial advocacy, focusing on legal argument rather than emotional appeal. Preparation for judicial questions about legal standards and case precedent. Development of concise responses to challenges to defense theories. Practice with hypothetical questions that test limits of legal arguments.

Robert Lin's oral argument focused on the fundamental unfairness of prosecuting conduct that was explicitly authorized by regulatory guidance when performed. West emphasized that due process requires fair notice of prohibited conduct and that Robert had reasonably relied on SBA guidance that permitted his application practices.

DEFENSE STRATEGY #140: *Appellate Advocacy Excellence*

Appellate advocacy requires mastery of legal writing and oral argument skills that focus on legal errors rather than factual disputes. Develop comprehensive appellate briefs that identify clear legal errors and present compelling arguments for reversal. Prepare thoroughly for oral arguments that focus on legal standards and constitutional principles. Present policy arguments that demonstrate broader implications of trial court errors.

Appellate advocacy excellence can achieve reversals and remands that provide opportunities for better outcomes even after trial defeats.

Case Management And Timing Strategy

Post-conviction proceedings involve complex timing requirements and strategic decisions about when to pursue different types of relief.

Appeal Timing Requirements:

Direct appeals must be filed within strict deadlines that cannot be extended except in extraordinary circumstances. Notice of appeal must be filed within fourteen days of sentencing. Appellate briefs must be filed according to court schedules that typically allow sixty to ninety days for preparation.

Collateral Attack Timing:

Habeas corpus petitions have different timing requirements than direct appeals. Federal habeas petitions must generally be filed within one year of conviction becoming final. Statute of limitations can be tolled for various reasons including pending direct appeals and newly discovered evidence.

Sentence Reduction Timing:

Various sentence reduction mechanisms have different timing requirements and eligibility criteria. Compassionate release motions can be filed at any time but require exhaustion of administrative remedies. Guideline amendment applications must be filed within specific time-frames after amendments become effective.

DEFENSE STRATEGY #141: *Strategic Timing and Case Management*

Post-conviction proceedings require careful timing and case management to preserve all available relief options. Meet all appellate deadlines while preparing comprehensive legal arguments and supporting evidence. Coordinate direct appeals with collateral attacks to maximize opportunities for relief. Time sentence reduction applications strategically to take advantage of changing legal standards and circumstances.

Strategic timing and case management ensures that all available post-conviction opportunities are preserved and pursued effectively.

Victory Through Persistent Advocacy

Robert Lin's conviction was overturned after eighteen months of appellate and post-conviction advocacy. The Ninth Circuit Court of Appeals ruled that his prosecution violated due process because it criminalized conduct that was explicitly authorized by SBA guidance when performed.

Appellate Victory Elements:

The appellate court's decision emphasized several factors that West had highlighted in her advocacy. Due process violations based on retroactive application of regulatory standards that were not in effect when Robert submitted his applications. Equal protection violations based on statistical evidence of discriminatory enforcement patterns targeting Korean American business owners. Evidentiary errors based on admission of algorithmic analysis that lacked proper foundation and reliability testing.

Broader Impact:

Robert Lin's victory established important precedents for other PPP defendants and changed how courts analyze these prosecutions. The decision clarified that defendants cannot be prosecuted for conduct that was authorized by contemporaneous regulatory guidance. It recognized that discriminatory enforcement patterns violate equal protection even when individual prosecutors lack discriminatory intent. It established higher standards for admission of algorithmic evidence in criminal prosecutions.

Personal Vindication:

Robert Lin's vindication had profound personal and community impact beyond the legal precedent. Robert returned to operating his restaurant and employing fifteen people in the Korean American community. His family was reunited after months of separation and financial hardship. Community trust in the justice system was partially restored through recognition that wrongful convictions can be corrected through persistent advocacy.

The Long Fight For Justice

Robert Lin's case demonstrates that post-conviction advocacy can achieve victory even after apparently hopeless trial defeats. This requires understanding that appeals and habeas proceedings operate under different rules and standards than trial proceedings.

Persistence Requirements:

Post-conviction success requires persistence through multiple proceedings and procedural obstacles. Direct appeals may be unsuccessful but still preserve issues for subsequent habeas corpus petitions. Sentence reduction motions may be denied initially but succeed after changed circumstances or legal standards.

Resource Investment:

Effective post-conviction advocacy requires significant investment in legal research, expert analysis, and evidence development. This investment often exceeds trial costs but can be justified by the stakes involved and the potential for complete vindication.

Strategic Coordination:

Successful post-conviction campaigns require coordination of multiple proceedings and strategic timing of different relief applications. Direct appeals should preserve all possible issues while collateral attacks develop constitutional claims that may not have been available during trial.

Your conviction may seem final, but the appellate process provides multiple opportunities to challenge legal errors, constitutional violations, and procedural mistakes that occurred during trial. Don't accept wrongful conviction as inevitable when persistent advocacy can achieve justice through the appellate system.

The fight for justice doesn't end with trial verdicts. Appeals and post-conviction proceedings represent different battlefields where legal expertise and constitutional principles can overcome factual disputes and jury emotions. Understanding these opportunities is crucial for defendants who refuse to accept unjust outcomes.

Post-conviction advocacy requires specialized knowledge and persistent effort, but it can achieve results that seemed impossible after trial defeats. The key is recognizing that appeals focus on legal errors rather than factual guilt, creating opportunities for victory even when trial evidence appeared overwhelming.

Remember that appellate courts can correct injustices that trial courts create through legal errors, constitutional violations, and procedural mistakes. Your challenge is identifying those errors and presenting them effectively through sophisticated appellate advocacy that transforms trial defeats into appellate victories.

CHAPTER 17

ACTUAL TIME SERVED

How Much Time Do You Actually Do?

David Greer stared at the federal sentencing order that condemned him to thirty-six months in federal prison for PPP fraud charges. The Korean American restaurant owner had pleaded guilty to inflating his payroll on loan applications by **$43,000,** hoping to avoid the ten-year sentence prosecutors had threatened if he went to trial. Now, sitting in his attorney's office three days before his surrender date, David felt overwhelmed by the prospect of leaving his wife and two young children for three years.

But his attorney, Maya Berry, had different news that would transform David's understanding of his sentence. "David, I know thirty-six months sounds terrifying, but the reality is that you'll likely serve less than half that time if we use every available program and reduction opportunity. The federal system has multiple mechanisms that can reduce your actual custody time, and PPP defendants are often ideal candidates for these programs."

Over the next two hours, Berry explained the complex web of federal programs, sentence reductions, and early release opportunities that could transform David's thirty-six month sentence into perhaps fifteen months of actual incarceration. The First Step Act, Second Chance Act, RDAP program, halfway houses, home confinement, good time credits, and compassionate release provisions all offered potential pathways to earlier freedom.

"The key," Berry explained, "is understanding that your sentence is not a fixed prison term, but a starting point for strategic reduction through multiple federal programs designed to reward rehabilitation, reduce recidivism, and promote successful reentry into society."

David's case would become a model for how PPP defendants can minimize their actual time served through strategic use of federal reduction programs. His thirty-six month sentence would ultimately result in eleven months in federal prison, four months in a halfway house, and six months of home confinement, with the remainder of his sentence served on supervised release.

Understanding Federal Sentence Structure

Federal sentences consist of multiple components that create opportunities for time reduction through various programs and mechanisms.

****Sentence Components:****

Federal sentences include incarceration time, supervised release periods, and potential alternative custody arrangements that can significantly reduce actual prison time. The Bureau of Prisons has authority to place inmates in community confinement including halfway houses and home detention for up to the final year of their sentences.

****Time Calculation Basics:****

Federal inmates typically serve approximately **85%** of their sentences before release, but this baseline can be reduced significantly through participation in programs and earning of good time credits. Good conduct time allows inmates to earn up to 54 days per year off their sentences for satisfactory behavior and program participation.

****Program Participation Benefits:****

The First Step Act expanded opportunities for sentence reduction through evidence-based recidivism reduction programming. Inmates can earn additional time credits for successful completion of programs including educational courses, vocational training, substance abuse treatment, and mental health counseling.

****DEFENSE STRATEGY #142:** *Comprehensive Time Reduction Planning***

Effective sentence reduction requires comprehensive planning that begins before incarceration and continues throughout the sentence. Identify all available time reduction opportunities including good time credits, program participation benefits, and community confinement eligibility. Develop a strategic timeline for program participation that maximizes credit earning potential. Coordinate with Bureau of Prisons staff to ensure proper documentation of program completion and credit calculation.

Comprehensive planning can reduce actual custody time by 40-60% through strategic use of available programs and mechanisms.

First Step Act Benefits And Implementation

The First Step Act of 2018 represents the most significant federal criminal justice reform in decades, creating new opportunities for sentence reduction and early release.

****Earned Time Credits:****

The First Step Act allows inmates to earn time credits for successful completion of evidence-based recidivism reduction programs. Credits can be applied toward pre-release custody including halfway houses and home confinement, effectively reducing prison time while maintaining supervision.

David Greer earned time credits through completion of financial literacy courses, business ethics training, and community service programs. His credits allowed him to serve the final ten months of his sentence in community confinement rather than federal prison.

****Recidivism Reduction** Programming:**

The Act requires the Bureau of Prisons to expand programming designed to reduce recidivism and promote successful reentry. Programs include educational courses, vocational training, substance abuse treatment, mental health counseling, and faith-based initiatives.

PPP defendants are often ideal candidates for financial literacy and business ethics programs that directly address the conduct underlying their offenses while providing practical skills for legitimate business operations.

****Risk Assessment Tools:****

The First Step Act implements risk assessment tools that evaluate inmates' likelihood of recidivism and their potential for successful participation in recidivism reduction programming. Lower risk inmates may qualify for expanded programming opportunities and community confinement placements.

****DEFENSE STRATEGY #143:** *First Step Act Maximization Strategy***

First Step Act benefits require strategic planning and active participation in available programming. Research available recidivism reduction programs and develop a participation timeline that maximizes credit earning. Ensure proper documentation of program completion and credit calculation through **Bureau**

of Prisons procedures. Coordinate program participation with community confinement planning to optimize sentence reduction benefits.

Strategic First Step Act utilization can reduce actual prison time by 15-25% through earned time credits and expanded community confinement eligibility.

Rdap And Substance Abuse Programming

The Residential Drug Abuse Program (RDAP) offers one of the most significant sentence reduction opportunities in the federal system, providing up to one year of sentence reduction for successful completion.

****RDAP Eligibility Requirements:****

RDAP participation requires documented substance abuse problems that contributed to the offense conduct. Many PPP defendants can establish substance abuse issues that affected their decision making during the pandemic crisis.

Documentation requirements include clinical assessments, treatment history, and evidence that substance abuse contributed to criminal conduct. Defense attorneys should gather this evidence during sentencing preparation to support RDAP eligibility.

****Program Components:****

RDAP involves intensive residential treatment lasting 9-12 months, followed by community-based transitional services. The program includes individual and group counseling, educational components, and work assignments designed to address addiction and promote recovery.

****Sentence Reduction Benefits:****

Successful RDAP completion can result in up to one year of sentence reduction through early transfer to community confinement. This reduction is in addition to good time credits and other program benefits.

****Alternative Substance Abuse Programs:****

Inmates who don't qualify for RDAP may participate in non-residential substance abuse programs that provide time credits under the First Step Act while addressing underlying addiction issues.

****DEFENSE STRATEGY #144:** *RDAP and Substance Abuse Program Strategy***

RDAP and substance abuse programming require early identification and documentation of eligibility factors. Assess defendant substance abuse history and document connection between addiction and criminal conduct. Gather clinical evidence supporting substance abuse diagnosis and treatment needs. Develop a timeline for program participation that maximizes sentence reduction benefits.

RDAP participation can reduce sentences by up to one year while providing valuable addiction treatment that supports successful reentry.

Educational And Vocational Programming

Educational and vocational programs provide time credits under the First Step Act while developing skills that support legitimate employment and business operations.

****GED and High School Equivalency:****

Inmates without high school diplomas are typically required to participate in GED programs, which provide time credits upon successful completion. These programs also support employment prospects upon release.

****College and University Programs:****

Many federal facilities offer college courses through partnerships with local institutions. Course completion provides time credits while developing advanced skills that support career advancement.

David Greer completed business administration courses that provided time credits while preparing him to operate his restaurant more effectively upon release. The courses also demonstrated his commitment to legitimate business practices to probation officers and community members.

****Vocational Training Programs:****

Vocational programs provide practical skills training in areas including construction, automotive repair, food service, and technology. These programs offer time credits while preparing inmates for employment in legitimate careers.

****Apprenticeship Programs:****

Federal facilities increasingly offer apprenticeship programs in partnership with labor unions and employers. These programs provide intensive training, time credits, and guaranteed employment opportunities upon release.

DEFENSE STRATEGY #145: *Educational and Vocational Programming Optimization*

Educational and vocational programming requires strategic selection that maximizes time credits while developing practical skills for reentry. Identify programs that align with the defendant's interests, abilities, and career goals upon release. Coordinate program participation with sentence timeline to optimize credit earning and skill development. Document program completion and achievements for use in early release applications and reentry planning.

Educational and vocational programming can provide significant time credits while developing skills that support successful reintegration into legitimate business and employment.

Halfway House And Community Confinement

Community confinement represents one of the most valuable opportunities for reducing actual prison time while maintaining employment and family relationships.

Halfway House Placement:

The Bureau of Prisons can place inmates in halfway houses for up to the final 12 months of their sentences, and up to six additional months under the First Step Act for inmates who have earned sufficient time credits.

Halfway houses allow inmates to maintain employment, participate in community programs, and gradually transition back to independent living while serving the remainder of their sentences under supervision.

Home Confinement Options:

Inmates may be eligible for home confinement during the final portion of their sentences, allowing them to serve time at home while maintaining employment and family responsibilities.

Home confinement typically involves electronic monitoring and requires approval based on factors including housing stability, employment prospects, and family support systems.

Community Confinement Benefits:

Community confinement allows inmates to maintain income, support families, and preserve business relationships that would otherwise be destroyed by extended incarceration. This continuity supports successful reentry and reduces recidivism risk.

David Greer's community confinement placement allowed him to resume restaurant operations while serving his sentence, maintaining employment for his staff and preserving his family's financial stability.

DEFENSE STRATEGY #146: *Community Confinement Maximization*

Community confinement requires early planning and documentation of eligibility factors including housing stability, employment prospects, and family support. Develop a comprehensive reentry plan that demonstrates community ties and commitment to legitimate activity. Coordinate with Bureau of Prisons staff to optimize placement timing and duration. Prepare housing, employment, and family documentation that supports community confinement applications.

Strategic community confinement planning can reduce actual prison time by 12-18 months while preserving employment and family stability.

Compassionate Release And Medical Considerations

Compassionate release provides opportunities for early sentence reduction based on extraordinary and compelling circumstances.

Extraordinary and Compelling Circumstances:

The First Step Act expanded compassionate release criteria to include various circumstances that may justify early release. Medical conditions that substantially diminish capacity for self-care or pose significant risk in institutional settings. Family circumstances including death or incapacitation of caregiver for minor children or spouse. Age-related factors for inmates over 65 who have served substantial portions of their sentences.

COVID-19 and Health Considerations:

The pandemic created new opportunities for compassionate release based on health vulnerabilities and institutional conditions that pose heightened infection risks.

Inmates with underlying health conditions including diabetes, heart disease, and respiratory problems may qualify for compassionate release based on COVID-19 vulnerability, particularly when institutional conditions cannot adequately protect their health.

Family Circumstances:

Compassionate release may be appropriate when family members depend on inmates for essential care that cannot be provided by others. This includes caregiving for disabled spouses, elderly parents, or minor children who lack alternative support systems.

DEFENSE STRATEGY #147: *Compassionate Release Strategy Development*

Compassionate release requires comprehensive documentation of extraordinary circumstances and compelling need for early release. Gather medical evidence supporting health vulnerabilities and institutional risk factors. Document family circumstances including dependent care responsibilities that cannot be fulfilled by others. Develop comprehensive release plans that address public safety concerns and demonstrate commitment to law-abiding behavior.

Compassionate release can provide significant sentence reductions for inmates facing extraordinary circumstances that justify early release on humanitarian grounds.

Good Time Credits And Behavior Management

Good conduct time represents the foundation of federal sentence reduction, providing automatic credits for satisfactory behavior and program participation.

Good Time Calculation:

Federal inmates can earn up to 54 days of good conduct time per year served, effectively reducing sentences by approximately 15% for inmates who maintain satisfactory behavior throughout their incarceration.

Good time credits are calculated annually and applied toward the earliest possible release date, creating incentives for continued positive behavior and program participation.

Behavior Requirements:

Good time credits require satisfactory behavior as determined by Bureau of Prisons staff based on factors including disciplinary record, work performance, and program participation.

Inmates who receive disciplinary infractions may lose good time credits, extending their actual service time beyond the minimum required under good conduct time calculations.

Program Participation Enhancement:

Active participation in educational, vocational, and treatment programs can enhance good time credit calculations while demonstrating commitment to rehabilitation and reentry preparation.

David Greer maintained exemplary behavior throughout his incarceration, earning maximum good time credits while participating extensively in educational and business programs that supported his reentry goals.

DEFENSE STRATEGY #148: *Good Time Credit Optimization*

Good time credit optimization requires consistent positive behavior and strategic program participation throughout incarceration. Maintain a disciplinary record free of infractions that could result in good time credit loss. Participate actively in available programs that demonstrate rehabilitation commitment while supporting early release applications. Document program achievements and positive behavior for use in early release applications and reentry planning.

Good time credit optimization provides automatic sentence reduction while creating foundation for additional programming benefits and early release opportunities.

Second Chance Act And Reentry Programming

The Second Chance Act provides funding and framework for reentry programming designed to reduce recidivism and support successful community integration.

Reentry Planning Services:

Second Chance Act programs provide comprehensive reentry planning including housing assistance, employment preparation, healthcare enrollment, and family reunification support.

These services begin during incarceration and continue post-release to ensure smooth transition and reduce likelihood of recidivism through comprehensive support systems.

Employment and Education Support:

Reentry programs provide job placement assistance, continuing education opportunities, and entrepreneurship training that support legitimate income generation upon release.

For PPP defendants with business backgrounds, reentry programs can provide resources for legitimate business development and regulatory compliance that prevent future legal problems.

Family Reunification Programs:

Second Chance Act initiatives include family reunification programs that address the impact of incarceration on spouses and children while preparing families for successful reunification.

These programs provide counseling, financial planning, and practical support that strengthen family stability and reduce factors contributing to recidivism.

DEFENSE STRATEGY #149: *Second Chance Act Program Utilization*

Second Chance Act programs require early engagement and active participation to maximize benefits for sentence reduction and reentry success. Identify available reentry programs and develop participation timelines that support early release applications. Engage family members in reunification programming that demonstrates stable support systems. Participate in employment and education programs that establish foundation for legitimate post-release income.

Second Chance Act programming provides comprehensive support for sentence reduction and successful reentry while addressing underlying factors that contributed to criminal conduct.

Strategic Timeline Development

Maximizing sentence reduction requires strategic timeline development that coordinates multiple programs and reduction opportunities.

Pre-Incarceration Planning:

Effective sentence reduction begins before incarceration with comprehensive planning that identifies available programs and develops participation timelines.

David Greer's pre-incarceration planning included RDAP assessment, educational program research, community confinement preparation, and family support system development that optimized his sentence reduction opportunities.

Early Incarceration Focus:

The first months of incarceration should focus on program enrollment, assessment completion, and establishment of a positive institutional record that supports later reduction applications.

Priority activities include substance abuse assessment, educational testing, vocational interest evaluation, and disciplinary record establishment that demonstrates commitment to rehabilitation.

Mid-Sentence Programming:

The middle portion of sentences should focus on intensive program participation that earns time credits while developing skills and demonstrating rehabilitation commitment.

This period typically involves completion of educational courses, vocational training, treatment programs, and work assignments that provide maximum credit earning opportunities.

Pre-Release Preparation:

The final portion of sentences should focus on community confinement applications, reentry planning, and transition preparation that supports successful release and supervision compliance.

DEFENSE STRATEGY #150: *Comprehensive Timeline Coordination*

Sentence reduction requires comprehensive timeline coordination that maximizes program benefits while preparing for successful reentry. Develop a detailed timeline that identifies optimal program participation sequence and credit earning opportunities. Coordinate program completion with community confinement applications and early release petitions. Prepare comprehensive documentation that supports all reduction applications and demonstrates rehabilitation commitment.

Strategic timeline development can transform lengthy sentences into manageable periods of incarceration followed by supervised community integration.

Case Study: David Greer's Actual Time Served

David's thirty-six month sentence was reduced to eleven months of actual prison time through strategic use of available programs and reduction opportunities.

****Sentence Reduction Timeline:****

Month 1-3: Assessment completion, GED program enrollment, RDAP eligibility documentation, and positive disciplinary record establishment.

Month 4-9: Intensive program participation including financial literacy courses, business ethics training, and community service work that earned significant time credits.

Month 10-11: Community confinement application preparation and approval based on program completion, time credit accumulation, and reentry plan development.

Month 12-15: Halfway house placement that allowed gradual reintegration while maintaining family and business relationships.

Month 16-21: Home confinement with electronic monitoring that permitted full-time restaurant operation while serving sentence remainder.

****Total Time Breakdown:****

11 months federal prison (31% of original sentence)

4 months halfway house (11% of original sentence)

6 months home confinement (17% of original sentence)

15 months supervised release (42% of original sentence)

****Program Benefits Achieved:****

First Step Act time credits: 4 months reduction

Good conduct time: 5 months reduction

Community confinement: 10 months reduction

Educational programming: 2 months additional credits

Substance abuse programming: 3 months reduction

DEFENSE STRATEGY #151: *Comprehensive Reduction Integration*

Maximum sentence reduction requires integration of multiple programs and reduction mechanisms that collectively transform lengthy sentences into manageable custody periods. Combine First Step Act credits with good time calculation, community confinement eligibility, and specialized programming benefits. Document all program participation and credit earning to ensure proper calculation and application. Coordinate reduction benefits with reentry planning that supports successful supervision completion.

Comprehensive reduction integration can reduce actual custody time by 60-70% while providing valuable rehabilitation programming and community support.

The Reality Of Federal Time

David Greer's experience demonstrates that federal sentences, while serious, can be significantly reduced through strategic use of available programs and reduction opportunities. Understanding these opportunities is crucial for defendants and families facing federal incarceration.

Key Insights:

Federal sentences are starting points rather than fixed terms, with multiple reduction opportunities available for inmates who participate actively in rehabilitation programming. Time reduction requires early planning, consistent program participation, and strategic coordination of available benefits. Community confinement and early release programs allow gradual reintegration that preserves family and business relationships while completing sentence requirements.

Planning Requirements:

Effective sentence reduction requires comprehensive planning that begins before incarceration and continues throughout the sentence period. This planning should involve coordination with experienced federal defense attorneys, Bureau of Prisons staff, and reentry service providers.

Family Preparation:

Families should understand that actual time served will likely be significantly less than sentenced time, but requires active participation in programming and consistent positive behavior throughout incarceration.

Your sentence may seem overwhelming, but remember that you have significant control over how much time you actually serve through strategic program participation and positive behavior. The federal system provides multiple pathways to early release for inmates who demonstrate genuine commitment to rehabilitation and community reintegration.

The key is understanding that incarceration is not just punishment, but opportunity for personal development, skill building, and demonstration of rehabilitation that can dramatically reduce your actual custody time while preparing you for successful reentry.

Take advantage of every available program, maintain exemplary behavior, and work with experienced counsel to optimize your sentence reduction opportunities. Your future depends not just on the sentence imposed, but on how effectively you use the time to demonstrate your commitment to positive change and community contribution.

Remember that thousands of federal inmates successfully reduce their sentences through strategic program participation. With proper planning and consistent effort, you can minimize your actual custody time while maximizing your preparation for successful return to your family and community.

CHAPTER 18

FEDERAL SENTENCE REDUCTION MECHANISMS

5K1.1, Rule 35, Minor Participant, And All Federal Reductions

Madeleine Robinson stared at the twenty-four month federal sentence that would separate her from her three young children and destroy the small bakery that had been her family's livelihood for twelve years. The Cuban American entrepreneur had pleaded guilty to PPP fraud charges involving **$89,000** in allegedly inflated payroll calculations, hoping to avoid the five-year sentence prosecutors had threatened at trial.

But her attorney, Hunter Smith, knew that Madeleine's case was far from over. Federal law provides numerous mechanisms for sentence reduction that could dramatically decrease her actual punishment, and PPP defendants are often ideal candidates for these reductions due to their typically clean criminal histories, community ties, and the technical nature of their violations.

"Madeleine," Smith explained during their post-sentencing meeting, "your twenty-four month sentence is just the starting point. Federal law provides multiple pathways to reduce your sentence, and we're going to pursue every available option. The **5K1.1 substantial assistance provision**, Rule 35 sentence reduction motions, minor participant adjustments, safety valve provisions, and acceptance of responsibility credits all offer potential relief."

Over the next eighteen months, Smith would systematically pursue every available sentence reduction mechanism, ultimately achieving a reduction of Madeleine's sentence from twenty-four months to eight months through a combination of cooperation credit, minor participant adjustment, and Rule 35 motion. Madeleine's case would demonstrate how strategic use of federal reduction mechanisms can transform seemingly harsh sentences into manageable periods of incarceration.

Understanding The Federal Sentence Reduction Ecosystem

Federal sentencing operates through a complex ecosystem of statutes, guidelines, and judicial discretion that creates multiple opportunities for sentence reduction when defendants and their attorneys understand how to navigate the system strategically.

The Layered Reduction System:

Federal sentence reductions operate through multiple layers that can be combined for cumulative effect. Guideline-based reductions including acceptance of responsibility, minor participant adjustments, and safety valve provisions that are calculated into the initial sentence. Statutory reductions including 5K1.1 substantial assistance departures and other congressionally mandated provisions that allow sentences below guideline ranges. Post-sentence reductions including Rule 35 motions, compassionate release, and sentence modification provisions that can reduce sentences after imposition. Administrative reductions including good time credits and program participation benefits that are applied during incarceration.

Timing and Coordination Strategy:

Different reduction mechanisms have different timing requirements and can often be combined for maximum effect. Some reductions must be pursued during initial sentencing proceedings, others can be sought post-sentence, and some accrue automatically through behavior and program participation.

Understanding these timing requirements allows strategic coordination that maximizes cumulative sentence reduction while preserving all available options throughout the sentence period.

PPP-Specific Opportunities:

PPP defendants present unique profiles that make them ideal candidates for many reduction mechanisms. First-time offenders with clean criminal histories who qualify for various first-offender provisions. Community-tied business owners who present low flight risk and strong reentry prospects. Technical violators whose conduct lacks traditional fraud characteristics like lavish lifestyle or victim harm. Crisis-motivated defendants whose actions were driven by pandemic business survival rather than greed.

DEFENSE STRATEGY #152: *Comprehensive Reduction Ecosystem Analysis*

Effective sentence reduction requires understanding the complete federal reduction ecosystem and developing strategies that maximize cumulative benefits. Map all available reduction mechanisms and their timing requirements to develop a comprehensive reduction timeline. Identify defendant characteristics that align with various reduction criteria to prioritize most promising opportunities. Coordinate reduction strategies to ensure they complement rather than conflict with each other.

Ecosystem analysis ensures no reduction opportunities are missed while optimizing the combination of available mechanisms for maximum sentence reduction.

5k1.1 Substantial Assistance Departures: The Crown Jewel

The 5K1.1 substantial assistance departure represents the most powerful sentence reduction mechanism in federal court, capable of reducing sentences below mandatory minimums and achieving reductions that would be impossible through any other mechanism.

****Understanding Substantial Assistance Standards:****

5K1.1 departures require that defendants provide substantial assistance to government investigations or prosecutions. The assistance must be truthful, complete, and of significant value to law enforcement efforts. Courts evaluate substantial assistance based on the significance and usefulness of information provided, the truthfulness and completeness of the defendant's cooperation, the nature and extent of assistance provided, and any injury suffered by the defendant as a result of cooperation.

****PPP-Specific Cooperation Opportunities:****

PPP cases present unique substantial assistance opportunities because they often involve broader schemes or systemic issues that investigators want to understand and address. Information about loan brokers, accountants, or attorneys who assisted multiple fraudulent applications can be extremely valuable. Details about lending institution practices that facilitated fraud can help the government understand systemic weaknesses. Explanations of industry practices that clarify whether conduct represents criminal fraud or regulatory violations. Assistance in identifying other potential violations within the defendant's industry or geographic area.

Madeleine Robinson's substantial assistance involved providing detailed information about Marcus White, the loan broker who had assisted her PPP applications and encouraged the inflated payroll calculations that formed the basis of her charges. Her cooperation revealed that White had been operating a sophisticated scheme across three states, using nearly identical inflation techniques with dozens of small business clients.

Government Motion Requirements and Negotiation:

5K1.1 departures can only be granted upon government motion, giving prosecutors significant leverage in cooperation negotiations. This requirement makes early cooperation discussions crucial for defendants seeking substantial sentence reductions.

Effective 5K1.1 negotiations require understanding what information would be valuable to government investigations while protecting defendant interests and maintaining ethical boundaries. Defendants must provide truthful, complete information without embellishing or manufacturing cooperation opportunities.

Smith negotiated Madeleine's cooperation agreement by demonstrating the genuine value of her information about White's operations while ensuring she would not be required to provide false or misleading testimony against other defendants.

Departure Magnitude and Judicial Discretion:

Courts have broad discretion in determining 5K1.1 departure extent based on cooperation quality and value. Departures can range from modest guideline reductions to sentences below statutory mandatory minimums, with some defendants receiving probationary sentences despite serious felony convictions.

The key factors courts consider include timeliness of cooperation, completeness and truthfulness of information, significance of assistance to investigations, personal risk undertaken by defendant, and defendant's motivation for providing assistance.

Protection and Safety Considerations:

5K1.1 cooperation can expose defendants to retaliation risks that courts must consider when evaluating assistance value and determining appropriate sentence reductions. Government witness protection programs may be available for defendants who face significant safety risks due to their cooperation.

****DEFENSE STRATEGY #153:** *5K1.1 Substantial Assistance Optimization***

5K1.1 departures require strategic cooperation that provides genuine value while protecting defendant safety and legal interests. Assess what information the defendant possesses that would be valuable to ongoing investigations without manufacturing cooperation opportunities. Negotiate cooperation agreements that provide meaningful sentence reduction guarantees in exchange for complete, truthful assistance. Document the extent and value of assistance provided to support government departure motions.

Strategic **5K1.1 cooperation** can achieve sentence reductions of 50-80% while contributing to legitimate law enforcement efforts and preventing future crimes.

Rule 35 Post-Sentence Reduction Motions: Ongoing Opportunities

Federal Rule of Criminal Procedure 35 allows courts to reduce sentences based on substantial assistance provided after sentencing, creating ongoing opportunities for sentence reduction through continued cooperation with government investigations.

****Post-Sentence Cooperation Framework:****

Rule 35 motions recognize that investigations often continue after sentencing and that defendants may discover additional valuable information or develop new cooperation opportunities. The rule allows government prosecutors to file motions for sentence reduction when defendants provide substantial assistance after their initial sentencing.

This mechanism is particularly valuable in complex cases like PPP prosecutions where investigations often span multiple years and involve numerous defendants across various jurisdictions.

****Rule 35 Requirements and Timing:****

Rule 35 motions must generally be filed within one year of sentencing, though this deadline can be extended when cooperation relates to information that was not reasonably available at the time of original sentencing.

The motion must be filed by the government and must demonstrate that the defendant has provided substantial assistance of significant value to investigations or prosecutions that occurred after the initial sentencing.

****Types of Post-Sentence Assistance:****

Rule 35 motions can be based on various types of post-sentence cooperation including providing additional information about criminal schemes that was discovered after sentencing, testifying in trials of co-defendants or other criminals that occur after defendant's sentencing, assisting in investigations of new criminal activity that was uncovered after initial cooperation, and helping government understand complex schemes or industry practices through ongoing consultation.

Madeleine Robinson's Rule 35 motion was filed eleven months after her sentencing when she provided crucial testimony in the prosecution of Marcus White, the loan broker whose scheme she had initially exposed. Her testimony was essential to White's conviction and helped recover over $2 million in fraudulent loans across multiple jurisdictions.

Strategic Considerations for Rule 35 Motions:

Rule 35 motions create ongoing incentives for defendants to seek out additional cooperation opportunities, which can be both beneficial and problematic. While continued cooperation can result in additional sentence reductions, defendants must avoid appearing to manufacture information or providing unreliable assistance to achieve further reductions.

Defense attorneys must balance clients' interests in additional sentence reduction with ethical obligations and the potential consequences of appearing over eager to cooperate.

Multiple Motion Possibilities:

Defendants can potentially file multiple Rule 35 motions based on different instances of substantial assistance, providing ongoing opportunities for sentence reduction throughout their incarceration and supervision periods.

Each motion must be based on new assistance that was not available at the time of previous motions, ensuring that defendants provide genuine ongoing value rather than recycling previous cooperation.

DEFENSE STRATEGY #154: *Rule 35 Motion Strategy Development*

Rule 35 motions require ongoing strategic planning that identifies legitimate cooperation opportunities while maintaining ethical boundaries. Monitor investigation developments that might create new cooperation opportunities without appearing to manufacture assistance. Prepare comprehensive documentation of post-sentence assistance and its value to government efforts. Coordinate Rule 35 motions with other ongoing sentence reduction mechanisms.

Strategic Rule 35 practice can provide additional sentence reductions of 25-50% through ongoing cooperation with evolving government investigations.

Minor And Minimal Participant Adjustments: Recognizing Limited Culpability

The federal sentencing guidelines recognize that not all participants in criminal schemes bear equal responsibility, providing reductions for defendants who played relatively minor or minimal roles compared to other participants.

Minor Participant Adjustment Framework:

Minor participant adjustments reduce offense levels by two points for defendants who were substantially less culpable than average participants in similar criminal activity. This adjustment recognizes that some defendants play lesser roles due to limited knowledge, reduced involvement, or manipulation by more culpable participants.

In PPP cases, minor participant adjustments often apply to small business owners who were guided or misled by professionals including accountants, attorneys, loan brokers, or business consultants who encouraged conduct that violated federal law.

Minimal Participant Benefits:

Minimal participant adjustments provide four-point offense level reductions for defendants who played truly minimal roles in criminal activity. This more substantial reduction applies to defendants who were essentially tools of others' schemes rather than willing participants in criminal conduct.

PPP defendants might qualify for minimal participant adjustments when they were manipulated by professionals who guided their applications without explaining legal requirements or when they were unknowing participants in broader fraudulent schemes.

Evidence Development for Participant Adjustments:

Participant adjustment claims require comprehensive evidence about the defendant's role relative to other participants, the scope and organization of criminal activity, defendant's knowledge and intent regarding illegal conduct, and the extent to which the defendant was manipulated or misled by others.

Madeleine Robinson's minor participant adjustment was based on extensive evidence that Marcus White, the loan broker, had guided every aspect of her application preparation. White had suggested the payroll inflations that became the basis of criminal charges, provided templates and calculations that Madeleine followed without understanding their illegal implications, and assured her that his guidance ensured compliance with all federal requirements.

Smith gathered evidence including email communications between Madeleine and White showing his guidance and her questions about legality, testimony from other White clients who received similar guidance and made identical mistakes, expert testimony about normal broker practices versus White's manipulative techniques, and documentation of Madeleine's attempts to verify White's advice with other sources.

Burden of Proof and Standard:

Defendants bear the burden of establishing entitlement to participant adjustments by preponderance of evidence. This requires systematic evidence development that clearly demonstrates limited culpability compared to other participants in similar schemes.

Courts evaluate participant adjustments based on the defendant's role in planning and executing criminal activity, defendant's awareness of the scope and structure of criminal schemes, benefits defendant received compared to other participants, and degree of control the defendant exercised over criminal conduct.

Comparison Group Analysis:

Participant adjustments require comparison of the defendant's role to other participants in the same scheme or similar criminal activity. This analysis must demonstrate that the defendant was substantially less culpable than typical participants in comparable crimes.

In Madeleine's case, Smith compared her limited role as a manipulated client to White's leadership role as scheme organizer and to other fraud defendants who independently planned and executed their violations without professional manipulation.

DEFENSE STRATEGY #155: *Participant Adjustment Evidence Development*

Participant adjustments require systematic evidence development that clearly demonstrates defendants' limited roles and reduced culpability. Document the defendant's limited involvement compared to other participants through communications, testimony, and expert analysis. Gather evidence of manipulation or misleading by professionals who guided defendant conduct. Show defendant's lack of knowledge about illegal nature of conduct and good faith efforts to comply with legal requirements.

Participant adjustment evidence can reduce sentences by 15-30% while demonstrating defendants' limited culpability and manipulation by more sophisticated criminals.

Safety Valve Provisions And Analogous Applications

The federal safety valve provision allows courts to sentence certain defendants below mandatory minimum sentences when they meet specific criteria demonstrating limited criminal involvement and cooperation.

****Traditional Safety Valve Criteria:****

Safety valve provisions traditionally apply to drug offenses and require that defendants have minimal criminal history (criminal history category I), did not use violence or possess weapons during criminal conduct, were not leaders, organizers, managers, or supervisors of criminal activity, and have truthfully provided all information about their offenses to government investigators.

While safety valve provisions don't technically apply to most PPP fraud cases, courts often consider similar factors when determining appropriate sentences for first-time, non-violent offenders.

****Analogous Safety Valve Application:****

PPP defendants can argue for safety valve-type consideration based on their profiles as first-time, non-violent offenders who played limited roles in criminal activity and have cooperated fully with investigations.

These arguments support downward departures or variances under 18 USC Section 3553(a) that achieve results similar to formal safety valve applications, particularly when combined with other reduction mechanisms.

****Documentation Requirements for Safety Valve-Type Arguments:****

Safety valve-type arguments require comprehensive documentation of defendants' minimal criminal involvement, complete cooperation with investigations, non-violent conduct throughout their backgrounds, and limited roles in criminal schemes.

Madeleine Robinson's safety valve-type argument emphasized her complete lack of criminal history, her full cooperation with the investigation of White's broader scheme, her non-violent conduct throughout the PPP application process, and her limited role as a manipulated participant rather than scheme organizer.

Policy Arguments for Safety Valve Application:

Defense attorneys can argue that safety valve principles should apply to PPP cases because they involve similar policy considerations including first-time offenders who pose minimal risk to public safety, technical violations that lack traditional criminal characteristics, and defendants whose cooperation serves important law enforcement purposes.

DEFENSE STRATEGY #156: *Safety Valve Principle Application*

Safety valve principles can support significant sentence reductions even when formal safety valve provisions don't apply to specific offenses. Document the defendant's minimal criminal history and non-violent conduct throughout their background. Show the defendant's limited role in criminal activity and complete cooperation with investigations. Argue that policy considerations supporting safety valve provisions apply equally to the defendant's circumstances.

Safety valve principle application can support sentence reductions of 20-40% for first-time, non-violent offenders who demonstrate limited culpability and cooperation.

Acceptance Of Responsibility: Automatic Reductions For Genuine Remorse

Acceptance of responsibility provides automatic sentence reductions for defendants who clearly demonstrate understanding of their wrongdoing and genuine commitment to making amends.

Three-Tier Reduction Structure:

Acceptance of responsibility reductions operate through a three-tier structure that can provide up to three points of offense level reduction. Two points for basic acceptance demonstrated through acknowledgment of wrongdoing and genuine remorse. One additional point for defendants who demonstrate acceptance early enough to permit government resource savings through avoided trials or simplified prosecutions.

Demonstration Requirements:

Acceptance of responsibility must be demonstrated through specific conduct including truthful admission to all elements of criminal behavior, genuine remorse expressed through allocution and conduct, assistance to government investigations when requested and appropriate, effort to make restitution to victims when possible, and acceptance of consequences without attempting to minimize culpability.

Madeleine Robinson's acceptance of responsibility was demonstrated through her immediate acknowledgment of mistakes in her PPP applications, her complete cooperation with the investigation that led to uncovering White's broader scheme, her proactive calculation and payment of restitution before it was ordered, and her genuine remorse expressed in court allocution that acknowledged harm to the PPP program and other legitimate borrowers.

Timing Considerations and Early Demonstration:

The third point of acceptance of responsibility requires that defendants demonstrate acceptance early enough in proceedings to permit government resource savings. This typically means entering guilty pleas before substantial trial preparation and avoiding unnecessary litigation over obvious facts.

Defense attorneys must balance early acceptance demonstrations with preservation of legal rights and development of mitigation evidence that supports favorable sentencing.

Balancing Acceptance with Legal Defenses:

Defendants can demonstrate acceptance of responsibility while preserving certain legal defenses, but they cannot minimize their conduct or shift blame to others while claiming acceptance credit.

The key is acknowledging specific criminal conduct while maintaining legal positions about sentencing factors, constitutional violations, or other issues that don't contradict acceptance of factual guilt.

Communication Strategy for Acceptance:

Acceptance of responsibility requires careful communication strategies that demonstrate genuine understanding and remorse without compromising legal positions or providing unnecessary ammunition for harsh sentencing.

Smith crafted Madeleine's acceptance communications to acknowledge her specific mistakes in PPP applications while emphasizing her good faith intent and the manipulation she experienced from White.

DEFENSE STRATEGY #157: *Acceptance of Responsibility Optimization*

Acceptance of responsibility requires strategic demonstration that maximizes reduction credit while preserving legal rights and developing favorable sentencing evidence. Demonstrate genuine remorse through consistent conduct and communications that acknowledge specific wrongdoing. Coordinate acceptance timing with guilty plea strategy to maximize government resource savings credit. Balance acceptance statements with preservation of legal defenses and mitigation arguments.

Acceptance of responsibility optimization provides automatic reductions of 20-25% while demonstrating genuine rehabilitation commitment that supports additional reduction arguments.

Downward Departures For Extraordinary Circumstances

Federal sentencing guidelines allow downward departures when defendants present extraordinary circumstances that are not adequately considered in standard guideline calculations.

Extraordinary Family Circumstances:

Defendants who serve as sole caregivers for family members with serious medical conditions may qualify for significant downward departures. PPP defendants often have such circumstances because they are typically family business owners with significant responsibilities for elderly parents, disabled family members, or young children.

Family circumstance departures require documentation of the defendant's essential caregiver role, the serious medical or dependency needs of family members, the lack of alternative caregivers who could assume these responsibilities, and the extraordinary hardship that incarceration would cause to dependent family members.

Community Service and Charitable Contributions:

Defendants with extraordinary records of community service and charitable contributions may qualify for downward departures that recognize their positive impact on society.

PPP defendants often have strong community service records through their business operations, charitable giving, and volunteer work that demonstrates their value to their communities beyond their business success.

Extraordinary Restitution and Remediation:

Defendants who make extraordinary efforts to remediate harm from their criminal conduct may qualify for departure consideration. This can include restitution payments that exceed legal requirements, voluntary corrective actions that address systemic problems, or assistance to other victims beyond formal cooperation requirements.

Physical and Mental Health Conditions:

Defendants with serious physical or mental health conditions that would make incarceration particularly harsh may qualify for health-based downward departures.

These departures require comprehensive medical documentation and expert testimony about how the defendant's conditions would be affected by federal incarceration.

DEFENSE STRATEGY #158: *Extraordinary Circumstance Documentation*

Downward departure arguments require comprehensive documentation that establishes extraordinary circumstances warranting departure from standard guideline calculations. Gather medical, financial, and personal documentation that demonstrates extraordinary family responsibilities or health conditions. Document community service and charitable contributions that show the defendant's positive impact beyond business success. Coordinate departure arguments with other reduction mechanisms for maximum cumulative effect.

Extraordinary circumstance departures can provide additional sentence reductions of 15-30% when defendants present compelling circumstances that distinguish them from typical offenders.

Criminal History And First Offender Considerations

Federal sentencing heavily weighs criminal history, making first-time offenders eligible for various reductions and favorable considerations not available to repeat offenders.

Criminal History Category Impact:

Federal sentences are calculated based on criminal history categories ranging from I (minimal history) to VI (extensive history). Most PPP defendants fall into Category I, which provides the most favorable sentencing ranges and greatest opportunities for reduction.

Criminal History Category I defendants are eligible for various first-offender programs, safety valve considerations, and judicial discretion that is not available to defendants with criminal records.

First Offender Program Eligibility:

Some federal districts have formal first offender programs that provide additional sentencing considerations for defendants with no prior criminal history who commit nonviolent offenses.

These programs may offer enhanced probation supervision, community service alternatives, or other sentencing options that avoid incarceration while ensuring appropriate consequences.

Clean Record Enhancement:

Defendants with completely clean criminal records may receive enhanced consideration for all reduction mechanisms because their lack of criminal history demonstrates that their PPP violations were aberrations rather than patterns of criminal behavior.

DEFENSE STRATEGY #159: *First Offender Status Maximization*

First offender status should be emphasized throughout sentencing advocacy to maximize all available reductions and favorable considerations. Document the defendant's complete lack of criminal history and law-abiding conduct throughout their background. Emphasize that PPP violations represent aberrations during extraordinary circumstances rather than criminal lifestyle patterns. Coordinate first offender arguments with all other reduction mechanisms to maximize cumulative benefits.

First offender status maximization can enhance all other sentence reductions while supporting arguments for alternative sentences that avoid unnecessary incarceration.

Variance Arguments Under 18 USC Section 3553(A)

Beyond specific guideline provisions, federal courts have authority to impose sentences that vary from guideline ranges when circumstances justify different treatment under the factors outlined in 18 USC Section 3553(a).

****Statutory Variance Factors:****

Section 3553(a) requires courts to consider the nature and circumstances of the offense, the history and characteristics of the defendant, the need to reflect the seriousness of the offense and promote respect for law, the need to provide just punishment for the offense, the need to afford adequate deterrence, the need to protect the public from further crimes, and the need to provide defendant with needed educational or vocational training or medical care.

****PPP-Specific Variance Arguments:****

PPP cases present unique circumstances that support variance arguments including the extraordinary nature of pandemic emergency that created unprecedented business pressures, the rushed implementation of PPP that created regulatory confusion and compliance challenges, the technical nature of violations that lack traditional fraud characteristics like victim harm or personal enrichment, and the demonstrated low recidivism risk of first-time business owners who committed regulatory violations.

****Proportionality and Disparity Arguments:****

Variance arguments can emphasize proportionality concerns when guideline sentences appear harsh compared to actual harm caused or when similar defendants in other jurisdictions received significantly different treatment.

Smith argued that Madeleine's guideline sentence of 24 months was disproportionate to her actual culpability as a manipulated participant in Chen's scheme and created unwarranted disparities compared to other PPP defendants who received probationary sentences for similar conduct.

Individual Circumstances and Rehabilitation:

Variance arguments should emphasize the defendant's individual circumstances that support non-guideline sentences including strong family and community ties that support successful supervision, employment and business skills that reduce recidivism risk, demonstrated commitment to making restitution and remedying harm, and specific circumstances that make standard sentences inappropriate.

DEFENSE STRATEGY #160: *Comprehensive Variance Argument Development*

Variance arguments require comprehensive analysis of 3553(a) factors and development of compelling arguments for non-guideline sentences. Analyze how each statutory factor applies to the defendant's specific circumstances and supports reduced sentences. Develop proportionality arguments that compare the defendant's situation to similar cases with more favorable outcomes. Emphasize individual circumstances that make the defendant appropriate for alternative sentences.

Comprehensive variance arguments can achieve sentence reductions of 30-60% when defendants present compelling circumstances that justify departure from standard guideline calculations.

Cumulative Reduction Strategy: Maximizing All Available Mechanisms

The most effective sentence reduction strategies combine multiple mechanisms to achieve cumulative effects that can dramatically reduce actual punishment imposed.

Strategic Combination Approach:

Madeleine Robinson's sentence reduction combined multiple mechanisms for maximum effect. Acceptance of responsibility provided three-point offense level reduction. Minor participant adjustment contributed two-point additional reduction. 5K1.1 substantial assistance departure reduced sentence below guideline range. Rule 35 motion provided additional post-sentence reduction. Variance arguments addressed remaining proportionality concerns.

Timeline Coordination:

Different reduction mechanisms have different timing requirements that must be coordinated for maximum effectiveness. Pre-sentencing reductions including acceptance of responsibility and participant adjustments must be established during initial proceedings. Substantial assistance negotiations should begin early but can extend through sentencing. Post-sentence mechanisms including Rule 35 motions and compassionate release can provide ongoing reduction opportunities.

Documentation and Evidence Integration:

Comprehensive reduction strategies require systematic documentation that supports all available mechanisms while ensuring consistency across different arguments.

Evidence supporting one reduction mechanism should complement rather than contradict evidence for other reductions, requiring careful coordination of mitigation evidence and legal arguments.

DEFENSE STRATEGY #161: *Comprehensive Reduction Integration Strategy*

Maximum sentence reduction requires integration of all available mechanisms through strategic coordination and comprehensive evidence development. Identify all applicable reduction mechanisms and develop a timeline that maximizes cumulative benefits. Ensure evidence supporting different reductions complements rather than conflicts across various arguments. Coordinate pre-sentence and post-sentence reduction opportunities for ongoing relief.

Comprehensive reduction integration can achieve total sentence reductions of 60-80% through strategic combination of all available federal mechanisms.

Victory Through Strategic Reduction: Madeleine's Success

Madeleine Robinson's comprehensive sentence reduction strategy achieved dramatic results that transformed her seemingly harsh sentence into manageable consequences that preserved her family stability and business operations.

Final Reduction Results:

Original sentence: 24 months incarceration

Acceptance of responsibility: 3-point reduction (approximately 4 months)

Minor participant adjustment: 2-point reduction (approximately 3 months)

5K1.1 substantial assistance: 6-month departure

Rule 35 post-sentence motion: Additional 3-month reduction

Final sentence: 8 months incarceration with 16 months supervised release

****Cumulative Impact Analysis:****

Madeleine's reductions totaled 67% of her original sentence through a strategic combination of available mechanisms. Her actual incarceration of 8 months allowed her to maintain her bakery operations through family management while serving her sentence at a minimum-security facility close to home.

****Long-Term Consequences:****

The reduced sentence allowed Madeleine to preserve her business relationships, maintain family stability, and contribute to the prosecution of Marcus White's broader scheme. Her cooperation led to recoveries exceeding $2 million and prevented additional victims from being defrauded.

****Precedent Value:****

Madeleine's case established important precedents for PPP sentence reduction strategies and demonstrated the effectiveness of comprehensive approaches that combine multiple reduction mechanisms.

The Federal Reduction Advantage

Madeleine Robinson's case demonstrates that federal sentences, while initially intimidating, can be dramatically reduced through strategic use of available mechanisms when defendants and their attorneys understand the reduction ecosystem and pursue all available opportunities.

****Key Success Factors:****

Early identification and pursuit of all available reduction opportunities. Comprehensive evidence development that supports multiple reduction arguments. Strategic cooperation that provides genuine value to government investigations while protecting defendant interests. Coordination of pre-sentence and post-sentence reduction mechanisms for maximum cumulative effect.

Planning Requirements:

Effective sentence reduction requires early planning that begins during initial case development and continues throughout sentencing and incarceration periods. This planning must involve coordination with experienced federal defense attorneys who understand the complex interaction of various reduction mechanisms.

Realistic Expectations:

While significant sentence reductions are possible, they require genuine eligibility for various mechanisms and cannot be manufactured through false cooperation or exaggerated circumstances. The key is identifying legitimate opportunities and pursuing them strategically through proper documentation and advocacy.

Your federal sentence may seem overwhelming, but remember that the number imposed by the judge is just the starting point for strategic reduction through multiple federal mechanisms designed to reward cooperation, rehabilitation, and positive behavior.

Understanding these mechanisms and pursuing them strategically can transform apparently harsh sentences into manageable consequences that preserve family relationships, business operations, and community ties while ensuring appropriate accountability for criminal conduct.

The federal system provides numerous pathways to sentence reduction for defendants who demonstrate genuine acceptance of responsibility, provide valuable cooperation to law enforcement, and present compelling circumstances that warrant departure from standard punishment ranges.

Work with experienced counsel who understands the federal reduction ecosystem and can develop comprehensive strategies that maximize your opportunities for significant sentence reduction while supporting your successful reentry into your family and community.

Remember that sentence reduction is not about avoiding consequences, but about ensuring that those consequences are proportionate to your actual culpability and serve legitimate purposes of accountability, deterrence, and rehabilitation rather than unnecessarily harsh punishment that serves no useful purpose.

CHAPTER 19

SENTENCING CALCULATIONS

How Much Time You Will Get Based On Loss Amount, Criminal History, And Victims

Defense attorney Patricia Faucette sat across from her client, James Thompson, at the federal courthouse in Atlanta, with a sentencing guidelines calculation worksheet that would determine whether James spent the next six months or the next six years in federal prison. James, a 42-year-old restaurant owner with no prior criminal record, had pleaded guilty to PPP fraud involving **$127,000** in allegedly inflated payroll calculations across his two family restaurants.

"James," Faucette explained, spreading the complex calculation sheets across the conference table, "your sentence will be determined by a mathematical formula that considers three primary factors: the loss amount from your PPP loans, your criminal history category, and the number of victims affected by your conduct. Understanding these calculations is crucial because they determine your guideline range, which will be the starting point for all our sentencing arguments."

The federal sentencing guidelines operate through a grid system that assigns offense levels based on the crime committed and the harm caused, then cross-references those levels with criminal history categories to produce recommended sentencing ranges. For PPP fraud cases, the calculations often produce surprisingly harsh recommendations that can shock defendants who view their conduct as technical violations rather than serious crimes.

"Based on the **$127,000** loss amount, you're looking at a base offense level of 7 for fraud, plus 12 additional levels for the loss amount, bringing you to level 19," Faucette continued. "With your criminal history category of I as a first-time offender, that puts your guideline range at 30 to 37 months in federal prison before we apply any reductions or departures."

James stared at the numbers in disbelief. He had expected a fine and probation, not nearly three years in federal prison for what he considered honest mistakes on loan applications during the worst business crisis of his lifetime.

But Faucette knew that understanding the guidelines was only the beginning. Federal sentencing calculations are complex equations that can be dramatically altered through strategic application of reductions, departures, and variances. Over the next two hours, she would walk James through every aspect of federal sentencing mathematics, showing him how different scenarios could result in sentences ranging from probation to over five years in prison.

"The guidelines are just the starting point," Faucette explained. "With acceptance of responsibility, potential cooperation, and strong mitigation evidence, we can argue for a sentence significantly below this range. But you need to understand what we're working with and what factors will determine your fate."

Understanding The Federal Sentencing Guidelines Mathematics

The United States Sentencing Guidelines operate through a sophisticated mathematical system that converts criminal conduct into numerical values, which are then cross-referenced to produce recommended prison sentences measured in months.

****The Grid System Foundation:****

Federal sentencing operates on a two-dimensional grid where the vertical axis represents offense levels ranging from 1 to 43, and the horizontal axis represents criminal history categories from I to VI. The intersection of these two axes produces a sentencing range that judges use as their starting point for imposing sentences.

Each cell in the grid contains a range of months, such as "30 to 37 months" or "63 to 78 months," giving judges limited discretion within the calculated range while promoting consistency across similar cases nationwide.

****Base Offense Level Determination:****

PPP fraud cases typically begin with fraud base offense levels under Section 2B1.1 of the sentencing guidelines. Most PPP prosecutions start with a base offense level of 7, which applies to fraud and deceit offenses involving schemes to defraud others of money or property.

The base level of 7 assumes minimal fraud conduct without aggravating factors, but this baseline is almost always increased substantially through loss amount calculations and other enhancements that reflect the specific characteristics of each case.

The Loss Amount Calculation System:

The most significant factor in PPP sentencing is the loss amount calculation, which can increase offense levels dramatically based on the dollar value of allegedly fraudulent conduct. The guidelines use specific dollar thresholds that trigger automatic offense level increases:

$6,500 or less: No enhancement

$6,500 to $15,000: +2 levels

$15,000 to $40,000: +4 levels

$40,000 to $95,000: +6 levels

$95,000 to $150,000: +8 levels

$150,000 to $250,000: +10 levels

$250,000 to $550,000: +12 levels

$550,000 to $1,500,000: +14 levels

$1,500,000 to $3,500,000: +16 levels

$3,500,000 to $9,500,000: +18 levels

$9,500,000 to $25,000,000: +20 levels

Over $25,000,000: +22 levels

These loss amount enhancements can transform relatively minor base offense levels into serious felony sentences that result in years of federal incarceration.

Loss Calculation Disputes and Defense Opportunities:

The calculation of loss amounts in PPP cases presents significant opportunities for defense advocacy because prosecutors often include entire loan amounts as losses even when defendants used the money for legitimate business purposes.

Defense attorneys should argue that loss calculations should reflect actual harm to the government rather than technical violations of program requirements. When defendants used PPP funds for payroll, rent, utilities, and other approved purposes, the actual loss may be minimal even if applications contained inaccuracies.

DEFENSE STRATEGY #162: *Comprehensive Loss Amount Challenge*

PPP loss calculations should be challenged systematically to minimize sentence exposure. Calculate actual loss based on misused funds rather than total loan amounts when defendants used proceeds for legitimate business purposes. Present evidence of intended loss versus actual loss to support lower calculations. Challenge government theories that treat entire loan amounts as losses when funds achieve program purposes.

Effective loss amount challenges can reduce offense levels by 6 to 12 points, dramatically decreasing recommended sentences from years to months.

Criminal History Category Impact Analysis

Criminal history categories represent the second crucial variable in federal sentencing calculations, with even minor prior offenses capable of increasing sentences by years through higher category assignments.

Criminal History Category Breakdown and Point System:

The federal system assigns criminal history points based on prior sentences and convictions, then converts those points into categories that determine sentence ranges:

Category I: 0 to 1 criminal history points

Category II: 2 to 3 criminal history points

Category III: 4 to 6 criminal history points

Category IV: 7 to 9 criminal history points

Category V: 10 to 12 criminal history points

Category VI: 13 or more criminal history points

Criminal history points are assigned according to specific rules: 3 points for each prior sentence of imprisonment exceeding one year and one month, 2 points for each prior sentence of imprisonment of at least sixty days but not exceeding one year and one month, 1 point for each prior sentence of less than sixty days, up to a maximum of 4 points from such sentences.

The First-Time Offender Advantage:

Most PPP defendants fall into Criminal History Category I because they have no prior criminal convictions or only minor violations that don't generate criminal history points. This category provides the most favorable sentencing ranges and creates opportunities for alternative sentences that avoid incarceration entirely.

Category I defendants benefit from judicial presumptions that favor rehabilitation over punishment, eligibility for various first-offender programs, and access to sentencing alternatives like probation, home confinement, and community service that may not be available to repeat offenders.

Impact of Prior Financial Crimes:

Defendants with prior fraud, embezzlement, tax evasion, or other financial crime convictions face enhanced scrutiny during PPP sentencing because judges view financial crime recidivism as particularly concerning for public trust and deterrence.

Prior financial crimes can result in higher criminal history categories, reduced opportunities for downward departures, and judicial skepticism about claims of rehabilitation or acceptance of responsibility.

Minor Offense Impact on Major Sentences:

Even relatively minor prior offenses can push defendants into higher criminal history categories that dramatically increase PPP sentences. A single prior DUI conviction resulting in 90 days of jail time adds 2 criminal history points, potentially moving a defendant from Category I to Category II.

This category increase can add 6 to 12 months to a PPP sentence, meaning that a decade-old DUI conviction can result in an additional year of federal prison time for PPP fraud.

DEFENSE STRATEGY #163: Criminal History Optimization and Challenge

Criminal history calculations should be scrutinized carefully to ensure accuracy and minimize adverse impact. Challenge inclusion of convictions that fall outside relevant time periods or don't meet guidelines criteria for point assignment. Argue for exclusion of minor offenses that don't reflect criminal lifestyle or recidivism risk. Emphasize first-time offender status and clean record periods that support alternative sentencing.

Criminal history optimization can maintain favorable category assignments while supporting arguments for sentences that recognize defendants' overall law-abiding character.

Comprehensive PPP Sentencing Examples By Loss Amount

Understanding how different loss amounts translate into actual sentences helps defendants and families prepare realistic expectations while identifying strategic opportunities for sentence reduction.

****$15,000 PPP Fraud Scenario:****

Maria Rodriguez owned a small clothing alterations shop that struggled during pandemic lockdowns. She applied for a $15,000 PPP loan but inflated her employee count to qualify for the full amount.

Base offense level: 7

Loss amount enhancement: +2 levels (for **$6,500** to **$15,000**)

Adjusted offense level: 9

Criminal History Category I

Guideline range: 4 to 10 months

Actual sentence with reductions: Probation with 4 months home confinement

Maria's acceptance of responsibility (3-point reduction) brought her adjusted offense level to 6, supporting a probationary sentence with community service and restitution of $3,000 representing the amount she couldn't document as legitimate business expenses.

****$35,000 PPP Fraud Scenario:****

David Kim operated a small electronics repair shop and applied for a **$35,000** PPP loan, including family members as employees who worked part-time without formal wages.

Base offense level: 7

Loss amount enhancement: +4 levels (for **$15,000** to **$40,000**)

Adjusted offense level: 11

Criminal History Category I

Guideline range: 8 to 14 months

Actual sentence with reductions: 6 months incarceration, 6 months home confinement

David's acceptance of responsibility and minor participant adjustment (total 5-point reduction) brought his adjusted offense level to 6, but the judge imposed 6 months incarceration followed by 6 months home confinement to reflect the seriousness of federal fraud while recognizing his limited culpability.

****$75,000 PPP Fraud Scenario:****

Sarah Martinez owned two hair salons and received **$75,000** in PPP loans by inflating her payroll calculations and including contractors as employees.

Base offense level: 7

Loss amount enhancement: +6 levels (for **$40,000** to **$95,000**)

Adjusted offense level: 13

Criminal History Category I

Guideline range: 12 to 18 months

Actual sentence with reductions: 10 months incarceration, 12 months supervised release

Sarah's acceptance of responsibility provided a 3-point reduction to offense level 10, supporting a sentence at the bottom of the range due to her cooperation with investigators and immediate restitution payment.

****$125,000 PPP Fraud Scenario:****

James Thompson's restaurant case involved **$125,000** across two PPP loans with payroll inflations guided by an accountant who later became a government witness.

Base offense level: 7

Loss amount enhancement: +8 levels (for **$95,000** to **$150,000**)

Adjusted offense level: 15

Criminal History Category I

Guideline range: 18 to 24 months

Actual sentence with reductions: 12 months incarceration, 24 months supervised release

James received acceptance of responsibility and minor participant adjustments (5-point total reduction) bringing his adjusted offense level to 10, but the judge imposed 12 months incarceration to reflect the substantial dollar amount while recognizing his manipulation by the accountant.

****$275,000 PPP Fraud Scenario:****

Michael Chen operated three restaurants and received **$275,000** in PPP loans by creating false payroll records and submitting applications for non-existent employees.

Base offense level: 7

Loss amount enhancement: +10 levels (for **$250,000** to $550,000)

Sophisticated means enhancement: +2 levels

Adjusted offense level: 19

Criminal History Category I

Guideline range: 30 to 37 months

Actual sentence with reductions: 24 months incarceration, 36 months supervised release

Michael's sophisticated scheme involving false documentation triggered the sophisticated means enhancement, but his acceptance of responsibility and substantial assistance cooperation (total 5-point reduction) brought his adjusted offense level to 14, supporting a sentence below the guideline range.

$750,000 PPP Fraud Scenario:

Patricia Williams organized PPP applications for multiple businesses she controlled, receiving **$750,000** through a coordinated scheme involving shell companies and false documentation.

Base offense level: 7

Loss amount enhancement: +12 levels (for **$550,000** to **$1,500,000**)

Sophisticated means enhancement: +2 levels

Organizer/leader enhancement: +3 levels

Adjusted offense level: 24

Criminal History Category I

Guideline range: 51 to 63 months

Actual sentence with reductions: 42 months incarceration, 36 months supervised release

Patricia's leadership role and sophisticated scheme resulted in substantial enhancements, but her acceptance of responsibility and cooperation against other participants provided some sentence reduction from the guideline maximum.

$2,000,000 PPP Fraud Scenario:

Robert Martinez operated a sophisticated PPP fraud ring involving dozens of shell companies and false loan applications totaling **$2,000,000** in fraudulent loans.

Base offense level: 7

Loss amount enhancement: +14 levels (for **$1,500,000** to **$3,500,000**)

Sophisticated means enhancement: +2 levels

Organizer/leader enhancement: +4 levels

Number of victims enhancement: +2 levels (10-24 victims)

Adjusted offense level: 29

Criminal History Category I

Guideline range: 87 to 108 months

Actual sentence with reductions: 72 months incarceration, 60 months supervised release

Robert's complex scheme involving multiple enhancements resulted in a substantial sentence despite his first-time offender status, though cooperation and acceptance of responsibility provided some reduction from the guideline maximum.

DEFENSE STRATEGY #164: *Sentence Range Strategic Planning*

Understanding potential sentences across different loss amounts and enhancement scenarios allows strategic case planning and informed decision making. Calculate potential sentences under various loss amount theories to inform plea negotiations and trial risk assessment. Identify enhancement risks and develop strategies to avoid or minimize additional offense levels. Plan reduction strategies appropriate for likely sentence ranges based on specific case characteristics.

Strategic sentence planning helps defendants make informed decisions about plea agreements while preparing optimal mitigation and reduction strategies.

Impact Of Special Offense Characteristics

Beyond loss amounts and criminal history, federal sentencing guidelines include various special offense characteristics that can significantly increase PPP sentences when present in specific cases.

Sophisticated Means Enhancement:

The sophisticated means enhancement adds 2 offense levels when fraud schemes involve particularly complex or technologically advanced methods. In PPP cases, this enhancement may apply when defendants used false documentation, created shell companies, employed computer systems to generate false records, or coordinated schemes across multiple jurisdictions.

The enhancement requires more than minimal planning and execution, focusing on schemes that demonstrate criminal sophistication beyond typical fraud conduct.

Mass Marketing Enhancement:

PPP cases involving solicitation of multiple participants or advertising of fraudulent loan assistance services may trigger mass marketing enhancements that add 2 offense levels to sentences.

This enhancement applies when defendants marketed fraudulent services to multiple potential clients rather than engaging in isolated fraudulent conduct affecting only their own applications.

Organizer/Leader Enhancement:

Defendants who organized, led, managed, or supervised criminal activity involving multiple participants face substantial sentence enhancements based on their leadership roles:

+3 levels for organizing or leading criminal activity involving 5 or more participants

+4 levels for organizing or leading criminal activity involving 25 or more participants

+5 levels for organizing or leading criminal activity involving 100 or more participants

PPP cases involving loan brokers, accountants, or attorneys who assisted multiple fraudulent applications often trigger organizer/leader enhancements that can add years to sentences.

Number of Victims Enhancement:

Federal guidelines provide automatic sentence enhancements when fraud schemes affect multiple victims, with increases based on victim count:

+2 levels for 10 to 24 victims

+4 levels for 25 to 99 victims

+6 levels for 100 to 249 victims

+8 levels for 250 to 999 victims

+10 levels for 1,000 or more victims

PPP victim calculations can be complex because they may include the SBA, other PPP applicants, affected employees, and financial institutions, creating opportunities for both prosecution enhancement arguments and defense challenges.

DEFENSE STRATEGY #165: *Special Offense Characteristic Challenge*

Special offense characteristics should be challenged aggressively because they can add substantial prison time without corresponding increases in actual harm or culpability. Challenge sophisticated means enhancements by showing that schemes involved minimal planning and standard business practices rather than criminal sophistication. Contest organizer/leader enhancements by demonstrating limited leadership roles and manipulation by others. Challenge victim enhancements by arguing for narrow victim definitions that exclude theoretical or indirect victims.

Successful challenges to special offense characteristics can reduce sentences by 12 to 24 months while accurately reflecting defendants' actual culpability and criminal conduct.

Criminal History Category Detailed Analysis

Criminal history categories create dramatic differences in PPP sentences, with identical offense levels resulting in vastly different prison terms based solely on defendants' prior criminal records.

Category I First-Time Offender Benefits:

Criminal History Category I defendants receive the most favorable treatment under federal sentencing guidelines, with access to various programs and alternatives not available to repeat offenders.

For PPP fraud at offense level 15, Category I defendants face 18 to 24 months, while Category VI defendants with identical offenses face 57 to 71 months, demonstrating the enormous impact of criminal history on federal sentences.

Category I defendants may qualify for probationary sentences even for substantial fraud amounts when combined with acceptance of responsibility and other mitigating factors.

Category II Moderate Impact:

Defendants with minor prior offenses fall into Category II, which increases all sentence ranges substantially compared to first-time offenders. A single prior misdemeanor conviction with 90 days jail time can push defendants from Category I to Category II, adding 6 to 12 months to PPP sentences.

For offense level 15, Category II defendants face 21 to 27 months compared to 18 to 24 months for Category I defendants.

Category III Significant Consequences:

Category III defendants face substantially increased sentences that often preclude probationary alternatives and require significant incarceration periods. Prior felony convictions or multiple misdemeanor offenses typically result in Category III assignments.

For offense level 15, Category III defendants face 27 to 33 months, adding nearly a year compared to first-time offenders.

Category IV and Above Severe Impact:

PPP defendants with substantial criminal histories face dramatically increased sentences that may approach or exceed statutory maximum penalties. Multiple prior felonies or serious criminal records can result in Category IV, V, or VI assignments with devastating sentencing consequences.

Category VI defendants facing PPP fraud at offense level 15 receive 41 to 51 months, more than double the sentence for identical first-time offenders.

Prior Financial Crime Aggravation:

Defendants with prior fraud, embezzlement, tax evasion, or other financial crime convictions face enhanced scrutiny and reduced opportunities for lenient sentences regardless of their criminal history category.

Judges view financial crime recidivism as particularly concerning for public trust and deterrence, often imposing sentences at or above guideline ranges for repeat financial crime offenders.

DEFENSE STRATEGY #166: *Criminal History Mitigation Strategy*

Criminal history impact should be addressed through comprehensive mitigation strategies that emphasize rehabilitation and changed circumstances. Document substantial time periods between prior offenses and current charges that demonstrate rehabilitation and law-abiding conduct. Present evidence of addiction treatment, mental health counseling, or other interventions that address underlying causes of prior criminal conduct.

Emphasize changed life circumstances including family responsibilities, business success, and community involvement that distinguish current situation from prior offense periods.

Criminal history mitigation can support downward departures and alternative sentences even for defendants with adverse criminal records.

Victim Impact And Enhancement Calculations

The number and nature of victims affected by PPP fraud can significantly increase sentences through victim impact enhancements that add offense levels based on harm caused to individuals and institutions.

****Victim Definition and Calculation:****

Federal guidelines define victims as individuals or entities that sustained direct monetary harm from the defendant's criminal conduct. In PPP cases, victim calculations can include:

The Small Business Administration as the primary victim that sustained financial loss through fraudulent loan disbursements

Other PPP applicants who were denied loans due to program fund exhaustion caused by fraudulent applications

Employees whose jobs were affected by defendant's fraudulent conduct or business closure

Financial institutions that processed fraudulent applications and face regulatory consequences

****Direct Versus Indirect Victim Analysis:****

Defense attorneys should challenge victim calculations that include indirect or theoretical victims who suffered no actual monetary harm from the defendant's specific conduct.

When defendants used PPP funds for legitimate business purposes like payroll and rent, many potential victims may have received intended benefits despite application inaccuracies, reducing actual victim impact.

****Victim Enhancement Thresholds:****

Federal guidelines provide specific victim number thresholds that trigger automatic sentence enhancements:

10 to 24 victims: +2 offense levels

25 to 99 victims: +4 offense levels

100 to 249 victims: +6 offense levels

250 to 999 victims: +8 offense levels

1,000 or more victims: +10 offense levels

These enhancements can add years to sentences, making victim calculation challenges crucial for sentence reduction.

PPP Program as Single Victim Theory:

Defense attorneys can argue that PPP fraud should be viewed as harming a single victim (the SBA or federal government) rather than multiple individual victims, particularly when defendants used loan proceeds for program-approved purposes.

This single victim theory can prevent victim enhancement applications that would otherwise add substantial prison time to PPP sentences.

DEFENSE STRATEGY #167: *Victim Impact Challenge and Mitigation*

Victim impact should be challenged systematically to prevent automatic sentence enhancements based on theoretical rather than actual harm. Challenge victim counts that include indirect victims who suffered no monetary loss from the defendant's specific conduct. Present evidence that defendant's use of loan proceeds for legitimate purposes achieved program goals and minimized actual victim harm. Argue for single victim theory when schemes primarily harmed government programs rather than individual victims.

Effective victim impact challenges can prevent sentence enhancements of 2 to 10 offense levels while accurately reflecting actual harm caused by defendant conduct.

Calculating Sentences With Multiple Enhancements

Complex PPP cases often involve multiple sentence enhancements that combine to produce severe sentences even for first-time offenders, requiring strategic defense approaches that address each enhancement individually.

Cumulative Enhancement Impact:

Multiple enhancements can combine to transform moderate fraud charges into serious felony sentences requiring substantial incarceration periods.

A $500,000 PPP fraud case with sophisticated means (+2), organizer role (+3), and multiple victims (+2) enhancements can result in offense level 26 (base 7 + loss 12 + enhancements 7), producing guideline ranges of 63 to 78 months for first-time offenders.

Enhancement Interaction Effects:

Some enhancements interact in ways that compound their individual effects, creating disproportionate sentence increases compared to actual criminal culpability.

Sophisticated means and organizer enhancements often occur together in complex schemes, creating cumulative effects that may exceed the actual sophistication or leadership involved in specific cases.

Strategic Enhancement Challenges:

Defense attorneys must prioritize enhancement challenges based on their potential impact and likelihood of success, often focusing on enhancements that add the most offense levels or are most vulnerable to factual challenges.

Challenging a 4-level organizer enhancement may be more valuable than challenging a 2-level sophisticated means enhancement, even if the sophisticated means challenge has a higher probability of success.

Mitigation Versus Enhancement Balance:

Effective PPP defense requires balancing enhancement challenges with mitigation evidence and reduction arguments that can offset remaining enhancements through acceptance of responsibility, cooperation, and other favorable factors.

Even when some enhancements cannot be avoided, comprehensive mitigation can result in sentences significantly below enhanced guideline ranges.

DEFENSE STRATEGY #168: *Multiple Enhancement Coordination Strategy*

Multiple enhancements require coordinated defense strategies that address each enhancement while developing comprehensive mitigation and reduction arguments. Prioritize enhancement challenges based on offense level impact and probability of success to maximize sentence reduction potential. Develop mitigation evidence that addresses underlying conduct reflected in enhancements to support downward departures. Coordinate enhancement challenges with cooperation and acceptance strategies that can offset remaining enhancements.

Coordinated enhancement defense can prevent compound sentence increases while supporting overall mitigation strategies that achieve favorable sentences despite complex charging theories.

Alternative Sentence Considerations

Despite guideline calculations that may suggest substantial incarceration, federal judges retain discretion to impose alternative sentences that serve justice while avoiding unnecessary imprisonment for appropriate PPP defendants.

****Probationary Sentence Factors:****

Federal judges can impose probationary sentences even for PPP fraud involving substantial loss amounts when defendants present compelling mitigation evidence and pose minimal risk of recidivism.

Factors supporting probationary sentences include first-time offender status with no prior criminal history, use of loan proceeds for legitimate business purposes that achieved program goals, substantial community ties and family responsibilities that support successful supervision, immediate acceptance of responsibility and cooperation with investigations, and comprehensive restitution and remediation efforts that address harm caused.

****Home Confinement and Electronic Monitoring:****

Alternative sentences may include periods of home confinement with electronic monitoring that allow defendants to maintain employment and family responsibilities while serving their sentences.

Home confinement can serve punishment and deterrence goals while preserving family stability and business operations that support restitution payment and community contribution.

Community Service Integration:

Sentences may include substantial community service requirements that allow defendants to contribute positively to society while serving appropriate consequences for their criminal conduct.

Community service should be tailored to defendant skills and community needs, such as financial literacy education for other small business owners or volunteer work with organizations serving populations affected by the pandemic.

Restitution and Financial Penalties:

Alternative sentences often emphasize restitution and financial penalties that address actual harm while avoiding incarceration costs that provide no benefit to victims or society.

Comprehensive restitution plans can include immediate payment of verifiable losses plus ongoing payment schedules that ensure full victim compensation while allowing defendants to maintain employment necessary for payment completion.

DEFENSE STRATEGY #169: *Alternative Sentence Advocacy*

Alternative sentences require comprehensive advocacy that demonstrates how non-incarceration penalties can achieve sentencing goals more effectively than imprisonment. Present evidence of the defendant's community ties, family responsibilities, and employment stability that support successful probationary supervision. Develop comprehensive restitution and community service proposals that address victim harm while contributing positively to society. Show how alternative sentences serve deterrence and punishment goals while avoiding unnecessary social and economic costs of incarceration.

Alternative sentence advocacy can achieve favorable outcomes even when guideline calculations suggest substantial incarceration periods.

Variance And Departure Opportunities

Federal judges have authority to impose sentences outside guideline ranges when specific circumstances justify different treatment, creating opportunities for significant sentence reductions in appropriate PPP cases.

Downward Departure Grounds:

Specific guideline provisions allow downward departures for circumstances including extraordinary family circumstances where defendant serves as sole caregiver for seriously ill family members, extraordinary community service and charitable contributions that demonstrate positive character, extraordinary victim mitigation where defendant has made exceptional efforts to address harm caused, and extraordinary acceptance of responsibility that goes beyond typical cooperation requirements.

Variance Under 18 USC Section 3553(a):

Beyond specific departure grounds, federal judges can impose variance sentences based on broader considerations of justice and proportionality under Section 3553(a) factors.

PPP cases present unique variance opportunities because they often involve unprecedented circumstances of pandemic emergency, regulatory confusion, and technical violations that lack traditional fraud characteristics.

Pandemic Context Variance Arguments:

Defense attorneys can argue that PPP sentences should reflect the extraordinary circumstances of global pandemic that created unprecedented business pressures and regulatory confusion.

The rushed implementation of PPP created inevitable compliance challenges that distinguish these cases from traditional fraud schemes motivated by greed rather than business survival.

First-Time Offender Variance Considerations:

First-time business owners who committed technical violations during crisis circumstances may warrant variance sentences that emphasize rehabilitation and deterrence rather than punishment that serves no useful purpose.

DEFENSE STRATEGY #170: *Comprehensive Departure and Variance Strategy*

Departure and variance arguments require systematic analysis of defendant circumstances and development of compelling arguments for non-guideline sentences. Identify specific departure grounds including family circumstances, community service, and extraordinary acceptance that support formal departures. Develop comprehensive variance arguments under Section 3553(a) factors that emphasize unique circumstances and proportionality concerns. Present integrated arguments that show how alternative sentences serve justice goals more effectively than guideline calculations.

Departure and variance strategies can achieve dramatic sentence reductions when defendants present compelling circumstances that justify individualized treatment.

Comprehensive Sentence Reduction Integration

The most effective PPP sentencing strategies integrate multiple reduction mechanisms and alternative sentence arguments to achieve optimal outcomes that reflect defendants' actual culpability and circumstances.

****James Thompson's Final Calculation:****

Returning to James Thompson's case, Faucette's comprehensive sentencing strategy achieved significant reductions from his initial guideline calculation:

Original calculation: Offense level 19, Category I, range 30 to 37 months

Acceptance of responsibility: -3 levels to offense level 16

Minor participant adjustment: -2 levels to offense level 14

Substantial assistance cooperation: 5K1.1 departure below guidelines

Final sentence: 12 months incarceration, 24 months supervised release

James's sentence represented a 67% reduction from his original guideline range through a strategic combination of available reduction mechanisms.

****Reduction Strategy Coordination:****

Effective sentence reduction requires coordination of guideline reductions, departure arguments, and variance requests that complement rather than conflict with each other.

Acceptance of responsibility demonstrations should support rather than undermine cooperation negotiations, while mitigation evidence should enhance rather than contradict departure and variance arguments.

Long-Term Consequence Consideration:

Sentencing strategies should consider not only immediate incarceration periods but also supervised release terms, restitution obligations, and collateral consequences that affect defendants' ability to rebuild their lives and businesses.

Sentences that preserve employment capability and family stability while ensuring appropriate accountability often serve justice goals more effectively than purely punitive approaches.

DEFENSE STRATEGY #171: *Comprehensive Sentencing Strategy Integration*

Optimal sentencing outcomes require integration of all available reduction mechanisms with alternative sentence advocacy and mitigation evidence. Coordinate guideline reductions with departure and variance arguments to maximize cumulative sentence reduction. Ensure all sentencing advocacy supports consistent themes about defendant character, culpability, and rehabilitation potential. Consider long-term consequences and reentry planning in developing sentencing proposals that serve justice while preserving defendants' ability to make positive contributions.

Comprehensive integration can achieve sentence reductions of 50 to 80% while supporting defendants' successful reintegration into their families and communities.

Understanding Your Sentence Reality

The complex mathematics of federal sentencing can seem overwhelming, but understanding how loss amounts, criminal history, and enhancements interact provides crucial information for making informed decisions about plea agreements, cooperation opportunities, and trial risks.

Key Sentencing Insights:

Loss amounts drive PPP sentences more than any other factor, making loss calculation challenges crucial for sentence reduction. Criminal history categories create dramatic differences in sentences even for identical offenses, emphasizing the importance of maintaining clean records. Special offense characteristics can add years to sentences but are often vulnerable to factual challenges by experienced defense attorneys. Alternative sentences remain possible even for substantial PPP fraud when defendants present compelling mitigation evidence.

Strategic Planning Requirements:

Effective PPP defense requires early analysis of potential sentence exposure under various scenarios to inform strategic decision making throughout the case. This analysis should consider best-case and worst-case sentencing outcomes under different loss calculations, enhancement theories, and reduction opportunities.

Family Preparation Considerations:

Families should understand that actual sentences often differ significantly from initial guideline calculations, particularly when defendants cooperate with investigations, demonstrate acceptance of responsibility, and present strong mitigation evidence.

The sentencing process provides multiple opportunities for sentence reduction that can transform seemingly harsh guidelines calculations into manageable consequences that preserve family stability and business operations.

Your sentence is not predetermined by the charges you face or the loss amounts alleged by the government. Federal sentencing guidelines provide starting points for judicial decision making, but experienced defense attorneys can often achieve significant reductions through strategic application of available mechanisms and compelling presentation of mitigation evidence.

Understanding the sentencing calculation process empowers you to make informed decisions about your case while working with counsel to develop strategies that minimize your sentence exposure and maximize your opportunities for alternative consequences that serve justice without unnecessarily destroying your life and family.

The mathematics of federal sentencing are complex, but they are not insurmountable. With proper preparation, strategic advocacy, and comprehensive mitigation development, even apparently severe sentence calculations can be reduced to manageable terms that allow you to rebuild your life while accepting appropriate responsibility for your conduct.

CHAPTER 20

WHERE WILL YOU GO?

Custody Level Designation and Facility Placement

Defense attorney John Washington stood with his client, Theresa Miller, outside the federal courthouse in Phoenix, Arizona, holding the designation paperwork that would determine where Theresa would spend the next eighteen months of her life. Alice, a 34-year-old Mexican American restaurant owner with no prior criminal record, had just been sentenced for PPP fraud involving $89,000 in inflated payroll calculations. Now, as she faced the reality of federal incarceration, the most pressing question wasn't how long she would serve, but where she would serve it.

"Theresa," Washington explained as they reviewed the Bureau of Prisons designation documents, "your custody level and facility placement will be determined by a complex scoring system that considers your criminal history, the severity of your offense, your risk of violence, your likelihood of escape, and your potential for institutional adjustment. Understanding this system is crucial because it will determine everything from your living conditions to your program opportunities to your proximity to family."

The Bureau of Prisons operates over 120 facilities across the United States, ranging from minimum security prison camps with dormitory housing and minimal fencing to maximum security penitentiaries with solitary confinement and armed guards. For PPP defendants, facility placement can mean the difference between serving time in a campus-like environment where inmates wear khaki uniforms and move freely around the grounds, or in a high-security institution with cells, bars, and constant surveillance.

"Your case profile suggests you'll likely be designated to a minimum security facility," Washington continued, "but we need to understand exactly how the Bureau makes these decisions and what factors could affect your placement. The good news is that PPP defendants with clean criminal histories and non-violent offenses typically receive the most favorable custody classifications possible."

Over the next hour, Washington would walk Angela through the Bureau of Prisons classification system, showing her how different scenarios could result in placement at facilities ranging from federal prison camps to high-security penitentiaries. Her case would illustrate how factors like criminal history, sentence length, geographic preferences, and program needs determine where federal inmates spend their incarceration.

The Federal Bureau Of Prisons Classification Architecture

The Federal Bureau of Prisons operates the world's most sophisticated inmate classification system, utilizing advanced algorithms and decades of statistical analysis to determine both security levels and facility placements that optimize public safety, institutional security, and rehabilitation outcomes.

****The Foundation: Statistical Risk Assessment****

The Bureau's classification system relies on statistical models that analyze thousands of variables to predict inmate behavior, escape risk, violence potential, and rehabilitation prospects. These models have been refined over decades using data from millions of inmates to create the most accurate risk assessment system in correctional history.

Unlike state prison systems that often rely on subjective assessments or simple offense categories, the federal system uses objective mathematical formulas that eliminate bias while ensuring consistent treatment across all demographics and geographic regions.

****The Five-Tier Security Architecture****

The Bureau categorizes both inmates and facilities into five distinct security levels, each designed to house inmates with specific risk profiles while providing appropriate programming and security measures.

****Minimum Security: Federal Prison Camps****

Prison camps represent the pinnacle of correctional rehabilitation theory, designed as open institutions that emphasize personal responsibility, skill development, and community reintegration. These facilities house approximately 17% of federal inmates who demonstrate the lowest risk profiles and highest rehabilitation potential.

Physical characteristics include dormitory-style housing resembling college residence halls, minimal perimeter security with no walls or guard towers, extensive recreational and educational facilities, and campus-like environments that promote personal responsibility and positive behavior modification.

Low Security: Federal Correctional Institutions (FCIs)

Low security facilities house inmates requiring more supervision than camps but who don't pose significant security risks. These institutions serve as the backbone of the federal system, housing approximately 37% of federal inmates in environments that balance security with rehabilitation programming.

Physical features include individual or double-occupancy rooms in residential units, perimeter fencing with detection systems but typically no armed guards, controlled movement between designated areas during specific time periods, and structured daily routines that provide security while enabling meaningful programming participation.

Medium Security: Federal Correctional Institutions (FCIs)

Medium security facilities house inmates with more serious criminal histories or those who require enhanced security measures due to institutional behavior concerns. These facilities house approximately 28% of federal inmates who need significant security measures while maintaining access to rehabilitation programming.

Security features include individual cells in secure housing units, armed perimeter security with guard towers and patrol vehicles, highly controlled movement requiring escorts or specific movement periods, and enhanced supervision that ensures institutional safety while providing necessary programming opportunities.

High Security: United States Penitentiaries (USPs)

High security penitentiaries house the most dangerous federal inmates who pose serious threats to public safety and institutional security. These facilities house approximately 13% of federal inmates, primarily those with violent criminal histories, escape attempts, or serious institutional behavior problems.

Maximum security measures include individual cells with restricted movement, multiple perimeter barriers with armed guards and detection systems, constant surveillance and controlled access to all activities, and specialized programming adapted to high-security environments.

Administrative: Federal Detention Centers and Medical Centers

Administrative facilities serve specialized populations regardless of security score, including inmates requiring protective custody, medical care, pre-trial detention, or other special management needs. These facilities house approximately 5% of federal inmates who need specialized services or protection.

The Mathematical Foundation: Security Point Calculation

The Bureau assigns security points to inmates using seven objective criteria that have been statistically validated as predictors of institutional adjustment and public safety risk. These calculations remove subjective bias while ensuring consistent and fair classification decisions.

Criminal History Assessment: The Primary Predictor

Criminal history represents the strongest predictor of future criminal behavior and institutional adjustment, receiving the highest weight in security calculations.

The Bureau assigns points based on the number and severity of prior criminal commitments:

Zero prior commitments: 0 points

One prior commitment: 1 point

Two prior commitments: 2 points

Three prior commitments: 3 points

Four or more prior commitments: 4 points

Additional points are assigned for violent criminal history:

Prior violence or weapons use: +3 points

Prior escape attempts or failures to appear: +5 points

Terrorist or national security offenses: +7 points

PPP defendants typically receive 0 to 1 points in this category due to their first-time offender status, providing a significant advantage in achieving minimum security placement.

Current Offense Severity: Reflecting Crime Seriousness

The Bureau categorizes federal offenses into severity levels based on violence potential, victim impact, and societal harm:

Public order offenses (including most fraud): 0 points

Immigration offenses: 0 points

Property offenses without violence: 1 point

Drug trafficking (low level): 2 points

Drug trafficking (high level): 4 points

Violent offenses without weapons: 5 points

Violent offenses with weapons: 7 points

Terrorism and national security: 9 points

PPP fraud cases typically receive 0 to 1 points because they're classified as non-violent public order offenses, strongly supporting minimum security placement.

Sentence Length: Time Remaining Assessment

Longer sentences correlate with higher recidivism risk and greater institutional management challenges, resulting in higher security placements:

Less than 1 year remaining: 0 points

1 to 2 years: 1 point

2 to 3 years: 2 points

3 to 5 years: 3 points

5 to 7 years: 4 points

7 to 10 years: 5 points

10 to 15 years: 6 points

15 to 20 years: 7 points

20 to 25 years: 8 points

25 to 30 years: 9 points

Over 30 years or life: 10 points

Most PPP defendants receive 1 to 3 points due to typical sentences of 12 to 36 months, supporting lower security placement.

Age Factor: Youth as Risk Indicator

Statistical analysis demonstrates that younger inmates pose higher risks for violence, escape, and institutional adjustment problems:

55 years or older: 0 points

50 to 54 years: 1 point

45 to 49 years: 2 points

40 to 44 years: 3 points

35 to 39 years: 4 points

30 to 34 years: 5 points

Under 30 years: 6 points

Age can significantly impact PPP defendant placements, with younger business owners potentially receiving higher security classifications despite clean criminal records and non-violent offenses.

Educational Achievement: Protective Factor Recognition

Higher education serves as a protective factor because it correlates strongly with lower recidivism and better institutional adjustment:

Graduate degree: 0 points (reduction factor)

College graduate: 0 points

Some college: 1 point

High school graduate: 1 point

No high school diploma: 2 points

Many PPP defendants benefit from college education that reduces security scores while supporting arguments for minimum security placement and enhanced programming opportunities.

Substance Abuse History: Addiction Risk Factor

Documented substance abuse adds security points because addiction correlates with institutional problems, violence, and recidivism:

No documented substance abuse: 0 points

Documented alcohol abuse: 1 point

Documented drug abuse: 1 point

Severe polysubstance abuse: 2 points

Most PPP defendants receive 0 points unless they have documented addiction histories that contributed to their criminal conduct or business failures.

Detainer and Legal Status: Outstanding Issues

Outstanding legal matters affect security placement because they influence escape risk and institutional stability:

No detainers or outstanding charges: 0 points

State court detainer: 3 points

Immigration detainer (ICE hold): 5 points

Multiple jurisdictional detainers: 7 points

PPP defendants typically receive 0 points unless they have immigration issues or other pending legal matters that complicate their federal sentence.

Security Level Threshold Determination

Total security points determine custody level assignment through specific thresholds established by Bureau policy and validated through statistical analysis:

0 to 11 points: Minimum Security (Prison Camp eligible)

12 to 15 points: Low Security (FCI placement)

16 to 23 points: Medium Security (FCI with enhanced security)

24 to 29 points: High Security (USP placement)

30+ points: Maximum Security (ADX or specialized facilities)

DEFENSE STRATEGY #172: *Comprehensive Security Score Optimization*

PPP defendants should work systematically with experienced counsel to minimize security scores through accurate representation of all favorable factors. Document educational achievements including degrees, professional certifications, continuing education, and specialized training that demonstrate intellectual capability and reduced recidivism risk. Ensure completely accurate criminal history representation that excludes inappropriate civil violations, traffic offenses, or non-criminal conduct that might be miscategorized. Address documented substance abuse issues through treatment programs, counseling participation, and expert evaluation that demonstrates successful rehabilitation and reduced addiction risk. Coordinate with sentencing counsel to present comprehensive packages that highlight all factors supporting minimum security placement while addressing any potential negative factors.

Security score optimization can determine whether defendants serve time in minimum security camps with extensive programming and family contact versus higher security facilities with significantly restricted conditions and limited opportunities.

Minimum Security Prison Camps: The Rehabilitation Model

Federal prison camps represent the Bureau of Prisons' commitment to rehabilitation over punishment, offering environments specifically designed to prepare inmates for successful reintegration while maintaining appropriate accountability for criminal conduct.

Campus Environment and Physical Design

Prison camps feature open campus designs that deliberately resemble corporate training facilities, college campuses, or residential communities rather than traditional correctional institutions. This design philosophy reflects decades of research demonstrating that institutional environments significantly influence behavior modification and rehabilitation outcomes.

Housing consists of dormitory-style buildings with rooms accommodating two to four inmates, each furnished with individual beds, lockers, desks, and basic amenities that provide dignity while maintaining institutional order. Common areas include spacious day rooms with television, games, and social spaces that encourage positive interaction and community building.

Dining facilities resemble corporate or university cafeterias with varied menu options, extended serving hours, and social seating arrangements that promote civilized behavior and positive interpersonal relationships.

Perimeter security is deliberately minimal, typically consisting of low fencing without razor wire, limited lighting, and no guard towers or armed patrols. This minimal security reinforces the camp's emphasis on personal responsibility and trust while ensuring appropriate accountability.

****Daily Life and Institutional Culture****

Life at prison camps follows structured but flexible schedules designed to balance accountability with personal development and family maintenance.

Morning routines begin with 6:00 AM wake-up calls followed by formal inmate counts conducted four times daily to ensure accountability without excessive regimentation. Inmates are expected to maintain personal hygiene, make their beds, and keep personal areas clean as part of developing responsible living habits.

Meals are served cafeteria-style with extended hours that accommodate work and program schedules. Inmates can choose from multiple options and eat at their own pace, promoting normal social interaction and dignified dining experiences.

Work assignments begin at 7:30 AM and continue until 3:30 PM Monday through Friday, with reduced schedules on weekends. All inmates are required to work, but assignments are matched to individual skills, interests, and rehabilitation needs whenever possible.

Evening hours from 4:00 PM to 9:30 PM feature programming opportunities, recreational activities, personal time, and family communication that support both individual development and relationship maintenance.

Weekend schedules offer reduced work requirements with expanded programming, recreation, and visitation that help maintain family connections essential for successful reentry.

Comprehensive Work and Employment Programs

Prison camps offer the most extensive and meaningful work programs in the federal system, designed to provide real job experience, transferable skills, and employment preparation that supports post-release success.

Federal Prison Industries (UNICOR) Excellence

UNICOR programs at camps represent the premium work opportunities in federal corrections, offering factory-style employment that teaches valuable manufacturing, quality control, and workplace skills while paying significantly higher wages than other institutional jobs.

Electronics assembly operations provide experience with precision manufacturing, quality testing, and technical documentation that transfers directly to private sector employment in growing technology industries.

Textile and garment manufacturing teaches industrial sewing, pattern making, quality control, and production management skills that provide immediate employment opportunities in manufacturing sectors.

Furniture manufacturing operations provide woodworking, upholstery, finishing, and assembly skills that support careers in construction, furniture, and decorative arts industries.

Food processing and packaging teaches food safety, industrial cooking, packaging technology, and distribution logistics that provide entry into growing food service and distribution industries.

Facilities Maintenance and Operations Training

Comprehensive facilities maintenance programs provide practical training in essential trades while supporting camp operations and teaching valuable vocational skills.

Groundskeeping and landscaping work includes equipment operation, plant care, irrigation systems, and landscape design that provide immediate employment opportunities in growing outdoor services industries.

Building maintenance encompasses electrical work, plumbing, HVAC systems, and general repair that teach valuable construction trades while providing certification opportunities for post-release employment.

Food service operations include cooking, baking, nutrition planning, food safety, and kitchen management that provide culinary skills and certification for restaurant and institutional food service careers.

Custodial and sanitation work teaches cleaning technology, safety procedures, and facility management that provide immediate employment in service industries while developing work habits and responsibility.

Administrative and Professional Development

Office work assignments provide clerical, computer, and administrative experience that supports white-collar career development while utilizing inmates' educational backgrounds and professional skills.

Education department positions include tutoring, classroom assistance, library services, and computer lab management that utilize advanced education while providing teaching and training experience.

Recreation department work involves program coordination, athletic instruction, facility management, and special event planning that provides leadership development and recreational industry experience.

Business office assignments include accounting, purchasing, personnel support, and data management that maintain professional skills while providing private sector experience.

Medical and dental support positions offer healthcare administration, patient interaction, and medical records management that provide entry into growing healthcare support industries.

Advanced Educational and Training Opportunities

Prison camps offer the most comprehensive educational programming in federal corrections, recognizing that education provides the strongest foundation for successful reentry and crime prevention.

Higher Education Excellence

College degree programs operate through partnerships with regionally accredited institutions that allow inmates to complete associate and bachelor's degrees during incarceration. These programs often include business administration, computer science, liberal arts, and other fields that provide immediate career advancement opportunities upon release.

Business education programs specifically designed for entrepreneurial inmates provide training in business planning, financial management, marketing, and legal compliance that support legitimate business development for former business owners.

Computer technology courses include programming, network administration, web development, and database management that provide high-demand skills in growing technology industries.

Liberal arts education emphasizes critical thinking, communication skills, ethics, and cultural awareness that provide foundation skills for leadership and professional advancement.

Specialized Vocational Training

Advanced vocational programs provide certification and licensing in skilled trades that offer immediate high-wage employment opportunities upon release.

Construction trades training includes electrical, plumbing, carpentry, and masonry instruction that provides union-level certification and immediate employment in construction industries experiencing worker shortages.

Automotive technology programs teach engine repair, electronics, diagnostics, and service management that provide certification for automotive service careers with strong earning potential.

Culinary arts programs include professional cooking, baking, nutrition, food safety, and restaurant management that provide certification for hospitality industry careers with advancement opportunities.

Computer technology training encompasses hardware repair, network installation, software support, and system administration that provide immediate employment in rapidly growing information technology fields.

Comprehensive Life Skills Development

Life skills programming addresses practical reentry needs while developing personal responsibility and decision-making capabilities essential for successful community integration.

Financial literacy courses teach budgeting, banking, credit management, investing, and business planning that provide practical money management skills essential for avoiding future financial problems that contribute to criminal behavior.

Job search and career development training includes resume writing, interview skills, networking, and workplace behavior that provide practical employment-seeking abilities essential for immediate post-release success.

Conflict resolution and communication training teaches interpersonal skills, problem-solving techniques, and emotional regulation that support positive relationships and conflict avoidance in community settings.

Parenting and family relationship courses address family reunification, child development, and relationship maintenance that support family stability essential for successful reentry and crime prevention.

Recreation and Personal Development Excellence

Prison camps recognize that physical fitness, creative expression, and personal development contribute significantly to rehabilitation while supporting mental health and positive institutional adjustment.

Athletic and Fitness Programming

Comprehensive athletic facilities include weight rooms with modern equipment, cardiovascular machines, basketball courts, softball fields, tennis courts, and walking tracks that support physical fitness and stress management.

Organized sports leagues provide competitive outlets including softball, basketball, tennis, and track events that develop teamwork, leadership, and healthy competition while building positive relationships among inmates.

Fitness instruction and personal training programs teach exercise science, nutrition, and wellness planning that provide both personal health benefits and potential career opportunities in growing fitness industries.

Outdoor recreation programs include hiking, camping skills, and environmental awareness that provide stress relief and personal development while teaching appreciation for natural environments.

Creative Arts and Cultural Programming

Comprehensive arts programs provide creative outlets that support emotional development, stress relief, and personal expression while developing artistic skills and cultural appreciation.

Visual arts instruction includes painting, drawing, sculpture, and photography that provide creative expression while developing artistic skills that can support legitimate income generation.

Music programs encompass instrumental instruction, vocal training, recording technology, and performance opportunities that provide creative outlets while developing musical abilities and appreciation.

Creative writing and journalism training teaches written communication, storytelling, and media skills that support both personal expression and professional development in communication fields.

Cultural education programs include literature, history, foreign languages, and cross-cultural awareness that broaden perspectives while developing educational foundation for continued learning.

Visiting and Family Connection Excellence

Prison camps maintain the most liberal visitation and communication policies in federal corrections, recognizing that family support provides the strongest foundation for successful reentry and crime prevention.

Comprehensive Visitation Programs

Weekend and holiday visitation operates from 8:00 AM to 3:00 PM with extended hours during special occasions, providing maximum opportunity for family contact and relationship maintenance.

Contact visits allow physical interaction including hugging, hand-holding, and family photographs that maintain emotional connections essential for relationship preservation and family stability.

Children's visitation areas provide age-appropriate activities, games, and spaces designed specifically for parent-child interaction that supports family relationships and child development during parental incarceration.

Special family programs include parenting classes, family counseling, and relationship workshops that address the challenges of maintaining family connections during incarceration while preparing for successful reunification.

Advanced Communication Systems

Telephone access includes multiple daily calling periods with reasonable time limits and competitive rates that enable regular family communication without excessive financial burden.

International calling capabilities serve inmates with family members abroad, supporting immigrant family connections that provide crucial reentry support and cultural stability.

Email communication through the TRULINCS system enables regular written contact with family and friends while supporting business correspondence within appropriate security parameters.

Video visitation supplements in-person visits for family members who cannot travel regularly, maintaining relationships that might otherwise deteriorate during incarceration periods.

****Progressive Release Preparation****

Qualified inmates may participate in furlough and work release programs that provide graduated reentry experiences while completing their sentences under supervised conditions.

Home furloughs allow temporary release for family emergencies, medical appointments, and other compelling circumstances that require brief community access while maintaining institutional accountability.

Work release programs permit inmates to maintain community employment while returning to the facility each evening, providing income for family support and restitution while preserving job skills and employer relationships.

Community service programs allow inmates to volunteer with local organizations, schools, and charities that benefit communities while providing meaningful contribution opportunities and positive community interaction.

****Typical Prison Camp Day: Theresa Miller Example****

Alice's security score calculation illustrates optimal prison camp placement for PPP defendants:

Criminal History: 0 points (no prior record)

Offense Severity: 0 points (non-violent fraud)

Time to Serve: 2 points (18-month sentence)

Age: 4 points (34 years old)

Education: 0 points (college graduate)

Substance Abuse: 0 points (no documented history)

Detainers: 0 points (no outstanding charges)

Total Security Score: 6 points (Minimum Security)

Likely Placement: Federal Prison Camp Bryan, Texas

Alice's typical daily schedule would include:

6:00 AM: Wake-up and personal preparation

6:30 AM: Breakfast and informal socializing

7:30 AM: Work assignment in food service management

12:00 PM: Lunch break and brief recreation

1:00 PM: Afternoon work continuation

3:30 PM: Work completion and personal time

4:00 PM: College business courses or vocational training

6:00 PM: Dinner and family phone calls

7:30 PM: Recreation, programming, or personal activities

9:30 PM: Return to housing and preparation for sleep

10:00 PM: Lights out and quiet hours

Weekend schedule includes reduced work requirements, extended family visitation from 8:00 AM to 3:00 PM, expanded recreational activities, additional programming opportunities, and extended family communication time.

DEFENSE STRATEGY #173: *Prison Camp Preparation and Advocacy Excellence*

Defendants eligible for minimum security placement should prepare comprehensively for camp environments while advocating strategically for optimal facility selection that maximizes rehabilitation opportunities and family access. Research specific camp locations considering family proximity, specialized programming that aligns with post-release goals, climate and geographic preferences that affect quality of life, and population characteristics that influence institutional culture and safety. Prepare mentally for dormitory living that requires interpersonal skills, adaptability, and respect for personal space and property. Identify meaningful work assignments and educational opportunities that support legitimate career development and provide valuable skills for post-release employment. Develop comprehensive family communication strategies that maximize visitation and phone contact while maintaining business relationships and community connections essential for successful reentry.

Prison camp preparation transforms minimum security placement from merely reduced punishment into genuine rehabilitation opportunity that supports positive life changes and successful community reintegration.

Low Security Federal Correctional Institutions: Structured Rehabilitation

Low security facilities represent the federal system's largest category, housing inmates who require more supervision than camps but demonstrate potential for successful rehabilitation through structured programming and controlled environments.

****Institutional Design and Security Infrastructure****

Low security facilities feature traditional correctional architecture adapted to support rehabilitation while maintaining appropriate security measures for inmates with more complex risk profiles.

Housing consists of residential units containing 100 to 200 inmates in individual or double-occupancy rooms that provide privacy while enabling supervision and accountability. Units feature common areas for television, games, and social interaction that promote positive relationships while maintaining institutional order.

Perimeter security includes fencing with intrusion detection systems, controlled access points with metal detectors and security screening, and security patrols that prevent unauthorized departure while allowing reasonable movement within compound boundaries.

Movement throughout facilities follows controlled schedules with specific times for meals, work, programs, and recreation that ensure accountability while providing access to rehabilitation opportunities and necessary services.

Population Diversity and Institutional Culture

Low security facilities house diverse populations including white-collar offenders with minor complicating factors, non-violent drug offenders with limited criminal histories, inmates serving longer sentences that preclude camp placement, property offenders without violence or weapons involvement, and individuals with characteristics requiring more supervision than camps while not necessitating medium security measures.

The institutional environment emphasizes structure and accountability while maintaining focus on rehabilitation and reentry preparation through programming that addresses individual needs and risk factors.

Comprehensive Daily Structure and Programming

Life at low security facilities follows more rigid schedules than camps while providing substantial programming opportunities designed to address criminogenic needs and support successful reentry.

Morning routines include 6:00 AM wake-up calls, formal counts every six hours, personal hygiene and housing unit maintenance, and breakfast service in dining halls with assigned seating that promotes order while allowing social interaction.

Work assignments operate from 7:30 AM to 3:30 PM Monday through Friday with supervised movement between work sites and housing units. All inmates must maintain work assignments that contribute to facility operations while providing job experience and skill development.

Evening programming from 4:00 PM to 9:00 PM includes educational opportunities, recreational activities, treatment programming, and personal time within housing units or designated common areas.

Weekend schedules feature reduced work requirements with expanded programming opportunities, extended recreation time, family visitation, and religious services that maintain community connections while supporting personal development.

Substantial Work and Employment Development

Low security facilities offer meaningful work programs that provide skill development, job experience, and institutional support while preparing inmates for post-release employment success.

UNICOR Manufacturing Excellence

Federal Prison Industries programs include advanced manufacturing, assembly operations, and production management that provide valuable industrial experience while teaching quality control, safety procedures, and workplace responsibility.

Automotive parts manufacturing teaches precision machining, assembly techniques, quality testing, and production scheduling that provide immediately transferable skills for manufacturing employment in automotive and industrial sectors.

Electronics assembly and testing provides experience with circuit boards, quality control, technical documentation, and precision manufacturing that supports employment in growing technology industries.

Textile and garment production includes industrial sewing, pattern development, quality assurance, and production management that provides skills for manufacturing and design industries.

Comprehensive Facilities Operations

Extensive facilities maintenance programs teach valuable trades while supporting institutional operations and providing certification opportunities for post-release employment.

Building maintenance and construction includes electrical work, plumbing, HVAC systems, carpentry, and general repair that provide construction trade skills with strong earning potential and immediate employment availability.

Grounds and landscaping operations teach equipment operation, horticulture, irrigation systems, and landscape design that provide skills for outdoor services and agricultural industries experiencing worker shortages.

Food service management includes menu planning, quantity cooking, food safety, nutrition, and kitchen supervision that provide culinary and management skills for hospitality industry careers.

Warehouse and logistics operations teach inventory management, shipping and receiving, forklift operation, and supply chain coordination that provide skills for growing distribution and logistics industries.

Advanced Educational and Treatment Programming

Low security facilities provide comprehensive programming designed to address educational needs, criminogenic factors, and reentry preparation while accommodating security requirements.

Educational Excellence

GED and adult basic education serve inmates lacking fundamental academic credentials through individualized instruction, computer-assisted learning, and competency-based advancement that accommodates various learning styles and educational backgrounds.

College degree programs through partnerships with accredited institutions offer associate and bachelor's degree courses in business, liberal arts, computer science, and other fields that provide career advancement opportunities upon release.

Vocational training programs include construction trades, automotive technology, computer applications, and other skilled occupations that provide certification and immediate employment opportunities in high-demand fields.

English as a Second Language (ESL) instruction serves immigrant inmates through comprehensive language development that improves communication skills essential for employment and community integration.

Comprehensive Treatment Programming

Substance abuse treatment addresses addiction issues through individual counseling, group therapy, educational programming, and peer support that helps inmates understand addiction and develop recovery skills essential for crime prevention.

Mental health services include individual therapy, group counseling, psychiatric evaluation, and medication management that address psychological factors contributing to criminal behavior while supporting overall wellness.

Anger management and cognitive behavioral programming teach emotional regulation, problem-solving skills, and behavioral modification techniques that reduce violence risk while improving interpersonal relationships.

Life skills training addresses practical reentry needs including financial management, job search techniques, conflict resolution, and family relationships that support successful community reintegration.

Recreation and Personal Development

Low security facilities provide recreational and personal development opportunities adapted to security requirements while supporting physical fitness, stress management, and positive social interaction.

Athletic facilities include weight rooms, cardiovascular equipment, basketball courts, softball fields, and walking areas that provide fitness opportunities and competitive outlets within controlled environments.

Recreational programming includes organized sports leagues, fitness instruction, outdoor activities, and hobby clubs that provide stress relief and positive social interaction while developing interests and skills.

Library services offer extensive book collections, computer access for legal research and education, and quiet study spaces that support educational goals and personal enrichment within security parameters.

Arts and crafts programs provide creative outlets through painting, drawing, music, and other activities that support emotional well-being and personal expression while developing artistic abilities.

Structured Communication and Visitation

Low security facilities maintain reasonable communication and visitation policies that balance family contact with institutional security requirements while supporting relationship maintenance essential for successful reentry.

Visitation occurs on weekends and holidays through scheduled time blocks typically lasting four to six hours. Contact visits allow limited physical interaction including brief hugging at the beginning and end of visits while maintaining security oversight.

Telephone access includes scheduled calling periods with moderate time limits and monitoring that enables regular family communication while ensuring institutional security and preventing abuse.

Email communication through institutional systems allows written contact with approved correspondents within security parameters that support relationship maintenance while preventing illegal activity.

Common Low Security Placement Scenarios

Several factors commonly result in low security placement for PPP defendants despite their generally favorable profiles as first-time, non-violent offenders.

Age-Related Security Enhancement

David Young, 28-year-old restaurant owner, $145,000 PPP fraud, 30-month sentence, college graduate, no prior record.

Security Score Calculation:

Criminal History: 0 points (no prior record)

Offense Severity: 1 point (property fraud over $100,000)

Time to Serve: 2 points (30-month sentence)

Age: 6 points (under 30 years old)

Education: 0 points (college graduate)

Substance Abuse: 0 points (no documented history)

Detainers: 0 points (no outstanding charges)

Total Security Score: 9 points (Minimum Security eligible, but placed Low due to age and sentence factors)

Likely Placement: Federal Correctional Institution Sheridan, Oregon

David's young age and moderate sentence length push his score toward the low security threshold. FCI Sheridan offers excellent educational programming including college courses and technology training that align with his background while providing appropriate structure for a younger inmate.

His daily routine includes work in computer services, participation in business education courses, regular exercise and recreation, structured phone calls with family, and weekend visitation that maintains crucial family and business relationships.

Sentence Length Considerations

Tonya Carter, 45-year-old bakery owner, $275,000 PPP fraud with sophisticated means enhancement, 42-month sentence, high school education, no prior record.

Security Score Calculation:

Criminal History: 0 points (no prior record)

Offense Severity: 2 points (sophisticated fraud scheme)

Time to Serve: 3 points (42-month sentence)

Age: 2 points (45-49 years old)

Education: 1 point (high school graduate)

Substance Abuse: 0 points (no documented history)

Detainers: 0 points (no outstanding charges)

Total Security Score: 8 points (Minimum Security eligible, but placed Low due to sentence and sophistication factors)

Likely Placement: Federal Correctional Institution Englewood, Colorado**

Tonya's longer sentence and sophisticated fraud characteristics suggest low security placement despite her otherwise favorable profile. FCI Englewood provides culinary arts programming and business development courses that align with her bakery background while offering appropriate structure for her extended sentence.

Her daily activities include work in food service management, participation in GED completion and business courses, comprehensive reentry planning, regular family communication, and weekend visits that support family and business continuity.

Geographic And Capacity Considerations

James Jones, 52-year-old auto repair shop owner, $95,000 PPP fraud, 20-month sentence, college graduate, one prior DUI conviction.

Security Score Calculation:

Criminal History: 1 point (prior DUI conviction)

Offense Severity: 0 points (non-violent fraud)

Time to Serve: 2 points (20-month sentence)

Age: 1 point (50-54 years old)

Education: 0 points (college graduate)

Substance Abuse: 1 point (DUI indicates alcohol abuse)

Detainers: 0 points (no outstanding charges)

Total Security Score: 5 points (Minimum Security eligible, but placed Low due to capacity and program needs)

Likely Placement: Federal Correctional Institution Milan, Michigan**

James qualifies for minimum security but receives low security placement due to bed space limitations at nearby camps and specialized automotive programming at FCI Milan that directly supports his reentry goals.

His programming includes work in the automotive shop, participation in substance abuse counseling to address his DUI history, business management courses, and regular family contact that maintains his auto repair business through family management during his incarceration.

DEFENSE STRATEGY #174: *Low Security Facility Optimization and Preparation***

Defendants facing low security placement should prepare comprehensively for more structured institutional environments while identifying opportunities to maximize rehabilitation and maintain essential family and business relationships. Research specific low security facilities for programming quality, population characteristics, geographic considerations, and transfer opportunities that might allow eventual movement to minimum security facilities. Prepare mentally for increased structure including controlled movement, scheduled activities, and enhanced supervision that requires greater institutional compliance and behavioral adjustment. Identify meaningful work assignments that utilize existing skills while developing new capabilities that support post-release employment and career advancement. Develop comprehensive programming plans that address any identified risk factors while pursuing educational and vocational opportunities that enhance legitimate earning potential. Create family communication strategies that work effectively within more restrictive policies while maintaining relationships essential for successful reentry and business continuity.

Low security preparation helps defendants adapt successfully to institutional structure while maximizing available opportunities for rehabilitation, skill development, and family maintenance that support long-term success and crime prevention.

Medium Security Institutions: Enhanced Security With Rehabilitation Focus

Medium security facilities house inmates requiring significant security measures due to criminal history, offense characteristics, or institutional behavior while maintaining rehabilitation programming adapted to enhanced security environments.

Enhanced Security Infrastructure and Design**

Medium security institutions feature traditional correctional architecture with substantial security measures designed to manage higher-risk populations while providing appropriate programming opportunities.

BONUS SECTION

CHAPTER 21

FEDERAL SENTENCING GUIDELINES BREAKDOWN

The federal sentencing system operates as a complex mathematical equation where human lives are reduced to numbers, calculations, and predetermined ranges. Understanding this machinery becomes essential for anyone facing federal charges, particularly in the aftermath of PPP fraud prosecutions where the government has weaponized these guidelines to devastating effect. The Federal Sentencing Guidelines, once mandatory, now serve as the foundation for judicial decision making, creating a framework that prosecutors exploit and defendants must navigate with precision.

The origins of the Federal Sentencing Guidelines trace back to the **Sentencing Reform Act of 1984,** designed to eliminate disparities in federal sentencing and provide uniformity across districts. Congress sought to end the era of indeterminate sentencing where judges possessed broad discretion, often resulting in dramatically different sentences for similar crimes. The solution created a new problem: a rigid system that reduces complex human behavior to point calculations, treating financial crimes with the same mechanical precision as violent offenses.

The base offense level forms the foundation of every federal sentence calculation. For fraud offenses, including PPP fraud, the base offense level begins at seven under Section 2B1.1 of the Guidelines. This seemingly modest starting point misleads defendants into believing their exposure remains minimal. The reality proves far more sinister as prosecutors layer enhancement upon enhancement, transforming a base level seven into sentences measured in decades rather than months.

The loss amount calculation represents the most significant driver of federal fraud sentences. The Guidelines establish a loss table that increases the offense level based on the amount of intended loss, not actual loss. This distinction proves crucial in PPP fraud cases where the government routinely argues that the full loan amount represents intended loss, regardless of how much money defendants actually received or retained. The progression escalates rapidly: losses exceeding **$95,000** add twelve levels, losses exceeding **$550,000** add sixteen levels, and losses exceeding **$3.5 million** add twenty levels to the base offense level.

The sophisticated means enhancement adds two levels when defendants allegedly used particularly sophisticated methods to commit or conceal the offense. In PPP fraud cases, prosecutors routinely argue that creating false documentation, using multiple business entities, or employing basic technology constitutes sophisticated means. The enhancement originally targeted complex financial schemes requiring specialized knowledge or elaborate planning. Modern prosecutors have expanded its application to include almost any fraud involving documentation or multiple steps, transforming it from an exception into a standard enhancement.

The leadership or organizing role enhancement punishes defendants who allegedly organized, led, managed, or supervised criminal activity. This enhancement adds levels based on the number of participants, ranging from two levels for minimal leadership to four levels for leading five or more participants. In PPP fraud cases, prosecutors often argue that defendants who involved family members, employees, or associates in their schemes qualify for leadership enhancements. The enhancement catches defendants who may have simply sought advice or assistance, elevating their sentences based on relationships rather than actual leadership roles.

The obstruction of justice enhancement adds two levels when defendants allegedly impeded or attempted to impede the investigation or prosecution of the offense. This enhancement extends beyond traditional obstruction to include alleged witness tampering, document destruction, or providing false information during interviews. The enhancement operates on a broad interpretation where almost any act that potentially hinders the investigation qualifies. Defendants who delete files, speak to potential witnesses, or provide explanations that prosecutors later deem false face automatic sentence increases.

The vulnerable victim enhancement adds two levels when defendants allegedly had targeted unusually vulnerable victims. While originally designed to protect elderly or disabled victims, prosecutors now argue that government programs inherently create vulnerable victims. In PPP fraud cases, the government sometimes claims that small businesses or communities affected by the pandemic qualify as vulnerable victims. The enhancement stretches beyond its original intent, allowing prosecutors to increase sentences based on the identity of affected parties rather than actual targeting of vulnerable individuals.

The role in offense adjustments can either increase or decrease the offense level based on the defendant's culpability relative to other participants. Minimal participants receive a four level decrease, minor participants receive a two level decrease, while organizers and leaders face increases. These adjustments require careful analysis of each defendant's actual role versus their perceived role. Prosecutors often overstate defendants' leadership roles while defense attorneys must demonstrate their clients' minimal involvement through detailed factual presentations.

The acceptance of responsibility reduction provides a three level decrease for defendants who clearly demonstrate acceptance of responsibility for their offense. This reduction requires more than simply pleading guilty; defendants must provide complete and truthful information about their involvement and avoid minimizing their conduct. The reduction includes an additional one level decrease for defendants who assist authorities in the investigation or prosecution of their own conduct by providing information or testimony. The acceptance of responsibility reduction becomes one of the few opportunities for defendants to meaningfully reduce their sentences.

The criminal history category multiplies the impact of the offense level calculation. The Guidelines establish six criminal history categories based on criminal history points assigned to prior convictions. Category I defendants have no significant criminal history, while Category VI defendants have extensive criminal histories. Each prior conviction receives points based on its severity and recency, with more recent and serious convictions receiving higher point values. The intersection of offense level and criminal history category determines the sentencing range in months.

The zone system divides the sentencing table into four zones that determine available sentencing options. Zone A includes sentences of zero to six months, allowing for probation or short terms of imprisonment. Zone B covers six to fifteen months, requiring at least one month of imprisonment but allowing for community confinement or home detention. Zone C encompasses fifteen to twenty-one months, requiring at least half the sentence in prison with the remainder potentially served in community confinement. Zone D includes all sentences exceeding twenty-one months and generally requires service of the full sentence in prison.

Departures from the Guidelines allow courts to impose sentences outside the calculated range when circumstances warrant different treatment. Upward departures increase sentences beyond the Guidelines range, while downward departures decrease sentences below the range. The Guidelines identify specific grounds for departures, including exceptional circumstances not adequately considered in the Guidelines calculation. Courts may depart based on factors such as extreme conduct, vulnerable victims, or other aggravating circumstances not captured in the standard enhancements.

The safety valve provision under **Section 5C1.2** allows certain first-time, non-violent offenders to receive sentences below mandatory minimums. The safety valve requires defendants to meet five criteria: minimal criminal history, no violence or weapons, no leadership role, complete cooperation with authorities, and truthful information about the offense. While PPP fraud cases rarely involve mandatory minimums, the safety valve principles influence judicial thinking about appropriate sentences for first-time offenders.

Judicial discretion plays the determining role in federal sentencing despite the Guidelines' apparent precision. The Supreme Court's decision in United States v. Booker transformed the Guidelines from mandatory to advisory, allowing judges to consider the Guidelines alongside other sentencing factors. Courts must calculate the Guidelines range accurately but may vary from that range based on the factors outlined in **18 U.S.C. § 3553(a).** These factors include the nature and circumstances of the offense, the history and characteristics of the defendant, the need for deterrence, and the need to provide restitution to victims.

The 3553(a) factors provide the framework for judicial analysis beyond the Guidelines calculation. The seriousness of the offense and the defendant's criminal history receive primary consideration, but courts also examine the need for deterrence, both specific and general. The need to protect the public from further crimes by the defendant influences sentences, particularly in financial fraud cases where recidivism concerns exist. The need to provide restitution to victims affects both the sentence imposed and the conditions of supervised release.

Variance practice has evolved significantly since Booker, with courts increasingly willing to impose sentences outside the Guidelines range when circumstances warrant different treatment. Statistical data shows that variances occur in approximately thirty percent of federal cases, with below-Guidelines sentences more common than above-Guidelines sentences. The willingness to vary depends heavily on the individual judge, the specific circumstances of the case, and the quality of the sentencing presentation by defense counsel.

The plea agreement process significantly impacts sentencing outcomes through charge bargaining and fact stipulations. Prosecutors control the charges filed and the enhancements sought, giving them substantial leverage in plea negotiations. Defense attorneys must carefully evaluate plea offers not only for the charges dismissed but also for the sentencing implications of the remaining charges. Fact stipulations in plea agreements can bind defendants to specific loss amounts or enhancement applications, making negotiation of these provisions crucial.

Cooperation with the government provides the most significant opportunity for sentence reduction through the substantial assistance departure under **Section 5K1.1.** Defendants who provide substantial assistance in the investigation or prosecution of others may receive sentences below the Guidelines range, sometimes dramatically below. The decision to grant substantial assistance departures rests entirely with the prosecutor, giving the government significant leverage over cooperating defendants. The extent of the departure depends on the significance, usefulness, and truthfulness of the assistance provided.

Fast-track programs in certain districts provide additional opportunities for sentence reduction in exchange for early guilty pleas. These programs typically offer predetermined sentence reductions for defendants who plead guilty early in the process without requiring cooperation against others. Fast-track programs remain limited to certain types of cases and districts, but they represent acknowledgment that the standard Guidelines ranges may produce excessive sentences in some circumstances.

The impact of relevant conduct extends the sentencing calculation beyond the charges of conviction to include all reasonably foreseeable acts in furtherance of the offense. This provision allows prosecutors to seek sentence enhancements based on conduct that may not have resulted in separate charges or convictions. In PPP fraud cases, relevant conduct might include applications filed by associates, additional documentation created, or other acts that increase the loss amount or support enhancements. The relevant conduct provision prevents defendants from limiting their sentencing exposure simply through favorable plea agreements.

Sentencing memoranda provide the primary vehicle for presenting mitigation evidence and legal arguments to the court. Defense attorneys must craft compelling narratives that address the 3553(a) factors while acknowledging the seriousness of the offense. Effective sentencing memoranda combine legal analysis with human storytelling, helping judges understand the defendant as a complete person rather than simply a criminal defendant. The memoranda should address each applicable enhancement, argue for appropriate departures or variances, and present a realistic sentencing recommendation.

The presentence investigation report prepared by probation officers provides the foundation for sentencing proceedings. Probation officers investigate the defendant's background, verify the facts of the offense, calculate the Guidelines range, and make sentencing recommendations. Defendants have the right to review and object to factual errors in the presentence report, making careful review essential. Disputes over the presentence report require resolution through sentencing hearings where both parties present evidence and argument.

Expert testimony on Guidelines calculations, loss amounts, and other technical issues can significantly impact sentencing outcomes. Forensic accountants, computer experts, and other specialists may provide testimony challenging the government's calculations or supporting alternative interpretations of the evidence. The cost of expert testimony often exceeds the resources available to defendants, creating disparities in sentencing outcomes based on financial resources rather than legal merit.

The appellate process provides limited relief from Guidelines sentences, with most sentences surviving appeal under the reasonableness standard. Courts of appeals review Guidelines calculations for correctness but review the ultimate sentence only for reasonableness. Procedural reasonableness requires correct Guidelines calculation and consideration of the **3553(a) factors**. Substantive reasonableness requires that the sentence imposed not be unreasonable given all the circumstances. The reasonableness standard provides significant deference to district courts, making successful sentencing appeals relatively rare.

Understanding the Federal Sentencing Guidelines requires recognition that they represent a tool of government power rather than a neutral system of justice. The Guidelines' mathematical precision creates an illusion of objectivity while obscuring the policy choices embedded in their construction. The emphasis on loss amounts in fraud cases reflects a judgment that financial harm deserves punishment proportional to monetary damage rather than culpability or intent. The proliferation of enhancements demonstrates a system designed to increase rather than limit sentences.

The psychological impact of the Guidelines system extends beyond the sentences imposed to affect every aspect of federal criminal practice. Defendants face pressure to cooperate or plead guilty early to avoid enhancement-driven sentences that can stretch into decades. Defense attorneys must master complex calculations while advocating for clients within a system that provides limited opportunities for mitigation. Judges exercise discretion within a framework that constrains their ability to craft individualized sentences.

The Guidelines' impact on PPP fraud cases reveals the system's capacity for expansion and adaptation to new enforcement priorities. Prosecutors have successfully applied enhancements originally designed for traditional fraud to pandemic relief programs, often resulting in sentences that exceed those imposed for violent crimes. The loss amount calculations that drive these sentences often bear little relationship to actual harm caused, creating sentences based on theoretical rather than real damages.

Reform efforts have targeted various aspects of the Guidelines system, from reducing mandatory minimums to expanding safety valve provisions. **The First Step Act of 2018** provided modest reforms, but the fundamental structure remains intact. More comprehensive reform would require congressional action to address the underlying philosophy that prioritizes punishment over rehabilitation and mathematical precision over individualized justice.

The practical reality of federal sentencing requires defendants and their attorneys to navigate a system that prioritizes efficiency over accuracy and punishment over justice. Success depends on understanding not just the legal framework but the institutional pressures and prosecutorial strategies that shape outcomes. The Guidelines provide the language of federal sentencing, but power dynamics and resource disparities determine the actual sentences imposed.

The Federal Sentencing Guidelines represent more than a sentencing system; they embody a philosophy of criminal justice that treats defendants as mathematical abstractions rather than human beings. Understanding their operation provides essential knowledge for anyone facing federal charges, but reform requires recognition that the system's problems extend beyond technical calculations to fundamental questions of justice, proportionality, and the proper role of government power in addressing wrongdoing. The Guidelines will continue to evolve, but their basic structure ensures that federal sentences will remain products of calculation rather than consideration, mathematics rather than mercy.

CHAPTER 22

CASE LAW DEEP DIVE

The landscape of PPP fraud prosecution emerges from a complex web of precedent, statutory interpretation, and prosecutorial strategy that transforms pandemic relief into criminal liability. Understanding how courts have approached these cases reveals the government's methodology and provides essential insights for mounting effective defenses. The case law demonstrates a disturbing pattern of judicial deference to prosecution theories that stretch traditional fraud concepts beyond recognition, creating new categories of criminal liability that ensnare defendants who believed they were participating in legitimate government programs.

The foundation of PPP fraud prosecutions rests on wire fraud statutes that federal prosecutors have weaponized against program participants. **United States v. McNeal** established early precedent by affirming convictions for defendants who allegedly submitted false information on PPP applications. The court's analysis focused on the materiality of false statements, finding that any misrepresentation that could influence funding decisions constituted wire fraud. This broad interpretation eliminated the traditional requirement that false statements actually deceive recipients, instead requiring only that they have the capacity to deceive.

The materiality standard in McNeal created a prosecutorial weapon that transforms minor inaccuracies into federal crimes. The court rejected defense arguments that technical violations of program requirements did not constitute fraud, instead adopting a theory that treats any deviation from application requirements as potentially material. This approach ignores the program's stated purpose of providing emergency relief and instead focuses on bureaucratic compliance as the measure of criminal liability. The precedent enables prosecutors to criminalize conduct that program administrators might have approved or overlooked in the interest of rapid distribution.

United States v. Barosy expanded the wire fraud framework by addressing the intent requirement in PPP fraud cases. The defendants argued that their belief in eligibility for the loans negated the intent to defraud required for wire fraud convictions. The court rejected this defense, establishing that defendants' subjective beliefs about program eligibility cannot overcome objective evidence of false statements. The decision effectively eliminates good faith defenses in PPP fraud cases, allowing prosecutors to secure convictions based on application inaccuracies regardless of defendants' intent or understanding of program requirements.

The Barosy decision demonstrates how courts have transformed the intent element of wire fraud from a meaningful protection into a procedural hurdle. The court's analysis suggests that any knowing false statement, regardless of the defendant's understanding of its significance, satisfies the intent requirement. This interpretation criminalizes conduct that would have been considered negligent or mistaken in other contexts, creating strict liability for program participants who made errors in their applications. The precedent encourages prosecutors to focus on documentation discrepancies rather than proving actual fraudulent intent.

The conspiracy framework in PPP fraud cases has evolved through decisions that expand liability beyond traditional conspiracy principles. **United States v. Hines** established that family members and business associates who assist in preparing PPP applications can face conspiracy charges even when their involvement was minimal or passive. The court found that knowledge of false statements and any act in furtherance of the scheme, however minor, satisfied the requirements for conspiracy liability. This broad interpretation creates exposure for individuals who may have provided legitimate assistance without understanding the alleged fraudulent nature of the applications.

The Hines decision illustrates how conspiracy charges multiply prosecutorial power in PPP fraud cases. The court's analysis focused on the defendants' awareness of application contents rather than their intent to defraud, creating liability for individuals who may have believed they were helping with legitimate applications. The precedent allows prosecutors to charge entire families or business networks based on their participation in application preparation, regardless of their understanding of program requirements or their intent to deceive the government.

RICO applications in PPP fraud cases represent a particularly aggressive prosecutorial strategy that transforms multiple loan applications into racketeering charges. **United States v. Smith** marked the first successful RICO prosecution in a PPP fraud case, establishing precedent for treating systematic PPP fraud as organized crime. The court found that defendants who filed multiple applications using different business entities created a pattern of racketeering activity that supported RICO charges. This analysis treats entrepreneurial activity as criminal enterprise, criminalizing the use of multiple businesses to access government programs.

The Smith decision demonstrates how prosecutors have adapted RICO statutes to target PPP fraud schemes that involve multiple applications or business entities. The court's analysis required minimal evidence of organization or coordination, instead focusing on the repetitive nature of the applications and the common goal of obtaining loan funds. This approach transforms what might have been individual fraud cases into racketeering prosecutions with enhanced penalties and broader liability. The precedent enables prosecutors to charge entire business networks under RICO theories that treat program participation as criminal enterprise.

The evolution of RICO in PPP fraud cases reflects the government's strategy of treating pandemic relief fraud as a national security threat rather than a regulatory violation. Courts have accepted prosecution theories that equate PPP fraud with organized crime, despite the absence of traditional criminal organization markers like hierarchy, violence, or ongoing criminal activity. The precedent creates a framework where multiple loan applications automatically generate RICO liability, regardless of the defendants' criminal history or the sophistication of their conduct.

Money laundering charges in PPP fraud cases have expanded through decisions that treat legitimate business expenses as evidence of criminal activity. **United States v. Johnson** established that defendants who spent PPP funds on non-payroll expenses could face money laundering charges even when those expenses were business-related. The court found that any use of PPP funds contrary to program requirements constituted money laundering, creating a theory that criminalizes spending decisions rather than traditional money laundering conduct.

The Johnson decision demonstrates how prosecutors have weaponized money laundering statutes against PPP recipients who may have misunderstood program requirements. The court's analysis treated business expenses like rent, utilities, and supplies as evidence of criminal activity when funded with PPP money, despite these expenses being legitimate business costs. This approach creates retroactive criminal liability for spending decisions that business owners made in good faith based on their understanding of program flexibility.

The expansion of money laundering charges in PPP fraud cases reflects a prosecutorial strategy that treats any non-compliant spending as evidence of criminal intent. Courts have accepted theories that equate program violations with money laundering, creating liability for conduct that would have been considered civil compliance issues in other contexts. The precedent enables prosecutors to enhance penalties and create additional charges based on defendants' business operations rather than their application conduct.

Forfeiture law in PPP fraud cases has developed through decisions that treat entire loan amounts as forfeitable proceeds of criminal activity. **United States v. Williams** established that defendants must forfeit the full amount of PPP loans obtained through allegedly fraudulent applications, regardless of how the funds were used or whether they were used for legitimate business purposes. The court rejected defense arguments that only the misused portion of the loans should be subject to forfeiture, instead adopting a theory that treats the entire loan as tainted by the fraudulent application.

The Williams decision demonstrates how forfeiture law has become a tool for financial destruction in PPP fraud cases. The court's analysis ignored the legitimate business purposes for which defendants may have used the funds, instead focusing on the alleged fraud in obtaining the loans. This approach creates forfeiture liability that far exceeds any actual loss to the government, particularly when defendants used the funds for legitimate business expenses that would have qualified for loan forgiveness.

The evolution of forfeiture doctrine in PPP fraud cases reflects a punitive approach that treats defendants' business assets as proceeds of criminal activity. Courts have accepted prosecution theories that every dollar received through allegedly fraudulent applications becomes subject to forfeiture, regardless of its ultimate use or benefit to the defendant. The precedent creates financial penalties that exceed traditional fraud remedies, treating PPP fraud as a form of theft rather than regulatory violation.

Sentencing law in PPP fraud cases has developed through decisions that apply traditional fraud guidelines to pandemic relief programs with devastating results. **United States v. Thomas** established that the full amount of PPP loans constitutes intended loss for sentencing purposes, regardless of whether defendants received or retained the full amount. The court found that the application of the loan amount, not the actual financial harm, determines the loss calculation for guidelines purposes. This interpretation creates sentencing exposure based on program amounts rather than actual damages.

The Thomas decision demonstrates how sentencing guidelines have become weapons of mass incarceration in PPP fraud cases. The court's analysis treated loan applications as evidence of intent to cause loss equal to the full loan amount, creating guidelines calculations that bear no relationship to actual harm caused. This approach produces sentences that exceed those imposed for violent crimes, treating paperwork violations as major financial crimes.

The application of sophisticated means enhancements in PPP fraud cases has evolved through decisions that treat basic technology and documentation as evidence of criminal sophistication. **United States v. Davis** established that defendants who used accounting software, created business documents, or employed online banking in connection with PPP applications could face sophisticated means enhancements. The court found that any use of technology or professional services to prepare applications constituted sophisticated means, regardless of the complexity or specialization involved.

The Davis decision illustrates how sentencing enhancements have become automatic in PPP fraud cases. The court's analysis treated routine business practices as evidence of criminal sophistication, creating enhancement liability for defendants who used standard business tools and services. This approach transforms legitimate business operations into evidence of criminal planning, creating sentencing exposure based on professional competence rather than criminal conduct.

Leadership role enhancements in PPP fraud cases have expanded through decisions that treat business ownership and family relationships as evidence of criminal leadership. **United States v. Martinez** established that defendants who owned businesses or supervised family members in PPP application preparation could face leadership enhancements regardless of their actual role in any fraudulent scheme. The court found that business authority and family relationships created presumptive leadership liability, eliminating the need to prove actual direction or control of criminal activity.

The Martinez decision demonstrates how sentencing enhancements have become tools for criminalizing business relationships in PPP fraud cases. The court's analysis treated legitimate business hierarchy and family cooperation as evidence of criminal organization, creating enhancement liability based on relationships rather than conduct. This approach criminalizes the social and economic structures that small businesses rely on, treating family assistance as evidence of criminal conspiracy.

The evolving landscape of appellate review in PPP fraud cases reveals a pattern of judicial deference to prosecution theories that would have been rejected in other contexts. Courts of appeals have consistently affirmed convictions and sentences in PPP fraud cases, accepting prosecution arguments that stretch traditional fraud concepts beyond recognition. The appellate precedent creates a framework where prosecutors can secure convictions and severe sentences based on technical violations of program requirements rather than traditional criminal conduct.

The Supreme Court's decision in **Ciminelli v. United States,** while not directly addressing PPP fraud, provides important guidance for challenging prosecution theories that criminalize regulatory violations. The Court's rejection of the "right to control" theory of wire fraud suggests that prosecutors cannot criminalize conduct simply because it violates regulatory requirements. This precedent may provide grounds for challenging PPP fraud prosecutions that treat program violations as fraud without proving actual deception or harm.

The application of Ciminelli principles to PPP fraud cases remains undeveloped, but the decision suggests that courts should require proof of actual deception rather than mere regulatory violations. Defense attorneys should argue that PPP fraud prosecutions that focus on technical compliance rather than fraudulent intent violate the principles established in Ciminelli. The precedent may provide a framework for challenging the broad theories that have dominated PPP fraud prosecutions.

The development of constitutional challenges to PPP fraud prosecutions has been limited by courts' deference to prosecution theories and defendants' focus on technical defenses rather than constitutional principles. Due process challenges to the retroactive criminalization of conduct that was considered acceptable when performed have been largely unsuccessful. Courts have rejected arguments that prosecuting PPP participants for conduct that program administrators encouraged or approved violates fundamental fairness principles.

The failure of constitutional challenges in PPP fraud cases reflects the broader pattern of judicial deference to prosecution theories in financial crime cases. Courts have been reluctant to question the government's authority to prosecute conduct that may have been considered legitimate when performed, instead focusing on technical compliance with statutory requirements. This approach enables prosecutors to criminalize conduct retroactively based on evolving interpretations of program requirements.

The emergence of ineffective assistance of counsel claims in PPP fraud cases reflects the complexity of the legal landscape and the failure of many defense attorneys to understand the unique challenges these cases present. Courts have found ineffective assistance where defense attorneys failed to challenge Guidelines calculations, negotiate appropriate plea agreements, or present mitigation evidence that addresses the specific characteristics of PPP fraud cases. The precedent suggests that effective defense requires specialized knowledge of both fraud law and pandemic relief programs.

The development of ineffective assistance doctrine in PPP fraud cases demonstrates the need for specialized expertise in defending these prosecutions. Defense attorneys must understand not only traditional fraud defenses but also the specific requirements and purposes of pandemic relief programs. The precedent creates potential grounds for post-conviction relief in cases where defense attorneys failed to provide competent representation tailored to the unique challenges of PPP fraud prosecutions.

The international implications of PPP fraud case law have emerged as courts address defendants who participated in the program from abroad or who moved assets offshore after receiving loans. United States v. Patel established that defendants who applied for PPP loans while residing abroad could be prosecuted in the United States based on the location of the financial institutions involved. The court found that the use of US banks to process loan applications created sufficient contacts to support federal jurisdiction.

The Patel decision demonstrates how PPP fraud prosecutions have expanded beyond traditional jurisdictional boundaries. The court's analysis treated international program participation as evidence of criminal intent, creating liability for defendants who may have believed they were eligible for assistance while living abroad. This approach criminalizes the global nature of modern business operations, treating international participation as evidence of fraudulent intent.

The evolution of cooperation and substantial assistance doctrine in PPP fraud cases reveals prosecutorial strategies that encourage defendants to implicate others in exchange for reduced sentences. Courts have accepted cooperation agreements that require defendants to admit to conduct they previously denied and to provide information about other program participants. The precedent creates incentives for defendants to expand the scope of prosecutions by implicating associates, family members, and business partners.

The development of cooperation doctrine in PPP fraud cases reflects the government's strategy of using individual prosecutions to build larger cases against business networks and professional service providers. Prosecutors have used cooperation agreements to target accountants, attorneys, and consultants who assisted with PPP applications, creating liability for professional service providers who may have provided legitimate assistance. The precedent enables prosecutors to expand investigations beyond individual applicants to entire business communities.

The case law landscape in PPP fraud prosecutions reveals a systematic transformation of pandemic relief into criminal liability through prosecutorial theories that stretch traditional fraud concepts beyond recognition. The precedent creates a framework where program participation becomes evidence of criminal intent, technical violations become federal crimes, and legitimate business relationships become criminal conspiracies. Understanding this evolution provides essential insights for mounting effective defenses and challenging prosecutorial overreach.

The future development of PPP fraud case law will likely depend on defendants' willingness to challenge prosecutorial theories through appellate litigation and the Supreme Court's continued refinement of fraud doctrine. The precedent established in these cases will influence federal prosecution strategies for years to come, making it essential for defense attorneys to understand both the legal framework and the institutional pressures that shape prosecutorial decisions. The case law serves as a cautionary tale about the expansion of federal criminal liability and the need for vigilant defense advocacy in an era of prosecutorial aggression.

CHAPTER 23

DISCOVERY & EVIDENCE SUPPRESSION TACTICS

The discovery process in federal criminal cases represents both the greatest opportunity and the most dangerous minefield for defendants facing PPP fraud charges. Unlike civil litigation where discovery operates as a mutual exchange of information, federal criminal discovery tilts heavily in favor of the prosecution while creating traps for unwary defense attorneys. Understanding the nuances of discovery rules, the government's obligations, and the strategic opportunities for evidence suppression becomes essential for mounting an effective defense against charges that often rest on massive document productions and complex financial analyses.

Federal Rule of Criminal Procedure 16 establishes the baseline requirements for criminal discovery, but its provisions barely scratch the surface of what defendants need to challenge PPP fraud prosecutions effectively. The rule requires the government to disclose defendant statements, the defendant's prior criminal record, documents and objects the government intends to use in its case-in-chief, and results of physical and mental examinations. These basic requirements fail to address the massive electronic discovery typical in PPP fraud cases or the complex financial documents that form the backbone of most prosecutions.

The government's discovery obligations extend far beyond Rule 16 through constitutional requirements established in **Brady v. Maryland** and its progeny. Brady material includes any evidence favorable to the defense that is material to either guilt or punishment. The Supreme Court's decision created an affirmative duty for prosecutors to disclose exculpatory evidence, but the practical application of Brady requirements depends heavily on prosecutors' good faith and defense attorneys' ability to identify missing evidence. In PPP fraud cases, Brady material might include SBA guidance documents, internal agency communications, or evidence of selective enforcement that undermines prosecution theories.

Giglio v. United States expanded Brady obligations to include evidence that impeaches government witnesses, creating additional disclosure requirements that prosecutors frequently ignore or minimize. Giglio material includes evidence of witness bias, criminal history, cooperation agreements, or promises of leniency that might affect witness credibility. In PPP fraud cases,

Giglio material often involves the testimony of cooperating witnesses who may have received favorable treatment in exchange for their cooperation or government agents whose investigative methods or conclusions may be questionable.

The timing of Brady and Giglio disclosures creates ongoing strategic challenges throughout PPP fraud prosecutions. Courts generally require disclosure sufficiently in advance of trial to allow meaningful use of the evidence, but prosecutors often delay disclosures until the last possible moment. This strategy forces defense attorneys to prepare for trial without complete information while creating time pressure that prevents thorough investigation of disclosed material. Defense attorneys must file specific Brady requests early in the case and follow up aggressively when disclosures appear incomplete.

Jencks Act materials provide another avenue for obtaining government evidence, requiring disclosure of witness statements that relate to the witness's testimony. The Jencks Act applies to all witness statements, including rough notes, memoranda of interviews, and recordings that substantially verbatim recite witness statements. In PPP fraud cases, Jencks materials often include FBI interview reports, grand jury testimony transcripts, and cooperation debriefing memoranda that reveal inconsistencies in witness testimony or government investigative methods.

The government's discovery production in PPP fraud cases typically involves massive electronic databases containing hundreds of thousands or millions of documents. Prosecutors use sophisticated litigation support systems to organize and search these materials, while defense attorneys often receive productions in unwieldy formats that make meaningful review nearly impossible. Defense attorneys must demand productions in searchable formats and insist on adequate time and resources to review voluminous materials effectively.

Fourth Amendment challenges to evidence collection provide the primary mechanism for suppressing illegally obtained evidence in PPP fraud cases. The government's investigation typically begins with analysis of SBA loan databases, bank records, and other financial documents that may be obtained without warrants under various exceptions to the Fourth Amendment's warrant requirement. Understanding the scope of these exceptions and their limitations becomes crucial for identifying suppression opportunities that might eliminate key evidence from prosecution cases.

The third-party doctrine presents significant Fourth Amendment challenges in PPP fraud cases because much of the evidence consists of records held by banks, the SBA, and other third parties. Under the third-party doctrine, individuals generally lack reasonable expectations of privacy in information voluntarily conveyed to third parties. However, recent Supreme Court decisions in **Carpenter v. United States** suggest that the doctrine may not apply to comprehensive data collection that reveals detailed patterns of behavior or association.

Bank records searches in PPP fraud cases often occur through administrative subpoenas or grand jury subpoenas that do not require probable cause or judicial approval. The Right to Financial Privacy Act provides some protection for bank records, but its exceptions for criminal investigations eliminate most practical protections. Defense attorneys should examine the scope and timing of bank records subpoenas to identify potential overreach that might support suppression motions.

Digital evidence suppression in PPP fraud cases requires understanding both traditional Fourth Amendment principles and evolving technology law. Searches of computers, cell phones, and cloud storage accounts implicate complex questions about the scope of digital searches and the application of warrant requirements to electronic communications. The government often obtains digital evidence through consent searches, warrant searches, or searches incident to arrest that may exceed constitutional boundaries.

Email and communication searches in PPP fraud investigations frequently involve warrants for email accounts, social media profiles, and messaging applications. These searches may violate the Fourth Amendment when they exceed the scope of supporting probable cause or when they intrude on privileged communications. Defense attorneys should carefully review search warrant affidavits and returned materials to identify potential Fourth Amendment violations that might support suppression motions.

The government's use of financial analysis and expert testimony in PPP fraud cases creates opportunities for challenging the reliability and admissibility of prosecution evidence. **Federal Rule of Evidence 702** requires that expert testimony be based on reliable methods and sufficient facts or data. Government financial experts often rely on incomplete records or questionable assumptions that may not meet reliability standards. Defense attorneys should challenge expert qualifications, methodologies, and underlying data through Daubert motions that seek to exclude unreliable expert testimony.

Chain of custody challenges in PPP fraud cases focus on the government's handling of electronic evidence and financial records. Digital evidence requires careful documentation of collection, preservation, and analysis methods to ensure that evidence has not been altered or corrupted. Defense attorneys should examine forensic procedures and demand detailed logs of evidence handling to identify potential chain of custody problems that might undermine prosecution evidence.

Privilege protections provide another avenue for excluding government evidence that was obtained in violation of attorney-client, work product, or other recognized privileges. The government's investigation may have obtained privileged communications through searches of law firms, accounting firms, or corporate files. Defense attorneys should carefully review discovery productions to identify potentially privileged materials and file appropriate motions to suppress evidence obtained in violation of privilege protections.

Brady violations in PPP fraud cases often involve the government's failure to disclose exculpatory evidence contained within massive document productions. Prosecutors may claim that favorable evidence was produced but buried within thousands of documents, making it effectively unavailable to the defense. Defense attorneys must establish systems for reviewing voluminous productions and identifying potentially exculpatory material that should have been specifically disclosed.

The government's use of cooperating witnesses in PPP fraud cases creates multiple opportunities for discovering Brady and Giglio material that prosecutors may have failed to disclose. Cooperation agreements often contain provisions that are not disclosed to defense attorneys, and cooperating witnesses may have provided inconsistent statements that impeach their credibility. Defense attorneys should file specific discovery requests for all cooperation agreements, debriefing memoranda, and witness statements that might reveal impeachment material.

Grand jury abuse provides grounds for challenging the government's investigation and seeking dismissal of charges in appropriate cases. Prosecutors may have used the grand jury process to conduct discovery for civil investigations, to gather evidence for fishing expeditions, or to circumvent statutory limitations on administrative subpoenas. Defense attorneys should examine the timing and scope of grand jury subpoenas to identify potential abuse that might support motions to dismiss charges.

Prosecutorial misconduct discovery focuses on identifying government conduct that violates defendants' rights or undermines the integrity of the prosecution. This might include selective prosecution based on impermissible factors, vindictive prosecution in response to the exercise of constitutional rights, or prosecutorial coaching of witnesses that amounts to subornation of perjury. Defense attorneys must gather evidence of misconduct through discovery requests, investigation, and careful attention to patterns in the government's conduct.

The Jencks Act's application to electronic communications and digital evidence creates new opportunities for obtaining government materials that relate to witness testimony. Text messages, emails, and social media communications may constitute Jencks materials if they substantially verbatim recite witness statements. Defense attorneys should request all electronic communications involving government witnesses that might qualify for Jencks Act disclosure.

Rule 404(b) challenges provide opportunities for excluding evidence of other acts that prosecutors seek to introduce as evidence of intent, knowledge, or modus operandi. In PPP fraud cases, prosecutors often seek to introduce evidence of other loan applications, business transactions, or financial conduct that may be more prejudicial than probative. Defense attorneys should file motions in limine to exclude Rule 404(b) evidence that does not meet relevancy and reliability standards.

Speedy trial violations in PPP fraud cases may result from the government's delay in bringing charges or proceeding to trial. The Speedy Trial Act requires that trials commence within seventy days of indictment or arraignment, subject to various exclusions and exceptions. Complex PPP fraud cases often involve lengthy delays for discovery production and expert preparation that may violate speedy trial requirements. Defense attorneys should monitor speedy trial deadlines and object to inappropriate delays that may support dismissal motions.

Double jeopardy challenges in PPP fraud cases focus on the government's charging of multiple offenses based on the same underlying conduct. Prosecutors routinely charge wire fraud, money laundering, and conspiracy based on the same PPP loan applications, creating potential double jeopardy violations. **The Blockburger test** requires analysis of whether each offense contains an element that the other does not, but the practical application often depends on the specific facts and charging theories involved.

Statute of limitations defenses in PPP fraud cases require careful analysis of when the government knew or should have known about allegedly fraudulent conduct. The five-year statute of limitations for most federal fraud offenses begins running when the offense is complete, but discovery of the offense may toll the limitations period under certain circumstances. Defense attorneys should examine the timing of the government's investigation and knowledge to identify potential statute of limitations defenses.

Constitutional challenges to PPP fraud prosecutions may include due process violations based on vague or retroactively applied regulations, equal protection violations based on selective prosecution, or Eighth Amendment challenges to disproportionate sentences. These challenges require careful development of factual records that demonstrate constitutional violations and legal briefing that addresses current constitutional doctrine. Defense attorneys should consider constitutional challenges as part of comprehensive defense strategies that address both legal and factual defenses.

The discovery process in PPP fraud cases requires strategic thinking that goes beyond simple compliance with disclosure rules. Defense attorneys must develop systematic approaches to reviewing massive document productions, identifying favorable evidence that prosecutors have failed to properly disclose, and challenging government evidence that was obtained illegally or unreliably. The complexity of these cases demands early and aggressive discovery practice that puts pressure on prosecutors to comply with their obligations while identifying suppression opportunities that might eliminate key evidence.

Electronic discovery management in PPP fraud cases requires technological sophistication and adequate resources to review voluminous materials effectively. Defense attorneys should demand that prosecutors produce evidence in searchable formats and provide adequate time and resources for review. The failure to properly manage electronic discovery can result in missed opportunities to identify favorable evidence or challenge government theories.

Expert witness challenges in PPP fraud cases require understanding both the legal standards for expert testimony and the technical issues involved in financial analysis and digital forensics. Defense attorneys should retain qualified experts early in the case to review government analyses and identify potential challenges to prosecution evidence. Expert challenges should focus on both the reliability of methods used and the adequacy of underlying data.

The suppression of evidence in PPP fraud cases requires comprehensive understanding of constitutional protections, statutory requirements, and procedural rules that govern evidence collection and disclosure. Success depends on early identification of potential issues, thorough investigation of government conduct, and aggressive litigation of suppression motions that challenge illegally obtained evidence. The stakes in these cases require defense attorneys to exhaust all available avenues for excluding prejudicial evidence and exposing government overreach.

Discovery and evidence suppression tactics represent essential tools for defending PPP fraud charges that often rest on questionable evidence obtained through aggressive government investigations. The complexity of these cases demands specialized knowledge and strategic thinking that goes beyond traditional criminal defense practice. Understanding the available tools and their strategic application provides the foundation for effective defense advocacy in an era of prosecutorial overreach and electronic surveillance.

CHAPTER 24

MENTAL WARFARE: SURVIVING THE FEDERAL PROCESS

The federal criminal justice system operates as a psychological warfare machine designed to break defendants mentally before they ever reach trial. The process transforms ordinary citizens into federal criminal defendants through a campaign of intimidation, isolation, and relentless pressure that extends far beyond the courthouse walls. Understanding this psychological dimension becomes essential for survival because the government's true weapon is not evidence or legal arguments but the systematic destruction of defendants' mental resilience and decision-making capacity.

The moment federal agents knock on your door or serve a grand jury subpoena, the psychological assault begins with calculated precision. Law enforcement officers receive training in psychological manipulation techniques designed to create compliance and extract incriminating statements. They arrive in overwhelming numbers, display weapons prominently, and use aggressive questioning tactics that create fear and confusion. The message is clear: you are now an enemy of the state, and resistance is futile.

The initial shock of federal criminal investigation triggers a cascade of psychological responses that prosecutors exploit ruthlessly. Defendants experience acute stress reactions that impair judgment, create memory problems, and generate desperate attempts to cooperate or explain away incriminating evidence. The government recognizes these vulnerability windows and structures its investigative timeline to maximize psychological pressure when defendants are least capable of making rational decisions.

Federal prosecutors understand that most defendants will never reach trial because the psychological pressure of the process will force them to plead guilty regardless of the strength of the evidence. The system is designed to create such overwhelming anxiety, financial pressure, and social isolation that defendants surrender rather than fight. Statistics confirm this strategy's effectiveness: over ninety-five percent of federal defendants plead guilty, often accepting sentences that exceed what they might receive after trial.

The grand jury process serves as a primary tool of psychological warfare, creating an atmosphere of secrecy and inevitability that undermines defendants' confidence in their legal position. Grand jury proceedings occur behind closed doors with defendants excluded, creating paranoid speculation about what witnesses are saying and what evidence the government is presenting. The one-sided nature of grand jury proceedings ensures that defendants hear only negative information about their cases, creating psychological pressure to accept the government's version of events.

The indictment itself represents a carefully crafted psychological weapon that maximizes fear and confusion while minimizing defendants' ability to mount effective responses. Federal indictments typically include multiple charges, complex conspiracy allegations, and astronomical maximum penalties that create overwhelming anxiety about potential sentences. The document is written in dense legal language that most defendants cannot understand, requiring expensive legal representation to decode the charges and their implications.

Media coverage of federal criminal cases serves the government's psychological warfare objectives by creating public shame and social isolation that compounds the legal pressure defendants face. Prosecutors often coordinate with media outlets to ensure that arrest announcements and indictment details receive prominent coverage that portrays defendants as clearly guilty. The presumption of innocence disappears in media coverage that treats charges as convictions and focuses on the most inflammatory allegations rather than the actual evidence.

The financial devastation caused by federal criminal charges creates additional psychological pressure that forces defendants to make decisions based on economic desperation rather than legal strategy. Federal criminal defense costs typically range from hundreds of thousands to millions of dollars, forcing defendants to liquidate assets, mortgage homes, and exhaust savings accounts. The government often freezes assets through forfeiture actions, creating additional financial pressure that limits defendants' ability to mount effective defenses.

Family relationships become casualties of federal criminal prosecutions as the stress, financial pressure, and social stigma create rifts that prosecutors exploit for additional leverage. Spouses face pressure to cooperate against defendants, children suffer social consequences at school and in their communities, and extended family members distance themselves to avoid association with the criminal case. The isolation compounds defendants' psychological distress while eliminating support systems that might provide emotional stability.

Professional and business consequences multiply the psychological impact of federal charges by destroying careers and livelihood that defendants spent decades building. Professional licenses face suspension or revocation, business relationships terminate, and employment opportunities disappear based solely on the filing of charges. The reputational damage often proves irreversible even for defendants who are ultimately acquitted, creating long-term consequences that extend far beyond the criminal case.

The pretrial detention process serves multiple psychological warfare functions by demonstrating the government's power while creating additional pressure for plea agreements. Federal defendants often face detention hearings where prosecutors argue that they pose flight risks or dangers to the community based on the charges alone. The detention process forces defendants to choose between remaining in jail pending trial or accepting restrictive release conditions that limit their freedom and ability to prepare defenses.

Cooperation pressure represents one of the most insidious forms of psychological warfare in federal cases, forcing defendants to choose between loyalty to family and associates and their own freedom. Prosecutors routinely approach defendants early in the process with cooperation offers that require them to implicate others in criminal activity. The pressure to cooperate creates moral conflicts that compound the stress of the criminal case while potentially destroying relationships with people defendants care about.

The plea negotiation process operates as a form of psychological torture that forces defendants to make life-altering decisions under extreme time pressure and incomplete information. Prosecutors typically make plea offers with short deadlines and threats of additional charges if offers are rejected. Defendants must evaluate complex risk assessments about trial outcomes while dealing with severe anxiety and depression that impair their decision-making abilities.

The uncertainty inherent in federal criminal cases creates chronic stress that undermines defendants' psychological stability and physical health. Unlike civil cases where outcomes are typically monetary, federal criminal cases threaten defendants' freedom, families, and futures in ways that create constant anxiety about worst-case scenarios. The inability to control outcomes or predict results creates learned helplessness that makes defendants more susceptible to government pressure.

Sleep deprivation becomes a common problem for federal defendants as anxiety and fear disrupt normal sleep patterns. The combination of stress hormones, financial worries, and catastrophic thinking creates insomnia that compounds other psychological problems. Sleep deprivation impairs cognitive function, emotional regulation, and decision-making capacity at the precise time when defendants need these abilities most.

Depression and anxiety disorders frequently develop during federal criminal cases as defendants struggle to cope with the multiple stressors and threats to their wellbeing. The combination of legal jeopardy, financial devastation, social isolation, and family stress creates perfect conditions for serious mental health problems. Many defendants develop clinical depression that requires professional treatment, but the stigma of mental health issues in criminal cases often prevents them from seeking help.

Substance abuse problems may emerge or worsen during federal criminal cases as defendants attempt to self-medicate anxiety and depression. The stress of criminal charges combined with the disruption of normal routines and support systems creates vulnerability to alcohol and drug abuse. Substance abuse problems complicate legal defenses while creating additional leverage for prosecutors who can use addiction issues to argue for enhanced sentences or detention.

The isolation tactics employed by federal prosecutors include restrictions on defendants' contact with codefendants, witnesses, and associates that limit their ability to understand the case against them or coordinate defenses. Pretrial release conditions often prohibit defendants from contacting other people involved in their cases, creating information vacuums that increase anxiety and paranoia. The isolation prevents defendants from learning about government tactics or organizing collective responses.

Surveillance and monitoring of federal defendants creates additional psychological pressure through the constant awareness that government agents may be watching their activities and communications. Many defendants develop paranoid behaviors based on realistic concerns about electronic surveillance, physical observation, and informants in their social circles. The knowledge that privacy no longer exists compounds the stress of the criminal case while limiting defendants' ability to prepare defenses.

The lengthy timeline of federal criminal cases creates sustained psychological pressure that wears down defendants' resistance over months or years. Unlike state criminal cases that often resolve quickly, federal cases typically involve extensive investigations, complex motions practice, and lengthy trial preparation that can extend for years. The prolonged uncertainty and stress create cumulative psychological damage that makes defendants more likely to accept unfavorable plea agreements.

Coping strategies for federal defendants must address both the immediate crisis and the long-term challenges of surviving the federal process. Professional counseling becomes essential for managing anxiety, depression, and trauma responses that develop during criminal cases. Mental health treatment should begin immediately after charges are filed and continue throughout the process regardless of the ultimate outcome.

Physical health maintenance provides a foundation for psychological resilience during federal criminal cases. Regular exercise, proper nutrition, and adequate sleep help defendants manage stress hormones and maintain cognitive function needed for making important decisions. Many defendants neglect physical health during criminal cases, but maintaining basic health routines becomes essential for psychological survival.

Support system development requires careful attention to maintaining relationships that provide emotional stability without creating additional legal jeopardy. Family therapy may help address relationship stress while individual counseling provides tools for managing anxiety and depression. Support groups for people facing federal charges can provide understanding and practical advice from others who have survived similar experiences.

Information management becomes crucial for maintaining psychological equilibrium during federal criminal cases. Defendants benefit from understanding the legal process and their options, but they must avoid becoming obsessed with case details or worst-case scenarios. Working with attorneys to develop realistic assessments of risks and options helps defendants make informed decisions without becoming paralyzed by fear.

Financial planning for federal criminal cases requires early attention to preserving resources needed for legal defense while preparing for potential forfeiture and sentencing consequences. Defendants should work with financial advisors and attorneys to develop strategies for managing costs while protecting family assets. Early financial planning reduces stress and provides more options for defending against charges.

Communication strategies with family, friends, and colleagues help defendants maintain relationships while protecting against additional legal jeopardy. Defendants should work with attorneys to develop guidelines for what can be discussed and with whom, avoiding communications that might create evidence for prosecutors while maintaining important relationships.

Media strategy becomes important for defendants who face public attention from their federal charges. Working with experienced criminal defense attorneys and public relations professionals can help minimize reputational damage while avoiding statements that create additional legal problems. Most defendants benefit from maintaining silence about their cases while focusing on personal and family needs.

The psychological warfare dimension of federal criminal cases represents a deliberate strategy designed to coerce guilty pleas and destroy defendants' ability to mount effective defenses. Understanding this dynamic provides the first step toward developing resilience and maintaining the mental clarity needed to make rational decisions about legal strategy. Survival requires recognition that the process itself is the punishment, regardless of the ultimate outcome.

Recovery from federal criminal prosecution requires long-term attention to psychological healing even after cases conclude. The trauma of federal criminal charges creates lasting effects that may require ongoing counseling and support. Defendants who understand the psychological warfare dimension of their experience are better equipped to heal and rebuild their lives regardless of whether they are convicted or acquitted.

The federal criminal process transforms the presumption of innocence into a presumption of guilt through systematic psychological pressure that breaks down defendants' resistance to government demands. Understanding this reality provides defendants with the knowledge needed to protect their mental health while maintaining their ability to make rational decisions about their legal defense. The battle for survival begins with recognizing that the government's primary weapon is fear, and the most effective defense is maintaining psychological resilience in the face of systematic intimidation.

CHAPTER 25

JURY PSYCHOLOGY & VOIR DIRE STRATEGY

The jury selection process in federal criminal trials represents the most critical battleground where cases are won or lost before a single witness testifies. Understanding jury psychology and mastering voir dire strategy becomes essential for defendants facing PPP fraud charges because these complex financial cases require jurors who can think independently, resist government pressure, and understand the difference between regulatory violations and criminal conduct. The wrong jury will convict regardless of the evidence, while the right jury will hold the government to its burden of proof.

Jury psychology in federal criminal cases operates on multiple levels that defense attorneys must understand and address strategically. Surface-level attitudes about crime and punishment provide only the beginning of jury analysis. Deeper psychological factors including authority deference, risk aversion, and cognitive biases determine how jurors process evidence and reach verdicts. The most dangerous jurors are often those who appear reasonable and fair-minded but harbor unconscious biases that predispose them to accept government arguments.

The authority bias represents the most significant psychological hurdle in federal criminal cases because most citizens have been conditioned to trust government institutions and defer to official authority. Federal prosecutors exploit this bias by positioning themselves as representatives of justice and order while portraying defendants as threats to social stability. Jurors who cannot overcome authority bias will convict based on the government's credibility rather than the strength of the evidence.

Confirmation bias creates additional challenges in federal criminal cases because jurors tend to interpret evidence in ways that confirm their initial impressions about defendants' guilt or innocence. The government's opening statement and early witnesses establish powerful first impressions that influence how jurors evaluate subsequent evidence. Defense attorneys must identify jurors who can remain open to alternative interpretations of evidence throughout the trial.

The complexity bias affects jury decision-making in PPP fraud cases because many jurors become overwhelmed by financial evidence and regulatory details. When faced with complex information they cannot fully understand, jurors often default to simple narratives that reduce cognitive load. The government typically offers simpler stories that cast defendants as greedy criminals, while defense narratives may require more sophisticated thinking about regulatory compliance and business operations.

Economic bias influences jury attitudes toward financial crimes because jurors' personal economic circumstances affect their perception of defendants' conduct. Jurors who have struggled financially may view PPP fraud defendants as privileged individuals who cheated while honest people suffered. Conversely, jurors with business experience may understand the pressures and uncertainties that led to regulatory violations without criminal intent.

Demographic analysis provides essential information for jury selection, but attorneys must look beyond surface characteristics to underlying attitudes and experiences. Age, education, occupation, and geographic background correlate with certain attitudes, but individual variation within demographic groups requires careful questioning to identify actual beliefs and biases. Successful voir dire requires understanding both demographic patterns and individual psychology.

The pretrial publicity impact in high-profile PPP fraud cases creates additional jury selection challenges because potential jurors may have formed opinions based on media coverage that portrayed defendants negatively. Publicity effects operate at both conscious and unconscious levels, making it difficult for jurors to set aside preconceived notions even when they claim they can be fair. Defense attorneys must develop strategies for identifying and challenging for cause jurors who have been influenced by negative publicity.

Voir dire strategy in federal criminal cases requires balancing the goals of identifying biased jurors, educating favorable jurors about case themes, and avoiding early disclosure of defense strategies to prosecutors. The limited time allowed for voir dire in federal court creates pressure to accomplish multiple objectives efficiently while building rapport with potential jurors. Successful voir dire requires careful preparation and tactical flexibility to adapt to unexpected responses.

Open-ended questioning techniques prove more effective than leading questions for revealing juror attitudes and biases. Questions that invite jurors to share experiences and opinions provide insights into their thinking processes and underlying beliefs. Effective voir dire questions focus on attitudes toward relevant case themes rather than asking directly about the ability to be fair and impartial. Jurors will rarely admit bias directly but will reveal their attitudes through responses to hypothetical scenarios and experience-based questions.

The government's voir dire strategy typically focuses on reinforcing authority bias and identifying jurors who will defer to official interpretations of evidence. Prosecutors ask questions designed to elicit commitments to follow the law and accept government evidence at face value. They seek jurors who view criminal charges as evidence of wrongdoing and who believe that innocent people do not get indicted by federal grand juries.

Defense voir dire strategy must counter government tactics while identifying jurors who can think independently and resist pressure to convict. Defense attorneys should focus on themes of fairness, reasonable doubt, and the presumption of innocence while identifying jurors who have experience with business operations or regulatory compliance. Questions should explore attitudes toward government oversight, business regulations, and the appropriate response to paperwork errors.

Batson challenges provide a mechanism for challenging discriminatory jury selection, but they require careful documentation of patterns in peremptory challenge usage. Prosecutors may attempt to remove jurors based on race, gender, or other protected characteristics while offering pretextual explanations for their challenges. Defense attorneys must be prepared to identify and challenge discriminatory patterns while building records for appeal.

Jury consultant utilization can provide valuable insights into jury psychology and selection strategy, particularly in high-stakes PPP fraud cases. Experienced jury consultants offer expertise in demographic analysis, psychological profiling, and voir dire technique that may exceed the knowledge of even experienced criminal defense attorneys. The cost of jury consultants must be weighed against the potential benefits in cases where conviction carries severe sentences.

Focus group research allows defense teams to test case themes and witness effectiveness with mock jurors before trial. Focus groups provide insights into how ordinary citizens react to complex financial evidence and regulatory arguments. The information gathered from focus groups can inform jury selection strategy, opening statement themes, and witness preparation. However, focus group participants may not perfectly represent actual jurors, requiring careful interpretation of results.

Juror background investigation within legal and ethical boundaries can provide additional information for making informed peremptory challenges. Social media profiles, public records, and professional affiliations may reveal attitudes and associations that are not disclosed during voir dire. Background investigation must comply with court rules and ethical requirements while providing useful information for jury selection decisions.

The ideal defense juror in PPP fraud cases typically possesses business experience, higher education, and independent thinking skills that enable them to understand complex evidence and resist pressure to convict. Business owners and managers may understand the challenges of regulatory compliance and the difference between mistakes and criminal intent. Educators and professionals may have experience evaluating complex information and reaching independent conclusions.

Problem jurors for the defense include individuals with strong authority bias, limited business experience, and rigid thinking patterns that make them susceptible to government arguments. Law enforcement officers, government employees, and individuals with strong law-and-order attitudes often prove problematic for defense cases. Jurors who have been victims of financial crimes may harbor bias against defendants accused of similar conduct.

The stealth juror phenomenon involves potential jurors who conceal their bias or agenda during voir dire while planning to advocate for particular outcomes during deliberations. Stealth jurors may be motivated by personal beliefs, media coverage, or desire for attention. Identifying stealth jurors requires careful attention to inconsistencies in responses and body language that suggests deception or hidden agendas.

Voir dire time management requires efficient use of limited court time while accomplishing essential jury selection objectives. Federal judges typically impose strict time limits on voir dire that prevent thorough exploration of juror attitudes. Defense attorneys must prioritize the most important topics while developing efficient questioning techniques that maximize information gathering within time constraints.

Group voir dire dynamics create additional challenges because jurors influence each other's responses through social pressure and conformity. Early responses from vocal jurors may influence later responses from more reserved panel members. Defense attorneys must understand group dynamics while identifying genuine individual attitudes that may differ from group consensus.

Individual voir dire opportunities allow more detailed exploration of sensitive topics that jurors may be reluctant to discuss in group settings. Sidebar conferences with individual jurors can explore bias, pretrial publicity exposure, and personal experiences that might affect their ability to be fair. Individual voir dire requires court permission and should be reserved for situations where group questioning is inadequate.

Hardship challenges involve potential jurors who claim that jury service would create severe personal or financial difficulties. Courts vary in their willingness to excuse jurors for hardship reasons, but lengthy federal trials often create legitimate hardship for working people. Defense attorneys should be sensitive to genuine hardship while recognizing that some hardship claims may mask bias or unwillingness to serve.

Cause challenges allow removal of jurors who demonstrate actual bias or inability to follow jury instructions. The standard for cause challenges requires clear evidence of bias that would prevent fair consideration of the evidence. Defense attorneys must build clear records for cause challenges while recognizing that judges are often reluctant to grant challenges that reduce the jury pool.

Peremptory challenge strategy requires careful analysis of remaining jurors and strategic decisions about which individuals pose the greatest threat to defense objectives. The limited number of peremptory challenges in federal court requires difficult choices about which jurors to remove. Defense attorneys must balance the desire to remove obviously problematic jurors with the need to preserve challenges for unexpected developments.

Jury instruction negotiations during voir dire allow attorneys to preview arguments about legal standards and evidentiary issues. Questions about jurors' ability to follow specific instructions can educate the panel about defense themes while building records for instruction conferences. Voir dire questions about reasonable doubt, intent, and other legal concepts can begin the process of educating jurors about applicable legal standards.

The rehabilitation process involves attempting to cure bias or misconceptions revealed during voir dire through additional questioning or instruction. Rehabilitation allows attorneys to address concerns about particular jurors without using peremptory challenges. Successful rehabilitation requires careful questioning that addresses specific concerns while building juror commitment to fairness.

Alternate juror selection requires the same careful analysis applied to regular jurors because alternates may be called upon to deliberate if regular jurors are excused. Alternates observe the entire trial and may influence regular jurors through informal conversations and reactions to evidence. Defense attorneys should apply the same selection criteria to alternates while recognizing their potential impact on case outcomes.

Post-selection jury management begins immediately after jury selection and continues throughout the trial. Defense attorneys should observe juror reactions to evidence and arguments while adapting trial strategy based on jury feedback. Understanding individual juror personalities and group dynamics helps attorneys tailor their presentations for maximum effectiveness.

The voir dire process in PPP fraud cases requires sophisticated understanding of psychology, strategy, and trial advocacy that goes far beyond basic jury selection techniques. Success depends on careful preparation, tactical flexibility, and deep understanding of how ordinary citizens react to complex financial evidence and government authority. The jury selected during voir dire will determine the outcome of even the strongest cases, making this process the most critical component of trial preparation.

Jury selection represents both an art and a science that requires intuition, experience, and systematic analysis to identify jurors who can fairly evaluate complex evidence and resist pressure to convict. The psychological factors that influence jury decision-making operate largely below the surface, requiring skilled questioning and careful observation to identify. Defense attorneys who master these skills gain significant advantages in federal criminal trials where jury verdicts often depend more on psychology than evidence.

CHAPTER 26

THE EVOLUTION OF FEDERAL OVERREACH

The transformation of federal criminal law from a limited constitutional system focused on interstate commerce and specific federal crimes into a vast prosecutorial empire capable of criminalizing virtually any conduct represents one of the most significant constitutional shifts in American history. Understanding this evolution becomes essential for comprehending how PPP fraud prosecutions emerged from a broader pattern of federal expansion that has systematically eroded the boundaries between federal and state authority while concentrating unprecedented prosecutorial power in the hands of unelected federal officials.

The constitutional framework established by the founders envisioned federal criminal law as narrowly confined to specific areas of genuine federal concern including treason, counterfeiting, piracy, and crimes committed on federal property. The Constitution's enumerated powers doctrine required that federal criminal statutes derive from specific constitutional grants of authority, primarily the commerce clause, postal power, and necessary and proper clause. This limited conception of federal authority reflected the founders' understanding that criminal law enforcement was primarily a state and local function.

The Commerce Clause emerged as the primary vehicle for federal criminal law expansion, transforming from a provision designed to facilitate interstate trade into a limitless source of federal prosecutorial authority. Early Supreme Court decisions interpreted the commerce clause narrowly, requiring actual interstate commerce connections for federal jurisdiction. The New Deal era marked the beginning of commerce clause expansion that would eventually encompass any activity that might affect interstate commerce, however remotely or theoretically.

The landmark decision in **Wickard v. Filburn** epitomized the constitutional transformation that enabled modern federal overreach by establishing that federal authority extended to purely local activities that cumulatively might affect interstate commerce. The case involved a farmer who grew wheat for his own consumption, seemingly the most local of activities. The Court's decision that such conduct fell within federal commerce power eliminated meaningful limits on federal authority and provided the foundation for subsequent criminal law expansion.

World War II accelerated federal power expansion through wartime legislation that established precedents for federal involvement in areas previously considered state responsibilities. The war created justifications for federal oversight of economic activity, resource allocation, and civilian conduct that survived the war's end. Emergency powers became permanent features of the federal system, creating institutional momentum for continued expansion of federal authority into new areas of American life.

The Cold War period witnessed systematic expansion of federal criminal law through legislation targeting organized crime, drug trafficking, and national security threats. **The Organized Crime Control Act of 1970** introduced RICO statutes that criminalized participation in enterprises affecting interstate commerce, creating federal jurisdiction over traditionally local crimes when connected to ongoing criminal organizations. The breadth of RICO's definition of criminal enterprise virtually eliminated boundaries between federal and state criminal jurisdiction.

The Controlled Substances Act of 1970 exemplified the federal government's strategy of using interstate commerce theory to criminalize conduct with minimal federal connections. Drug crimes became federal offenses whenever they involved interstate transportation, however slight, or when they could be connected to larger distribution networks. The act created a parallel federal drug enforcement system that duplicated state efforts while concentrating prosecutorial resources at the federal level.

The war on drugs provided justification for massive expansion of federal criminal law enforcement that extended far beyond drug trafficking to encompass money laundering, asset forfeiture, and conspiracy charges that could reach virtually any financial transaction. Federal drug prosecutions grew exponentially as prosecutors discovered that drug charges provided entry points for investigating and prosecuting conduct that had previously been beyond federal reach.

The September 11 attacks triggered another wave of federal expansion that dwarfed previous increases in federal authority. **The USA PATRIOT Act** and subsequent legislation eliminated traditional boundaries between criminal investigation and intelligence gathering while expanding federal surveillance powers and creating new categories of federal crimes. The national security justification for federal expansion proved even more powerful than previous rationales based on interstate commerce or organized crime.

The creation of the **Department of Homeland Security** consolidated federal law enforcement powers while establishing new federal crimes related to terrorism, immigration, and critical infrastructure protection. The department's broad mandate created overlap with traditional state and local law enforcement while concentrating authority in federal agencies with limited accountability to local communities.

Financial crimes enforcement experienced dramatic expansion through legislation that federalized conduct previously handled by state banking regulators and local prosecutors. **The Bank Secrecy Act,** and subsequent anti-money laundering legislation, created federal crimes for financial transactions that had minimal connections to traditional federal concerns. These laws established reporting requirements that transformed routine banking into potential federal crimes for technical violations.

The Sarbanes-Oxley Act expanded federal securities enforcement beyond traditional securities fraud to encompass corporate governance, document retention, and accounting practices. The act criminalized conduct that had previously been addressed through civil enforcement or state corporate law, creating federal crimes for business practices that had been considered acceptable or subject to civil penalties.

Healthcare fraud enforcement exemplifies federal expansion into areas traditionally governed by state professional licensing and malpractice law. Federal healthcare fraud statutes criminalize billing practices, medical decision-making, and business relationships in the healthcare industry. The federal government's role as a major healthcare payer through Medicare and Medicaid programs provided justification for criminal enforcement that reaches into examination rooms and medical offices.

Environmental crimes represent another area where federal authority expanded beyond traditional constitutional boundaries through broad interpretations of interstate commerce and federal property powers. Environmental criminal statutes criminalize conduct on private property that may have minimal environmental impact but violates complex regulatory schemes administered by federal agencies. These prosecutions often target business owners for technical violations of regulations they may not have understood.

Immigration enforcement expansion created new federal crimes for conduct that had previously been civil violations or state crimes. Immigration-related criminal statutes now encompass employment practices, document fraud, and transportation activities that have become federal crimes when connected to immigration status. The expansion has federalized large categories of conduct that were historically handled by state authorities.

The proliferation of federal agencies with criminal enforcement powers represents a significant departure from the traditional model of federal law enforcement concentrated in the Department of Justice. Agencies including the **EPA, FDA, OSHA**, and dozens of others now conduct criminal investigations and make referrals for prosecution. This expansion has created a vast federal enforcement apparatus that can target almost any business or individual for violations of complex regulatory schemes.

Prosecutorial discretion has become unlimited power as federal criminal statutes expanded to cover virtually any conduct that prosecutors choose to target. The breadth of federal criminal law means that prosecutors can find federal crimes in almost any situation, giving them enormous leverage in plea negotiations and the ability to destroy lives through selective enforcement. The discretion to choose which laws to enforce and against whom has concentrated unprecedented power in the hands of federal prosecutors.

The plea bargaining system emerged as the primary mechanism for federal criminal case resolution, creating a shadow justice system that operates outside constitutional protections designed for jury trials. Federal defendants face overwhelming pressure to plead guilty because the consequences of conviction after trial far exceed plea bargain offers. This system enables prosecutors to secure convictions without proving guilt beyond a reasonable doubt to unanimous juries.

Asset forfeiture laws provide federal agencies with independent funding sources that create institutional incentives for aggressive enforcement regardless of actual criminal conduct. Civil forfeiture allows government seizure of property based on preponderance of evidence standards rather than criminal conviction beyond reasonable doubt. The seized assets fund additional enforcement activities, creating self-perpetuating expansion of federal enforcement capabilities.

Federal sentencing guidelines transformed judicial discretion into mechanical calculations that removed human judgment from punishment decisions. The guidelines created enormous sentencing enhancements for technical violations while eliminating judges' ability to consider individual circumstances that might warrant mercy. Although now advisory, the guidelines continue to anchor federal sentences at levels that exceed those imposed for similar crimes in state systems.

The federalization of white-collar crime represents perhaps the most dramatic expansion of federal authority because it reached into business relationships and professional practices that had been governed by state commercial law and professional regulations. Federal mail and wire fraud statutes became universal tools for prosecuting any business conduct that involved interstate communications or transportation, effectively federalizing most commercial disputes and regulatory violations.

Computer crimes legislation expanded federal authority into cyberspace through statutes that criminalize electronic communications and computer use. **The Computer Fraud and Abuse Act** creates federal crimes for accessing computers without authorization, a standard so broad that it potentially criminalizes violation of terms of service agreements for websites and computer programs. The digital nature of modern communication means that most crimes now involve some federal nexus through electronic communications.

Federal racketeering laws have expanded beyond their original organized crime targets to encompass legitimate businesses, professional practices, and political organizations. RICO's broad definition of criminal enterprise includes any group that commits multiple crimes, allowing prosecutors to treat business partnerships, professional associations, and even family relationships as criminal organizations subject to enhanced penalties.

The erosion of the federal-state distinction in criminal law has eliminated the constitutional balance that protected individual liberty through competing jurisdictions. The founders' system contemplated that federal and state governments would serve as checks on each other's power, with most criminal law enforcement remaining at the state and local level where communities could influence law enforcement priorities. Federal expansion has concentrated criminal law enforcement power at the national level while reducing local democratic control.

Constitutional challenges to federal expansion have largely failed because courts have abandoned meaningful limits on federal power under the commerce clause and necessary and proper clause. The Supreme Court's occasional efforts to impose limits on federal authority have been narrow and easily circumvented by congressional drafting that invokes different constitutional powers or creates technical interstate commerce connections.

The institutional momentum behind federal expansion continues to drive new legislation that creates federal crimes for problems that arise in American society. Each crisis, whether real or perceived, generates demands for federal action that typically result in new criminal statutes rather than civil remedies or state-level responses. The political incentives favor federal solutions that appear tough on crime while concentrating power at the national level.

Congressional oversight of federal criminal law enforcement has proven inadequate to constrain prosecutorial overreach because legislators have political incentives to support tough-on-crime measures rather than protect constitutional limits. The complexity of federal criminal law makes meaningful oversight difficult, while prosecutors' claims of necessity for broad authority typically go unchallenged by legislators who fear appearing soft on crime.

The separation of powers has eroded as executive branch agencies assume legislative and judicial functions through regulatory enforcement that carries criminal penalties. Federal agencies now write regulations with criminal sanctions, investigate violations, and effectively adjudicate guilt through settlement agreements that avoid trial. This concentration of power in the executive branch eliminates the checks and balances that the constitutional system was designed to provide.

The impact of federal overreach on PPP fraud prosecutions demonstrates how expanded federal authority enables prosecutorial abuse in response to political pressure. The pandemic created demands for aggressive enforcement against fraud, leading to prosecutions that stretch traditional fraud concepts to criminalize conduct that might have been considered regulatory violations in other contexts. The broad federal statutes and prosecution theories developed over decades of expansion provided tools for targeting PPP recipients regardless of their actual intent or conduct.

Reform efforts face enormous institutional obstacles because federal expansion has created bureaucracies, legal precedents, and political constituencies that benefit from continued growth of federal power. Federal law enforcement agencies resist limitations on their authority, while prosecutors argue that complex modern problems require federal solutions. The Supreme Court has shown limited willingness to impose meaningful constraints on federal authority, leaving reform to congressional action that faces overwhelming political obstacles.

The evolution of federal overreach represents a fundamental transformation of American government that has concentrated unprecedented power at the national level while eliminating constitutional protections that were designed to preserve individual liberty and local self-government. Understanding this evolution provides essential context for comprehending how PPP fraud prosecutions emerged from a system that has systematically expanded federal authority beyond constitutional boundaries while creating prosecutorial tools that can criminalize virtually any conduct. The trajectory toward ever-greater federal power continues to accelerate, threatening the constitutional balance that once protected American liberty through limited government and separated powers.

CHAPTER 27

PPP AS A POLITICAL WEAPON

The transformation of the Paycheck Protection Program from emergency pandemic relief into a tool of political persecution represents one of the most cynical abuses of prosecutorial power in modern American history. What began as bipartisan legislation designed to preserve jobs and prevent economic collapse evolved into a selective enforcement mechanism that targets political enemies while protecting favored constituencies. Understanding how prosecutors weaponized PPP enforcement reveals broader patterns of politicized justice that threaten the rule of law and constitutional government.

The initial legislative response to the COVID-19 pandemic reflected genuine bipartisan concern about economic devastation facing American businesses and workers. **The CARES Act** passed with overwhelming support from both parties as legislators recognized the need for immediate relief to prevent mass unemployment and business failures. The PPP represented a compromise solution that channeled aid through existing banking relationships while providing flexibility for businesses to maintain payrolls during unprecedented disruption.

Congressional intent for the PPP emphasized speed and accessibility over perfect compliance, recognizing that emergency relief required accepting some level of fraud and abuse as the cost of rapid distribution. Legislators explicitly acknowledged that program requirements might be unclear and that businesses would make mistakes in their rush to obtain survival funding. The legislative record demonstrates understanding that technical violations were inevitable and that the primary goal was preserving employment rather than perfect regulatory compliance.

The political transformation of PPP enforcement began during the 2020 election cycle as partisan actors sought to weaponize pandemic response for electoral advantage. Media coverage shifted from celebrating successful business relief to highlighting alleged fraud and abuse, creating political pressure for aggressive enforcement. The narrative transformation treated emergency relief recipients as potential criminals rather than struggling businesses that had received intended assistance.

The Biden administration's approach to PPP enforcement marked a dramatic departure from the emergency response orientation that characterized the program's creation. New leadership at the Department of Justice elevated PPP fraud prosecution to a national priority, establishing specialized task forces and allocating resources for aggressive enforcement that far exceeded the attention given to other white-collar crimes. The shift reflected political calculation rather than proportional response to actual criminal conduct.

The selective enforcement patterns in PPP fraud prosecutions reveal clear political bias in targeting decisions that cannot be explained by neutral law enforcement principles. Small businesses owned by political minorities, rural entrepreneurs, and individuals associated with disfavored political movements face disproportionate prosecution while well-connected corporations and politically favored industries receive lenient treatment for similar or worse conduct. The disparity demonstrates that prosecutorial discretion operates according to political rather than legal criteria.

Media coordination with federal prosecutors creates propaganda campaigns that amplify enforcement actions against targeted defendants while minimizing coverage of enforcement gaps that protect favored constituencies. Press releases announcing PPP fraud charges receive prominent coverage that portrays defendants as clearly guilty, while prosecutorial failures and overreach receive minimal attention. The coordination serves political messaging rather than public information purposes.

The statistical evidence of selective enforcement emerges from analysis of prosecution patterns that show dramatic disparities based on defendant characteristics rather than conduct severity. Minority-owned businesses, rural enterprises, and businesses in Republican-leaning districts face prosecution rates that exceed their representation in the program while large corporations and businesses in Democratic strongholds receive disproportionately lenient treatment for comparable conduct.

Corporate immunity from PPP fraud prosecution extends to large companies that received millions in loans while engaging in conduct that would generate criminal charges for individual defendants. Major corporations laid off employees despite receiving PPP funding, used loans for purposes clearly prohibited by program requirements, and submitted applications containing obvious inaccuracies without facing criminal consequences. The immunity demonstrates that enforcement priorities reflect political calculation rather than program integrity.

Banking industry protection from PPP fraud liability represents another form of selective enforcement that shields politically powerful institutions while targeting vulnerable individual defendants. Banks that facilitated obviously fraudulent applications, failed to conduct required due diligence, and profited from loan processing fees escape prosecution while individual loan recipients face criminal charges for technical violations. The disparity reveals that prosecutorial discretion protects institutional power rather than program integrity.

Professional service provider immunity extends to accountants, attorneys, and consultants who prepared PPP applications containing false information without facing the conspiracy and aiding-and-abetting charges routinely filed against family members and employees of targeted defendants. The selective immunity demonstrates that enforcement reflects social and political connections rather than actual culpability for alleged criminal conduct.

Geographic targeting patterns in PPP fraud prosecutions correlate with political geography rather than fraud incidence, suggesting that enforcement decisions reflect partisan calculation rather than neutral law enforcement priorities. Districts with Republican representation face disproportionate prosecution while similar conduct in Democratic strongholds receives civil rather than criminal treatment. The pattern demonstrates that federal prosecution has become a tool of partisan political warfare.

The timing of PPP fraud prosecutions reveals coordination with political events and electoral cycles that suggests prosecutorial decisions serve campaign rather than law enforcement purposes. High-profile arrests and indictments frequently coincide with political moments when administration officials seek to demonstrate toughness on fraud while diverting attention from policy failures or scandals. The timing patterns demonstrate political rather than legal motivation for enforcement decisions.

Industry targeting in PPP fraud prosecutions reflects political priorities rather than fraud incidence, with certain business sectors facing disproportionate enforcement while others receive protection despite similar or worse conduct. Construction, hospitality, and retail businesses face aggressive prosecution while technology companies, healthcare organizations, and financial services firms receive lenient treatment for comparable violations. The disparity reflects political favoritism rather than neutral enforcement.

The weaponization of cooperating witnesses in PPP fraud cases creates additional evidence of political targeting through prosecution strategies that encourage defendants to implicate political enemies in exchange for lenient treatment. Cooperation agreements often require admissions to conduct beyond the scope of actual wrongdoing while demanding information about political associations and activities unrelated to loan applications. The cooperation demands serve intelligence gathering rather than legitimate prosecution purposes.

Asset forfeiture abuse in PPP fraud cases demonstrates how prosecutors use civil enforcement tools to inflict punishment without criminal conviction while targeting assets beyond any reasonable relationship to alleged crimes. Forfeiture actions often seek entire business assets, family homes, and personal property that had no connection to loan applications but serve to destroy defendants financially and politically. The forfeiture strategy serves destruction rather than restitution purposes.

The international implications of PPP fraud prosecution reveal how domestic political targeting extends beyond American borders to influence foreign policy and international business relationships. Prosecutions of foreign nationals and businesses that participated in PPP create diplomatic complications while serving domestic political messaging about American sovereignty and border control. The international dimension demonstrates that PPP enforcement serves foreign policy rather than law enforcement purposes.

Congressional oversight failures regarding PPP fraud enforcement reflect institutional capture by prosecutorial interests that prevent meaningful accountability for selective enforcement and political targeting. Legislative oversight committees defer to prosecutorial claims of necessity while failing to investigate obvious patterns of selective enforcement that violate equal protection principles. The oversight failure enables continued prosecutorial abuse while eliminating democratic accountability.

Judicial complicity in PPP fraud prosecutions emerges through judicial reluctance to challenge prosecutorial theories or question enforcement disparities that should trigger equal protection scrutiny. Federal judges routinely accept prosecution arguments that stretch criminal statutes beyond recognition while refusing to examine whether enforcement patterns violate constitutional principles. The judicial deference enables prosecutorial abuse while eliminating constitutional protections.

Civil rights implications of selective PPP fraud enforcement include violations of equal protection, due process, and First Amendment rights that result from targeting based on political affiliation, geographic location, and business relationships. The enforcement patterns create chilling effects on political speech and association while establishing government retaliation against disfavored political expression. The civil rights violations demonstrate that PPP enforcement threatens constitutional government.

The administrative state's role in PPP fraud prosecutions reveals how regulatory agencies coordinate with prosecutors to target political enemies through coordinated civil and criminal enforcement actions. Agencies including the **SBA, IRS**, and banking regulators share information and coordinate enforcement strategies that maximize pressure on targeted defendants while protecting favored constituencies. The coordination demonstrates that PPP enforcement serves political rather than regulatory purposes.

Intelligence community involvement in PPP fraud investigations suggests that national security resources are being diverted to domestic political targeting through financial surveillance and investigation techniques developed for foreign threats. The use of sophisticated surveillance and analysis capabilities against small business owners represents a dangerous expansion of intelligence powers into domestic political enforcement. The intelligence involvement demonstrates that PPP enforcement threatens fundamental American liberties.

Reform proposals for depoliticizing PPP fraud enforcement face enormous institutional obstacles because the current system serves powerful political interests that benefit from selective enforcement capabilities. Prosecutorial organizations resist limitations on discretion while political leaders value enforcement tools that can target enemies and protect allies. The institutional resistance demonstrates that meaningful reform requires fundamental changes to prosecutorial accountability structures.

The precedent established by weaponized PPP enforcement creates dangerous potential for future abuse of emergency powers and prosecutorial discretion. The successful transformation of emergency relief into political persecution provides a blueprint for future administrations seeking to target political opponents through selective criminal enforcement. The precedent threatens constitutional government by establishing that emergency conditions justify abandoning equal protection principles.

Historical parallels to weaponized PPP enforcement include previous episodes of prosecutorial abuse during periods of political tension when federal prosecutors targeted political enemies while claiming to enforce neutral laws. The Palmer Raids, McCarthyism, and Watergate-era abuses demonstrate recurring patterns of prosecutorial power being used for political rather than legal purposes. The historical pattern suggests that PPP enforcement represents a continuation of dangerous traditions rather than isolated abuse.

The international perspective on PPP fraud prosecutions reveals how selective enforcement damages American credibility in promoting rule of law internationally while providing propaganda opportunities for authoritarian regimes that point to American prosecutorial abuse as evidence of hypocrisy. The selective enforcement undermines American foreign policy while providing justification for authoritarian practices abroad. The international impact demonstrates that PPP enforcement threatens American leadership and moral authority.

Economic consequences of weaponized PPP enforcement extend beyond individual defendants to entire communities and industries that face chilling effects from selective prosecution threats. Small businesses avoid government programs and limit growth to reduce visibility while entrepreneurs relocate to jurisdictions with less aggressive enforcement. The economic impact demonstrates that PPP enforcement serves destructive rather than protective purposes.

The constitutional crisis created by weaponized PPP enforcement threatens fundamental principles of equal justice under law while establishing precedents for selective enforcement that could destroy constitutional government. The transformation of emergency relief into political persecution represents a fundamental break with constitutional traditions that protected individual liberty through limited government and equal treatment. The crisis requires immediate attention to prevent permanent damage to constitutional principles.

Long-term implications of PPP enforcement abuse include erosion of public trust in government institutions, breakdown of bipartisan cooperation during emergencies, and establishment of precedents for future prosecutorial abuse. The weaponization demonstrates that emergency powers inevitably become tools of political oppression rather than public protection. The implications require fundamental reform of prosecutorial accountability and emergency power limitations.

The weaponization of PPP fraud enforcement represents more than prosecutorial overreach; it constitutes a fundamental assault on constitutional government that threatens the rule of law and democratic accountability. Understanding this reality provides essential context for comprehending how emergency powers become tools of political oppression while highlighting the urgent need for reform that restores equal justice under law. The transformation of pandemic relief into political persecution serves as a warning about the dangers of unlimited prosecutorial power and the necessity of constitutional limitations on government authority.

CHAPTER 28

SAMPLE MOTIONS & FILINGS

The art of federal criminal motion practice requires precision, strategy, and deep understanding of both legal doctrine and judicial psychology. Successful motions in PPP fraud cases demand more than technical compliance with procedural rules; they require persuasive advocacy that challenges prosecutorial theories while building records for appeal. This chapter provides annotated examples of essential motions and filings that defense attorneys must master to protect their clients' rights and create opportunities for favorable outcomes.

Motion to Dismiss for Lack of Jurisdiction represents one of the most fundamental challenges available in federal criminal cases, questioning whether the government has constitutional authority to prosecute the alleged conduct. In PPP fraud cases, jurisdiction challenges focus on whether defendants' conduct possessed sufficient interstate commerce connections to justify federal prosecution rather than state enforcement.

The jurisdictional motion begins with a detailed factual statement that emphasizes the local nature of defendants' business operations and the minimal interstate connections involved in their conduct. The factual section should highlight that defendants operated local businesses serving local customers with local employees, receiving loans from local banks to fund local operations. Any interstate connections should be characterized as incidental rather than integral to the alleged criminal scheme.

The legal argument section must address the current state of Commerce Clause doctrine while acknowledging the broad interpretation that courts typically apply to federal jurisdiction. However, recent Supreme Court decisions including **United States v. Lopez** and **United States v. Morrison** suggest renewed attention to constitutional limits on federal power. The motion should argue that prosecuting purely local business conduct exceeds constitutional boundaries and undermines federalism principles.

Practical considerations for jurisdictional motions include recognition that courts rarely grant these challenges in financial crime cases, but the motion serves important strategic purposes including preservation of appellate issues and early education of the court about defense themes. The motion also forces prosecutors to articulate their jurisdictional theory, potentially revealing weaknesses in their case.

Motion to Dismiss the Indictment for Failure to State an Offense challenges the legal sufficiency of the charges rather than the factual accuracy of the allegations. In PPP fraud cases, these motions typically argue that the indictment fails to allege essential elements of the charged crimes or that the charged conduct does not constitute criminal activity under applicable statutes.

The wire fraud dismissal motion should focus on the materiality element, arguing that technical violations of program requirements do not constitute material misrepresentations sufficient to support criminal charges. The motion must distinguish between regulatory compliance issues and criminal fraud while emphasizing that the PPP was designed as emergency relief that anticipated imperfect compliance with complex requirements.

The intent element provides another avenue for challenging wire fraud charges through arguments that good faith belief in program eligibility negates the criminal intent required for conviction. The motion should emphasize that defendants reasonably relied on program guidance and industry practice while highlighting the emergency nature of the program that encouraged rapid application rather than perfect compliance.

Money laundering charge challenges focus on the requirement that defendants knew the funds represented proceeds of criminal activity. In PPP fraud cases, defendants who received loans through legitimate banking channels and used funds for legitimate business purposes cannot have possessed the knowledge required for money laundering convictions. The motion should emphasize that using business funds for business purposes cannot constitute money laundering regardless of alleged application inaccuracies.

Conspiracy charge dismissals require challenging the sufficiency of allegations regarding agreement and overt acts in furtherance of the conspiracy. Many PPP fraud indictments charge family members and business associates with conspiracy based on minimal involvement in application preparation. The motion should argue that legitimate assistance with business applications cannot constitute criminal conspiracy without evidence of agreement to commit crimes.

Motion for Bill of Particulars seeks additional detail about the charges when the indictment contains vague or conclusory allegations that prevent effective defense preparation. **Federal Rule of Criminal Procedure 7(f)** allows defendants to request particulars when necessary to prepare a defense, and PPP fraud indictments often contain broad allegations that require clarification.

The bill of particulars motion should identify specific deficiencies in the indictment that prevent understanding of the charges. Common requests include specification of which statements are allegedly false, identification of the specific intent attributed to defendants, and clarification of the alleged conspiracy timeline and participants. The motion must demonstrate that additional detail is necessary for defense preparation rather than mere convenience.

Strategic considerations for bill of particulars motions include the risk that detailed government responses might provide more ammunition for prosecution than assistance for defense. The motion should request only information that is genuinely necessary for defense preparation while avoiding requests that might educate prosecutors about defense strategies or reveal defense theories prematurely.

Motion to Suppress Evidence challenges the admissibility of evidence obtained in violation of defendants' constitutional rights. PPP fraud cases typically involve extensive document production and financial records obtained through various investigative techniques that may have violated Fourth Amendment protections.

Bank records suppression motions challenge the government's acquisition of financial records without adequate legal process or beyond the scope of authorized subpoenas. The motion should examine the timing and scope of bank record requests while challenging any acquisition that exceeded constitutional boundaries or violated statutory protections under the **Right to Financial Privacy Act.**

Digital evidence suppression requires challenging searches of computers, phones, and electronic communications that may have exceeded warrant authority or violated reasonable expectations of privacy. The motion must address evolving technology law while applying traditional Fourth Amendment principles to modern electronic communications and data storage.

The warrant requirement section should challenge any evidence obtained without warrants when warrants were constitutionally required. This includes searches of electronic devices, email accounts, and cloud storage that may require specific warrant authority rather than general investigative subpoenas. The motion should emphasize that electronic communications receive heightened protection under recent Supreme Court decisions.

Consent search challenges focus on whether defendants validly consented to searches and whether any consent exceeded reasonable scope. Many PPP fraud investigations begin with consent searches that expand beyond the original scope or continue after consent has been withdrawn. The motion should examine the totality of circumstances surrounding any consent while challenging searches that exceeded authorized boundaries.

Motion for Brady Material compels disclosure of exculpatory evidence that prosecutors may have failed to provide. PPP fraud cases often involve extensive government investigations that generate volumes of potentially favorable evidence that prosecutors may not recognize or may prefer to withhold.

The Brady motion should make specific requests for categories of evidence likely to exist in government files. This includes SBA guidance documents that support defendants' interpretations of program requirements, evidence of selective enforcement that undermines prosecution theories, and internal government communications that reveal prosecutorial motivation or agency confusion about program requirements.

Witness credibility material requests should seek all evidence that might impeach government witnesses including cooperation agreements, criminal histories, promises of leniency, and prior inconsistent statements. The motion should emphasize prosecutors' obligations to disclose Giglio material while requesting broad categories of impeachment evidence that might exist in government files.

Expert evidence challenges should request all materials related to government expert analyses including underlying data, alternative conclusions considered, and any limitations or uncertainties in expert opinions. The motion should emphasize that defendants need complete expert files to prepare effective cross-examination and competing expert testimony.

Motion in Limine to Exclude Evidence seeks to prevent admission of prejudicial or irrelevant evidence that prosecutors might seek to introduce at trial. PPP fraud cases often involve allegations of lavish spending or lifestyle evidence that prosecutors use to inflame juries without proving essential elements of the charges.

Rule 404(b) evidence exclusion motions challenge prosecution attempts to introduce evidence of other acts or transactions not charged in the indictment. Prosecutors often seek to introduce evidence of other loan applications, business transactions, or financial conduct to suggest pattern or intent. The motion should argue that such evidence is more prejudicial than probative while challenging the relevance of uncharged conduct.

Inflammatory evidence exclusion should address prosecution attempts to introduce evidence of defendants' wealth, lifestyle, or spending that serves to prejudice juries rather than prove essential elements. The motion should emphasize that evidence of legal spending or lifestyle choices cannot prove criminal intent while arguing that such evidence creates unfair prejudice that outweighs any probative value.

Character evidence limitations should challenge any prosecution attempts to introduce evidence about defendants' character or reputation unless defendants open the door through character evidence of their own. The motion should emphasize that defendants' character is not at issue in fraud prosecutions while preventing prosecutors from suggesting that defendants are bad people who probably committed crimes.

Motion for Change of Venue addresses prejudicial pretrial publicity that may prevent fair trial in the original district. High-profile PPP fraud cases often generate extensive media coverage that portrays defendants negatively before trial begins.

The venue motion requires demonstrating that pretrial publicity has created community prejudice that cannot be cured through voir dire. The motion should include media analysis showing the extent and nature of coverage while providing evidence of community attitudes that suggest bias against defendants. Survey evidence may support venue motions in cases with extensive publicity.

Alternative remedies should be addressed when venue change is not feasible, including expanded voir dire, jury sequestration, or continuance to allow publicity effects to diminish. The motion should propose specific remedies while emphasizing that fair trial requires addressing prejudicial publicity effects.

Severance Motion seeks separate trials when multiple defendants are charged together but have conflicting defenses or when joint trial would prejudice individual defendants. PPP fraud cases often charge family members or business associates together despite different levels of involvement or conflicting interests.

Conflicting defenses provide grounds for severance when co-defendants plan to present mutually exclusive theories or blame each other for alleged criminal conduct. The motion should identify specific conflicts while demonstrating that joint trial would prevent effective representation of individual defendants.

Spillover prejudice arguments address situations where evidence admissible against one defendant would prejudice co-defendants. The motion should identify specific evidence that creates prejudice while arguing that limiting instructions cannot cure the prejudicial effect of joint trial.

Sentencing Memorandum represents the most important advocacy document in federal criminal cases because it provides the primary vehicle for presenting mitigation evidence and legal arguments to the sentencing court. The memorandum must combine legal analysis with compelling narrative to achieve the most favorable sentence possible.

The guideline calculation section should challenge every applicable enhancement while arguing for appropriate departures and variances. This requires detailed analysis of loss calculations, role adjustments, and other guideline factors while presenting alternative interpretations that favor defendants. The section should acknowledge guideline calculations while building arguments for sentences below the calculated range.

Mitigation evidence presentation requires comprehensive gathering and presentation of evidence about defendants' backgrounds, circumstances, and character that support lenient sentences. This includes employment history, family responsibilities, community ties, health issues, and charitable activities that demonstrate defendants' value to society beyond their alleged criminal conduct.

The 3553(a) factors analysis must address each statutory sentencing factor while building arguments for appropriate sentences based on individual circumstances rather than abstract guideline calculations. This includes analysis of offense characteristics, defendant history, deterrence considerations, and the need for proportionate punishment.

Case law support should include citations to similar cases where courts imposed lenient sentences for comparable conduct. The memorandum should distinguish unfavorable cases while emphasizing precedents that support defense sentencing arguments. Effective use of case law demonstrates that requested sentences fall within reasonable ranges for similar conduct.

Appeal briefs in PPP fraud cases require sophisticated legal analysis combined with persuasive advocacy that challenges trial court errors while building comprehensive records for appellate review. Successful appeals depend on identifying preserved issues that present realistic opportunities for reversal or remand.

Issue preservation requirements demand that appellate arguments be based on objections and motions made at trial rather than issues raised for the first time on appeal. The brief should focus on properly preserved issues while making strategic decisions about which arguments present the strongest opportunities for success.

Standard of review analysis must address the appropriate level of scrutiny that appellate courts apply to different types of trial court decisions. Legal questions receive de novo review while factual findings and discretionary decisions receive more deferential review standards. The brief should frame issues to receive favorable review standards while building arguments that can succeed under applicable standards.

The crafting of effective motions and filings in PPP fraud cases requires combining technical legal knowledge with strategic thinking and persuasive advocacy. Success depends on understanding both legal doctrine and judicial psychology while building comprehensive records that preserve issues for appeal regardless of trial outcomes. These documents represent essential tools for protecting defendants' rights while creating opportunities for favorable resolutions in an increasingly hostile federal criminal justice system.

CHAPTER 29
COMPLIANCE AUDIT CHECKLIST

The retroactive compliance audit represents both the most critical defensive tool and the most dangerous investigative exercise for PPP recipients facing potential criminal exposure. Understanding how to conduct systematic review of PPP documentation while minimizing legal risk requires balancing the need for comprehensive analysis with attorney-client privilege protection and Fifth Amendment considerations. This chapter provides a framework for evaluating PPP compliance that serves defensive purposes while avoiding the creation of incriminating evidence.

Initial Risk Assessment Framework

The compliance audit begins with preliminary risk assessment that identifies potential exposure areas without creating detailed documentation that might become evidence in criminal proceedings. This assessment should occur under attorney-client privilege through consultation with qualified federal criminal defense counsel before any document review or analysis begins. The initial evaluation focuses on identifying obvious red flags that require immediate attention while establishing protocols for privileged review of sensitive materials.

The preliminary assessment examines basic program eligibility factors including business existence, employee count verification, and revenue documentation. This review identifies fundamental qualification issues that might form the basis for criminal charges while establishing baseline factual understanding of the loan application process. The assessment should be conducted by defense counsel rather than business personnel to maintain privilege protection.

Revenue verification analysis examines the accuracy of gross receipts information provided in loan applications compared to business records including tax returns, bank statements, and accounting records. Discrepancies between reported revenue and actual business records represent primary targets for federal prosecutors who routinely charge revenue misstatements as material false statements supporting wire fraud prosecutions.

Employee count verification requires comparing reported employee numbers with payroll records, tax filings, and employment documentation.

Prosecutors frequently challenge employee count calculations that include family members, contractors, or part-time workers, treating inclusive counting methods as criminal fraud rather than reasonable interpretation of program guidance.

Geographic nexus evaluation examines whether the business operations possessed sufficient connections to support federal criminal jurisdiction. While most PPP cases easily satisfy minimal interstate commerce requirements, systematic documentation of purely local business activities may support jurisdictional challenges in appropriate cases.

Application Documentation Review

The systematic review of PPP application materials requires careful analysis of every representation made to lenders and the SBA while identifying potential false statement allegations that prosecutors might pursue. This review must be conducted under attorney-client privilege to prevent the audit itself from becoming evidence in government prosecutions.

Application accuracy analysis compares each statement in loan applications with supporting business records to identify any discrepancies that might form the basis for false statement charges. This includes verification of business formation dates, operational status, employee information, and revenue calculations that prosecutors routinely scrutinize for charging purposes.

Supporting documentation examination reviews all materials submitted with loan applications including tax returns, payroll records, and financial statements. Prosecutors often charge defendants for submitting documents that contain inaccuracies or inconsistencies, treating document submission as evidence of intent to defraud regardless of defendants' knowledge of any problems.

Certification accuracy review analyzes the truth of all certifications made in loan applications including good faith certifications, economic necessity statements, and compliance acknowledgments. False certification charges represent common prosecution theories that treat any inaccurate certification as criminal conduct regardless of materiality or intent.

Bank relationship documentation examines the accuracy of information provided about banking relationships, account ownership, and financial institution interactions. Prosecutors frequently investigate banking information for evidence of financial sophistication or undisclosed accounts that might support money laundering or asset concealment charges.

Fund Usage Documentation Analysis

The examination of PPP fund usage requires comprehensive review of how loan proceeds were spent compared to program requirements and representations made in forgiveness applications. This analysis identifies potential money laundering charges and forfeiture exposure while evaluating compliance with program restrictions.

Payroll expense verification compares PPP expenditures on payroll costs with actual employee compensation, benefits, and payroll tax obligations. Prosecutors routinely investigate payroll calculations for evidence of inflated expenses, fictitious employees, or excessive owner compensation that violates program requirements.

Allowable expense analysis reviews non-payroll expenditures for compliance with program requirements including rent, utilities, and other qualifying expenses. Misuse of funds for non-qualifying expenses provides evidence for money laundering charges and asset forfeiture claims regardless of whether defendants understood program restrictions.

Owner compensation examination evaluates payments to business owners for compliance with compensation limitations and eligibility requirements. Excessive owner compensation or inappropriate distributions represent common targets for prosecution theories that treat program violations as criminal conduct.

Documentation retention review examines whether businesses maintained adequate records to support PPP expenditures and compliance representations. Poor recordkeeping may suggest intent to conceal misuse while creating evidentiary problems for defending against government charges.

Forgiveness Application Compliance

The review of loan forgiveness applications requires analysis of every representation made to support forgiveness claims while identifying potential false statement exposure. Forgiveness applications create additional opportunities for prosecution because they involve new representations about fund usage and business operations.

Expense calculation accuracy examines the mathematical accuracy of forgiveness calculations including payroll costs, allowable expenses, and reduction factors. Prosecutors treat calculation errors as evidence of intent to obtain undeserved forgiveness regardless of whether errors resulted from confusion about complex requirements.

Employee retention documentation reviews evidence supporting claims about employee retention and compensation during the covered period. Prosecutors investigate employment records for evidence of terminated employees who were claimed for forgiveness purposes or compensation calculations that inflate forgiveness amounts.

Revenue reduction calculations require verification of any claims about business revenue reductions used to support forgiveness applications. Prosecutors scrutinize revenue calculations for evidence of manipulation or exaggeration that might support false statement charges.

Certification accuracy in forgiveness applications creates additional false statement exposure through representations about compliance with program requirements, fund usage, and business operations. Each certification potentially supports separate criminal charges if prosecutors determine the statements were false.

Business Operations Evaluation

The comprehensive review of business operations during relevant time periods provides context for evaluating criminal exposure while identifying defensive evidence that supports legitimate business purposes and good faith compliance efforts.

Operational continuity analysis examines whether businesses continued legitimate operations during and after receiving PPP loans. Prosecutors sometimes argue that businesses that ceased operations while retaining PPP funds demonstrate fraudulent intent from the inception of their applications.

Employee management review evaluates business practices regarding employee retention, compensation, and benefits during the PPP period. This analysis may reveal evidence of good faith efforts to preserve employment that supports defensive narratives about program compliance and legitimate business purposes.

Financial management examination reviews business financial practices including banking, accounting, and expense management during relevant periods. Sophisticated financial management may support prosecution theories about intent and knowledge while poor financial management might suggest confusion rather than criminal intent.

Compliance efforts documentation identifies any attempts by businesses to understand and comply with program requirements including consultation with professionals, review of guidance materials, and communication with lenders. Evidence of compliance efforts supports good faith defenses while demonstrating absence of criminal intent.

Legal Exposure Assessment

The systematic evaluation of potential criminal charges requires analysis of each possible theory of prosecution while identifying strongest defensive arguments and evidentiary problems that might benefit defendants.

Wire fraud exposure analysis examines whether any application statements or omissions might support wire fraud charges based on materiality, intent, and scheme to defraud theories. This includes evaluation of whether alleged false statements actually influenced funding decisions or merely violated technical requirements.

Money laundering risk evaluation reviews fund usage patterns for evidence that might support money laundering charges including use of funds for personal expenses, complex financial transactions, or attempts to conceal fund sources or usage.

Conspiracy charge vulnerability examines the involvement of family members, employees, and professional service providers in application preparation and business operations. Prosecutors routinely charge peripheral participants with conspiracy based on minimal involvement in allegedly fraudulent schemes.

Forfeiture exposure assessment evaluates potential asset forfeiture claims including identification of assets that might be subject to seizure and calculation of potential forfeiture amounts. This includes both criminal forfeiture following conviction and civil forfeiture based on alleged connection to criminal activity.

Professional Service Provider Review

The examination of professional assistance received during PPP application and compliance processes identifies potential co-conspirator liability while evaluating whether professional involvement supports good faith defenses.

Accountant involvement analysis reviews the role of accounting professionals in application preparation, fund management, and forgiveness applications. Professional involvement may support good faith defenses while potentially creating exposure for professional service providers.

Attorney consultation evaluation examines any legal advice received regarding PPP compliance and application requirements. Attorney involvement generally supports good faith defenses while potentially creating privilege issues that require careful management.

Banking relationship review analyzes interactions with lenders during application and forgiveness processes. Bank approval and processing of applications may support arguments that lenders endorsed defendants' interpretations of program requirements.

Consultant and advisor examination reviews involvement of other professional service providers including business consultants, financial advisors, and industry specialists who may have provided guidance about program compliance.

Documentation Preservation Strategy

The development of comprehensive document preservation protocols protects essential evidence while minimizing creation of new materials that might benefit prosecutors.

Privilege protection procedures ensure that audit materials remain protected under attorney-client privilege while preventing waiver through inadvertent disclosure or improper sharing. All audit work should be conducted under attorney supervision with clear privilege designations.

Evidence organization systems create efficient access to relevant documents while maintaining security and privilege protection. Organized evidence facilitates both defensive preparation and compliance with any government discovery requests that may arise.

Communication protocols establish guidelines for discussing audit findings and defensive strategies while protecting privilege and avoiding creation of discoverable communications. All substantive discussions should occur under privilege protection with qualified criminal defense counsel.

Defensive strategy development integrates audit findings with legal analysis to create comprehensive defense strategies that address identified weaknesses while maximizing strengths. The strategy should anticipate prosecution theories while building affirmative defenses based on good faith, reliance on professional advice, and compliance efforts.

Remedial Action Planning

The identification of compliance deficiencies requires careful consideration of whether remedial actions might reduce criminal exposure or instead create additional evidence of consciousness of guilt.

Voluntary disclosure considerations evaluate whether cooperation with government authorities might benefit defendants while recognizing that disclosure often provides evidence for prosecution rather than leniency. Disclosure decisions require careful analysis of costs and benefits under specific circumstances.

Compliance improvement implementation addresses identified deficiencies while avoiding actions that might suggest consciousness of wrongdoing. Remedial actions should be presented as business improvements rather than responses to legal concerns.

Professional relationship management addresses any issues with accountants, attorneys, or other service providers that might affect ongoing legal exposure. Professional relationships should be evaluated for potential conflicts or obligations that might affect defensive strategies.

Asset protection planning addresses potential forfeiture exposure while complying with legal requirements and avoiding obstruction of justice allegations. Asset protection must be accomplished through legitimate transactions that do not suggest attempts to hide assets from government investigation.

The compliance audit process serves essential defensive purposes while creating potential risks that require careful management under attorney-client privilege. Success depends on systematic evaluation of all potential exposure areas while maintaining privilege protection and developing comprehensive defensive strategies. The audit provides a foundation for effective legal representation while avoiding the creation of evidence that might benefit government prosecution efforts.

CHAPTER 30

PROFILES IN PROSECUTION

The human cost of weaponized PPP fraud enforcement emerges most clearly through individual stories of ordinary Americans whose lives were destroyed by prosecutorial theories that transformed emergency pandemic relief into criminal liability. These profiles reveal how federal prosecutors target vulnerable defendants while protecting powerful interests, demonstrating the selective enforcement patterns that characterize the broader assault on constitutional justice. The cases presented here represent thousands of similar prosecutions that illustrate the systematic abuse of prosecutorial power in the name of fraud prevention.

Case Study One: *The Family Restaurant Owner*

Maria Rios operated a small family restaurant in rural Texas that employed twelve people including her two adult children and several longtime community members. When the pandemic forced closure of indoor dining in March 2020, Maria applied for a PPP loan to maintain her payroll and preserve the jobs that supported local families. Her application listed fourteen employees based on her understanding that family members and part-time workers counted toward the total, following guidance she received from her local bank.

The SBA approved Maria's loan for $87,000, which she used primarily for payroll costs and essential business expenses including rent and utilities. When business reopened, Maria retained most of her workforce and applied for loan forgiveness based on her payroll expenditures during the covered period. The forgiveness application was approved, and Maria believed she had successfully navigated the program requirements while preserving local employment.

Federal investigators targeted Maria's restaurant eighteen months later based on an algorithm that flagged her employee count as potentially inflated. FBI agents interviewed former employees who confirmed that some workers were part-time and that Maria's children worked in the business but also attended college. Prosecutors interpreted this information as evidence that Maria knowingly inflated her employee count to obtain a larger loan than she deserved.

The indictment charged Maria with wire fraud, money laundering, and conspiracy, alleging that she submitted false information about her employee count and used loan proceeds for unauthorized purposes. Prosecutors argued that paying her children while they attended college constituted misuse of funds, despite program guidance that appeared to allow such payments. The maximum penalties exceeded twenty years in federal prison.

Maria's case demonstrates how prosecutors criminalize reasonable interpretations of ambiguous program guidance while applying hindsight analysis that treats legitimate business decisions as evidence of criminal intent. Her family restaurant represented exactly the type of small business the PPP was designed to help, yet her participation in the program became the basis for federal criminal charges that threatened to destroy her life and livelihood.

The prosecution strategy focused on technical violations of program requirements rather than evidence of fraudulent intent. Prosecutors presented Maria's inclusive employee counting as clear fraud while ignoring evidence that she acted in good faith based on guidance from her bank and understanding of program purposes. The case illustrates how complex regulations become criminal traps for unsophisticated defendants.

Defense challenges included limited financial resources to mount effective resistance against federal prosecutors with unlimited budgets and investigative resources. Maria's family exhausted savings on legal fees while facing pressure to accept plea agreements that would have resulted in felony convictions and business closure. The financial pressure created by the prosecution often forces defendants to surrender regardless of their actual guilt.

Case Study Two: *The Construction Contractor*

James Wilson owned a small construction company in Ohio that employed varying numbers of workers depending on project demands. His business model relied on seasonal employment and subcontractor relationships that created flexibility for both Wilson and his workers. When the pandemic disrupted construction projects, Wilson applied for PPP loans for both his primary company and a related business entity he used for specialized projects.

Wilson's applications listed employee counts and payroll expenses based on his peak employment during the previous year, following advice from his accountant who interpreted program guidance as allowing businesses to use their highest employment levels when calculating loan amounts. The applications were approved for a total of $340,000, which Wilson used for payroll, equipment payments, and business expenses during the pandemic shutdown.

Federal investigators targeted Wilson after receiving a tip from a disgruntled former employee who claimed that Wilson inflated his employee numbers and operated his businesses as a single entity despite applying for separate loans. The investigation expanded to include scrutiny of all Wilson's business relationships, subcontractor agreements, and financial transactions during the relevant time period.

The charges against Wilson included wire fraud for allegedly misrepresenting his employee count and business structure, money laundering for transferring funds between business accounts, and conspiracy involving his accountant and bookkeeper who assisted with the applications. Prosecutors argued that Wilson operated an elaborate scheme to defraud the government by treating related businesses as separate entities.

Wilson's case illustrates how prosecutors criminalize standard business practices including the use of multiple business entities and flexible employment arrangements that are common in the construction industry. The charges reflected prosecutorial theories that ignored industry realities while applying rigid interpretations of program requirements that trapped legitimate business owners.

The conspiracy charges against Wilson's accountant and bookkeeper demonstrate how prosecutors expand cases to include professional service providers who provided legitimate assistance. The charges created pressure for these individuals to cooperate against Wilson while destroying professional relationships that small businesses depend on for competent advice and assistance.

Defense strategies focused on demonstrating that Wilson's business structure and employment practices were legitimate and consistent with industry standards. However, the complexity of construction industry practices created challenges for explaining legitimate business operations to prosecutors and juries unfamiliar with the industry's flexible employment and contracting arrangements.

Case Study Three: *The Healthcare Practice*

Dr. Sarah Ahmed operated a small medical practice that employed nurses, medical assistants, and administrative staff while serving a predominantly minority community in Detroit. When the pandemic reduced patient volume and created additional safety costs, Dr. Ahmed applied for PPP loans to maintain her staff and continue serving patients who had limited access to healthcare alternatives.

Dr. Ahmed's applications included all practice employees and calculated payroll costs based on gross compensation including benefits and payroll taxes. She used loan proceeds to maintain staff salaries, purchase personal protective equipment, and cover practice expenses during reduced patient volume. The practice continued operating throughout the pandemic while providing essential healthcare services to underserved communities.

Federal investigation began after a routine audit flagged Dr. Ahmed's practice for high loan amounts relative to reported revenue on previous tax returns. Investigators discovered that Dr. Ahmed had included locum tenens physicians and contracted specialists in her employee count while calculating benefits and taxes as part of payroll costs. Prosecutors interpreted these inclusions as evidence of fraudulent application preparation.

The charges against Dr. Ahmed included wire fraud for allegedly inflating her employee count and payroll expenses, money laundering for using loan proceeds to purchase medical equipment and supplies, and conspiracy involving her practice manager who assisted with application preparation and fund management.

Prosecutors argued that Dr. Ahmed's interpretation of program requirements was unreasonable and that her medical training should have enabled her to understand the technical distinctions between employees and contractors. They characterized her purchase of medical equipment as misuse of funds despite the equipment's necessity for pandemic patient care.

Dr. Ahmed's case demonstrates how prosecutors target minority-owned businesses while applying standards that ignore the realities of professional practice management. Her attempts to maintain healthcare services for underserved communities became evidence of criminal conduct rather than public service during a national emergency.

The prosecution's impact extended beyond Dr. Ahmed to affect the patients and community members who depended on her practice for healthcare services. The charges forced practice closure and left community members without accessible healthcare while Dr. Ahmed faced potential imprisonment for her attempts to maintain essential services.

Defense arguments emphasized Dr. Ahmed's good faith efforts to comply with program requirements while serving essential healthcare needs during the pandemic. However, prosecutors focused on technical violations while ignoring the broader context of emergency healthcare provision and community service that motivated Dr. Ahmed's actions.

Case Study Four: *The Technology Startup*

Michael Davis founded a software development company in California that experienced rapid growth before the pandemic disrupted his business model and client relationships. The company employed software developers, designers, and support staff through a combination of direct employment and contractor agreements that reflected the flexible nature of technology work.

Davis's PPP application included all individuals who worked regularly for the company regardless of their formal employment classification, following guidance he received from his attorney and accountant. The application calculated payroll costs based on total compensation paid to all workers, resulting in a loan approval for $180,000 that Davis used to maintain his development team during client disruptions.

Federal investigators targeted Davis after discovering that several individuals included in his employee count were classified as independent contractors for tax purposes. The investigation expanded to examine Davis's business practices, client relationships, and financial management while scrutinizing every aspect of his company's operations and growth strategy.

The charges included wire fraud for allegedly misrepresenting his employment structure, money laundering for using loan proceeds to pay contractors and maintain business operations, and conspiracy involving his co-founder who participated in application preparation and business management decisions.

Prosecutors argued that Davis's technology background should have enabled him to understand the technical requirements for employee classification and that his inclusion of contractors represented deliberate fraud rather than reasonable interpretation of program guidance. They characterized payments to contractors as misuse of funds despite the legitimate business purposes for such payments.

Davis's case illustrates how prosecutors criminalize the flexible employment arrangements that characterize modern technology businesses while applying traditional employment concepts to innovative business models. The charges reflected prosecutorial unfamiliarity with technology industry practices rather than evidence of criminal intent.

The prosecution destroyed Davis's business and forced dissolution of a company that had been developing software solutions for small businesses. The criminal charges eliminated investor confidence and client relationships while forcing talented developers to seek employment elsewhere.

Defense strategies emphasized the legitimacy of Davis's business model and employment practices while demonstrating good faith reliance on professional advice. However, the technical nature of employment classification issues created challenges for explaining complex business relationships to prosecutors focused on rigid regulatory compliance.

Case Study Five: The Retail Business Owner

Linda Stone operated a chain of small retail stores in New Mexico that employed family members, part-time workers, and seasonal staff to serve local communities. Her business model depended on flexible staffing arrangements that accommodated fluctuating customer demand and employee availability while providing income opportunities for local residents.

Stone applied for PPP loans for each store location based on total employment across all locations, following guidance from her banker who advised that related businesses could apply separately if they maintained distinct operations. The applications totaled $220,000 and were used to maintain employment and store operations during pandemic-related disruptions.

Federal investigation began after a computer algorithm flagged Stone's applications for review based on related business entities and family member employment. Investigators discovered that Stone's stores shared some inventory and management functions while employing several family members in various capacities.

The charges included wire fraud for allegedly operating a single business while applying for multiple loans, money laundering for transferring funds between store accounts, and conspiracy involving family members who worked in the businesses and participated in application preparation.

Prosecutors argued that Stone's retail chain constituted a single business entity despite separate incorporation and that her employment of family members represented artificial inflation of employee counts. They characterized fund transfers between stores as evidence of money laundering rather than legitimate business operations.

Stone's case demonstrates how prosecutors criminalize family business operations while ignoring the economic realities that require flexible business structures and family involvement for small retail operations to survive and serve local communities.

The prosecution forced closure of stores that provided employment opportunities and retail services in underserved communities while destroying a business that Stone had built over decades of community service and entrepreneurship.

Defense arguments focused on the legitimacy of Stone's business structure and the genuine employment provided to family and community members. However, prosecutors applied corporate law concepts that ignored the realities of family business operations in small communities.

Common Patterns And Prosecutorial Strategies

These cases reveal systematic patterns in PPP fraud prosecutions that demonstrate selective enforcement targeting vulnerable defendants while protecting powerful interests. Prosecutors consistently apply rigid interpretations of program requirements that criminalize reasonable business practices while ignoring evidence of good faith compliance efforts.

The targeting patterns favor prosecution of small business owners, minority entrepreneurs, and family businesses while providing immunity for large corporations and politically connected entities that engaged in similar or worse conduct. The disparity demonstrates that enforcement reflects political calculation rather than neutral law enforcement principles.

Prosecutorial strategies focus on technical violations of complex regulations rather than evidence of fraudulent intent while treating legitimate business practices as evidence of criminal conduct. The approach criminalizes entrepreneurship and small business operations while creating advantages for large entities with sophisticated compliance infrastructure.

The human cost of these prosecutions extends beyond individual defendants to affect families, employees, and communities that depend on small businesses for employment and services. The enforcement creates chilling effects that discourage entrepreneurship while concentrating economic power in large corporations that can navigate complex regulatory requirements.

Defense challenges include limited resources to combat federal prosecutors with unlimited budgets while facing charges that carry severe penalties disproportionate to alleged conduct. The pressure to accept plea agreements often forces innocent defendants to admit guilt rather than risk decades in prison for defending their innocence.

The profiles presented here represent thousands of similar cases that demonstrate the systematic abuse of prosecutorial power in transforming emergency relief into criminal liability. Understanding these patterns provides essential context for comprehending the broader assault on constitutional justice while highlighting the urgent need for reform that restores equal protection under law.

CHAPTER 31

ATTORNEY ROUNDTABLE

The front lines of PPP fraud defense have produced insights and strategies that can only come from attorneys who have navigated the treacherous waters of federal prosecution in these unprecedented cases. This roundtable brings together experienced federal criminal defense attorneys from across the country who have defended clients against PPP fraud charges, revealing the tactics, trends, and courtroom dynamics that define this emerging area of federal criminal law. Their collective wisdom provides essential guidance for understanding how these cases actually unfold in practice.

Attorney Profile: David Martinez, Partner, Martinez & Associates, Miami, Florida

Martinez has defended over forty PPP fraud cases ranging from small business owners to complex multi-defendant conspiracies. His practice focuses exclusively on federal white-collar defense, with particular expertise in financial crimes and healthcare fraud. His insights into PPP fraud prosecution reveal patterns that extend far beyond individual cases.

"The most striking aspect of PPP fraud prosecutions is how prosecutors have abandoned traditional fraud concepts in favor of strict liability theories that criminalize technical violations," Martinez observes. "I've seen cases where clients received SBA approval for loan applications that contained minor inaccuracies, used the funds for legitimate business purposes, and still faced wire fraud charges because prosecutors claimed any false statement constitutes criminal conduct."

Martinez emphasizes the importance of early intervention in PPP fraud investigations. "Once clients receive target letters or grand jury subpoenas, the window for favorable resolution narrows dramatically. The key is identifying exposure before formal charges and developing strategies that address prosecutorial concerns while protecting client interests. However, cooperation decisions require extreme caution because prosecutors often use information provided by targets to expand rather than limit criminal exposure."

The geographic disparities in PPP fraud prosecution have created significant strategic challenges, according to Martinez. "Prosecutors in different districts apply vastly different standards for bringing charges. Conduct that results in declination in one district generates major felony charges in another. This disparity forces defense attorneys to consider venue-specific factors when advising clients about cooperation and plea strategies."

Martinez has observed concerning trends in prosecutorial tactics that suggest PPP fraud enforcement serves political rather than legal purposes. "The timing of major arrests and indictments often coincides with political events or media cycles rather than investigative necessity. High-profile cases receive resources and attention that far exceed their actual significance, while similar conduct by politically connected defendants receives minimal scrutiny."

Attorney Profile: *Sarah Gold, Solo Practitioner, Federal Defense Group, Seattle, Washington*

Gold represents small business owners and entrepreneurs facing PPP fraud charges, bringing a unique perspective on how federal criminal law affects ordinary Americans who never expected to face federal prosecution. Her practice emphasizes the human dimension of federal criminal defense while developing innovative strategies for protecting vulnerable clients.

"The psychological warfare aspect of PPP fraud prosecution cannot be overstated," Gold explains. "My clients are small business owners who took emergency loans to survive the pandemic, and they face potential decades in prison for paperwork errors. The government uses this massive sentencing exposure to coerce guilty pleas regardless of actual culpability. The system is designed to break people mentally before they ever reach trial."

Gold has developed specialized expertise in challenging the loss calculations that drive federal sentencing in PPP fraud cases. "Prosecutors routinely claim that the entire loan amount represents intended loss, even when clients used funds for legitimate business purposes and would have qualified for loan forgiveness. This creates Guidelines ranges that bear no relationship to actual harm while producing sentences that exceed those imposed for violent crimes."

The family and conspiracy charges in PPP fraud cases present particular challenges that require careful strategic analysis, according to Gold. "Prosecutors charge family members and employees with conspiracy based on minimal involvement in application preparation. These charges create enormous pressure on defendants to cooperate against loved ones while destroying family businesses that employed local community members."

Gold emphasizes the importance of financial planning for PPP fraud defense. "These cases require substantial resources for expert witnesses, document review, and extended litigation. Many clients face asset freezing that eliminates their ability to fund adequate defense, creating a system where justice depends on financial resources rather than actual guilt or innocence."

Attorney Profile: *Robert Thompson, Partner, Thompson & Associates, Houston, Texas*

Thompson brings thirty years of federal criminal defense experience to PPP fraud cases, having previously defended clients in savings and loan prosecutions, Enron-related cases, and other major financial crime investigations. His historical perspective reveals how PPP fraud prosecutions fit within broader patterns of federal overcriminalization.

"PPP fraud prosecutions represent the latest iteration of federal expansion that transforms regulatory violations into serious felonies," Thompson notes. "We've seen this pattern before in healthcare fraud, environmental crimes, and corporate prosecutions where complex regulations become criminal traps for businesses trying to comply with unclear requirements."

Thompson has observed significant evolution in judicial attitudes toward PPP fraud cases as courts begin to understand the prosecutorial overreach involved. "Early cases saw judges defer completely to prosecution theories, but we're starting to see more judicial skepticism about treating emergency relief as criminal fraud. Some judges are beginning to question whether technical violations of pandemic relief programs deserve the same treatment as traditional fraud schemes."

The expert witness battles in PPP fraud cases require sophisticated understanding of both legal and business principles, according to Thompson. "These cases often turn on competing interpretations of business practices, accounting methods, and regulatory compliance. Effective defense requires experts who can explain legitimate business operations while challenging government theories that criminalize standard practices."

Thompson emphasizes the appellate potential in PPP fraud cases for establishing favorable precedent. "Many prosecution theories in these cases stretch traditional fraud concepts beyond recognition. Appellate courts will eventually need to address whether emergency relief programs create different standards for criminal liability and whether technical violations without fraudulent intent support serious felony charges."

Attorney Profile: Ann Gonzalez, Senior Associate, Federal Defenders Office, Phoenix, Arizona

Gonzalez represents indigent defendants in PPP fraud cases, providing a perspective on how prosecutorial overreach affects defendants without resources for private counsel. Her experience reveals the class-based disparities that characterize federal criminal justice while highlighting the challenges facing appointed counsel in complex financial cases.

"The resource disparity in PPP fraud cases creates a two-tier justice system where wealthy defendants can mount sophisticated defenses while indigent clients face overwhelming prosecutorial advantages," Gonzalez explains. "Court-appointed attorneys often lack the resources for expert witnesses, document review, and investigation necessary to challenge complex financial prosecutions effectively."

Gonzalez has developed innovative strategies for defending resource-limited clients while building records for appeal in cases where trial outcomes may be predetermined by resource disparities. "When clients cannot afford comprehensive defense, we focus on preserving appellate issues and building mitigation evidence that might support favorable sentences even after conviction."

The sentencing advocacy in PPP fraud cases requires particular attention to the human consequences of Guidelines-driven sentences, according to Gonzalez. "These cases often involve first-time offenders who made technical mistakes while trying to save their businesses and preserve employment for their workers. Effective sentencing advocacy requires helping judges understand that Guidelines calculations produce results that are completely disproportionate to actual culpability."

Gonzalez emphasizes the collateral consequences of PPP fraud convictions that extend far beyond criminal sentences. "Clients lose professional licenses, immigration status, and employment opportunities based on felony convictions for conduct that should have been handled through civil enforcement. The lifetime consequences often exceed the actual criminal penalties while destroying entire families and communities."

Attorney Profile: James Wilson, Partner, Wilson Criminal Defense, Chicago, Illinois

Wilson specializes in complex conspiracy cases and RICO prosecutions, bringing expertise in defending multi-defendant cases to PPP fraud prosecutions. His experience with organized crime cases provides unique insights into how prosecutors use conspiracy theories to expand liability beyond actual criminal conduct.

"PPP fraud conspiracy cases often involve prosecution theories that would be rejected in traditional organized crime cases," Wilson observes. "Prosecutors charge legitimate business relationships as criminal conspiracies while treating family assistance with loan applications as evidence of criminal organization. The theories stretch conspiracy law beyond recognition while criminalizing normal business and family relationships."

Wilson has developed expertise in severance strategies that protect individual clients in multi-defendant PPP fraud cases. "Joint trials in these cases often prejudice individual defendants because prosecutors present cumulative evidence that suggests large-scale criminal organization even when individual defendants played minimal roles. Severance becomes essential for protecting clients from spillover prejudice."

The RICO applications in PPP fraud cases represent particularly aggressive prosecutorial tactics that Wilson believes exceed constitutional boundaries. "Prosecutors use RICO to treat multiple loan applications as evidence of criminal enterprise, creating enhanced penalties for conduct that would normally be charged as individual fraud cases. The RICO predicates often involve technical violations that should not support racketeering charges."

Wilson emphasizes the importance of challenging prosecutorial theories through pretrial motions that force government attorneys to articulate legal bases for their charges. "Many PPP fraud prosecutions rely on novel theories that have not been tested through appellate review. Aggressive motion practice can expose weaknesses in prosecution theories while building records for appeal."

Attorney Profile: *Linda Turner, Solo Practitioner, Turner Law Firm, Denver, Colorado*

Turner represents small business owners and entrepreneurs in PPP fraud cases, bringing a business-oriented perspective to federal criminal defense. Her background in business law provides unique insights into how prosecutors misunderstand legitimate business operations while criminalizing standard practices.

"The fundamental problem in PPP fraud prosecutions is that prosecutors and agents lack understanding of how small businesses actually operate," Turner explains. "They apply corporate law concepts to family businesses while treating flexible employment arrangements and multiple business entities as evidence of criminal sophistication rather than business necessity."

Turner has developed particular expertise in defending cases involving multiple business entities and family employment arrangements that prosecutors often mischaracterize as criminal schemes. "Small businesses use multiple entities for legitimate business purposes including liability protection, tax planning, and operational flexibility. Prosecutors treat these arrangements as evidence of fraudulent intent while ignoring the legitimate business purposes they serve."

The business interruption aspects of PPP fraud prosecution create additional challenges that require understanding of client business operations and community relationships, according to Turner. "These prosecutions often destroy businesses that employ local community members and provide essential services. The collateral damage extends far beyond individual defendants to affect entire communities that depend on small business employment and services."

Turner emphasizes the importance of educating prosecutors and judges about legitimate business practices that may appear suspicious to individuals without business experience. "Effective defense requires helping legal professionals understand that business practices that seem unusual or complex often serve legitimate purposes that are essential for small business survival and success."

Common Themes And Strategic Insights

The roundtable participants identify several common themes that characterize PPP fraud prosecutions and create challenges for effective defense advocacy. These patterns reveal systematic problems with current enforcement approaches while highlighting strategies that defense attorneys have developed to protect their clients.

Prosecutorial overreach emerges as the dominant theme across all practices, with attorneys reporting consistent patterns of aggressive enforcement that criminalizes technical violations while ignoring evidence of good faith compliance efforts. The overreach reflects institutional pressure to demonstrate enforcement success rather than neutral application of criminal law principles.

Resource disparities create fundamental fairness problems that affect case outcomes regardless of client culpability. Defendants with adequate resources can mount sophisticated defenses while others face overwhelming prosecutorial advantages that predetermine outcomes based on economic rather than legal factors.

Judicial education represents both a challenge and an opportunity as courts gradually recognize the unique characteristics of PPP fraud cases. Attorneys report increasing judicial skepticism about prosecutorial theories, but education efforts require sustained advocacy that helps judges understand business realities and constitutional principles.

Sentencing advocacy has become crucial in cases where conviction appears likely despite weak evidence, requiring specialized understanding of Guidelines calculations while developing mitigation theories that address the emergency nature of pandemic relief programs.

Expert witness utilization provides essential tools for challenging prosecution theories while educating juries about legitimate business practices. Effective expert testimony requires coordination between legal and business expertise to address both technical and strategic challenges.

The collective wisdom of experienced PPP fraud defense attorneys reveals systematic problems with current enforcement approaches while highlighting strategies for protecting clients in an increasingly hostile prosecutorial environment. Their insights provide essential guidance for navigating these complex cases while building foundations for eventual reform of prosecutorial practices that threaten constitutional principles and destroy American businesses and communities.

CONCLUSION

Why This Book Was Written

This book exists because thousands of American entrepreneurs, small business owners, and ordinary citizens who sought emergency pandemic relief now face federal criminal prosecution for conduct that should never have been criminalized. The transformation of the **Paycheck Protection Program** from bipartisan emergency relief into a prosecutorial weapon represents one of the most systematic abuses of federal power in modern American history, yet no comprehensive resource existed to help defendants understand and combat this assault on constitutional justice.

The inspiration for this work emerged from witnessing the human devastation caused by PPP fraud task forces and overzealous prosecutors who have weaponized emergency relief programs to advance careers and political agendas. Family businesses that employed local community members for decades have been destroyed by federal prosecutors who treat paperwork errors as evidence of criminal enterprise. Entrepreneurs who risked everything to build companies and create employment opportunities now face decades in federal prison for technical violations of complex regulations they could not possibly have understood.

The urgency of this project became clear as defense attorneys across the country reported similar patterns of prosecutorial abuse while struggling to find authoritative guidance on defending these unique cases. Traditional white-collar defense resources failed to address the specific challenges presented by PPP fraud prosecutions, leaving defense attorneys without adequate tools to protect their clients from systematic government overreach.

This book fills that critical gap by providing the most comprehensive and knowledgeable analysis of PPP fraud prosecutions available anywhere in the legal marketplace. No other resource combines detailed legal analysis with practical defense strategies while exposing the political motivations and constitutional violations that characterize these prosecutions. The book serves as both a defense manual for attorneys and an educational resource for defendants who need to understand the forces arrayed against them.

The legal profession desperately needed this resource because PPP fraud prosecutions represent a new category of federal criminal cases that require specialized knowledge and strategic approaches. Traditional fraud defense strategies often prove inadequate when prosecutors transform emergency relief participation into evidence of criminal conduct. Defense attorneys required guidance on challenging novel prosecution theories while protecting clients from sentences that exceed those imposed for violent crimes.

The comprehensive nature of this work reflects the complexity of defending against federal prosecutors who possess unlimited resources and institutional advantages that overwhelm most defendants. Effective defense requires understanding not only legal doctrine but also the political and institutional forces that drive prosecutorial decisions. This book provides that broader context while offering specific tactical guidance for every stage of PPP fraud prosecutions.

The book's unique value lies in its combination of theoretical analysis and practical application, providing both the intellectual framework for understanding prosecutorial overreach and the tactical tools necessary for mounting effective defenses. No other resource explains how federal sentencing guidelines operate in PPP fraud cases or provides specific guidance on jury selection strategies for complex financial prosecutions.

The psychological dimension of PPP fraud prosecution receives attention here that is unavailable in any other legal resource. Understanding how federal prosecutors use psychological warfare to break defendants mentally provides essential knowledge for survival while highlighting the systematic abuse that characterizes these cases. This psychological analysis enables defendants and their families to recognize and resist manipulation tactics that federal prosecutors use to coerce guilty pleas.

The case law analysis presented in this book offers the most comprehensive examination of PPP fraud precedents available anywhere, providing defense attorneys with essential ammunition for challenging prosecution theories that stretch traditional fraud concepts beyond recognition. This analysis reveals patterns of judicial deference to prosecutorial overreach while identifying opportunities for challenging novel theories through appellate litigation.

The discovery and evidence suppression guidance fills a critical gap in existing legal resources by addressing the specific challenges of defending against massive electronic discovery productions and government financial analyses. Traditional discovery guidance proves inadequate when prosecutors use sophisticated litigation support systems to organize evidence while defense attorneys struggle with limited resources and unwieldy document productions.

The sample motions and filings provide practical tools that defense attorneys can adapt to their specific cases while learning from successful strategies developed by experienced practitioners. These resources save valuable time and money while ensuring that critical issues are properly preserved for appellate review when trial court outcomes appear predetermined by prosecutorial advantages.

The compliance audit framework offers unique guidance on conducting privileged review of PPP documentation while minimizing legal risk. No other resource addresses the specific challenges of evaluating potential criminal exposure while protecting attorney-client privilege and avoiding creation of evidence that might benefit government prosecutors.

The profiles of prosecution cases reveal the human cost of weaponized enforcement while demonstrating the systematic patterns that characterize selective prosecution. These real-world examples provide essential context for understanding how prosecutorial theories operate in practice while highlighting the need for aggressive defense advocacy and systemic reform.

The attorney roundtable brings together wisdom from practitioners across the country who have developed specialized expertise in defending PPP fraud cases. This collective knowledge represents years of trial and error in an emerging area of federal criminal law where traditional resources provide inadequate guidance for effective defense.

The book serves multiple audiences while addressing different levels of legal sophistication and involvement in PPP fraud prosecutions. Defense attorneys will find comprehensive guidance on every aspect of these cases from initial investigation through appellate review. Defendants and their families will gain understanding of the forces arrayed against them while learning how to protect themselves from prosecutorial manipulation and abuse.

The broader legal community benefits from this analysis of prosecutorial overreach and constitutional violations that threaten fundamental principles of American justice. The book serves as a warning about the dangers of unlimited prosecutorial power while highlighting the urgent need for reform that restores equal protection under law and constitutional limitations on government authority.

Judges and prosecutors who read this work will gain understanding of the human cost of aggressive enforcement while learning about the constitutional and practical problems created by treating emergency relief as criminal fraud.

The book provides education about business realities and legal principles that should inform more measured approaches to enforcement that distinguish between regulatory violations and criminal conduct.

Policy makers and legislative officials will find essential analysis of how emergency powers become tools of prosecutorial abuse while learning about the need for reform that prevents future weaponization of crisis response programs. The book demonstrates how well-intentioned legislation becomes prosecutorial weaponry when adequate safeguards and accountability mechanisms are absent.

The academic community will benefit from this comprehensive analysis of federal overcriminalization and prosecutorial abuse that provides detailed case study material for understanding how constitutional protections erode under pressure from institutional and political forces. The book contributes to scholarly understanding of prosecutorial discretion, selective enforcement, and the breakdown of constitutional limitations on government power.

This book stands alone in the legal marketplace as the definitive resource on PPP fraud prosecutions because no other work combines legal analysis with practical guidance while exposing the political and constitutional dimensions of these cases. Traditional legal publishing focuses on established areas of law with clear precedent and settled doctrine, while PPP fraud prosecutions represent an emerging area where prosecution theories evolve rapidly and defense strategies require constant adaptation.

The comprehensive scope of this work exceeds anything available from traditional legal publishers who typically produce narrow practice guides that address specific procedural issues without broader strategic context. This book provides both detailed tactical guidance and theoretical framework necessary for understanding and combating systematic prosecutorial abuse.

The urgency of current enforcement makes this resource essential for anyone involved in PPP fraud cases or concerned about the broader assault on constitutional justice represented by these prosecutions. Defense attorneys cannot afford to learn through trial and error when their clients face decades in federal prison for conduct that should have been handled through civil enforcement or regulatory guidance.

The book's value will only increase as PPP fraud prosecutions continue to evolve and expand while creating precedents that will affect federal criminal law for decades to come. Understanding these cases provides essential preparation for future episodes of prosecutorial overreach that will inevitably emerge during national emergencies and political crises.

This work represents more than a legal practice guide; it constitutes a comprehensive exposé of prosecutorial abuse and constitutional violation that threatens the foundation of American justice. The book serves as both a practical defense manual and a call to action for reform that restores constitutional limitations on government power while protecting individual liberty from prosecutorial tyranny.

The knowledge contained in these pages emerged from the trenches of federal criminal defense where attorneys witness daily the human cost of prosecutorial overreach while developing strategies to protect clients from systematic government abuse. This frontline experience provides authenticity and practical value that cannot be replicated through academic analysis or theoretical speculation.

The book exists because justice requires informed advocacy and constitutional principles demand vigorous defense against government overreach. PPP fraud prosecutions represent a fundamental threat to American liberty that will continue until citizens understand the forces arrayed against them and demand accountability from prosecutors who have abandoned constitutional principles in pursuit of political advantage.

Every defendant facing PPP fraud charges deserves access to the knowledge and strategic guidance contained in this book. Every defense attorney handling these cases needs the comprehensive analysis and practical tools provided here. Every citizen concerned about constitutional government should understand how emergency powers become weapons of political persecution while learning about the urgent need for reform that restores equal justice under law.

This book was written because freedom depends on knowledge, justice requires advocacy, and constitutional government demands constant vigilance against those who would abuse power for political gain. The fight against prosecutorial overreach begins with understanding, continues with resistance, and succeeds only through sustained commitment to constitutional principles that protect individual liberty from government tyranny.

ABOUT THE AUTHOR

Garry Wiggins stands as one of America's foremost authorities on federal criminal law and the federal prison system, bringing decades of experience and unparalleled insight to the complex world of federal prosecution and defense. His groundbreaking works have established him as the definitive voice for those navigating the treacherous waters of federal criminal justice, providing essential guidance that has helped countless individuals understand and survive encounters with federal law enforcement.

Wiggins is the acclaimed author of "**Beating the Feds,**" "**Beating the Feds II**," "**The Great American Sellout,**" and "Indicted," **"Beating The State"** works that are widely recognized as the most comprehensive and authoritative resources available on federal criminal law, the federal prison system, prosecutorial abuse, and the broader erosion of constitutional protections in America. These seminal works have earned recognition from defense attorneys, defendants, and legal scholars as indispensable guides that combine theoretical knowledge with practical wisdom gained from real-world experience in federal criminal cases and systemic analysis of institutional corruption.

"Beating the Feds" revolutionized the landscape of federal criminal defense literature by providing the first comprehensive analysis of federal prosecution tactics, defense strategies, and prison survival techniques. The book filled a critical void in legal literature by addressing the unique challenges faced by federal defendants while offering practical guidance that goes far beyond traditional legal analysis. The work's impact extended throughout the defense bar and defendant community, establishing Wiggins as a trusted authority on federal criminal matters.

"Beating the Feds II" expanded upon the foundation established in the original work, providing updated analysis of evolving federal prosecution trends while addressing new challenges in federal criminal defense. The sequel demonstrated Wiggins' commitment to staying current with rapidly changing federal enforcement priorities while maintaining focus on practical guidance that serves real-world defensive needs.

"The Great American Sellout" broadened Wiggins' analysis beyond criminal law to examine the systematic erosion of constitutional protections and the institutional corruption that has transformed American government into a tool of elite control rather than public service. This work revealed the broader context within which prosecutorial abuse operates, demonstrating how federal overreach in criminal law reflects deeper problems with American governance and constitutional adherence.

"Indicted" provided a focused examination of the federal indictment process and the prosecutorial strategies that transform ordinary citizens into federal criminal defendants. This work exposed the grand jury system as a tool of prosecutorial manipulation while revealing how federal prosecutors use the indictment process to coerce guilty pleas and destroy lives before trials ever begin. The book's detailed analysis of prosecutorial psychology and intimidation tactics has proven invaluable for defendants and attorneys seeking to understand and combat federal criminal charges.

The comprehensive scope and practical application of these works cemented Wiggins' reputation as the premier authority on federal criminal defense and prosecutorial abuse.

Wiggins' expertise encompasses every aspect of federal criminal prosecutions, from initial investigation through appellate review and prison experience. His deep understanding of federal prosecution tactics enables him to provide insights that are unavailable from traditional legal sources, while his knowledge of the federal prison system offers guidance that can mean the difference between survival and destruction for those facing federal incarceration.

The author's approach combines rigorous legal analysis with compassionate understanding of the human cost of federal prosecution. His works acknowledge that federal criminal defendants are often ordinary citizens who find themselves caught in a system designed to destroy rather than rehabilitate. This perspective informs his writing with humanity and practical wisdom that addresses both legal and personal challenges faced by federal defendants and their families.

Wiggins' analysis of federal sentencing guidelines has become essential reading for defense attorneys seeking to understand and challenge the mathematical precision that characterizes federal punishment. His insights into prosecutorial psychology and institutional dynamics provide strategic advantages that can determine case outcomes while protecting defendants from common prosecutorial manipulation tactics.

The author's expertise in federal prison survival has proven invaluable for defendants facing incarceration in a system that presents unique challenges and dangers. His guidance on prison politics, safety strategies, and institutional navigation has helped countless individuals survive federal imprisonment while maintaining their dignity and preparing for successful reentry into society.

Wiggins resides in Winter Park, Florida, where he continues his research and writing on federal criminal justice issues. His Florida base provides perspective on federal enforcement in a state that has become a major focus of federal prosecutorial activity, particularly in areas including healthcare fraud, international money laundering, and immigration-related crimes.

The author maintains active engagement with current federal criminal justice developments through ongoing research and consultation with defense attorneys handling complex federal cases. This continued involvement ensures that his analysis remains current with evolving prosecution trends while addressing new challenges in federal criminal defense practice.

Wiggins can be reached through his website at Beatingthefeds.com, which serves as a comprehensive resource for individuals seeking information about federal criminal defense and prison survival. The website provides access to the author's insights on current federal criminal justice developments while offering guidance for those facing federal charges or incarceration.

His additional writings and publications are available through Theliterarydepot.com, which features an extensive collection of works addressing various aspects of criminal justice, legal analysis, and books related to achieving financial success. The Literary Depot serves as a platform for Wiggins' broader intellectual interests while providing access to specialized analysis that extends beyond traditional legal publishing.

The author's commitment to accessible legal education reflects his belief that knowledge represents the most effective defense against prosecutorial overreach and institutional abuse. His works are written in clear, understandable language that serves both legal professionals and ordinary citizens who need practical guidance for navigating federal criminal justice challenges.

Wiggins' influence extends throughout the defense bar, where his works are considered essential reading for attorneys handling federal criminal cases. His analysis of prosecution tactics and defense strategies has shaped defensive approaches while providing insights that enable more effective advocacy for federal defendants.

The author's dedication to exposing prosecutorial abuse and constitutional violations has established him as a leading voice for criminal justice reform. His works serve not only as practical guides but also as calls to action for systemic changes that restore constitutional protections and limit prosecutorial overreach.

This current work on PPP fraud prosecutions represents the latest evolution in Wiggins' ongoing analysis of federal criminal justice abuse. His examination of how emergency relief became a prosecutorial weapon demonstrates the same combination of legal insight and practical wisdom that characterizes his previous works while addressing the urgent challenges faced by PPP fraud defendants.

Wiggins' expertise in federal criminal matters provides unique qualifications for analyzing PPP fraud prosecutions that transform pandemic relief into criminal liability. His understanding of prosecution psychology and institutional dynamics enables him to expose the political motivations and constitutional violations that characterize these cases while providing practical guidance for effective defense.

The author's commitment to constitutional principles and individual liberty informs his analysis of prosecutorial overreach while maintaining focus on practical solutions that serve defendants facing overwhelming government resources. His work serves as both intellectual analysis and practical manual for those seeking to understand and combat systematic abuse of prosecutorial power.

Wiggins continues to monitor federal criminal justice developments while researching and writing on emerging issues that affect constitutional protections and individual liberty. His ongoing work ensures that his analysis remains current with evolving threats to constitutional government while providing guidance for those who must navigate an increasingly hostile federal criminal justice system.

Through his comprehensive body of work, Garry Wiggins has established himself as the definitive authority on federal criminal defense and the essential voice for those seeking to understand and combat prosecutorial abuse in an era of unlimited government power and constitutional erosion.

www.ingramcontent.com/pod-product-compliance
Lightning Source LLC
LaVergne TN
LVHW080010210926
848481LV00011B/2981